The Defence and Fall of Greece 1940–1941

The Defence and Fall of Greece 1940–1941

John C. Carr

Pen & Sword
MILITARY

First published in Great Britain in 2013
and reprinted in this format in 2020 and 2021 by
PEN & SWORD MILITARY
An imprint of
Pen & Sword Books Ltd
47 Church Street
Barnsley
South Yorkshire
S70 2AS

Copyright © John C. Carr 2013, 2020, 2021

ISBN 978 1 52678 182 6

The right of John C. Carr to be identified as the Author of this Work has been asserted by him in accordance with the Copyright, Designs and Patents Act 1988.

A CIP catalogue record for this book is
available from the British Library.

All rights reserved. No part of this book may be reproduced or transmitted in any form or by any means, electronic or mechanical including photocopying, recording or by any information storage and retrieval system, without permission from the Publisher in writing.

Typeset by Concept, Huddersfield, West Yorkshire.

Printed and bound in England by CPI Group (UK) Ltd, Croydon, CR0 4YY.

Pen & Sword Books Ltd incorporates the Imprints of Pen & Sword Aviation, Pen & Sword Family History, Pen & Sword Maritime, Pen & Sword Military, Pen & Sword Discovery, Wharncliffe Local History, Wharncliffe True Crime, Wharncliffe Transport, Pen & Sword Select, Pen & Sword Military Classics, Leo Cooper, The Praetorian Press, Remember When, Seaforth Publishing and Frontline Publishing.

For a complete list of Pen & Sword titles please contact
PEN & SWORD BOOKS LIMITED
47 Church Street, Barnsley, South Yorkshire, S70 2AS, England
E-mail: enquiries@pen-and-sword.co.uk
Website: www.pen-and-sword.co.uk

Contents

Preface vi
List of Plates x
Maps xi

Chapter 1   'Incoming Torpedo!': Greece on the Eve of War   1
Chapter 2   Over the Edge 16
Chapter 3   Punch and Counterpunch 37
Chapter 4   Mud, Blood and Cold Steel 61
Chapter 5   In the Teeth of the Blizzard 74
Chapter 6   Fiats and Gladiators 100
Chapter 7   Metaxas: 'Let us fall like men' 116
Chapter 8   Apocalypse on Hill 731: The Spring Offensive 139
Chapter 9   Falling Stars 163
Chapter 10 'This one's for the *Elli*!': The Naval War 173
Chapter 11 The Allies Arrive 191
Chapter 12 6 April 1941: The Saga of Fort Rupel 203
Chapter 13 Final Countdown 217
Chapter 14 Behind the Wire 237

Appendix 243
Notes 244
Sources 252
Index 254

Preface

Warfare has always been a potent generator of myth. Ever since Homer brought the sacrifices and sufferings of war to lasting attention in *The Iliad*, people have wanted to remember and commemorate them, to find some way of assuring themselves that those tribulations and vanished lives meant something, that what happened was for some meaningful purpose.

Wars beget myths in proportion to how 'right' they are perceived to be. Hollywood and the global media industry have made colossal profits out of this largely artificial distinction. Even now, the Allied viewpoint in the Second World War prevails in the public mind as supposedly a clear case of punishing an evil tyrant, be it Hitler or Tojo. More recent wars such as Vietnam or the two Gulf conflicts have not had the benefit of such a Manichaean framing. The presumed moral guidelines of the later wars were far less clear and hence less liable to myth-making.

I employ the term 'myth' in its sociological rather than colloquial sense. A myth need not be outright fiction. It can refer to an undoubted historical event. The myth-making consists of elevating and refining – and distorting – the memory of that event until it becomes a defining cultural trait, a part of who a people are. An essential element in this process is the imposition of a moral framework, 'a good guy, bad guy' narrative, with ourselves, of course, as the good guys. To take one example, books and films about the Battle of Britain from the 1950s to the 1970s were all about fresh-faced, insouciant and jokey British lads shooting down legions of grim-jawed, beetle-browed *Sieg Heil*-barking Luftwaffe pilots, even though in real life the characters of both classes of men were pretty much the same. Both included heroes and cowards, bad apples and near-saints as well as ordinary chaps. The moral distinction between them was nil. They were simply men in uniform called on to fight for their country. Yet even today the myth of 'good' RAF versus the 'bad' Luftwaffe persists.

To turn to the subject of Greece, few modern Greek myths have been more potent, more igniting of national pride, than the story of the Italian invasion of October 1940 and subsequent repulse in the mountains of Albania in the ensuing months. It remains one of the few examples of such myths (again, in the sociological sense) largely justified by the historical record. The pride the Greeks still feel in this fully rivals, if it does not exceed, the pride the British feel for the Battle of Britain in the same year. For the past seventy-odd years the Greek media and schools have been part of a great campaign of historical parallelism, likening the Albania campaign to the glories of Marathon and Thermopylai, endlessly repeating Churchill's facile hyperbole that it ought to be said not that Greeks fight like heroes, 'but heroes fight like Greeks'. In Italy, on the contrary, the post-war tendency has been to forget about the whole thing like a bad dream. As one Italian friend put it to me some years ago, the present-day Italian military establishment shame-facedly regards the Albania debacle as '*la vergogna del corpo*' – the disgrace of the corps (in this case the Alpine troops).

That said, however, Mussolini's aggression on hitherto-neutral Greece was frankly as naked as it gets. If there is such a thing as completely unprovoked aggression, 28 October 1940 came close, on a par with Hitler's march into Poland, the Japanese attack on Pearl Harbor and the Iraqi invasion of Kuwait in 1990. In the Greek case, even a good portion of the Italian military establishment was aghast at the decision. And when within a matter of days the Greeks threw the aggressor well back into Albania, the Allied world applauded. Here, it seemed, was justice on a divine scale. It was thus especially tragic that Hitler, to drag Mussolini out of the mire of an Axis defeat, steamrollered over Greece and wiped out all the country's gains in April and May 1941.

Yet a serious historian cannot rely on myths, however well-grounded in fact they might be. It is all too easy to approach a study of the Albania campaign with a predisposition in favour of the victim Greece. The purpose of this history is not to 'justify' Greece at the expense of Italy, nor indeed to 'justify' the Allies against the Axis. That is the task of the myth-driven mass media, not the military historian. When the guns begin to speak, issues of 'right and wrong' have a tendency to quickly evaporate in the reciprocal struggle to survive. It's the fate of all soldiers in all uniforms, from the youngest private to the top field marshal, to struggle through the fog of all wars. The arms are the man, not what the politicians say he has to fight for.

To provide as authentic a picture of the campaign as possible, I have relied mostly on the earliest possible sources, written when memories were fresh. These include the memoir of General Papagos, the Greek commander-in-chief. Though it is mostly a ponderous and dull chronicle of the technical details of the campaign and has little narrative 'meat', it has the merit of scientific impartiality. By far the best writer on the Italian side is Mario Cervi, whose classic and admirably balanced *Storia della Guerra di Grecia* (available also in English as *Hollow Legions*) draws on all the key original sources in a unified and perceptive narrative, though the author's rather too-obvious anti-Mussolini animus is a drawback in that it tends to pile blame on a single leader. The standard Greek history of the campaign is Angelos Terzakis' *Greek Epic 1940–1941* (available in Greek only), a strongly-written work which, however, suffers from the defect of sensationalism – a necessary attribute, it must be admitted, for a market among the Greek public. During my initial researches I was extremely fortunate to discover the *War Diaries* of Prince Peter of Greece, who served as a liaison officer with the British Military Mission in Greece in 1940. The prince's direct observations, which I believe have never been translated into English, throw a fascinating and often startling light on the thinking and activities of Greece's British allies at the time. The last volume of the diaries of Ioannis Metaxas is crucial for an understanding of what went on in the mind of that great statesman in the months before his death. Another diary, a hastily-scrawled one by an Evzone soldier named Miltiades Nikolaou, illustrates the ordeals of the men at the front.

I have taken the story up to the fall of Athens and the eve of the Battle of Crete, i.e. the end of April 1941. As many excellent books have been written about the Battle of Crete, to merely summarize it in a final chapter would not have contributed much. To all intents and purposes, Greece had already fallen before the first German paratrooper landed on the beleaguered island.

The reader may excuse me for recommending my own first book under the Pen & Sword imprint, *On Spartan Wings: The Royal Hellenic Air Force in World War Two*, for those who would like more details of the air war.

Ultimately I have tried to avoid loading the text with armchair strategy. A certain amount of background explanation, of course, is necessary, and this can be found in Chapters 1 and 2. This is a book of description, not theory. I am one of those inclined to believe that, whatever men may plan and do, the influence of the Divine Arbiter of Events is decisive. Socrates and C.S. Lewis were right when they said that ultimately, none of us can ever 'know' anything by sheer mental exercise. When a considerable time has passed between a particular campaign and the writing about it, and the smoke has long ago dissipated, we think we can see, for example, where so-and-so went wrong and what the result of such-and-such a move was. As a corrective, I have chosen to try and recreate that smoke, as it were, to portray what it must have been like during the action. Unless he has been a soldier himself, and in a rare case (in this era) actually been in combat, the military historian must approach his task in a spirit of humility and constant respect for those in any uniform who risked and gave their lives for a cause greater than themselves.

George Mermingas was of enormous help, as always, with his extensive library on Greek military history, plus his research team, including Wing Commander Pantelis Vatakis HAF, Constantine Lagos, Ioanna Georgakopoulou and Captain Nikolaos Garbatsis of the EEES Kirikio Cultural Foundation. Yannis Korodimos of the Hellenic War Museum was there with his usual unstinting help and encouragement, especially noted in a time of crunching economic austerity when the museum budget was being relentlessly squeezed. My friend and fellow-author Alex Martin stepped in at just the right time

Preface ix

with help on naval issues. Special thanks also go to Nasos Athanasiou, George Tassos for his hospitality while I was doing research at the Albanian border, John Chatwin for providing more facts about Squadron Leader 'Pat' Pattle, and Dimitris Pitellos, whose contribution to research on the naval war went considerably above and beyond the call of duty.

A note on style: to avoid reader confusion over the numbers of Italian and Greek army corps, I spell out the Italian and German (e.g. Fourth Corps, Twenty-sixth Corps) while leaving the Greek in classic Roman numeral form (e.g. I Corps, II Corps). As a conscientious journalist I have tried to give the full names of everyone mentioned in the text, though in a few cases only rank and surname have been available and I have had to make do with those.

John C. Carr
Athens
October 2012

List of Plates

1. Ioannis Metaxas and Lieutenant General Alexander Papagos (Hellenic War Museum)
2. Sketch of Italian bombers over Kalyvia, 28 October 1940 (with permission)
3. Greek conscripts go off to war, 28 October 1940 (Hellenic War Museum)
4. Greek cavalry fords the Kalamas River, November 1940 (Hellenic War Museum)
5. The village of Elefthero (Author's photograph)
6. Bicycle used by Italian Bersaglieri, in the Kalpaki Museum (Author's photograph)
7. Greek troops in the snows of Albania, December 1940 (Hellenic War Museum)
8. Greek artillery is placed in position in Albania (Hellenic War Musem)
9. Greek soldiers with captured Italian tank (Hellenic War Musem)
10. Ground crew refuel a RHAF PZL24 fighter (Hellenic War Musem)
11. The Mertzani Bridge over the Aoos River today (Author's photograph)
12. The rear deck of the RHN destroyer Queen Olga (Hellenic War Musem)
13. Commander Athanasios Spanidis on the submarine Katsonis (Hellenic War Musem)
14. German infantry attack Fort Rupel, 6 April 1941 (George Mermingas collection)
15. Germans pinned down in front of the Metaxas line (Hellenic War Musem)
16. Major George Douratsos, commander of Fort Rupel (Hellenic War Musem)
17. Death notice of Gefreiter (Private) Franz Rothmeier (George Mermingas collection)
18. Field Marshal Wilhelm List (Hellenic War Musem)
19. Greek officer surrenders Fort Rupel (George Mermingas collection)
20. German 92mm howitzer at the Rupel National Memorial (Hellenic War Musem)

Maps

1. Operations 28 October–14 November 1940
2. Repulse of the 3rd 'Julia' Division, 28 October–13 November 1940
3. Line of farthest Greek advance in Albania, February 1941
4. Route of RHN destroyers and submarines, 1940–41
5. The Metaxas Line and German invasion, April 1941

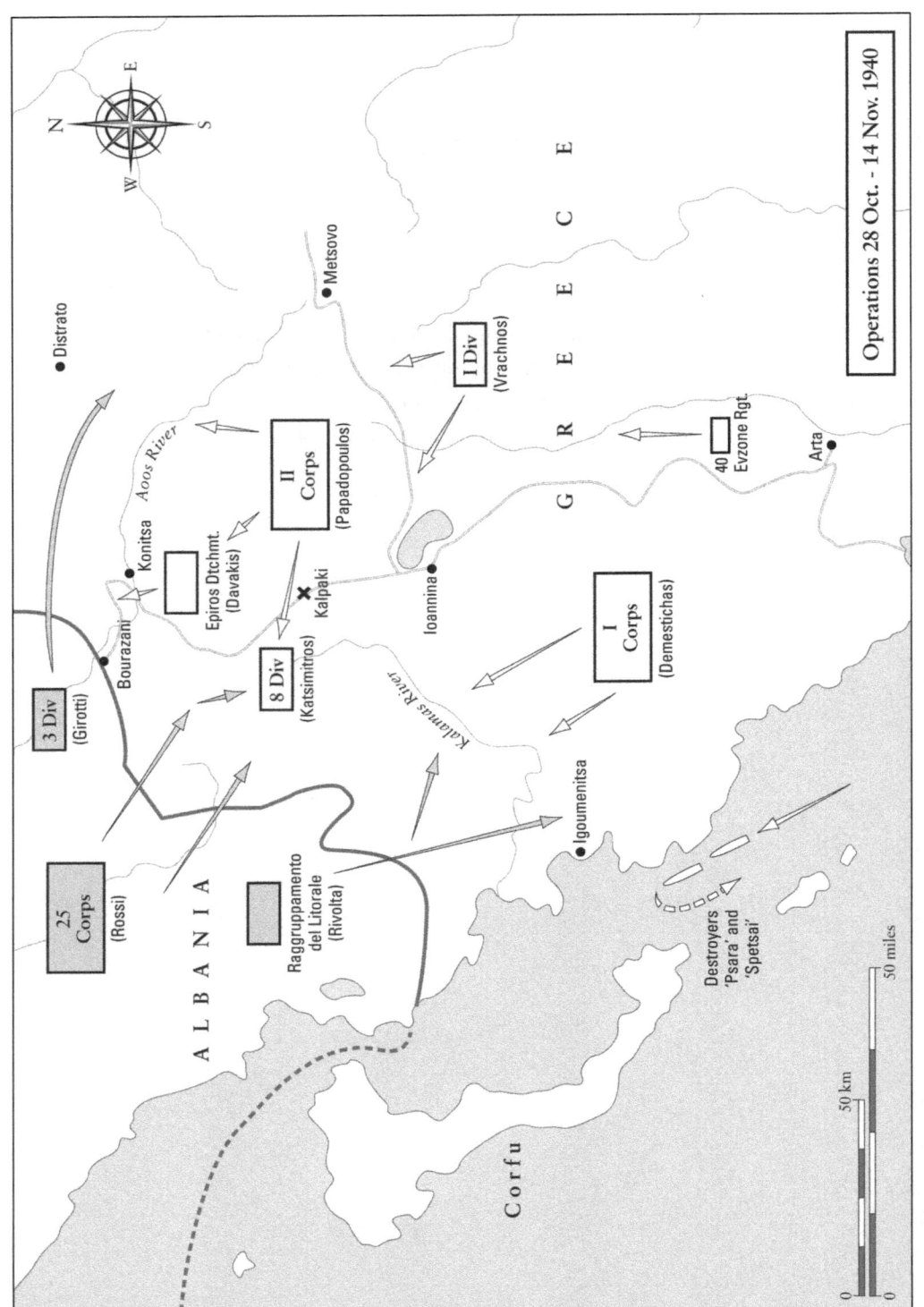

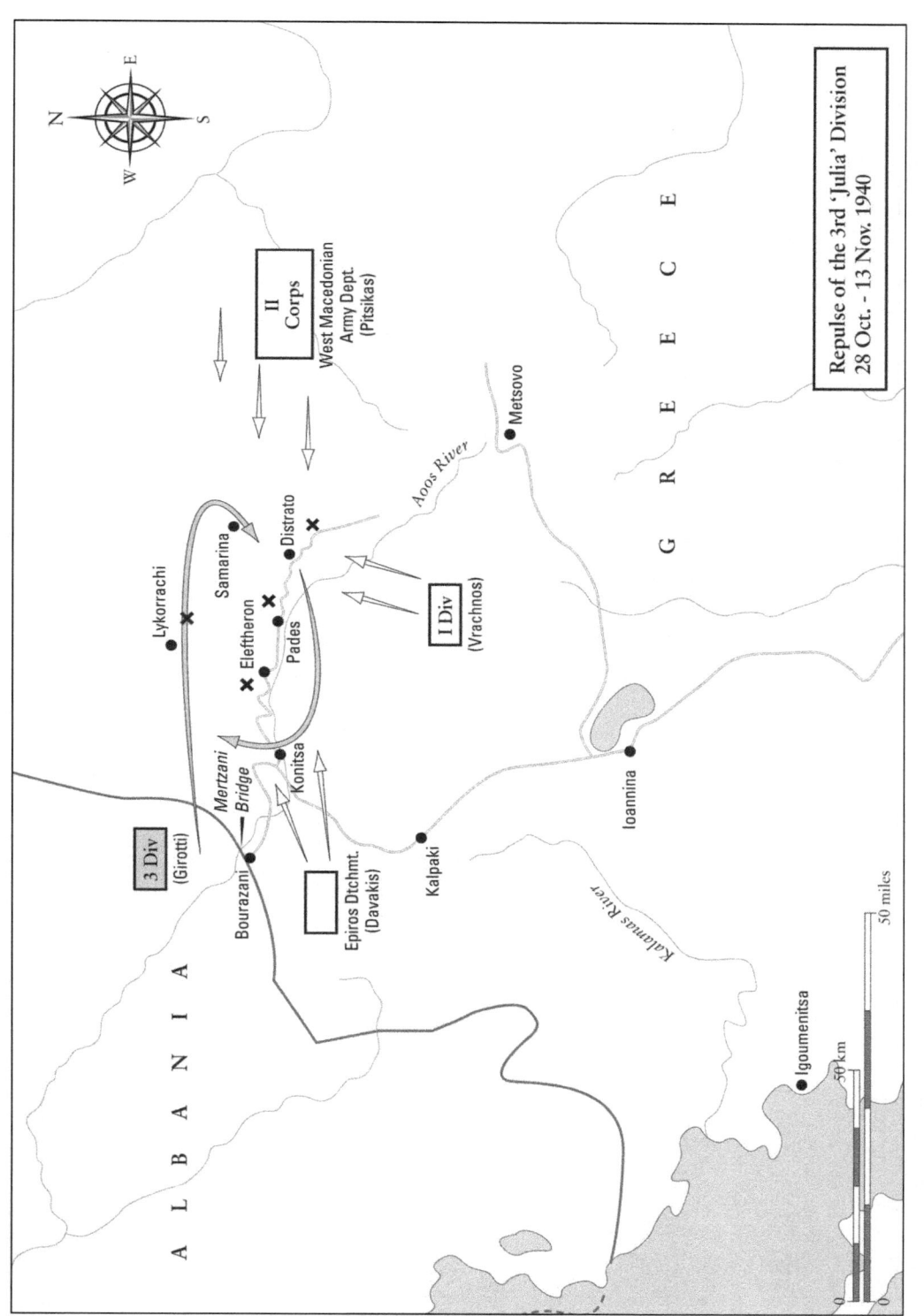

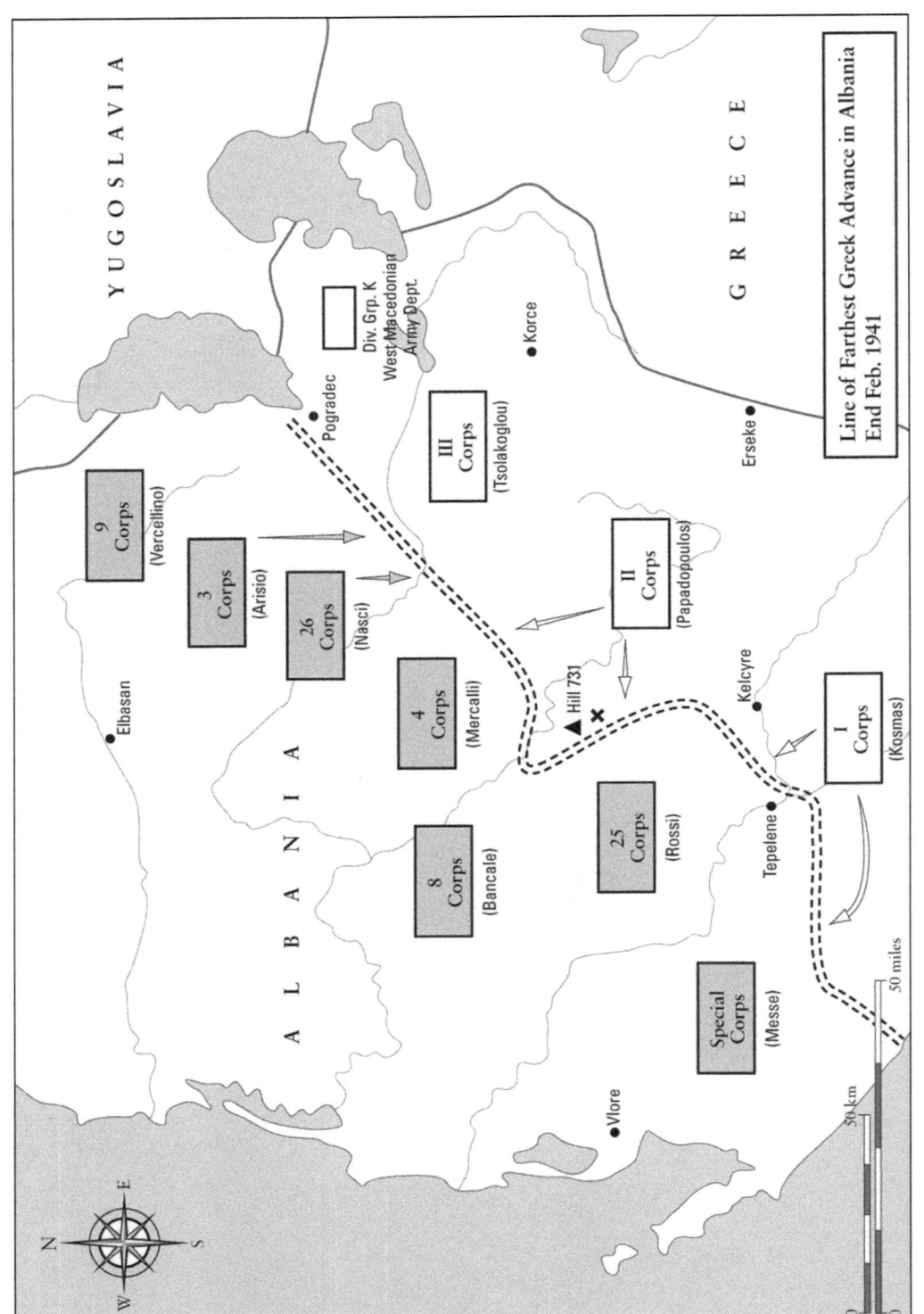

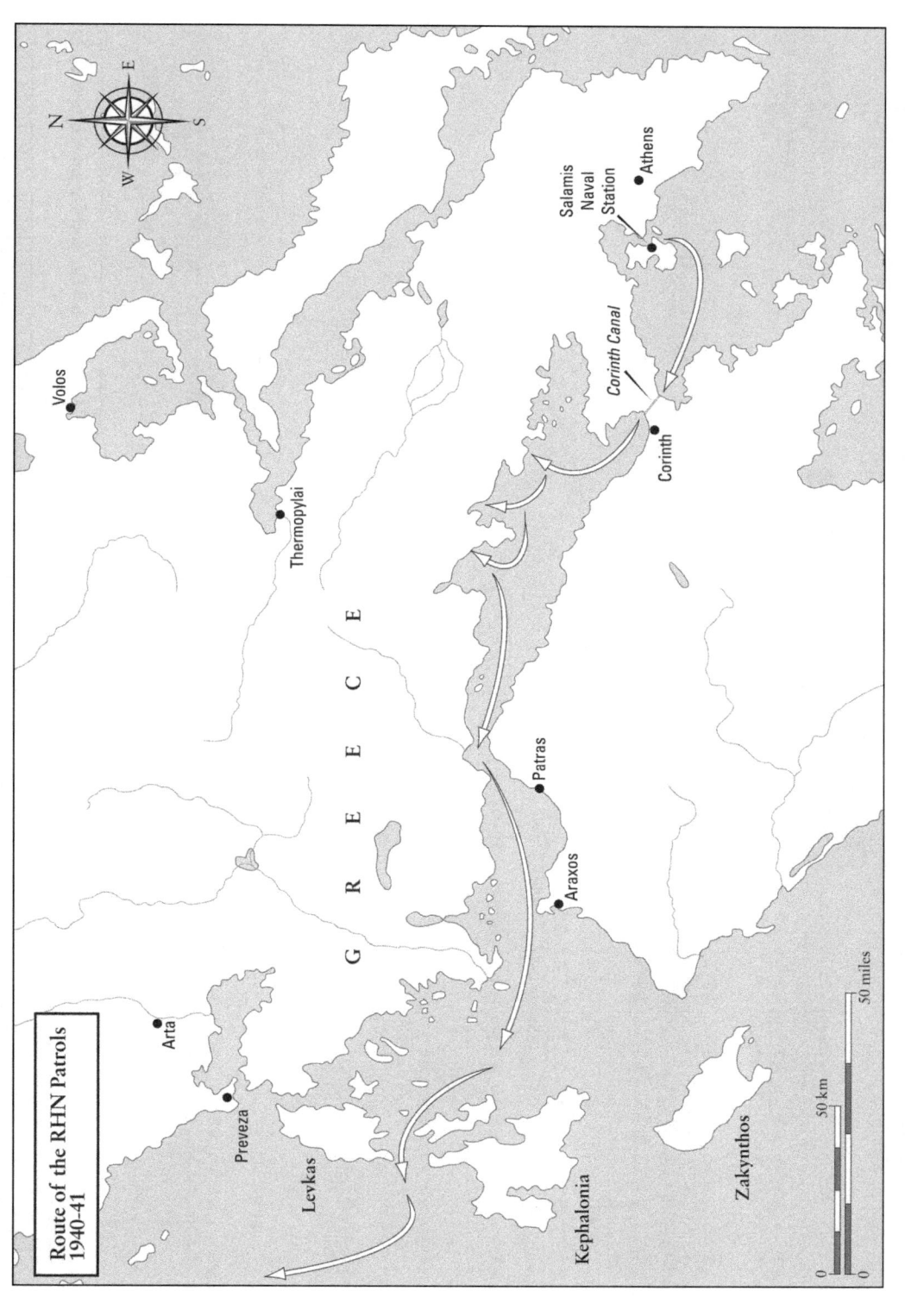

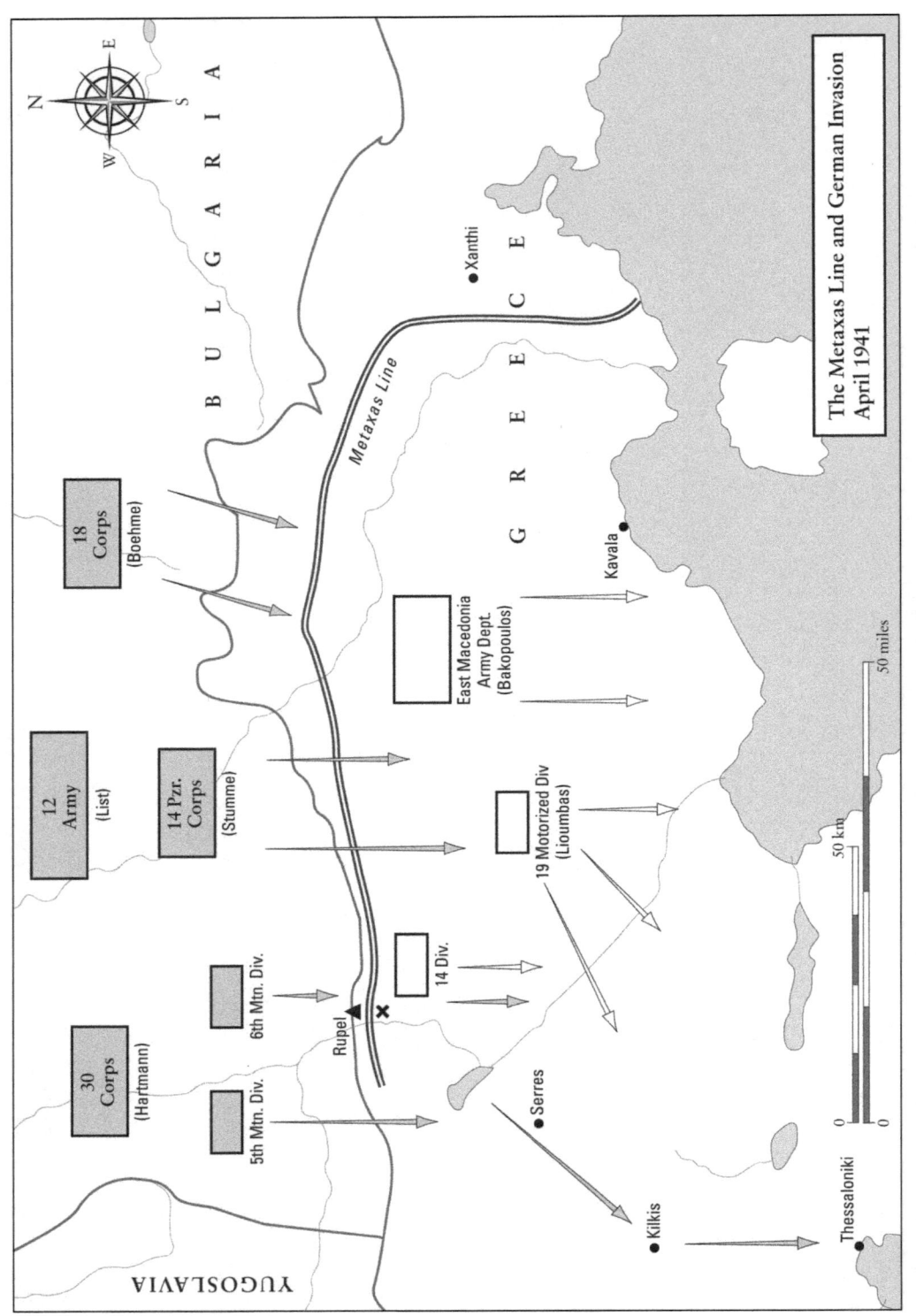

Chapter 1

'Incoming Torpedo!': Greece on the Eve of War

The sinking of the Elli – Italian sneak attacks on the RHN – trepidation in Rome – the career and character of Metaxas – Third Hellenic Civilization – economy and armaments – seeking an alliance with Britain

> *Far from this surf and surge keep thou thy ship.*
>
> Homer, *The Odyssey* XII 219

Through the warm night of 14–15 August 1940 an aging Royal Hellenic Navy light cruiser, the *Elli*, nosed slowly north-westwards through the calm waters of the Aegean Sea. Shortly before 6.00 am it reduced speed and made a gentle port turn towards its destination, the small island of Tinos.

That day was, and is, one of the holiest in the Greek Orthodox calendar, marking the death and taking up into heaven of the Virgin Mary. Tinos has been closely associated with the holiday ever since 1823, when a farmer discovered an old icon of the Virgin buried in the ground. Cleaned up and framed with silver, the icon was on display in a magnificent white marble-faced church dominating the height behind the small port town of Tinos. Even today, thousands of pilgrims sail to the island each 15 August to worship the icon, to which many miraculous healings have been attributed.

The 10,000-ton *Elli*, built in the United States for the Chinese navy and subsequently sold to Greece, had sailed from its base on the island of Milos as the RHN's official escort to the sacred holiday. Forty of its crew, including eight officers, had been detailed to help carry the flower-bedecked miracle-working icon in solemn procession around the town in the annual ritual. As the ship approached Tinos in the pre-dawn twilight, the crew could make out scores of pinpricks of light stretching up the hill from the port – flickering candles borne by the day's first worshippers making their way up to the brilliantly-lit church. At anchor nearby was the passenger ship *Esperos* which a few hours before had unloaded the last of the pilgrims from the mainland. A warm breeze blew from the south as the *Elli* slowed down to make a curving approach to the port. It was going to be a hot day. As the ship dropped anchor about 6.30 am, the bugle sounded to deploy the ceremonial flags. Below decks, the freshly-shaved honour guards were donning dress whites in preparation for their sacred task.

Nonetheless, tension was in the air. The Greek navy was abuzz with what had happened a month before, when aircraft believed to be Italian had bombed and strafed the supply ship *Orion* that had been offloading provisions at a remote lighthouse at Grambousa on the westernmost tip of Crete. It had been pure luck that no-one was hurt, the only victim of the bullets being an unfortunate seagull.[1]

The *Elli* was the Greek navy's biggest active warship. Its task was to patrol the Aegean Sea and islands in company with the destroyers *Psara*, *Hydra*, *Spetsai* and *Koundouriotis*, while the *Queen Olga* and *King George* were tasked with protecting the western approaches to the Ionian Islands and Crete. Having been built in Italian shipyards, these destroyers were sometimes mistaken for Italian vessels by the Royal Navy as their outlines were similar.

The *Hydra*, in fact, had already seen action of sorts, having sped to the aid of the *Orion*. To avoid provocation, the *Hydra* had sailed from its station at Milos with its 37mm 'pom-pom' guns loaded and ready, but with the barrels depressed. As the destroyer was heading south at twenty knots, three unidentified aircraft appeared and dropped a string of bombs. The ship shook violently in the near-misses. The shock of the explosions shattered porthole glass, wrenched doors from their hinges and smashed the ship's crockery. The ratings, kept below decks, were thrown around like dolls. On the decks, the officers gave the orders to fire. The first salvo from the *Hydra* missed the raiders that were flying just out of the guns' range. The formation turned away, only to return a few minutes later for a second attack. One of the planes began to dive on the ship; before it could unload its bombs, a shell from the *Hydra* winged it and it veered off, leaving a trail of smoke. The ship's crew couldn't tell if the plane eventually crashed or not. But they raised a lusty cheer anyway.[2]

Faced with strong protests by the Greek Admiralty, the Italian embassy in Athens vehemently denied that the attackers were Italian, hinting that they could have been British. But other incidents had strengthened the Greeks' suspicions. In the following two weeks, similar attacks were made on a submarine station at Itea in the Gulf of Corinth and on the *Queen Olga* and *King George* off Nafpaktos, again without casualties. The Greek Admiralty, admittedly, could establish no conclusive proof that Italy had staged the attacks, and news of them had been strictly censored. Then as the glorious August sun rose over Tinos on 15 August, the mask dropped.

As the *Elli*'s crew were preparing to go ashore, an aeroplane droned overhead. It was coming in from the east and its markings appeared to have been painted over. As it overflew the port at about 4,000 feet, the gunners rushed to their stations. Some of the worshippers trudging up to the church waved at the plane, thinking it was a Greek one come to salute the sacred holiday. After circling the port twice, the plane flew off to the west.

Just after 8.25 am, with the sun well up, a junior officer was about to go ashore to light a candle at the icon when Petty Officer Papanikolaou of the engine room asked him for a favour – to light a candle for him too. Papanikolaou had been one of those deputed to stay on board. The officer's reply, whatever it was, was drowned out by a shout from the bridge: 'Incoming torpedo from starboard!' Moments later, a shattering explosion almost lifted the *Elli* out of the water. The torpedo had hit the ship squarely in the middle of the starboard side, blowing out one of the boilers. Within seconds the oil and fuel tanks went up. Petty Officer Papanikolaou, who had asked that a candle be lit for him, was killed in the blast. Men and pieces of metal were flung overboard. Soon the whole ship was engulfed in flames. Captain Angelos Hatzopoulos, the ship's commander, had been trying to get a nap in his cabin when the blast threw him out of his bunk; cabin furniture tumbled all around him. His first thought was that the main ammunition magazine above his cabin had exploded, or perhaps a boiler had gone up.

Hatzopoulos rushed up to the already listing deck to find a chaos of flame, leaking fuel and blackened rubble. A crater several feet wide yawned between the smokestacks, smoking like a volcano. The starboard side of the ship had been split open from rail to waterline. Crewmembers were floundering in the sea, some of them injured and badly burned. The captain's first order was for the tender to be lowered to take on the injured. Then came a second torpedo. This one missed the *Elli* but slammed into the rocks near the jetty, giving a woman a fatal heart attack. That's when Hatzopoulos realized they were under attack.

A third torpedo also missed the ship, hitting a breakwater and raising a huge plume of water, shattering windows on the seafront that was now packed with panicked people heading for the hills. Hatzopoulos was now seriously worried about the fire spreading to the main magazine that had 120 depth charges in its racks. That would mean that not only the *Elli*, but also a goodly part of the port, would be blown to smithereens. He gave the order to flood the magazines with seawater, but the vents were jammed. That left the only alternative – to take the ship out and beach it on a remote stretch of shore, praying there would be enough time. But the steam power had been knocked out. A request for a tow went out to the captain of the *Esperos* passenger ship at anchor nearby, but that ship's fires had been banked and there wasn't enough steam pressure. The master ordered the fires to be re-stoked as quickly as possible, but to get up the requisite steam would take some time.

By the now the *Elli* was beginning to go under. Hatzopoulos remained on deck supervising the transfer of the wounded to the tender. Two medical orderlies trapped in the ship's dispensary were only just rescued from drowning by a heroic effort. When the *Esperos* got up steam it tried towing the stricken light cruiser out of the port, but the tow rope broke twice. Hatzopoulos then ordered the eight officers remaining with him on deck to abandon ship. They pleaded with him to go with them, and at first he seemed to comply. But according to one of the officers:

> As we began to descend to the tender with heavy hearts, seeing our ship vanish, the captain pulled back to stay. Then all together we quickly climbed back on the deck. The two strongest of us physically grabbed him, lifted him up and made him get down with us.[3]

By 9.00 am all that remained of the *Elli* above water was its upper mast. A fourth torpedo, meanwhile, had veered off course and gone out to sea.

Given the naval tensions of the past month, there was little doubt about who fired the torpedoes. That same day, investigators came across fragments of one of the torpedoes that had hit the rocks; the Italian manufacturer's marking stood out clearly.

Some of the first sailors to swim to shore vented their fury on a little Catholic church that happened to have an Italian flag flying from it, smashing the windows and tearing the flag down. There was no man among the crew of the *Elli* that day who did not pray for a chance at revenge.

South of Tinos Lieutenant (*Tenente di Vascello*) Giuseppe Aicardi, commander of the Italian submarine *Delfino*, lowered his periscope with satisfaction. His orders had been clear: to attack British and Allied shipping in the Aegean in expectation of a war with Greece. Clearly thinking he had completed an important mission, he turned the *Delfino* round and headed for his base on the Italian-occupied island of Leros, to await congratulations from his superiors.

Yet Aicardi's military and political bosses in Rome were rattled. Count Galeazzo Ciano, the Italian foreign minister, fretted that the sinking of the *Elli* would reflect badly on his country, especially as the attack was carried out on a religious holiday which the Catholic Italians actually shared with the Greek Orthodox. To this day mystery surrounds the motives for Aicardi's action. The chief of the Italian Naval Staff (*Supermarina* in service telegraphese), Admiral Domenico Cavagnari, had issued specific instructions to Italian naval units operating in the Aegean Sea to strangle British trade and supplies moving through the Dardanelles and the Aegean. The admiral believed the best time for such a campaign would be in late August, in which period, to quote his orders: 'any submarines [involved in the attacks] should sink without warning any vessels trading on behalf of the enemy, even under a neutral flag [and] the action carried out in such a way that the nationality and identity of the submarine cannot be discovered ...'[4]

What remains far from clear is why a RHN ship carrying out a ceremonial religious duty visible to all should have been considered 'aiding the enemy'. It was highly improbable that the sub commander could have mistaken it for a British warship. Aicardi himself later blamed a 'vagueness of orders' by his immediate superiors on Leros, and claimed that when he looked through his periscope and saw the *Elli* steaming up to Tinos he 'had no choice' but to sink it. The excuse rings hollow, even to Mario Cervi, the leading Italian historian of the war with Greece, who admits: 'The torpedoing could not have been worse timed.'[5] The upshot was that after 15 August the Greeks could have no doubt in their minds that they would soon be victims of a more substantial Italian aggression.

The casualty count from the sinking of the *Elli* remains a matter of dispute. The official record indicates that one crewman, Petty Officer Papanikolaou, was confirmed killed, and one other engine room petty officer and three firemen ratings were missing. Spyros Melas, a leading Greek authority, says the engine room personnel were blown to bits as they were at the precise spot where the first torpedo hit. Twenty-two other crewmen were wounded. There were claims that the Greek government covered up the true casualty figure so as not to stoke public indignation at Italy.

Be that as it may, no-one was more aware of the Italian threat than Ioannis Metaxas, the Greek prime minister, who had been ruling with dictatorial powers for four years. During this period he had been trying manfully to keep Greece neutral. Though a fascist by conviction and a former general, Metaxas despised his fellow-dictator Benito Mussolini, whom he viewed as little more than a theatrical windbag. Trained in the German authoritarian tradition, he was nonetheless an ardent patriot who made no secret of his preference for an alliance with Great Britain. The torpedoing of the *Elli* taxed his self-control to the utmost. He could not retaliate because Greece could not afford to be stampeded into war with the Axis. A few days afterwards he received an encouraging message from Winston Churchill citing Greek valour in the ancient battles of Marathon, Thermopylai and Salamis, and by implication urging the Greeks to similar heroism. Though flattered, Metaxas was not deceived by such claptrap. He needed not words but weapons. On 23 August he quietly called up the army's 8th and 9th Divisions as a trial run for a real mobilization. The results heartened him. 'The machine,' he wrote in his diary, 'is running exceptionally well.'[6]

Ioannis Metaxas at the time was 69 years old, and had ample reason to believe that his best years were behind him. He was not a prepossessing figure by any means. Short and pudgy, with thinning grey hair and owl-like spectacles, he was often misjudged by friend and foe alike. Yet the penetrating look from his clear hazel eyes revealed the razor-keen brain behind them. A native of the western Greek island of Kephalonia, Metaxas had displayed a talent for soldiering and strategy at an early age, graduating at the top of his class from the *Scholi Evelpidon*, the Greek Military Academy, in 1889. His abilities as a young field officer in the brief and disastrous Greek-Turkish war of 1897 impressed his Commander-in-Chief, Crown Prince Constantine (later King Constantine I) enough to suggest that he attend higher military studies at the German *Kriegsakademie* in Berlin.

As Constantine was a cousin of Kaiser Wilhelm II, the young Metaxas might have been expected to receive privileged treatment. Yet he proved to be extraordinarily competent in almost anything handed to him – mechanics and chemistry, art and literature, philosophy and battle tactics. By the time he graduated, his awestruck professors avowed that no problem was insoluble for '*den kleinen Moltke*' – 'little Moltke', a reference to the legendary General Helmuth von Moltke, the chief of the Prussian general staff and architect of victory in the Franco-Prussian War in 1871.

Back in Greece Metaxas rose in the army hierarchy thanks to distinguished service in the Balkan Wars of 1912–13. His unwavering loyalty to the Greek throne in the face of attacks by liberals placed him firmly in the camp of the now pro-German King Constantine during the First World War. While Greece was neutral for most of that conflict, the royalist-liberal rift worsened into a brief civil war in 1916. As the Allies fought their way to victory and took control of Greece, the king was forced into exile. Metaxas, one of the king's chief aides, was also exiled and sentenced to death in absentia. After Greece's shattering defeat in Asia Minor at the hands of a revived Turkey in 1922, Metaxas' death sentence was revoked. But the anti-royalist politicians in power forced him again into exile, from which he returned in 1924 only after a general amnesty.

Metaxas found himself repelled by the dishonesty and corruption of the political class and alarmed by the rise of the militant far left. 'It makes one sick,' he wrote in his diary on 28 November 1924. 'This is why we don't go forward. In the evening I help the children with their homework. The best thing I can do is retire to a happy family life.' He was now past fifty. But the desire to serve and reform his country, however unrewarding, kept him like a moth to a flame. He formed the Libertarian Party whose policy was to heal the chronic and bitter royalist-liberal rift and build up Greece's trade and industry. He gained enough votes in 1926 to become minister of communications, signing off on extensive road-building and irrigation projects in impoverished country districts. Two years later, out of office, he took up his pen as a newspaper columnist. He refused all calls to re-enter politics. Typical is a diary entry in 1931:

> The mere idea of running from grocer to grocer, from village to village, pleading for votes, excusing myself for the complaints [voters] may have, humiliating myself ... having to lie and flatter people I have no regard for, to praise scoundrels, to act unjustly toward able people and be good to incompetents ... to harm my home financially and make my family suffer – all this fills me with horror.

Yet Greece continued to need him. Partly as a consequence of long-term economic mismanagement and partly because of the world economic crisis, the country slid into bankruptcy in May 1932. To avert social chaos Metaxas agreed to serve as interior minister. While suppressing strikes, he kept the price of bread low by working out an agreement among bakers, flour suppliers and consumers.

His commentary columns helped him form a picture of Greece that thereafter would remain dear to him: the heiress of classical Athens and the Orthodox Byzantine Empire, a historically-continuous mystic entity that was being scandalously ill-served by the mean-spirited political class and deserved far better. He rejected as defeatist the idea that Greece should pull in its horns and take care only of its own house. While dreaming of the revival of classical and mediaeval greatness he damned the moneyed classes for living lives of decadence and unconcern for the welfare of the less fortunate. 'Youth cannot live without ideals,' he wrote in his final newspaper column on 23 January 1935. 'A vague and nebulous leftism has become the vogue. Others have turned towards fascist reaction [because] they are disappointed that their lives have become bereft of a higher purpose. "Human being" has become a mere zoological term ...'

The words betray the depression that intermittently plagued him. Sometimes he would spend long periods doing nothing but seeking escape in reading detective novels. 'I despise myself and the whole world,' he confided to his diary on 5 September 1935, in the midst of one such crisis. 'I don't feel very well.' And the following day: 'I feel I'm worth nothing. I no longer work ...'

Revisionist commentators, mainly on the left, have pointed to such passages as signs of incipient mental illness that were soon to blossom into a full-fledged megalomania and urge to become a dictator. Yet it is equally possible, in fact probable, that Metaxas' journeys into the 'dark night of the soul' were simply the trials of a sensitive and highly intelligent man who saw his best years wasted in inaction and felt deep inside himself that he was cut out for better things, namely, to save the country he loved from terminal political decline.

In hindsight, he need not have fretted. Six months after his darkest diary jottings, the time came for him to act. In early 1936 the military and the right wing were spooked by a political cooperation agreement between the liberals and the rising Greek Communist Party (KKE). For the first time, there was a possibility that the communists could enter the government. King George II moved to head off the threat by appointing Metaxas as war minister. But barely had Metaxas time to settle in to his new job when a month later Constantine Demertzis, the prime minister, died unexpectedly and the king promptly moved Metaxas into the vacant seat.

There is little doubt now that he was the best man for the job at the time. The international horizon was darkening by the day. Italian forces were active in Abyssinia in a telling demonstration of the aggressive power of Greece's western neighbour. Two days after Metaxas had become war minister, Hitler had marched into the Rhineland. In this worrisome atmosphere, when Metaxas unveiled his policy statements in the Parliament on 25 April he found many willing ears. His priority, he told the nation, was to maintain Greece's harmonious relations with other powers while at the same time building up the military for any eventuality. It all made eminent sense, and by an overwhelming vote of 241 out of 300 deputies, Metaxas was handed extraordinary powers to rule by decree for the next five months.

Metaxas' first challenge as national leader came from tobacco workers in the northern port of Thessaloniki who were striking for better pay and working conditions at the instigation of the communist KKE. He ordered the army to quell riots in that city, resulting in a number of deaths. It is not true, as many have claimed, that he was against parliamentary democracy in principle; he had a soft spot for the working class and also well knew what pitfalls a dictatorship could fall into. Yet he saw Greek parliamentary democracy as fatally ill and vulnerable to destruction by the communists. The philosophy of Marxism filled him with dread. In communism he saw the one virus that could destroy the Greeks' patriotism, Orthodox faith and family values which he held dear.

Metaxas' tough stand against the strikers mobilized the full force of the KKE against him. Between January and the end of July 1936 there were 247 strikes costing the national economy 195 million drachmas in lost wages. From the pyrite mines of Lavrion to the shipyards of Volos and the textile mills of Serres, the streets seethed with protests. To cap the scattered unrest, a coordinated nationwide general strike was called for 5 August. The nation's police were placed on the alert. Many predicted bloodshed.

In the afternoon of 4 August Metaxas conferred with King George. To thwart the expected violence, he recommended darkly, it might be wise to suspend some articles of the constitution. The king at first opposed the idea; autocratic measures would do nothing for his own uncertain popularity. But Metaxas talked the king round. He hoped he wouldn't have to do it, but at the head of a democratic government full of squabbling ministers he felt hamstrung.

An authoritarian regime was the only solution. By midnight the king had signed the royal decree suspending some articles of the constitution and dissolving the Parliament. King George II has been accused of acting unconstitutionally.[7] But in May 1935 the Parliament had passed an act authorizing any government to suspend constitutional articles when it deemed it necessary.[8] Metaxas had simply pushed at an already open door. The Dictatorship of 4 August – or the Third Hellenic Civilization, as its adherents preferred – had begun.

Metaxas' Third Hellenic Civilization – which inevitably gave rise to comparisons with Hitler's Third Reich – depended heavily on a Bismarckian tradition of industrial progress and social justice resting on a prospering middle class and muscular military establishment. Technically the Metaxas regime was a fascist one, ideologically underpinned by a glorification of the Greek past, in control of the media and mobilizing a national youth movement modelled on the *Hitlerjuegend*. But if Metaxas was a fascist, he was an unusual one. His social conscience moved him to set up Greece's social security system, the Social Insurance Foundation (IKA) which to this day provides most Greeks with their medical coverage and pensions. Building up Greece was his job. He was a fanatical believer in the great potential that he was convinced still lay hidden in the putative descendants of Perikles and Leonidas, of Alexander the Great, of the emperors of Christian Byzantium. Balancing this romantic idealism, however, was his training in the German school of pragmatism. He knew how power relationships worked and saw curtailed civil liberties as a lesser evil than the alternative.

The magnitude of Metaxas' task left him no time to write in his diary for some months. The first entry after 4 August comes under the date of 31 December, where he exults: 'It's the renaissance of Greece, and my own renaissance as well.' Guiding a country in a Europe careening towards a major crisis, he was in his element. Hitler had shown how to get results through a combination of guile and force. Soviet Russia under Stalin was busy trying to spread communism over the continent. Only Britain and France remained on overtly friendly terms with Greece. Days after Metaxas assumed dictatorial powers, King Edward VIII of England (in one of the very few official acts of his momentary reign) paid Greece an official visit. Sir Reginald Leeper, the British ambassador, noted wryly that Metaxas' penchant for banishing politicians had somewhat cramped the 'game of politics, the king of sports in Greece'.[9] But if Metaxas could guarantee an oasis of stability in the uncertain Mediterranean, Britain wished him well.

Metaxas' foreign policy, followed meticulously from August 1936 to October 1940, can be described as 'free of [obligations to] sentiment, friendship, ideological orientation and promises'.[10] In a word, classic *Realpolitik*. For him, democratic Britain was a more natural ally of Greece in the Mediterranean than his fellow-fascist ideologue in Rome. Greece also shared naval interests with Britain, as Greece's convoluted coastline and many islands would be of advantage to anyone controlling the waves.[11] Despite his insistence on military prowess and discipline, he knew that his own Greeks were strongly against becoming entangled in the string of European crises that darkened the latter half of the 1930s. Yet Metaxas was no isolationist. On the contrary, he engaged actively with the great powers, angling for Greece's national interests. These were, in short, to stay on good diplomatic terms with all the neighbours – Italy, Albania, Yugoslavia, Bulgaria and Turkey – and avoid getting on the wrong side of the Axis to preserve national strength for the showdown he was sure would come. It wasn't easy. The policy was fraught with traps. For example, Greece depended heavily on German exports of industrial and consumer goods, including pharmaceuticals, yet despite pressure from Berlin, Metaxas steadfastly refused to accept any German military mission on Greek soil; on the contrary, he retained a British naval mission as an overt sign of where he believed Greece's interests lay. 'The one solid benefit of his years of rule was . . . to establish the military, material and psychological foundations on which Greece could face the calamity of 1940,' writes one of Britain's foremost authorities on modern Greece.[12]

Until the late 1930s Greece's strategic worries centred on Bulgaria to the north. In the Second Balkan War of 1912–13 Greece had stymied Bulgaria's attempts to force an outlet to the warm Aegean Sea, and most northern Greeks still cultivated a dark distrust of their Slavic neighbours. Strategists in Athens feared that Italy might back a renewed Bulgarian drive southwards, and so in February 1937 Metaxas signed a pact with Bulgaria to head off that potential threat. Lieutenant General Alexander Papagos, the chief of the Greek General Staff, protested that as a result Greece would be on a potential collision course with Italy. But Metaxas, with his faith in British and French aid, was willing to take that risk. The one fence which he felt he could mend was that with Turkey to the east – ironically, the very power he had fought as a young officer in the Balkan Wars. Turkey and Greece signed a political cooperation agreement in 1937, removing a potential source of friction in the Aegean area and freeing Greece's military establishment to grow unhindered by concerns on the eastern frontier.

The diplomatic and military balancing act which Metaxas was called upon to perform would have overwhelmed a lesser man. Helping him maintain his balance was his firm belief in Britain as Europe's most trustworthy great power. As early as March 1934, two years before he assumed power, he asserted in the Parliament that 'Greece may enshrine as political doctrine that in no case can it find itself in any camp opposite to that to which Britain belongs'.[13] In the summer of 1936 he bluntly informed his military staff chiefs that he foresaw war between the British and German alliance systems – a war that would prove 'far worse than the previous one'. He added, with a warning to the top brass to keep it under their braided hats: 'I will do all I can for Greece not to get involved, but unfortunately it will be impossible.'[14] Papagos was sent to Paris to sound out the possibilities of French military support but came back disappointed. The republican French had never quite forgiven Metaxas' royalist record and his attack on a French expeditionary force to Athens in 1916 that was sent to topple Constantine I. The French, in fact, nursed grand plans to enrol Greece in a French-led *Armèe de l'Orient*, but nothing ever came of them.

Metaxas' economic burden at home was quite as daunting as the diplomatic one. The Greek economy in 1936 was in a parlous state, running a budget deficit of 844 million drachmas and dependent on a constant stream of foreign loans. In a country of about five million people, 135,000 were unemployed. Hundreds of thousands of ethnic Greek refugees from Turkey, uprooted after the war of 1920–22, were still living in hovels. Legions of farmers faced ruin at the hands of loan sharks. Metaxas moved to placate simmering unrest in the working classes by establishing holidays with full pay, banning child and Sunday labour, building child care centres and setting up the IKA social security system. However, strikes were all but outlawed. Farmers had their debts slashed and became entitled to buy out their tenancies with soft state loans. Irrigation and drainage projects added thousands of acres for growing crops. The farm reforms helped wheat production to rise from 531,000 tonnes in 1936 to 983,000 tonnes in 1938. Exports of olives, olive oil and tobacco soared, while cotton was introduced as a new crop.

The Greek drachma was stabilized and corporate and luxury taxes raised. Metaxas had no love for the moneyed class. In a 1937 speech in the town of Ioannina he lambasted the rich as 'a few thousand people . . . sitting in Athens making all the social, economic and political decisions, sucking Greece dry without giving anything back'. Democracy in Greece up to that point, he concluded, had been a rich men's game, orchestrated by a press servile to the media barons and believed in by 'slaves who think they are free'. Metaxas frankly prescribed his corporate state as 'anti-communist, anti-parliamentarian and totalitarian, based on labour and agriculture and, as a consequence, anti-plutocratic'. His political party was designed to include 'the whole people except for the unrepentant communists and the reactionary old politicians'.[15] The regimen largely worked. Exports in 1938 rose by more than fifty-seven per cent over the previous year. Currency reserves grew and the Athens Stock Exchange was consistently bullish. Greece's merchant shipping tonnage in 1938 hit 1.87 million tons, making Greece the world's ninth biggest commercial maritime power.

In 1939, however, colder economic winds began to blow. Metaxas poured every available drachma into building up Greece's industry and military establishment, and as a result, the country's borrowing bill soared. Between

1936 and 1940 some fifteen billion drachmas had gone into rearmament.[16] Greece was sinking into a sea of red ink. Whereas in 1935 Greece's public deficit stood at 373 million drachmas, by 1937 it had yawned to 1.7 billion drachmas, dipping to 341 million in 1938 and climbing back up to 1.5 billion in 1939. In April 1939 the Greek government was paying out up to forty per cent on Greek state bonds, with jittery London lenders demanding sixty-five per cent. Britain's credit institutions were fretting over Greek orders for warplanes and other military materiel, fearing that a European war might erupt before they could get their money back. Greece already had a shaky record of defaults going back to the 1840s. Greece's neighbours to the north, meanwhile, were changing their stance in the face of the growing German menace. Bulgaria let its arms-limitation agreement with Greece lapse, while Italy delivered a nasty surprise by occupying Albania on Easter Monday 1939. In the circumstances Metaxas felt he had no choice but to accept an informal guarantee of Greece's territorial integrity by Britain and France. Somehow, the London City lenders were fobbed off, but grumbling continued.

To aid national rearmament Metaxas promoted a domestic steel industry, though against the opposition of Britain and Germany which feared the loss of a market for their own steel. Some industries had to be bullied into building up national power.

The War Ministry made itself unpopular, for example, when it ordered the textiles industry to come up with nearly three million metres of khaki fabric for military uniforms at a price set by fiat. The dissident voices were silenced when the chairman of the League of Greek Industry (SEBB), Andreas Hadjikyriakos, was co-opted into Metaxas' administration as national economy minister. Hadjikyriakos' ministerial career was short-lived. In May 1937 the SEBB board unanimously decided to launch a nationwide collection for the purchase of modern warplanes for the six-year-old fledgling Royal Hellenic Air Force. When the collection came up with forty million drachmas in short order, Metaxas was delighted. But his joy soon turned to fury when a financial newspaper published a list of contributions by captains of industry against their recorded profits, showing that those men enjoying the highest profits had contributed the least. To keep Greece's infant war industry afloat, Metaxas passed a new law in January 1938 allowing the seizure of industrial property assets.

Though the economics were worsening, Metaxas could not afford to slow down his war preparations. Major items such as aircraft, warships, artillery pieces, machine guns and rifles had to be purchased abroad. Britain, Germany, France, the United States and even Poland and Yugoslavia were approached, as part of the prime minister's plan not to be too dependent on a single power. Britain was the favoured supplier of the big-ticket weapons such as ships and aircraft, as the Royal Hellenic Navy had been organized by the British, who also were influential in the RHAF. The French, who had organized the Greek army, had a near-monopoly on arms supplies and munitions for land warfare. The RHAF, the young newcomer to the services, had to make do with a truly mixed bag of warplanes from four countries, complicating the supply and technical processes. Three days before Metaxas' parliamentary coup, Lieutenant General Papagos, a staunch royalist, had been appointed to the post of Chief of the Greek Army Staff. Once in his job he reorganized and streamlined the staff to include quartermaster, transport and industrial warfare sections. His calls for military credits to meet these new requirements, however, were not always heeded by the Defence Ministry.[17]

When the Second World War broke out on 1 September 1939 Greece was quick to proclaim its neutrality. But few had the illusion that the country could stay uninvolved for long. When France fell in May 1940 Metaxas ordered some reservists called up, a move which rattled Italy. As early as 18 January the Italian daily *Corriere della Sera* was spouting the official Rome propaganda line that Greece was preparing for a mountain war in Albania 'with such obviously offensive tactical plans'.[18] Metaxas' vehement protestations of neutrality were ignored. Crews of the Italian airline Ala Littoria were instructed to spy on the Greek island ports they overflew and the Greek aerodromes they used. Metaxas was becoming increasingly troubled. 'Will everything collapse?' he mused in his diary in June. 'If so, I'll go with the army and seek to be killed.'

The *Elli* incident of 15 August was the catalyst for the Greek realization that war was imminent and Metaxas was the man to lead the country when it came. Many on the left as well as right shared that view. A young Athens University professor of sociology named Panayotis Kanellopoulos, jailed for his liberal activism, was moved enough to write to Metaxas personally, assuring him that if war should break out, the dictator may rest assured that Greece would in the end defeat the Axis. Kanellopoulos, destined to become an accomplished historical philosopher and serve briefly as a conservative Greek prime minister in 1967, said later that he contacted the dictator 'because whether I liked it or not, he held in his hands the fortunes of Greece'.[19]

Metaxas had bigger worries than what Greece's liberals thought of him. He hoped that Hitler, whom he believed to be an eminently realistic politician, would restrain Mussolini from a mad jaunt in the Balkans. But the cordiality of the meeting between Hitler and the Duce at the Brenner Pass in October dashed that hope. He knew now beyond doubt what was coming, and could only hope that an Italian invasion could be held up by token defence actions until full mobilization could be complete. Britain was Greece's great hope, but even there the news was bad. The British Expeditionary Force had been driven out of Europe at Dunkirk and the Royal Air Force was fully occupied in the fight for Britain's life. Metaxas felt keenly the humiliation of a small country dependent on stronger powers for survival. 'If the Germans prevail, we will be their slaves,' he wrote gloomily in his diary on 14 July. 'If the British prevail, we will become theirs. If neither, then Europe will crumble. Dear God, what melancholy!'[20]

Metaxas had been pressing for an alliance with Britain for two years. In late 1938, just after the Munich appeasement, he had asked Sir Sidney Waterlow, the British ambassador, to request that London upgrade what until now was a vague British pledge of support into something stronger. 'An alliance with Great Britain is what I want,' he said in his official note.[21] He wouldn't get it. Neville Chamberlain, the British Prime Minister, was basking in his appeasement at Munich while in Rome the British ambassador, Lord Perth, was fretting to Chamberlain that any formal alliance between London and Athens would have 'destructive consequences' for Anglo-Italian relations.[22]

In June 1940 a dapper and debonair figure appeared in Metaxas' office. It was Prince Peter, a cousin of the king, an explorer and anthropologist who had spent most of his time in European capitals and the Far East but recently had felt the call of patriotism and enlisted in the Greek army with the rank of captain. The cosmopolitan and well-educated prince, no fan of dictatorships, nonetheless suggested to Metaxas that he be allowed to form a Military Liaison Bureau to work with allied military missions. Metaxas perked up at the idea and told the dashing prince (who with his clipped moustache and handsome profile resembled a Hollywood character actor) to go ahead. 'If we go to war,' Metaxas informed the prince, 'we'll fight on the side of the British. Don't believe anything else!'[23]

Nazi Germany, meanwhile, already had Greece's fate mapped out. Germany was Greece's biggest trading partner. The German business and political establishment planned to recruit the whole of southern and eastern Europe into a so-called 'Complementary Space' (*Ergaenzungsraum*) designed to supply raw materials exclusively for the Fatherland which in turn would export industrial and consumer goods in a closed system – in short, total economic domination. To be sure, few Balkan countries had much choice, as German industrial and consumer goods, from trains to clocks, were essential to the growth of their economies. Hitler himself boasted of his admiration for the ancient Greeks. Josef Goebbels, the German propaganda minister, wreathed in smiles, posed for the press cameras with Metaxas during a visit to Athens in September 1936.

It took the Italian occupation of Albania in April 1939 to jolt the British into giving Metaxas some of what he had been insistently demanding. It came in the form of a verbal guarantee of Greece's territorial integrity in case Greece had to defend itself against aggression. The guarantee was deliberately kept vague in case London found its resources too stretched to help a country 2,000 miles away. Metaxas, of course, would have preferred an outright alliance, but it was a step in the right direction. The bond became tighter in January 1940, when Greece's wealthy shipping establishment agreed to lend the British government several dozen merchant vessels totalling half a million tons.[24]

By September 1940 Athens could have no doubt about what was looming. Security in Rome was not of the best, not to mention Mussolini's lack of discretion in his public utterances. In Athens Emanuele Grazzi, the Italian ambassador, and Colonel Luigi Mondini, his military attaché, were sending home long and urgent cables detailing the efficient mobilization measures of the Greeks; reservists, they fretted, were being called up by the thousands. For a long time Greek defence planners had been divided as to whether Bulgaria or Italy was the greater threat. After the sinking of the *Elli*, however, all ambiguity had vanished. The gradual build-up of Italian forces in Albania had pushed concerns over Bulgaria to the sidelines.

One prescient officer who had foreseen that, if an attack on Greece were to come, it would come from the direction of Albania, was General Haralambos Katsimitros, the commander of the 8th Division based in the north-western city of Ioannina. Since taking up his command in 1938 Katsimitros had devoted his energies, despite a chronic shortage of military credits, to beefing up defences in Epiros, the northwest corner of Greece abutting Albania. Defying disapproval by his boss Papagos, he dotted the craggy countryside with tank traps and caves in which to hide artillery. Some of these preparations spooked commentators in Rome. On 18 January 1940 the Italian daily *Corriere della Sera* had asked in an editorial 'how come those Greeks are equipped for a mountain war with such obviously offensive plans?' Within ten months the 8th Division had built up its full strength to ten infantry battalions (three of which were made up of called-up reservists), joined by the 9th Division with six battalions of infantry and a reduced-strength 1st Division held in reserve, accompanied by artillery.

There was more where that came from. Greece could field a total of five army corps consisting of fifteen infantry divisions and one cavalry division, fifteen regiments of mountain artillery and five of field artillery, plus scattered anti-aircraft units. The bulk of Greece's rearmament, in fact, had overwhelmingly benefited the Army, with the underequipped Royal Hellenic Navy (all of ten destroyers, thirteen torpedo boats and six submarines, a handful of minesweepers and the ancient hulk of an armoured cruiser as a reserve) and the flimsy Royal Hellenic Air Force (barely 130 front-line aircraft) left to manage as best as they could.[25]

Chapter 2

Over the Edge

Overconfidence in Rome – Mussolini's character – Esigenza G – Visconti Prasca plans a walkover – the crucial war council of 15 October – an army show – the Metaxas Line – Greece's evolving defence doctrine – mobilization – Grazzi delivers his ultimatum – C'est la guerre

> *We have the men and means sufficient to annihilate every Greek resistance. British aid [to Greece] will not be able to hinder us in attaining this firmest of purposes.*
>
> Benito Mussolini, addressing a conference of
> Fascist Party officials, 18 November 1940

In the autumn of 1940 Benito Mussolini had been at the helm of Italy for eighteen years. In that time he had built up his country along authoritarian corporatist lines which, though involving some political thuggery by the ruling Fascist Party, had satisfied most ordinary Italians who cared little for politics, enjoyed economic and social security and indeed were proud to see their country respected as a new military power. Mussolini would periodically re-stoke public adulation from the balcony of his office overlooking the Piazza Venezia. '*Vinceremo!*' he roared to a huge crowd from the balcony on 10 June 1940 when Italy entered the war on the side of Germany. 'We will win!' Yet a great foreboding was also in the air. Rome newspapers advised readers to avoid the upper floors of their *palazzi* during air raids. Ancient statues were taken indoors. People found themselves queuing for olive oil, pasta and shoes. Buses had to run on diluted fuel. 'Rome,' writes one historian, 'took on the aspect of a country town.'[1]

Pope Pius XII, on the papal throne for just a year, issued a fervent call for peace. The Duce's administration took not the slightest notice of him. Mussolini wasn't going to let a bookish Catholic priest divert him from his grand aims. By 1940 these had included gaining control of Greece. That country, with its long and convoluted Mediterranean coastline and plethora of islands, was too good a prize to be left to the British who, once their Royal Navy got control of the place, would seriously cramp the Duce's Balkan ambitions.

And so, Greece had to 'go'. But the more Mussolini pondered on how to do it, the less he could come to a final decision. Part of the Duce's character was his desire to be all things to all men, a key element in his innate desire for power. People close to him noted that 'he always tended to agree with the person to whom he had last spoken'.[2] This trait, in fact, dominated the whole tortured course of the diplomatic cat-and-mouse game between Italy and Greece. Mussolini would blow hot and cold on Greece as the mood – or influence of the day – took him. One day he might nurse the darkest suspicions of Greece, and the next he might well give way to hope that his sunny neighbour to the east might be cajoled into forming part of his Caesaresque sphere of influence. Disseminating the latter message was the task of Radio Bari, a powerful transmitting station on the heel of Italy which served as an international broadcasting arm of the *Ente Italiano Audizioni Radiofoniche* (Italian Radio Listening Organization) national radio network. Inaugurating regular Greek-language programming in the middle of 1937, Radio Bari avoided crude propaganda in favour of an audience-friendly news and entertainment format that gained a respectable listenership in Greece. Radio Bari made a point of overtly supporting the Metaxas regime, contributing to the impression among many that war between Italy and Greece was improbable.[3]

Yet no-one could deny that relations between the two countries had steadily deteriorated since 1928, when they had signed a much-ballyhooed treaty for Mediterranean cooperation. That was the year of the Kellogg-Briand Pact that eyebrow-raisingly sought to 'outlaw war as an instrument of national policy'. Greece had attached itself to an influential European club consisting of Britain, France and Italy, and public optimism at the time was high. The emergence of Hitler, of course, had changed all that. Ten years after the burst of idealism of Frank Kellogg, the American secretary of state, and Aristide Briand, the French foreign minister, their pact had been consigned to history's dustbin. When the 1928 treaty came up for renewal in September 1939, Metaxas refused to renew it. Grazzi, the Italian ambassador in Athens, expected as much when Metaxas the previous month had asked him to convey to Mussolini Greece's determination to defend itself if attacked from any quarter.

Did Mussolini relay this message to his service chiefs? Or did he assume that Metaxas was a paper tiger, a sabre-rattler like himself – if true, a fatal miscalculation? Metaxas, of course, was not saying anything new; every country on the globe is (or ought to be) prepared to defend itself if attacked. Metaxas, uncomfortably aware of Greece's relative weakness, still hoped he could stay out of a conflict, and Mussolini knew it. Throughout the tense summer of 1940 Mussolini tested the Greeks' resolve at sea and in the air. The sinking of the *Elli* was merely the most egregious of such acts.

The Duce tended to rely for support on flamboyant characters like himself. Thus he found a kindred spirit in General Sebastiano Visconti Prasca, the commander of the Italian occupation forces in Albania. Shallow and delusional, but with a strong ambitious streak, he harboured one great desire – to spring to the ultimate rank of *Maresciallo d'Italia*, his country's highest. Visconti Prasca imagined his designated grand role as the Roman general who would replicate the achievement of his 2nd century BC predecessor, Titus Quinctius Flamininus, who had conquered Greece and brought it into the Roman orbit. Suspecting that his general might overplay his hand, Mussolini gave Visconti Prasca the command in Albania in May 1940 urging him to use 'tact, tact!' in his dealings with the Albanians.[4] Visconti Prasca was willing enough to comply, as long as he could admire his five 'beautiful divisions' (*'belle divisioni'*): the Ferrara, Arezzo and Venezia infantry divisions, the crack 3rd Alpine Division – better known as the Julia – and the 131st, or Centauro, Armoured Division. There was also the proud 3rd Sardinian Grenadier Regiment and two divisions or so of Albanian auxiliaries.

The divisions might be *belle* in their commander's eyes, but they were in Albania for a purpose, and here is where the strategic thinking became fuzzy. In his years of absolute power Mussolini had transformed himself from a radical social reformer and peacenik into an out-and-out militarist. War, he told his military men as early as 1931, was the truly ennobling fact of human experience. A nation was useless without it. 'The more enemies,' he told his fascist party chiefs, 'the greater the honour.'[5] He yearned to emulate Hitler's *Blitzkrieg* tactics in Poland and Western Europe. Yet he was realist enough to realize that though lesser races in Africa had been mown down by the Italian bayonet, poison-gas shell and aeroplane, a modern European army like that of Greece would be a quite different proposition. Levering Greece out of the sphere of British influence would need careful handling. The first stage would be a 'limited-range offensive', the preparation for which was given to General Carlo Geloso, Visconti Prasca's predecessor in Albania, now at a senior staff desk in Rome. Geloso's initial draft envisaged an advance into the north-western Greek provinces of Epiros and Akarnania as far as the town of Mesolonghi. During this operation, the navy would help secure the Ionian Islands – Corfu, Kephalonia, Zakynthos and Levkas. Geloso estimated that eleven divisions would be enough, including one for the occupation of Corfu and three to move up against the Yugoslav border to deter the Yugoslavs from intervening.

Thus was born *Esigenza G*, or Contingency G (sometimes known as *Emergenza*, or Emergency G). What the G stood for remains vague. It's generally taken to refer to *Grecia* (Greece), though it could also be Geloso's initial. The planned operation, if successful, would give Italy control of the western end of the Gulf of Patras, a key shipping route leading to the Corinth

Canal. Meanwhile, Ciano in the Foreign Ministry was hatching a parallel plan. This was to detach a triangular wedge of Greek territory running from the Albanian border south to the Preveza promontory, the home of a non-Greek ethnic group related to the Albanians called the Chams. Mostly Muslims, the Chams were a forgotten remnant of the old Ottoman Empire. Naturally, separatist sentiment had taken root among some of them, though most of the Cham element had become assimilated into Greek society and was apparently content to stay there. In the eyes of the gung-ho Ciano, an independent 'Chamuria' under Italian tutelage would be a valuable foothold on the Ionian Sea.

Mussolini put *Esigenza G* and the 'Chamuria' plan before Visconti Prasca, who was unexpectedly hesitant. He replied that preparing for it would take at least two weeks. He also needed more units in Albania, especially horse-drawn mountain artillery. And what if, he said, Greece and Yugoslavia reacted more quickly than expected? There is a reluctant, cautious tone here which, admittedly, does not sound like the Visconti Prasca who was preening himself as the imminent vanquisher of the Greeks. And the historian is right to treat it with caution, because the source is the general's own highly unreliable post-war memoir, written when he was anxious to restore his tattered reputation. In fact, Ciano, in his more reliable diary, notes that Visconti Prasca's reaction to Contingency G was in fact enthusiastic, 'on condition that we hurry it up.' To detach 'Chamuria' would probably trigger a fight with the Greeks, so Visconti Prasca said he would need two more divisions of infantry, four artillery battalions, three alpine battalions, four battalions of Blackshirts and 10,000 rifles for the Albanian auxiliaries – a 'striking fist'.[6]

If Visconti Prasca saw himself as the owner of this fist, his superiors did not share that view. The chief of the Italian General Staff, Marshal Pietro Badoglio (*Superesercito* in the cablese of the day), could not bring himself to believe that Mussolini took seriously the amateurish and frankly dangerous escapade that Contingency G prescribed. Badoglio saw far more clearly than Visconti Prasca that an attack on Greece would be no simple matter of a few divisions marching over a border. When Visconti Prasca dutifully informed Badoglio of the plan, the marshal's grave doubts about the Duce's strategic sense became graver. 'He's mad,' Badoglio said. 'Now he wants Greece as well.'

Greece had been rankling in the Duce's mind for years – since 1923, in fact, a year after he had become prime minister of Italy. In that year an Italian general working on an international commission trying to delineate the Greek-Albanian frontier was murdered on Greek soil. The culprits were probably Albanian brigands, but Mussolini immediately blamed Greece and launched a swift punitive strike, landing troops on the Greek island of Corfu. To add more injury to insult, an incautious naval officer bombarded the town of Corfu, killing several children in a refugee camp. The resulting international outcry forced Mussolini to pull his soldiers out of Corfu a month later, though not without issuing dire threats against Britain which had stood up for the Greeks. For him, Greece represented unfinished business.[7]

Recent Italian writers, doubtless conscious of the unflattering record of the Italians in Abyssinia in the 1930s, have played down Mussolini's overseas ambitions, intimating that his targeting of Greece was something of a spur-of-the-moment decision.[8] Yet there was also more that a grain of truth in Greek suspicions that Mussolini had his eyes on southeast Europe for some time. As early as 1927 he had been arming Macedonian terrorists and meddling in the affairs of Albania in the hope of one day turning it into an Italian colony. Since as far back as 1912 the ethnically-Greek islands of the Dodecanese had been under Rome's control; a control that by the late 1920s had become frankly oppressive to the point at which the native Greeks were forbidden to use their own language, even on their tombstones. To be sure, most of this can be put down to the Duce's desire to strut large on the world stage and enjoy his undoubted nuisance value, as an American journalist put it. But when in his speeches he held forth about the Italians whom he was about to forge into 'a single mass ... a thunderbolt that I can hurl against anyone anywhere,' neighbouring governments naturally became extremely jittery.[9]

The Germans were quite well aware of the shaky ground the Duce was standing on. As early as March 1940 Hitler, after meeting with Mussolini, noted shrewdly that the Italian leader resembled 'a schoolboy who has not done his homework'. Mussolini's own view of Hitler was undergoing a slow but steady transformation. In the beginning he was inclined to see the German dictator as a half-mad simpleton nowhere near as politically sophisticated as himself; yet at the same time German military strength and the German military's coldly rational strategic sense – particularly as regards the Balkans – impressed him mightily. He marvelled at the German invasion of Norway in April as a model for his own hoped-for conquest in the south. The Italian attack on southern France in June was expected to be a dry run for a more ambitious campaign in the east, but it quickly petered out because of poor staff work. The Duce blamed not only his generals but also the Italian soldiery for 'not being worthy of his leadership'. A future campaign, he told himself, would toughen the Italians to the required degree.[10]

But the weak Greece of the 1920s was quite different from the newly-rearmed Greece of 1940 under the resolute Metaxas, as Rome was undoubtedly aware. So why didn't Badoglio, Italy's top soldier, apply stronger brakes? The answer lies probably in the marshal's lack of inner steel. There is strong evidence that a creeping depression seized him in the latter half of 1940. The depression – nurtured probably by his growing disillusionment with Mussolini personally – gave rise to passivity and a debilitating lack of interest in what his boss was doing. By October much of the top staff work was being done by Badoglio's deputy, General Mario Roatta, who was not exactly a paragon of optimism himself. In response to Visconti Prasca's howls for more men and materiel, Roatta ordered three infantry divisions, the Parma, Siena and Piemonte, to sail to Albania, beefed up by one motorized machine gun battalion, other motorized units, two battalions of sappers and engineers and twelve field hospitals. Once off the troopships, these units were swept up in a confusing kaleidoscope of redeployments and transfers. Soldiers were marched back and forth with no apparent aim; observing their officers themselves confused by the incessant rain of orders and countermands, they soon lost their morale. That vital ingredient of warfare, a confidence in the senior command, was largely lacking among the Italian troops in Albania.[11]

Visconti Prasca might be excused his hasty arranging and rearranging, as he had been given an attack date of 1 September, the first anniversary of Hitler's march into Poland that had triggered the war in Europe. Roatta, doing his best to keep up with the ever-changing demands, was not helped by the Duce's own frequent changes of mood. The deadline obviously could not be kept, and so a week before the end of August, the planned attack on Greece was put back a month, to 1 October. On 31 August it was postponed yet again – to 20 October.

The cause of all the delay was Mussolini's continuing uncertainty about what to do. There were three choices before the Italian General Staff: (a) an attack on Greece; (b) an attack on Yugoslavia with a holding operation on the Greek border; and (c) static defence, without action, on both borders. All three were mutually exclusive, and the Duce just couldn't seem to decide on one. He desperately needed to be militarily useful, anyhow, anywhere. For example, one day he might hatch the bright idea of annexing parts of southeastern France, which would in turn lead his thoughts to the possibility of occupying Corsica. He would then fire off a peremptory communiqué to the General Staff to start working on the idea. The senior brass, of course, could hardly refuse. Thus an initial plan would be followed by re-draftings and modifications whenever Mussolini had another idea and picked up the phone to Badoglio, who was in short order driven to distraction. The fatalistic feeling inside the General Staff can be summed up as: 'Let's get into the war, then we'll see.'[12]

Italian hopes were also pinned on what many in Rome believed was widespread defeatism in the Greek military. Papagos was a capable but not a popular commander. Tall and supercilious, he had a more than passing resemblance to another tall and haughty European soldier, a certain Colonel Charles de Gaulle in France. He easily made enemies among his underlings. But for all his character flaws, Papagos was a patriotic and capable general. When one of his staff subordinates, Major General Constantine Platis, suggested that Greece was veering too much towards British influence and needed to be conciliatory with the Axis, Papagos had him cashiered and clapped under house arrest. There was to be none of that talk if he could help it.

Nonetheless, the Italian delusion of a Greek unwillingness to fight persisted. Visconti Prasca himself appeared convinced that the Greek troops would rebel against their officer corps and that a fifth column in Athens was preparing to welcome the Duce's minions as conquering heroes! Even the leading Italian military historian of the period, Mario Cervi, is at a loss to explain this tragic delusion. The case of Platis, of course, had been duly transmitted to Rome by Grazzi, there to be magnified under the glass of wishful thinking. To be sure, there were pro-German officers in the Greek military, numerous enough to worry Metaxas himself. But they had not, to anyone's knowledge, betrayed any intention of not fighting if their country was attacked. Grazzi knew the score. In a crucial despatch to Ciano dated 3 October he advised his boss to ignore 'the exaggerations of informers', adding:

> without doubt Greece has about 250,000 men under arms, most of them deployed on the frontiers ... it is therefore to be assumed that the Metaxas government intends to repulse any attempt at invasion, and it will not be possible to obtain from it, without the use of force, any cession of territory [or] consent for the occupation of strategic zones or points ... never before has Prime Minister Metaxas had behind him such unanimity of agreement ...[13]

Though Badoglio himself was aware of the true situation, the delusions at the top persisted. They seem to have been nurtured by the head of the Italian occupying authority in Albania, Lieutenant General Francesco Jacomoni, himself deluded by revived Roman dreams of empire and busy preparing the ground for an independent 'Chamuria'. Ciano boasted of a brimming war-chest that was emptying fast as Greek politicians and military men were being bought off. Yet there remains not the slightest evidence that any high-level Greek pocketed Italian money to betray his country in 1940. Given the state of public opinion in Greece, such bribery is indeed hard to imagine. After the war Grazzi claimed to be nonplussed at the delusions his boss Ciano laboured under. The faithful ambassador, one of the best diplomats Italy could field, was staggeringly ill-served by his superiors. He often wondered what was the point of maintaining an Italian embassy in Athens staffed, in Rome's apparent view, by 'cretins or traitors'.[14]

By mid-October, however, more of a sense of reality was beginning to kick in. Greek opinion was stiffening by the day, especially after Joachim von Ribbentrop, the German foreign minister, had tactlessly advised the Greek ambassador in Berlin that Athens, for its own good, should submit to Italy's planned dominance of the Mediterranean. The plan for this dominance was now taking shape. Mussolini had personally outlined it to Ribbentrop: Italy's advance along the North African coast towards Egypt would force the British fleet out of Alexandria, while the conquest of Greece would deprive that fleet of a refuge in the Aegean islands. Yet a wider problem now presented itself: to secure Greece would also have to entail neutralizing Yugoslavia to the north. There were as many Italian troops on the Albanian-Yugoslav border as there were on the border with Greece. The Italian general staff, in a typical burst of Mussolinian enthusiasm, had been ordered to plan for an invasion of Yugoslavia as well. Thirty-seven divisions based in northern Italy were available for driving into Yugoslavia from the north. Another advantage of an attack on Yugoslavia was that it would satisfy popular sentiment for long-standing Italian demands for a large part of Dalmatia (now a part of Croatia) going back to aftermath of the First World War. Finally, it would be militarily a simpler task than butting through the Albanian and Greek mountains.

Berlin killed the Yugoslav plan. Prince Paul, the Yugoslav regent, was pro-German and could be relied on to keep his country out of a Balkan conflagration which was the last thing Hitler needed at that moment. Nonetheless, the plan for an *Emergenza E* (Emergency E for East), designating an invasion of Yugoslavia, remained on the drawing board until it was placed on the back burner after the crucial 15 October meeting. Six hundred thousand reservists were told to stand down, leaving just twenty battle-ready divisions. The Duce seems to have feared the moral effects of large-scale mobilization, as industry and farming had been denuded of vital manpower, and the effects on the national economy were already being felt.

All attention was now concentrated on Greece, but the Italian leadership was not all of one mind. Badoglio had by now become used to Mussolini's frequent changes of mood. 'The troops in Albania,' the marshal told his staff chiefs on 25 September, 'are enough to keep Greece in place ... after having put in place three divisions [the Parma, Siena and Piemonte], we consider the situation stabilized, [and that] the Greek problem, like the Yugoslav, can be resolved at the peace table.'[15] If this sounds curiously pacific coming from the head of the Duce's military establishment, to General Francesco Pricolo, the chief of the Regia Aeronautica, it was positively surreal. For Pricolo's air commander in Albania, General Ferruccio Ranza, had just informed him that the army was requesting 'air reinforcements for a forthcoming operation against Greece'. It was the first that Pricolo had heard of such a 'forthcoming operation;' his reaction was to disingenuously conclude that the secrecy had been necessary for security!

This ambiguity transmitted itself down through the command echelons. Roatta ordered Visconti Prasca to pull back the Siena division from the Greek border. But for many of the 40,000 Italian troops in Albania the immediate future was another winter of cold and discomfort. Badoglio, though, sounded convinced that Greece was off the board for the time being, and was relieved. The Duce was now preoccupied with the Italian advance against the British in North Africa – another move that Badoglio thought foolish but did not protest.

Mussolini finally concentrated his mind on 14 October at a high-level council of war at the Palazzo Venezia in Rome. *Esigenza G*, he proudly informed Visconti Prasca, who had been called to Rome for the occasion, at last was on. Greece, he said, was doomed – serve it right for helping the British. The key to his decision was the news four days before that Hitler had deployed Luftwaffe units in Romania to protect the Ploesti oil fields – without consulting his Pact of Steel ally. The omission had rankled.

The Hitlerian *fait accompli* did more than anything else to reawaken old inferiority complexes and persuade Mussolini that his time to act had come. Having lost the battle to invade Britain, Hitler was turning his eyes eastwards. If Mussolini wasn't on the ball, as far as he was concerned his German ally might grab the whole Balkans. 'I'll pay [Hitler] back in his own coin!' the Duce fumed to Ciano. 'He'll learn from the newspapers that I've occupied Greece.'

To Roatta, for one, the decision came as a shock. Only the day before he had messaged Pricolo that *Esigenza G* was still on the back burner. This was one of two totally contradictory messages the air chief received that day. The other was from Badoglio ordering him to have his squadrons in Albania ready for action in twelve days! Roatta was soon put in the loop by Mussolini, who rationalized his decision as the result of Greece's being 'overly supportive of the Allies'. (The true reason, the Duce's pique, was of course hidden.) Thus galvanized into action, Roatta with Badoglio's agreement came up with a campaign plan for twenty divisions to be used for the initial thrust into Greece, to be backed up by twelve more divisions ferried over the Adriatic over the next three months.[16]

Historians have seen this cumbersome plan as a way for Badoglio and Roatta to hold up the operation, or at least give Mussolini time to change his mind (again). The two officers had tacit support from King Vittorio Emanuele III, whom Mussolini had buttered up by appointing him joint *primo maresciallo dell'Impero* (first marshal of the Empire) along with himself. On the other hand, Jacomoni was fuelling Mussolini's ardour with fictitious reports that the Muslim Chams were ready to revolt from Greece and Visconti Prasca seemed raring to go. But was he? The meeting on the 14th seems to have concentrated minds. A quarter of a million Greek troops, Italian intelligence suggested with scarcely credible exaggeration, were lying in wait. Jacomoni suggested that any action be lightning quick, with the maximum element of surprise.

The final war council, to outline 'the *modus operandi* in its general character that I [Mussolini] have decided to initiate against Greece,' convened at 11.00 am the following day, 15 October, at the Palazzo Venezia with Ciano, Jacomoni, Visconti Prasca, Badoglio and Roatta in attendance. Incredibly, neither Admiral Cavagnari, the navy chief, nor Pricolo, the air force commander, had been invited. Roatta was the last to arrive, entering the room after the discussion had started. What he heard as he took his seat appalled him. The Duce, apparently ignoring Roatta's plan of the previous day, was going ahead with the invasion after all. Mussolini brushed aside all doubts; he and Visconti Prasca and the aggressive Ciano carried the day. Those of a contrary opinion, such as Badoglio and Roatta, were intimidated into silence.

The general plan was to invade the Greek province of Epiros to secure the independence of 'Chamuria' as a first stage, the second stage being to extend the operation to the occupation of Greece itself, knocking the country out of the potential Allied camp. Visconti Prasca and his nine-division 'mailed fist' would carry out the initial strike on 26 October. The twenty divisions planned by Roatta would be employed in the second stage. 'This is an action,' the Duce boasted, 'that I have been maturing for months and months before our entry into the war and indeed before the start of the conflict.'

Delusion piled upon delusion. Mussolini turned to Jacomoni. 'What's the state of mind of the Greek population?' he asked, as if he didn't have adequate information from Grazzi.

'Apparently, profoundly depressed,' Jacomoni replied.

'Most Greeks', Ciano chimed in, 'are indifferent to anything that might happen after our invasion.' This comment from Ciano sounds scarcely credible, given the precise opposite picture painted by Grazzi in Athens and the *Servizio Intelligenza Militare*, Italy's military intelligence. The otherwise capable foreign minister had allowed wishful thinking to overcome his reasoning powers. As regards morale in the ranks, Visconti Prasca, who detested Roatta as a desk man, assured his listeners that it was 'very high, with top-grade enthusiasm,' adding (with scant respect for his own fighting men) that 'the only cases of indiscipline involve officers and soldiers unwilling to go forward and fight through excess of anxiety'. That was a curiously impolitic thing to tell the Duce, who, whatever else could be marked against him, was never a coward and detested cowardice on the battlefield. But that defect, the general opined, would be offset by Italy's superiority in numbers. 'Don't worry about losses,' Mussolini replied.

Ciano promised to fabricate a border incident on 24 October to serve as an excuse for the invasion. Visconti Prasca said 'five or six divisions' would be in Athens within days and even reach Thessaloniki in the north. Badoglio roused himself to object that the nine divisions now poised to attack would be nowhere near enough to occupy all Greece. He was ignored. Fascist salutes were raised, boot heels clicked, and the meeting broke up.

There were still plenty of high-level worries. On October 16 Badoglio made his own clear to Jacomoni over lunch. 'The Greeks are good fighters,' the marshal said darkly. 'They showed it in their last war [1920–22] with Turkey. They were defeated but they fought valiantly.' After that comment, Jacomoni reported, Badoglio abruptly changed the subject. In fact, he was seriously considering resigning, dissuaded only by General Ubaldo Soddu, the deputy chief of the army staff. It is likely that Badoglio for some time had been disillusioned by Mussolini's lack of military common sense and had decided to let him go ahead and get Greek egg on his face in an absurd military campaign after which he, Badoglio, might hopefully return Italy to rationality. (It would be three years before he actually got the chance to do so.)

Another doubter was Pricolo, the air force chief, who moreover felt slighted at not having been invited to the 15 October meeting. General Quirino Armellini, a senior staff officer, had the task of reassuring him that as Greece wouldn't put up much resistance, significant air force operations would probably not be necessary – another disastrously wrong assumption.[17] Yet Armellini was no fool. He saw a potentially fatal rift opening up in the Rome hierarchy, between Ciano who was obsessed with the prestige of expanding Italy's domains, and Badoglio, who shrank from actions that he feared could set the Balkans aflame. The Germans, moreover, tended to agree with Badoglio.

King Vittorio Emanuele wasn't briefed on the 15 October meeting until five days later. The briefing didn't change his opposition to the plan, yet as a weak and diffident monarch whose continued presence on the throne of Italy depended directly on the Duce's favour, Vittorio Emanuele didn't have the moral fibre to be able to pull rank, even though he had the broad agreement of all three of Italy's staff chiefs – Badoglio for the army, Cavagnari for the navy and Pricolo for the air force. An invasion of Greece could all too easily slide into disaster, as any strong resistance by the Greeks would cost the army more men and equipment than it could afford.

But whatever the uncertainties at the top, Contingency G now had been brought forward as a rush job. Mussolini had to act fast before Hitler could stop him. Visconti Prasca worked on his battle order. He placed the Parma division on the left, against the Yugoslav border. Thus protected on his left flank, he assigned the Julia Alpine Division the task of spearheading the invasion of Greece in the centre. The Julia was to drive southwards to take the key town of Ioannina and then veer eastwards to Metsovo to entrap the bulk of the Greek force in a pincer movement. The bottled-up Greeks would then be hammered by the Ferrara Division backed up by the armoured 131st Centauro. The job of the Venezia division was to open the main southward road as far as Kalpaki to enable the Centauro to trundle into Ioannina and hopefully get as far south as Arta, cutting off north-western Greece altogether. The Siena and other smaller units were to secure the right flank at the coastal town of Igoumenitsa opposite Corfu, while the Piemonte would be held in reserve to guard a 'liberated Chamuria'. It would be a *passeggiata*, Visconti Prasca harrumphed at the Palazzo Venezia on 15 October – a walkover. All he needed was half a dozen or so divisions. They could be in Athens within two days.

Technically, the plan was a good one. But it was based on two false assumptions. The first was that the Greeks would put up a mere token resistance and fall apart after the initial determined thrust. The second was that the Italian army itself had the equipment and stamina to carry out an invasion. Perceptive Italians such as Grazzi, the ambassador in Athens, were in no doubt of the Greeks' iron resolve to defend their country if attacked. Moreover, though the nine Italian divisions already in Albania were formidable on paper, they lacked a great deal, mainly in mobile armour, artillery and field hospitals. Supplying those forces was proving to be a clumsy and slow process, as most Albanian ports were too shallow for the larger supply ships and troop transports. Badoglio, having just ordered the demobilization of 300,000 men after France was knocked out of the war, was now asked to put in motion a major campaign in just thirteen days – 28 October was the final D-day. On that date the Duce was to meet with Hitler in Florence and give him the good news.

At this late stage, some thought was finally given to what the role of the Regia Aeronautica would be. Mussolini had a curious blind spot where his own air force was concerned, even though he himself was an aviator and his sons Bruno and Vittorio bomber pilots. Perhaps he believed that his powerful air force could pretty much take care of itself. The day was yet to come when air force strategy would assume much importance in the minds of southern European military planners. Aircraft were seen to be mere army auxiliaries, like lorries or bullets. Pricolo commanded a formidable force. Based at Albanian aerodromes at Tirana, Korce, Gjirokaster, Berat, Sarande and Vlore were 225 top-line bombers, 179 fighters and fifty-nine reconnaissance patrollers. Other squadrons could reach Greece from bases in the heel of Italy such as Lecce, Bari and Grottaglie. There were even more aircraft of various types available at the headquarters of the Regia Aeronautica's Fourth Air Force at Brindisi, including twenty Junkers Ju87 Stuka dive-bombers. But not all of the Duce's planes were new and shiny. There were many obsolete Fiat CR32 biplanes serving as front-line fighters, for example, plus a variety of other aging types which unnecessarily burdened the supply and repair services.

With such a force at his command, why was Pricolo not more assertive? The answer lies in his own conflicting loyalties. He had let himself be caught up in the game of political influence and feared losing his position in the Duce's charmed circle. When Ranza, his air commander in Albania, had asked him what the air support plans were for the planned invasion of Greece,

Pricolo had to admit he didn't know! Mussolini at last decided to personally brief his top airman, telling him that Italian forces had to be in Greece 'before the British turn it into a base against us'. Pricolo asked if the Duce had any proof of that. The reply was: 'Of course,' without elaboration. And that pretty much was that.

The exchange reveals that Pricolo didn't quite buy his boss' rationalization of the planned Greek campaign. He also resented the fact that, as was becoming obvious, Mussolini intended to give all the glory to the Italian army. Yet he continued to serve his leader. In fact, throughout the Greek campaign Pricolo would never be more than a rubber-stamp air commander on the sidelines, leaving air tactical decisions to his subordinates.

The situation in the navy, the Regia Marina, was even more precarious. In April Cavagnari had been given a typically vague and woolly order of the day that his fleet should be prepared at all times to attack 'at once' all over the Mediterranean, and even beyond. The senior admirals had the presence of mind to question this impossible order, or at least ask to have it broken down into manageable specifics, but they waited in vain. Basic naval considerations such as how to invade and secure key points such as Corsica, Malta, the strategic Tunisian port of Bizerta (the only one with cranes big enough to unload supply ships) and even the coast of Egypt remained unanalyzed. Because of deficiencies in supply by sea, the Italian troops sweltering in the Libyan desert were chronically short of lorries and even drinking water.[18]

Just how ill-prepared the Regia Marina was became sadly clear on 9 July when it blew an enviable opportunity to hammer a British fleet on manoeuvres off Punta Stilo near the toe of Italy. Italian intelligence had done a good job of intercepting and deciphering messages from the Royal Navy base at Alexandria, but at the last minute, the Italian naval commanders at Punta Stilo, despite adequate support from shore-based aircraft, simply dared not take any initiatives not expressly approved by the Duce. They knew, moreover, that he was unwilling to risk naval capital ships this early in the war. The result was the loss of a never-to-be-repeated chance to block the central Mediterranean to British shipping.[19] To compensate, The Regia Marina authorized hit-and-run attacks on British shipping which sometimes caught the Greeks as well, the worst incident being that of the *Elli*.

In the senior ranks of the army, meanwhile, as the date of the invasion of Greece drew nigh, other generals jostled for a piece of the action. Visconti Prasca knew this and fretted that he might be relegated to a mere corps commander in the operation, and his hoped-for rise to the top of the military hierarchy derailed as a result. On 25 October the Duce himself reaffirmed his faith in the general, putting his mind at rest. 'Attack with maximum decisiveness and violence,' was the Duce's order of that day. 'The success of the action depends above all on its speed.'[20] Mussolini could brook no delay now, as he was preparing to make his momentous announcement to Hitler in three days' time.

Ciano naively believed that a single bombing of Athens would be enough to make the Greeks capitulate, and if they didn't, he plotted to have King George II assassinated. The Duce proclaimed to all and sundry that half a million of his soldiers were poised on the Yugoslav frontier and 200,000 more facing Greece – at least twice the actual figure. He further boasted that 'a hundred heavy tanks' were in position and ready to roll – the purest fantasy. To the naysayers he crowed that 'if anyone makes any difficulties about beating the Greeks I shall resign from being an Italian'.[21] Few other figures in history have set themselves up with such diligent sound and fury for the inevitable fall.

Among the bizarre developments of those few days, one in particular stands out – Mussolini's eleventh-hour attempt to get Bulgaria on board. On 16 October he had sent an emissary to Sofia, the Bulgarian capital, with a bombastically-worded invitation to join in the attack on Greece. Before King Boris III was dangled the prize of an outlet to the warm Aegean Sea, long coveted by the Bulgarians. But Boris was not to be stampeded into hasty adventures. Responding in elegantly-written French, the Bulgarian king politely declined on the grounds that he feared a Turkish encroachment on southeast Bulgaria and moreover, Bulgaria's military was not ready for war with a neighbour. 'Lily-livered monarchs, no good for anything!' the Duce fumed when he read Boris' reply. 'We'll manage by ourselves.'[22]

And so, with almost all of Italy's top military leadership doubtful, with the Germans frowning, with Bulgaria shying away, with the Greek embassy in Rome sending Athens accurate reports of what was going on (security in Rome was atrocious) and the Greeks bracing for a major showdown, Mussolini single-mindedly pushed for his great adventure. Metaxas in Athens was on tenterhooks. 'No Italian attack today,' he jotted, relieved, in his diary on 25 October. And on the following day: 'No attack today either.'

Inside the ornate Italian embassy in Athens, Grazzi and Mondini might be biting their nails over the growing military preparedness of the Greeks through 1940, but the view from the Greeks' own high command was less than completely rosy. Some senior officers were unhappy with some of Metaxas' policy choices. One of them had been the leader's preoccupation with Bulgaria as Greece's prime potential foe in the Balkans. This worry had given rise to the Metaxas Line, a 300km complex of underground reinforced concrete bunkers and surface gun positions running just south of the Bulgarian frontier along the top of the Rodopi mountain range and turning south to the coast near Xanthi. It was a massive and costly project, carried out in what secrecy could be achieved at the time. By the time it was completed just before the outbreak of war in Europe, it included twenty-one major redoubts taking up

26km of underground corridors and bunker living quarters, linked by more than 200km of interior roads. Some 108,000 tonnes of reinforced concrete had been used in them, plus 1,300km of telephone line and 90km of barbed wire. Fort Rupel, the largest complex, was manned by forty-four officers and 1,300 men and protected by two 75mm field guns, five 37mm German-made PAK antitank guns, three 20mm antiaircraft guns, five 81mm Brand mortars, eighty-five heavy Saint-Etienne machine guns, twenty-five lighter machine guns and fifty-three grenade launchers.

Manning the entire Metaxas Line were just over 10,000 men with a total of seventy-five heavy guns, twenty-six antitank guns and several hundred machine guns. Chemical filters in the air conditioning protected the bunkers against gas attack. It was one of the most advanced defensive works in Europe at the time; the French military attaché, given a tour of the line, pronounced it superior in several ways to the fabled Maginot Line it was modelled on. It would have been invulnerable to attack by the likes of the Bulgarian Army, but like the Maginot Line it was destined to be overrun by the Wehrmacht in short order. Weaknesses of the Metaxas Line included the basic fact that it could protect only one portion of Greece's northern frontiers, that it could stockpile ammunition and supplies for at most ten days of combat, and that when war came, the line would have to be weakened by urgent transfers of men and weapons to other fronts.[23]

Papagos has been blamed in hindsight for concentrating almost exclusively on the Metaxas Line to the exclusion of almost everything else, including the more vulnerable Albanian border. There were also criticisms about the construction. One senior officer suspected that the private contractors employed to build the hive of complexes 'had no idea of the requirements of fortifications' and that the General Staff was spending money on huge static fortifications when, say, the purchase of armoured vehicles would have been more useful. It was a prescient criticism.

The Greek Army had acquired its first armour in 1931 – two 6-ton Vickers Mark E light tanks and two smaller 1½-ton Carden Lloyd Mark IV tankettes. Four years later the Tank Battalion was created in expectation of the delivery of fourteen British and French tanks to make the unit viable. War broke out before they could arrive, and so the essentially armourless army had to content itself with what was called the Cavalry Division Motorized Regiment, consisting of six companies of a total of 165 all-terrain vehicles, the best of which were forty-four Mercedes-Benz G5s.[24]

Metaxas had a cogent motive for not strengthening defences on the Albanian border – a reluctance to overly antagonize Italy. This reluctance did not arise out of fear but of a sense of national self-respect. Metaxas did not wish to be perceived as panicking in front of a bully. 'I will not bow my head to the Italians,' he confided to his diary on 28 August. Five days before, the

8th and 9th Divisions had been called up, with as much secrecy as could be managed. In case of an invasion over the Albanian border, Metaxas figured, Greek units might manage a token defence in a few sectors to hold up the attackers until full mobilization could be complete. 'The machine is running exceptionally well,' he wrote in his diary.

That was perhaps being a tad overoptimistic. Military credits available for the defence of the Albanian border remained unspent. Worried cables from the Italian embassy in Athens notwithstanding, Rome's intelligence could not fail to be well aware of the weakness of the Greek position in the northwest.[25] For Metaxas that was a risk that had to be taken. In light of the subsequent success of Greek arms, Metaxas has been criticized for initially agreeing to a strategy by which in the event of an attack the Greek front line should withdraw 200m from the frontier (apart from the token resistance moves already mentioned), and if the invasion was overwhelming, to pull back all the way to Mount Othrys on the east coast, leaving the whole northwest of the country in enemy hands so that defence could concentrate on the east coast – 'a gross staff planning error', according to one critic. Not all senior officers were of a defensive frame of mind. Lieutenant General Dimitrios Papadopoulos, the II Corps Commander, insisted that an army's morale was best maintained by offence.[26] Papadopoulos' 8th Division commander, Major General Haralambos Katsimitros, was of like mind and had no intention of retreating that easily if it came to a fight.

With Visconti Prasca's jump-off date now a few days away, one final detail needed seeing to – the fabricated border incident scheduled for 25 October and designed to provide a flimsy fig leaf for the act of aggression to come. First, an unmarked Italian aeroplane was sent to drop leaflets on Albanian territory with a purported exhortation to join the Greeks and British against the Italian masters. This was then shown to be 'proof' of Allied treachery. On Jacomoni's secret orders, bombs exploded in the Italian authorities' premises in Sarande (officially renamed Porto Edda after Mussolini's daughter). The blasts were timed to coincide with a report from the state-controlled Stefani news agency that a 'band of Greeks' had been caught trying to attack Italian positions near Korce; six of the assailants were reported captured, while two Albanian accomplices were reported killed and three others wounded. The 'incident' was never proven, and the consensus now is that several hapless Albanians were dressed up in Greek uniforms and gunned down to provide the story. Athens issued an immediate and strong denial that it had authorized any such covert operation – one of those times in history when such denials ring true – and agreed to send a team of officers to join the Italians in an on-the-spot investigation on 27 October. The Italians, however, claimed a lack of authority and the probe was halted because Visconti Prasca, of course, had an invasion to begin. At dusk on that date he was more or less ready. The attack on Greece was to begin at two points, the first through the Kalamas River valley with the immediate objective of reaching Ioannina, and the second some 50km to the northeast, over the southern spurs of Mount Grammos and through the defiles of the Pindos range to the town of Metsovo, more than 100km away. The aim was to weaken the defending Greeks by forcing them to fight on disparate fronts in forbidding country.

The advance on Ioannina was tasked to the Twenty-fifth Corps (*Corpo d'Armata*) commanded by General Carlo Rossi and comprising the Ferrara and Siena divisions plus the armoured Centauro equipped with 163 Fiat light tanks, many of which were not in the best shape – some 30,000 men in all, including a legion of Blackshirts to stiffen the Ferrara, which included 3,500 Albanian volunteers of questionable trustworthiness. The corps fielded 134 artillery pieces, with the Centauro operating an additional twenty-four anti-aircraft and anti-armour guns.

The eastern prong of the attack was entrusted to the Julia Division under General Mario Girotti, which included some of the best and toughest soldiers Italy could boast, men from the Italian Alps who knew the techniques of mountain combat. With 10,800 men and twenty artillery pieces, the crack Julia was entrusted with the demanding assignment of punching its way to Metsovo to outflank the Greek defence north of Ioannina.

The twin attacks would be supplemented by an advance down the western Greek coast by the so-called Coastal Group (*Raggruppamento del Litorale*) under General Carlo Rivolta, consisting of the 3rd Grenadier Regiment and the 3rd Cavalry Regiment 'borrowed' from the Aosta, Milano and Parma Divisions, totalling about 5,000 men including Albanian volunteers. The aim of Rivolta's group was to secure the coast down to the town of Preveza and the island of Corfu, in order to ease incoming supplies by sea.

Yet farther to the northwest, between the Albanian town of Korce and the Yugoslav border, the Twenty-sixth Corps under General Gabriele Nasci waited for the order to attack through Greek Macedonia. This corps consisted of the Parma Division in the front line with the Piemonte held in reserve, and included twenty-four gun batteries and ten light tanks. Its task, if deployed, was to cut off the important northeast Greek port of Thessaloniki, which was the main entry point for Greek troop reinforcements from the islands and the north. The total Italian invasion force (not counting Nasci's corps) was somewhere in the vicinity of 87,000 men (Greek sources place the total at 105,000). But they were ranged along a front of 250km of some of the toughest terrain soldiers have ever been called on to fight in.[27]

Opposing the invaders were about 50,000 Greeks of the II Corps, of which only the 8th and 9th Divisions were up to strength. Mobilization was in full spate, with Papagos estimating that he could eventually field eighteen divisions for the defence of Epiros. Katsimitros' 8th Division was to block the planned

Italian advance on Ioannina, while the 9th Division under Major General Christos Zygouris, beefed up by 4 Brigade, occupied a large swath of mountain country opposite the Italian Twenty-sixth Corps in Albania. Seven battalions of infantry were placed in the second line.[28] Papagos had the advantage of fairly limited options. He knew which way the Italian attacks would have to come and, thanks to the few well-defined valleys, where to block them. He also was well aware of what the Julia Division would try to do – outflank the Greek right – though Girotti himself feared that the Greeks might outflank the Julia's left. Papagos' first line of defence stretched from the Kalamas River eastwards along the crags of Mount Tymfi to Mount Smolikas. But he was by no means confident of having enough forces to hold it. If that line were to be breached, a second defence was organized at the Arachthos River north of Arta, extending eastwards to the plain of Thessaly and ending up in Greek Macedonia.

In 1940 the Greek army was made up of five army corps comprising fifteen divisions. The I Corps was based in Athens, the II Corps in Larissa, the III Corps in Thessaloniki, the IV Corps in Kavala and the V Corps in Alexandroupolis. The brunt of operations, in case of invasion through Albania, would be borne by the II and III Corps, with the relevant sector divisions, namely, the 8th Division in Ioannina, the 9th Division in Kozani and the 11th Division in Thessaloniki, plus the separate Thessaloniki-based Cavalry Division. The divisions contained thirty-nine battle-ready infantry regiments plus the Athens-based Royal Evzone Guards company, the picturesque skirted elite unit of over-six-footers charged with standing guard outside the Tomb of the Unknown Soldier in front of the Parliament building.

The Greek artillery corps was organized into fourteen regiments of regular artillery, two of field artillery, four of heavy artillery and four of anti-aircraft units. The cavalry was organized into ten regiments, including one mechanized regiment, a mounted machine gun company and a mounted Royal Guards company. The engineer corps included four regiments of sappers, railwaymen and signallers, plus independent units such as bridge-builders.[29]

The V Corps had been formed in 1936 to beef up the Metaxas Line along the Bulgarian border, along with the 14th Division of the IV Corps. Papagos had long fretted that the slender coastal corridor of northeast Greece, served by only one railway line, was particularly vulnerable to Bulgarian aggression. An enormous amount of staff work, in fact, had gone into preparing for a possible Bulgarian attack. In the northwest, Katsimitros' 8th Division was given considerable freedom of action – a tribute to the prescient persistence of its commander. That division was also liberally supplied with field artillery, which would soon come in very useful.

The mobilization plan in force, revised in 1939, provided for the immediate call-up of fifty-six infantry regiments, each of which would be equipped with four mortars and a battery of mountain artillery; twenty-four regiments of divisional mountain and field artillery and four of anti-aircraft artillery. Anti-armour gun batteries were also included in the II, III IV and V Corps, plus a separate unit in the 8th Division. Some of the mobilization had already taken place, followed by a partial mobilization of the 10th Division, then of the II Corps. At the same time the 6th, 7th and 14th Divisions were to mass at the Bulgarian frontier as a precaution. More corps and divisions would be readied according to the progress of operations.[30]

The defence of the Albanian front in particular was defined by so-called Plan IB, anticipating an Italian attack, which after April 1939 replaced Bulgaria as the prime threat to be met. Greek staff chiefs suddenly found they had to tear up the ponderous reams of instructions for the Bulgarian front and re-think everything. Even then, Plan IB (Italy-Bulgaria) presupposed a *simultaneous* fight against Bulgaria and Italy. In fact, not until the actual Italian invasion did Bulgaria recede in importance in military minds. The plan called for eight divisions and two brigades of infantry, plus a cavalry brigade, to meet the attackers at the Albanian border and form a line of defence along the Kalamas River, and eastwards to Mount Smolikas as far as the Yugoslav frontier.[31]

Greek intelligence did not have an overly demanding task. As we have seen, Italian security fell far short of ideal. By 27 October Papagos knew full well that an invasion was imminent. On that day he summoned Mondini to warn him that every metre of Greece's frontiers was being heavily guarded. That evening, while the eighteenth anniversary of Mussolini's seizure of power was being celebrated in a glittering gala in an Italian cultural centre in Athens, the decoding machines in the backrooms of the Italian embassy were humming with instructions for war.

Well after midnight Grazzi and Mondini, accompanied by an embassy interpreter, walked down the front steps of the embassy and got into Mondini's car. The streets of Athens were deserted and the night was very mild. Mondini took his seat behind the wheel and started the ignition, driving up Vassilissis Sophias Avenue, the main northbound thoroughfare which leads to Kifissias Avenue, the principal road to the affluent northern suburbs of Athens. Mondini took time to admire the 'marvellous sky of Attica with its myriad stars'. His passenger, Grazzi, probably didn't say much during the drive, and with good reason, because the moment he dreaded had come. What followed was an iconic moment in Greek and indeed European history, a moment that has been justifiably compared to the ringing defiance of Spartan King Leonidas I to the massed Persians of Xerxes at Thermopylai in 480 BC, and all the more striking because the details are authentic.

The two-storey house where Metaxas lived is still standing in a quiet, leafy block in the upscale district of Kifissia, and still owned by his family. The house and grounds are pretty much as they were when, at about 2.45 am in the morning of 28 October 1940, Mondini drew up at the security guard post at the iron gate. The head guard, partly dazzled by the headlights, mistook the tricoloured Italian flag over the front right wheel for the French one and telephoned the in-house guard who woke up the prime minister.

Metaxas had not been feeling well the previous day and had no doubt hoped for an uninterrupted night of rest. Heaving himself out of bed, he didn't bother to change out of his old-fashioned nightshirt but slipped on a dressing gown decorated with little white flowers and a pair of slippers, and went downstairs where he saw that his nocturnal visitor was not a French diplomat but Grazzi. At that moment he must have known what was about to happen, but put on a pleasant diplomatic face.

'*Ah, monsieur le ministre,*' Metaxas began civilly. '*Comment allez-vous?*' (French was still the *par excellence* diplomatic language of the time.) He showed Grazzi, Mondini and the embassy interpreter into a small parlour, motioning Grazzi to a comfortable brown leather armchair. Still speaking French, Grazzi formally informed the Greek leader that his government had instructed him to communicate the following urgent note, whereupon he handed Metaxas a sheet of paper. Metaxas read it through carefully, shaking his head. In contrast to the civility of the men in the room, the note was blunt. It accused Greece of violating its declared neutrality by being partial to the British. It went on, without providing any proof, to enumerate several so-called instances of neutrality violation, including a nonexistent 'threat' to Albania.

'All this,' the note concluded on a note of aggressive triumph, 'cannot lately be tolerated by Italy.' If Greece wanted to stay safe, the note warned, 'as a guarantee of neutrality by Greece and of the security of Italy, the Italian government requests the facility of occupying, with its armed forces and for the duration of the conflict with Great Britain, some strategic points in Greek territory.' Then came the threat. 'The Italian government asks the Greek government not to oppose such an occupation and not to hinder the free passage of troops ... Wherever the Italian troops meet resistance, such resistance will be met by force and the Greek government will assume responsibility for the consequences.' And that was not all. Greece had three hours – until 6.00 am – to agree.

Metaxas finished reading, his hands trembling slightly, his eyes moist. Grazzi, to his credit, felt almost as bad. The Greek leader raised his eyes to the ambassador and in an even voice said, '*Alors, c'est la guerre.*' 'Well then, it's war.' In his own extreme discomfiture, Grazzi felt he had to sweeten the pill somewhat. He suggested to Metaxas that he cave in to the ultimatum. 'What are these "strategic points" that Italy wants to occupy?' Metaxas asked. The ambassador was stumped. He simply didn't know. There were, of course, no such specific 'points'. 'So you see, it's war,' Metaxas repeated. Grazzi could do little but say lamely that he would be in his embassy until 6.00 am in case Metaxas had a change of heart. Coldly Metaxas saw Grazzi and Mondini to their car. 'You are the stronger ones,' he said. Grazzi stayed in his office until six, as he promised, but of course Metaxas was already strapping on Greece's armour.

Chapter 3

Punch and Counterpunch

The Greeks rush joyfully to war – Prince Peter rushes back – the Italians push across the border – Athens and Patras are bombed – The Julia Division invades – the 8th Division digs in at Kalpaki – Battle of Kalpaki – air hero Mitralexis rams a bomber – the Julia is halted and knocked out – Italian army reorganized – British help arrives – the death of Sgt Merifield – D'Albiac's inner doubts

The date of 28 October 1940, a Monday, left an indelible impression on every Greek who lived through it. It has become a modern Greek icon, repeated and amplified endlessly in the national media and history books. The prevailing image is that of a Greece unwillingly dragged into war, but once the conflict came, jumping eagerly to the colours. That was certainly the impression of the average individual volunteer who on the morning of 28 October quit his job with the blessing of his employers, joined the delirious crowds thronging central Athens and crowded onto the tram to head for the recruiting offices. And certainly it was the impression of the majority of junior and middle-grade officers, many of them rushed into the service from civilian life and nervous in their new shoulder insignia. They read the same newspapers and listened to the same patriotic radio programmes.

Of course, there could be no question of going back to bed for Metaxas. His first telephone call was to the king, followed by others to his ministers for an emergency cabinet meeting. He then threw on some clothes and got into his official car. It was not yet 4.00 am when he drew up at the downtown residence of Sir Michael Palairet, the British ambassador, and implored him to urgently notify Admiral Sir Andrew Cunningham, the Senior Royal Navy Commander in the Mediterranean, based at Alexandria, to send British warships to block feared Italian naval moves on Corfu and the Ionian islands and discourage an attempt on the Peloponnese. Palairet wanted time to code the message but Metaxas insisted there wasn't time for that, so the message went out *en clair*. Still, in the best of situations, the British fleet would need two days to steam from Alexandria to Souda Bay in Crete.

Metaxas also used the ambassador for an immediate appeal to Churchill for air force help. Sleepless and mentally shattered, he was prone to fears and doubts. What if the Duce's boasts about an invincible army came true and the Greek defenders were hurled back? Could Athens itself be held? Might not ancient history repeat itself and the free Greeks be confined to resistance in the Peloponnese, as almost happened in the Persian Wars of the fifth century BC? And would the Germans join in? Anything was possible. Of course, that did not mean that the Greeks should submit. 'The war we confront today is thus solely a war for honour,' Metaxas' message to Churchill read. 'The outcome of the world war will not be decided in the Balkans.'

It was a curiously-worded statement, revealing the Greek leader's apprehensions that Britain might shy away from a heavy Balkan involvement. He was concerned that the British, facing a possible German invasion across the English Channel and hard-pressed in North Africa, should not think that Greece would be too big a strain on their resources. The Greeks, Metaxas implied, would not hesitate to fight their own fight; but if the British could show their support with military help, they might fight even better. The five army corps which comprised the whole Greek land force might enjoy high morale, but until the last minute it remained underequipped, besides being scattered along the entire northern Greek frontier and through the Aegean islands. After a brief cabinet meeting including the king, Metaxas issued his first war directives, including a proviso that 'no Greek will become richer out of this war'. He needed all the working-class support he could now get.[1]

By 4.30 am Metaxas was at the Foreign Ministry meeting with King George and Crown Prince Paul. An hour later, just as the first Italians were crossing into Greece, the full cabinet had convened in emergency session. After briefing the cabinet on what had just happened in his home, he asked for their signatures on the general mobilization order. 'If anyone disagrees, he may resign,' Metaxas concluded. No-one spoke. 'I'll sign first,' he said, crossing himself on his breast and putting his pen to the paper. 'God save Greece,' he breathed when he had signed.[2] At 6.00 am air raid sirens woke the Athenians who quickly filled the streets and squares in a paroxysm of patriotic fervour. Newspapers rushed out special Monday morning editions with screaming headlines and ecstatic editorials whipping up public enthusiasm – if it really needed whipping up – for a stern lesson to be delivered to the 'macaroniboys' (*makaronades*). State radio broadcast and re-broadcast Metaxas' ringing messages of defiance. 'Our forces are defending the homeland,' ran the terse official communiqué issued at lunchtime, accompanied by the strains of the national anthem. Call-up lists were hurriedly pasted on the city's walls. At 11.00 am Metaxas and the king took a short drive in an open car through the centre of the city soaking up the adulation. At one point he left his car and walked. Girls tossed flowers at him. Cab drivers wanted to throw their arms around him. He remarked to a cabinet minister with him: 'At last, at 70 years old, the time of recognition has come for me. They say the Greeks have always been ungrateful to their politicians since ancient times. I don't buy that.'[3]

At that moment it would have been very hard to find a foe of the regime. Literally overnight, a fascist dictator had become a national hero. Kanellopoulos, the anti-fascist intellectual, cabled Metaxas with congratulations and asked to be released from confinement to join the war effort, a wish granted four days later. Thousands of other liberal and left-wing Greeks felt the same and flocked to the cause. The national media condensed Metaxas' polite French response to Grazzi's ultimatum into a single word, as powerful as a right hook to the jaw: '*Ochi!*' 'No!' (Which is how it remains in legend today.) Far away in London, a former British army officer and intelligence operative named Compton Mackenzie heard of 'the great negative' on BBC radio. 'I never,' Mackenzie wrote later, 'wanted to shake any man so warmly by the hand as I wanted to shake the hand of Metaxas.'[4] The confession is remarkable since Mackenzie had been one of a team of British officers and diplomats in Greece during the First World War secretly aiding liberal parties and fighting royalist stalwarts such as Metaxas! In Britain, it was especially appreciated that 'Greece was the only country to enter the war voluntarily on the allied side when Britain stood alone'.[5]

Prince Peter, taking a short break in Istanbul, was awakened before dawn by a hammering on his hotel room door. He opened the door to see a distraught employee of the Greek consulate who blurted out the news. He and his wife hurriedly packed their bags and called for their travelling car, making a brief halt at the Orthodox church of Saint Mary of the Mongols to light candles for their deliverance. Arriving in Athens three days later – after witnessing an Italian bombing raid on Larissa – he went straight to his office at the ornate Grande Bretagne Hotel in Syntagma Square that had been commandeered as General Staff headquarters.[6]

As the Greek nation enthusiastically went to war, those Italians living in Athens found themselves victimized. The local office of the Ala Littoria airline and Italian schools and cultural offices were trashed, and leading members of the Italian community arrested. Grazzi, himself sleepless and shaken by the turn of events, spoke on the telephone to Ciano, who made light of it all. The Italian foreign minister at the time was in the same room with Mussolini. 'Grazzi tells me that everything is all right,' the ambassador heard his boss tell the Duce.

'I didn't tell you that,' Grazzi retorted.

'You'll see,' Ciano reassured Grazzi. 'We're now sending twenty divisions to Albania and in fifteen days it will all be over.' Grazzi was hardly reassured. Shortly afterwards he and his staff were expelled from Athens. As a reward for his faithfulness to the Duce despite his own misgivings, he was sent on 'holiday leave' under a cloud.[7]

When Visconti Prasca ordered his legions to cross the Greek border at 5.30 am, he found his first unexpected foe in the weather. Autumn in the Balkans can be a riot of gold and ochre-coloured forests wreathing the sunlit mountains. But for two days the rain had come down in torrents, turning the dusty mountain tracks into brown quagmires sucking down boot and hoof. Ordinarily gentle mountain gullies became raging cataracts. Men and horses and mules struggled through the mire. But Visconti Prasca was unperturbed; bad weather, he figured, would be bad for the enemy as well. What he apparently failed to realize was that though mud and rain indeed affected all alike, they were immeasurably harder on an advancing army than on one in a defensive position.

Rossi's Twenty-fifth Corps, dubbed the 'Chamuria,' advanced in the centre, while in the west, hugging the grey and choppy Ionian Sea, a regiment of the Raggruppamento del Litorale under Colonel Enrico Andreini pushed through sheets of rain into Greek territory, while to the east the first two regiments of the Siena Division, Colonel Carloni's 31 Infantry and Colonel Roberto Gianani's 32 Infantry crossed the frontier. On their left the Ferrara also advanced, with the 47 Infantry (Colonel Trizio) and the 48 (Colonel Sapienza) in the lead. Trundling towards the Kalamas River valley were a regiment of Centauro Division armour and feather-hatted *bersaglieri* under Colonel Solinas. None of these units at first encountered any resistance, as Papagos' Plan IB had provided for an initial strategic withdrawal to more defensible positions along the Kalamas River. Greek border and customs posts stood abandoned. Italian soldiers noted plates of half-eaten food on the tables and portraits of Metaxas and King George still on the walls. Behind the advance units of the Ferrara lumbered the rest of the Centauro's light tanks, their tracks skidding in the mud but making progress nonetheless. Well might Visconti Prasca triumphantly cable later in the day, as Mussolini was in conference with Hitler in Florence: 'Our troops are proceeding with great enthusiasm across the frontier.'

Peasants in the Greek frontier villages rushed from their fields as the air shook with artillery fire and ran to huddle around their fireplaces. Only the lucky few with radios had any idea what was happening. Villagers gazed impassively at the Italians in their grey-green uniforms tramping southwards through the damp and narrow streets. The Italians were just the latest invaders of Epiros over the ages, after the Ottoman Turks, Slavs, Goths, Gauls and Romans. These, too, would come and go. Thanks to this history, each mountain village had its secret caves where the population could flee to if things got really rough.

Papagos, ready or not, had to deploy what he had, and fast. His defence plan included a transfer of the 13th and 17th Infantry Divisions from the Bulgarian border to beef up the 8th Division, plus 16 Infantry Brigade, though the units would need time to complete their transfer. These divisions would be under the ultimate command of I Corps in Athens, while the 2nd, 3rd and 4th Divisions would muster east of the Pindos mountain range to be sent to the front via Arta. Rather than split his forces to meet the two separate waves of invaders, Papagos risked temporarily giving up some Greek territory in order to maintain contact between his forces and forge a defensive wall of men.[8] Even so, Papagos' front was more than 240km across, the 8th Division alone responsible for some 100km. Time was impossibly short. National mobilization was still far from complete. Men would have to be called up, given basic training and sent into battle within days. Some of the delays in preparation had been understandable. Metaxas, for cogent reasons, hadn't wanted to make the mobilization too obvious. Moreover, the Greek military had not fought a war since the demoralizing Asia Minor debacle of 1922, and as a result strategic and tactical thinking had not progressed much since then. For Metaxas, however, the period of agonizing uncertainty had come to an end, and he could throw himself into his task with a clear mind.

Bad weather over Albania and Northern Greece had grounded all the Regia Aeronautica units based in Albania. But those bombers based in southern Italy had no such impediment. Barely had Grazzi got back into his car after delivering the Duce's ultimatum when a squadron of Savoia-Marchetti SM81s took off, appearing at 20,000 feet over the Royal Hellenic Air Force College at Tatoi north of Athens around lunchtime. The sirens sounded in Athens again around 9.30 am but no-one bothered to run to a shelter. The war was just too exciting. The college commandant, Group Captain George Falkonakis, thought the planes were Greek. Either the fine art of aircraft recognition had yet to be taught in Greece or it took time for the RHAF officer corps to realize that Greece was actually at war. Only when the first bombs came whistling down did he order the sirens to be sounded and his flying cadets to don their helmets and man the anti-aircraft guns. One of them was Constantine Hatzilakos, a keen student flier barely into his first year at the air force college, finally glad, as he put it much later, 'to get into the fight' even if not yet airborne. Pilot Officer Doros Kleiamakis, a young flight instructor, was in the air testing a French-made Bloch MB151 fighter when he puzzled over the black puffs dotting the sky around him. Realizing what was happening, he managed to land without getting hit by his own side's anti-aircraft fire. Falkonakis' delay in mobilizing the defences got him court-martialled.[9]

In the dusty village of Kalyvia, 15km east of Athens, it was the start of an ordinary school week for 9 year old Sotiris Kollias. He was in the playground with his friends when the sound of a distant loud explosion made them stop their games. A few minutes later the SM81s that had just bombed Tatoi roared overhead at 3,000ft. The young Sotiris counted ten of them, four in front and six in two formations of three each. 'All of us, teachers and pupils, stood there not making a sound,' he recalled, as the bombers banked over Mount Pan to the south of Kalyvia and headed for the coast. When he got home he sketched his vivid impression on a piece of paper.[10] The raiders went on to bomb the port of Piraeus, the Corinth Canal and the city of Patras, with much loss of life.

Around 4.00 am, while it was still dark, General Mario Girotti, the commander of the 3rd Julia Alpine Division, ordered his front ranks across the border into Greece. The Julia was a separate command, independent of either Rossi in the west or Nasci in the east. Girotti's point of attack was a hundred or so kilometres northeast of Rossi's advance, the left segment of a great pincer that Visconti Prasca hoped would trap the Greeks in a vice. The Julia, consisting of 8 Alpine Regiment on the left and 9 on the right, could field some of the best mountain fighters Italy had. Occupying the centre sector between Rossi and Nasci, the Julia was reinforced with twenty-four pieces of mountain artillery and a cavalry squadron. As Visconti Prasca's spearhead, the Julia was joined with the Venezia and Arezzo divisions to bring some 35,000 men to bear at the initial point of attack.

The great impediment to Girotti's advance was not human but geological – the 10,000ft mass of Mount Smolikas that loomed before the advancing Alpini. Colonel Vincenzo Dapino's 8 Regiment was to flank the mountain from the left, Colonel Gaetano Tavoni's 9 from the right. Both regiments were supported by artillery and Albanian auxiliaries. Ranged against Girotti were a mere 2,000 men of the Greek army's Epiros Detachment of the 8th Division. This paltry force was under the command of Colonel Constantine Davakis, who moreover had to defend a mountainous front of 35km where visibility and communications were hellishly difficult. With two infantry regiments, a single gun battery and a few dozen cavalrymen from the 1st Troop of B Reconnaissance Company, Davakis had to fall back. Girotti continued his advance, with the aim of outflanking the Greek 8th Division main force to the east. His objective was the town of Metsovo, some 70km to the south. But he would have to move over some of the most rugged terrain in Europe, with mountains over 5,000ft high divided by a maze of gullies and ravines.

The filthy weather continued into the second day of hostilities. Rome matter-of-factly informed Visconti Prasca that rough seas in the Adriatic had temporarily stopped the supply ships from sailing from the heel of Italy. The mud-caked men of the Ragruppamento del Litorale had yet to meet any defenders in force, but they stared in dismay at the foaming brown mountain rivers, swollen by the rains and dotted with the carcasses of farm animals. The Greeks had taken the precaution of blowing up the main bridges and the Italians lacked fording equipment. The Kalamas River in particular was impassable. In the northern sector the Julia Division was finding a similar rushing obstacle in the Sarandaporos River, where the 8 Alpine was falling behind.

There were plenty of men in the Italian army who were quite prepared to believe that they were on a mission of national glory and who swallowed the Duce's bombast whole. This did not necessarily mean they were fascists by conviction, although many were. Most, in fact, were simple clear-eyed patriots whose families had benefited from Mussolini's earlier efforts to organize Italy and had found a sense of mission. One of them was a grenadier lieutenant in the Raggruppamento del Litorale called Genserico Fontana who on the eve of the invasion, about half a kilometre from the Greek border, was keyed up by nervous excitement.

> The night is dark and rainy [Fontana wrote in his diary]. War will be here tomorrow. The captain is nervous and often wipes his glasses. He's a volunteer as well ... It's as if he's performing a sacred rite in silence. Tomorrow we may hope that Mars [the Roman god of war] will favour us. They tell us we have to look sharp, as we're only a few divisions and haven't been able to send a declaration of war. Even though we're few, we have no fear. We have our hand grenades in our pockets and they don't weigh much. For two hours now we're flat on the ground under a light but penetrating rain. Here comes the dawn, dismal and soundless. No-one is moving.[11]

Lieutenant Fontana's view of why he was about to invade Greece is revealing. 'We haven't been able to send a declaration of war,' the troops were told. He does not seem to have been bothered by the irregularity. If the Duce had his reasons for not issuing a formal declaration of war on Greece, surely there was a good reason for it. (Much later, he would radically change his mind, and pay with his life for it.) Even if he had qualms, the sheer excitement of soldiering on active service would have silenced them. As dawn broke, a senior officer peered through his binoculars through the thick mist, his cape collar turned up against the cold. Then the sudden thunder of a cannonade signalled that the war was on.

On the right of the front, the Siena Division managed to reach its first objective of Filiates within twenty-four hours, but the weather had prevented a planned conjunction of Trizio's 47 Infantry and Solinas' *bersaglieri* of the Ferrara in front of the Kalamas. The result was that the armoured Centauro was pressing on the Ferrara's rear, causing some confusion. Away in Rome Armellini on Badoglio's staff wrote in his diary that the situation had already deteriorated into 'complete bedlam'. Mussolini put on a bold front, but he, too, was concerned enough to move his headquarters temporarily to Grottaglie, an air base near Bari, to be nearer to the action. In response to messages of confusion coming in from the front he promised his commander that the Bari Division would disembark at Vlore on 1 November on its way to occupy Corfu, with more divisions and armoured vehicles following by the middle of the month. 'I am convinced,' the Duce wrote to Visconti Prasca, 'that you will continue to press on the complex of operations that rapid pace which events, rather than doctrine, peremptorily impose.'[12] A cloud of uncertainty is discernible through the ambiguous and lapidary phrasing. 'Events rather than doctrine' were already spoiling Mussolini's plans. Translation: stop complaining and get on with it. Pricolo, the Air Force Chief, pressed into service as Mussolini's messenger, flew to Albania to boost morale.

On the Greek side the 39 Evzone Regiment of the 3rd Division was force-marched to Arta to join the 8th Division. To the northeast, various scattered commands were being filtered up to meet the Julia's advance, mostly by long and exhausting marches over mountain tracks. Papagos ordered the II Corps to move northwest from its base at Larissa. The corps' cavalry division was tasked with joining up with the 8th to keep the Greek line intact, while the III Corps in Thessaloniki was told to get ready for a possible counter-thrust into Albania to outflank the Italian advance.[13]

Ciano, meanwhile, was chafing at the bit. At the time one of the most militant of fascist leaders, and a pilot to boot, he yearned to add a genuine combat medal to the shining array on his uniform. As long as the weather kept him grounded he vented his frustration on the General Staff, accusing it of half-heartedly preparing for the Albania campaign – a charge that contained more than a germ of truth. Then on 1 November the weather cleared enough for Ciano to fly on his coveted combat mission over Greece. His target was the port of Thessaloniki, which he bombed without much of a result except to narrowly miss obliterating a building full of Italian civilians about to be shipped out as enemy aliens. The 'spectacular bombing' he boasted about in his diary is certainly a gross fantasy, as is his claim of downing two Greek fighters. (The Greek air force reported no losses for that day.) However, he did confess to feeling 'very uncomfortable' at the sight of enemy fighters on his tail.[14]

By 2 November the weather had cleared enough for the Siena, Ferrara and Centauro divisions to shake the mud off their boots and tank treads and advance on Kalpaki, some 30km inside Greek territory and half way to the Italians' first objective of Ioannina. For some time Katsimitros had been digging in his 8th Division for a solid defence at Kalpaki, where the main road runs through a valley. The brass in Athens had been strongly urging Katsimitros to line up his defence deeper into Greek territory. Katsimitros ignored the urging, which had the peremptoriness of an outright order. He was convinced that the main battle would be at Kalpaki and nothing would make him budge. Moreover, to beef up morale in the division he had ensured that a plurality of his soldiers came from Epiros. These men were fighting for their own mountains and villages. To leave the province to the enemy – however transiently for strategic purposes – would be to risk a mutiny.[15] By his disobedience of top-level orders, Katsimitros, a stand-and-fight soldier of the classic kind, served his country exceedingly well.

Katsimitros had been awakened by telephone at 3.45 am on 28 October. In driving rain spiked with thunder and lightning, he moved his field headquarters out of Ioannina and up the road towards Kalpaki. It was still dark when advance posts sounded the alarm; the Italians were sighted. 'To arms!' As the call went down the line, galvanizing men and horses into action, the first Italian artillery shells came howling over, adding their own thunder to that of the elements. Katsimitros kept cool, pulling back advanced units to congregate at Kalpaki. His Order of the Day was uncompromising. The shadow-boxing was over.

> The decisive fight against the enemy will take place in this location [Kalpaki]. Stout defence of our positions until the last. No-one should have any notion of retreat.[16]

Rossi's Twenty-fifth Corps advanced with motorcyclists first, armoured cars second and infantry last, on foot. The mood in the ranks was bright. One Albanian villager overheard an Italian officer make confident plans to *prendere il caffè* (take coffee) in Ioannina the following evening. Another Italian was seen riding his motorbike with a live sheep on his back, to roast when he got to Ioannina. Behind them were the light tanks of the Centauro, tasked with punching through the Greek defence at Kalpaki to lead the advance on Ioannina, but one of its columns got lost, didn't show up in time, and hence weakened the thrust. West of the road, and dominating the approaches north and south, stands Grambala Hill. And here is where the Italians found the Greeks of the 8th Division waiting for them, backed up by the 2nd, 3rd and 4th Infantry Divisions, and the tall, skirted fighters of the 39 Evzone Regiment.

Katsimitros' divisional headquarters intercepted a message from Rossi calling for air support to take advantage of the better weather. At 9.00 am waves of Italian bombers hit Kalpaki and positions south, all the way to Ioannina and its airfield. At noon the Italian artillery joined in with a massive bombardment that was answered by the Greeks in a two-hour cannonade. The Italians were employing a classic World War One tactic, softening up the enemy with shellfire before an infantry attack. This time, however, the Greek artillery was far from discomfited, and opened up again as soon as the waves of grey-green uniforms of the Siena and Ferrara began to advance over the small plain towards Grambala Hill. The Greek guns also homed in on a unit of Italian engineers trying to repair a destroyed bridge behind their lines. The first shell landed among them, killing five and wounding as many more.

Attempts by Italian guns to reply to what they called the 'ghost battery' (the Greeks' guns were well-concealed) resulted in their own destruction.

During the night of 1 November an elite Italian unit beefed up with Albanian volunteers seized Grambala Hill after scaling its steep northern face in a surprise attack, driving off two Greek companies. It was still night, and a thunderstorm had broken, but Katsimitros ordered the hill retaken immediately at all costs; if it remained in enemy hands it would split the defence in half. At 5.00 am on 2 November, when the storm finally abated, Greek artillery opened up on Grambala Hill to prepare for an infantry counterattack entrusted to fresh reserves. Bayonets fixed and levelled, the Greeks charged up the hill, the junior officers clearing the way with hand grenades. The Italians put up a fanatic resistance but eventually had to fall back, leaving twenty men dead and six prisoners, machine guns, mortars and ammunition; their expected reserves had failed to come up.

Later in the morning the Italians re-took Grambala. At about 4.00 pm the Centauro armour rolled within sight of Kalpaki – some fifty Fiats in two columns flanked by motorcycle troops, an impressive and alarming sight from the Greek position. The front tanks of the Centauro caught the first rain of Greek shells and were turned into blazing hulks that blocked the road, forcing those behind to swerve into the fields. There several came to grief stumbling on tank traps and mines. 'Like beasts gone mad,' the Centauro tanks scattered wildly. Some Greek soldiers hid in ditches as they approached, throwing blankets under their treads to immobilize them, and then killing their crews.[17] The Italians on Grambala Hill were again driven off in yet more savage close-order combat. Peasants streamed down from the adjacent hills, shouting their encouragement to the Greek artillerymen: 'Hit 'em, captain! Give 'em hell!' Italian motorbikes lay abandoned, sprawled on the road and in shell craters, as their riders fled on foot. Several Fiats were captured and eventually incorporated into the Greek Army's Mechanized Regiment.[18] The much-vaunted Centauro armour was proving alarmingly deficient from the first. Two of the Fiats had previously been neutralized at Bourazani just inside Greek territory when they tumbled into one of Katsimitros' well-concealed anti-tank ditches. Two others were attempting to skirt the ditch when they hit mines and blew up.

The Centauro's tank crews were admittedly ill-prepared for what they found. At the height of the battle of Kalpaki an Italian tank commander had radioed his headquarters (intercepted by Greek intelligence) complaining desperately that 'the forward-thinking and crafty Greeks placed their artillery where it could not be seen ... I am being hit on all sides by heavy enemy small and medium-calibre artillery fire ... This artillery fire is devastatingly accurate'. Katsimitros received a despatch from an Evzone battalion commander pooh-poohing the tanks. 'This weapon of Mussolini's has been rubbished.'[19]

In the Ragruppamento del Litorale opposite Corfu, Colonel Gianani's 32 Infantry Regiment of the Siena had moved out of Filiates to ford the lower reaches of the Kalamas River where it was 50yds wide and swollen to boot. Lancer Lieutenant Riccardo Avati stripped to his undergarments and, his pistol under his armpit, rode his horse gingerly through the treacherous currents to locate a crossing place that wasn't too deep. Some of his men, good swimmers, wanted to try their luck but Avati refused; he wanted the honour of being the first across. Eventually he managed to get a rope across, as a guide for a fragile raft that ferried Gianani and his staff, plus a machine gun platoon, to the south bank. Most of the regiment had got over and was gingerly feeling its way south when a burst of Greek fire killed both Gianani and Avati. (Avati was awarded a posthumous gold medal for valour.) Papagos had ordered the Greeks in that sector to pull back, abandoning the coastal town of Igoumenitsa to the Italians, to form a line farther south, but there were plenty of traps for the Italians. Despite the loss of its commander, the 32 Regiment had formed a solid bridgehead on the south side of the Kalamas and could have gone farther had not other Italian units run into serious trouble elsewhere.[20]

On its way to Kalpaki the Twenty-fifth Corps had come under sporadic Greek air attack. On 1 November Metaxas personally ordered a night bombing attack on the Italian position at Doliana, a few kilometres northwest of Kalpaki. It was the first time the RHAF had flown operationally at night. Three crews of Larissa-based 31 Bombing *Mira* (squadron) were selected. They were frankly scared as they climbed into the cockpits of their French-built twin-engine Potez 63s; none of them had ever flown a night mission, but Metaxas was adamant that it be done, even if it were to prove fatal. After a half hour's anxious flight on instruments alone the mission leader, Pilot Officer Anastasios Vladousis, successfully dive-bombed the lights of the Italian columns, weaving away through the flak, followed by the others.

The RHAF, in fact, had a dual mission on its hands: to defend Greek cities against bombing while acting as long-range artillery for the army in Epiros. The former was the task of the air force's four pursuit *mirai* based (thanks to Metaxas' foresight) mostly in central and northern Greece. While the army was trying to absorb the Italian incursions in the northwest, the Regia Aeronautica regularly bombed Greek strategic and civilian targets, making little distinction between them. On 2 November the pilots of 22 Pursuit Mira based at Thessaloniki were scrambled to meet a formation of Italian bombers of 50 Gruppo converging on the city at 20,000 feet. Eight Polish-built PZL24 monoplane fighters sporting the blue and white Greek roundel climbed to meet them. Pilot Officer Marinos Mitralexis caught a three-engined CantZ1007 – a sinister-looking machine painted in lizard-like camouflage – in his gunsight and sent a stream of 8mm bullets into it. Not seeing any immediate effect, he pressed the firing button again, but found he was out of ammunition.

His next act, witnessed by an amazed wingman, was to aim his PZL straight into the CantZ's tail section. The impact sheared off part of one of the twin rudders, throwing the plane into a spin. The crew – minus the pilot who was apparently killed by Mitralexis' initial burst – baled out.

Mitralexis, too, survived, having nursed his robust fighter to the ground with surprisingly minimal damage. Once down, he found the Italian crew seemingly about to be lynched by a mob of peasants. Drawing his pistol, he warned the peasants off and personally led the enemy bomber crew into captivity. Mitralexis' ramming feat became an immediate *cause celebre*. Scores of airmen, actual and aspiring, longed to be able to imitate him. (A few tried, but were unlucky.) The RHAF College received a huge surge of applicants. The sturdy PZL24, with its gull wing and raucous engine, became the object of desire of every air cadet.

That same day Captain Luigi Mariotti was leading a dozen Fiat CR42s of 363 Squadriglia on a bomber escort to Thessaloniki when they were jumped by four fighters of 22 Mira. Sergeant Constantine Lambropoulos in his fighter engaged the Fiats but soon had the worst of the encounter. As bullets smashed into his plane from every side he tried to bale out but caught his flying boot lace in the cockpit. With the plane plunging down vertically, his chances of survival were rapidly dwindling to zero when a shell burst in the cockpit, snapping the lace and allowing him to fall free. Seconds later the plane disintegrated, and as Lambropoulos drifted down the Italians kept firing at him – a contemptible practice which sullies the otherwise impressive record of the Italian air force in the Greek campaign. He remained unpunctured, but his parachute had more than fifty holes in it.

Savoia-Marchetti SM79 bombers of 107 Gruppo based at Grottaglie raided Thessaloniki and Larissa, killing scores of noncombatants. CantZs of 47 Stormo, including bombers skippered by Mussolini's two sons, Bruno and Vittorio, were met by defenders of 21 Mira but suffered no losses. In retaliation, British-made Bristol Blenheim IV bombers of the RHAF 31 Bombing Mira hammered the Italian air base at Korce inside Albania, killing nineteen Italian airmen in the base operations room.

The Regia Aeronautica's bombers might fly blithely over Greek skies to bomb the towns and factories, but they seemed to be in short supply over the front itself. Though Greek sources mention waves of Italian bombers over the front, General Rossi, the Twenty-fifth Corps commander, fumed at the perceived lack of air support on 4 November after the failure of the first Italian attempt to break the line at Kalpaki.[21] The Greeks, however, reported shooting down two Italian aircraft on 5 November, as Italian artillery renewed its bombardment of the Greek position. At about 10.00 pm the Siena and Ferrara divisions launched a fresh assault, backed by about sixty tanks of the

Centauro. The attack was beaten back, with fifteen Fiats immobilized in the bogs of the Kalamas River.

That evening Rossi felt he had to give his battered units a breather. The staff of the 8th Division intercepted an Italian despatch that graphically described what the invaders were up against:

> The Greeks, known for their stubbornness and persistence, have since peacetime organized the naturally rough and uneven territory of Epiros with such method and diligence that every rock is an artillery nest and every cave a defensive bulwark. [The Greeks] are so fierce in battle that more and stronger means are required to drive them off.[22]

If it was Rossi who composed the message, he may have been overly melodramatic. If he shared Visconti Prasca's vision of an Italian-style *Blitzkrieg* that would shatter the Greeks, then the resistance at Kalpaki would have come as a stern corrective. Yet in this petulant despatch there is no sign that any senior Italian commander understood the message of the battle at Kalpaki so far. The prevalent thinking was that 'more and better' would do the trick.

Keeping an eye on the cautious advance of the Raggruppamento del Litorale in the west, Katsimitros gambled that if he kept the Italians at bay at Kalpaki, the Raggruppamento would hesitate to wheel east and join up with Rossi's hard-fought corps. All day on 7 November Rossi threw infantry and cavalry into futile attacks on the Greeks. At sunset Italian artillery pounded Grambala Hill afresh in preparation for an all-or-nothing night charge. What followed was a second scaling of the steep north slope by Italian crack troops known as *fanti della morte*, or soldiers of death, distinguishable by the skulls on their metal dog-tags. Once at the top, the *fanti* drove back the Greek reservists holding the hill. At midnight two Greek companies counterattacked with bayonets, in pitch blackness lit only by grenade flashes reflected on the cold steel. After a vicious fight, the *fanti* had to retreat, leaving forty-five of their number fulfilling the ominous emblem around their necks.

The following day opened with a lull. Italian artillery was seen re-grouping to the rear. The Centauro's tanks were nowhere to be seen. Two days later, on 8 November, a chastened Visconti Prasca received the order to halt all offensive operations. By now, however, the single Greek victory at Kalpaki was only one of the *Esercito* high command's worries. For on the left of the front, Girotti's Julia Division had also got into serious trouble.

The Alpini of the Julia, ordered to advance on the left of the invasion front, had taken the border village of Lykorrachi and were moving through a series of winding valleys leading to their objective of Metsovo. While the main Greek defence had concentrated at Kalpaki, the moves against the Julia were of necessity piecemeal. In charge of the Greek defence north of Metsovo was the 1st Division under Major General Vasilios Vrachnos. But his force was nowhere near up to strength, as most of the division had yet to be called up! Nevertheless, he rallied Colonel Davakis' scattered commands plus the Cavalry Division Motorized Regiment under Lieutenant Colonel Epaminondas Asimakopoulos whose obsolete Vickers light tanks had to trundle a considerable distance over fearsome cliffs from Thessaloniki; several soldiers had already lost their lives in accidents on the way.

From Lykorrachi the Dapino and Tavoni regiments in the van of the Julia proceeded cautiously southwards towards Mount Smolikas. They found their way blocked by units of the Greek 1 and 7 Cavalry regiments on the north bank of the swollen Aoos River. At dawn on 1 November Vrachnos ordered a counterattack on Lykorrachi from three points. Davakis was assigned command of the middle detachment with orders to occupy Prophitis Ilias Hill, while the other two were to snipe at the advancing Julia from the flanks. At 7.30 am cavalry scouts located an Italian column of 300 men plus baggage mules marching east of Lykorrachi. The officer in charge placed his cavalrymen on one side and mortar and machine gun units on the other. The coordinated burst from both sides stopped the Italian column in its tracks and sent it scurrying back to the shelter of the houses of Lykorrachi, where more Italians were waiting to move out. Holed up in the village, the Alpini poured withering fire into the Greeks for three hours.

At 11.00 am two more companies of Greek infantry under Lieutenant Colonel Misyris turned up but failed to dent the stubborn Italian resistance. Misyris fell wounded but stayed on to encourage his men, like an ancient Spartan king, declining the attentions of the medics. It wasn't until about 5.00 pm that the exhausted men of the Julia, unable to hope for reinforcements, threw up their hands. Two hundred and ten Italian soldiers were taken prisoner, and 120 provisions-loaded mules were captured, in this first Greek victory of the war. Only then did the wounded Misyris allow himself to be carried to the rear. The battle at Lykorrachi cost the Greeks thirty-one dead and wounded.

The Italians, it must be admitted, had come totally unprepared for the war they were called on to fight. Whipped by sleet and rain from the coast to the Yugoslav border, they marched soaked to the skin, their puttees stiff with ice and little to eat except dry biscuits that flaked in the humidity and resembled 'the skin of a leper'. Most of the Italians, with perhaps the exception of the hardy Alpini of the Julia, had not been trained for this. The sands and heat of Libya, where many had been transferred from, had been a very different proposition from the bitter cold and wet of Albania and northern Greece. Many if not most of the defending Greek conscripts, on the other hand, had grown up in hill country and could skip along the perilous goat-tracks with ease; many were also familiar with firearms from an early age.

Davakis took Prophitis Ilias Hill in a bayonet charge by 2 Company of the 51 Infantry Regiment, led by Second Lieutenant Spyropoulos who personally neutralized an enemy machine gun nest with hand grenades. Davakis himself was seriously wounded. A reservist warrant officer led a similar charge on a machine gun post. Though wounded twice, he refused to leave his men. A little to the south a company under Lieutenant Alexander Diakos, bayonets fixed, charged the height of Tsouka held by strong Italian forces. This may have been the first time that the Greeks' war cry of '*Aera!*' ('Wind!') echoed among the mountains of Epiros. It was an exhortation to the soldiers to attack like the wind, blowing all before them, and quickly became a national rallying-cry. Diakos' company at first drove the Italians from Tsouka but lost it again to a determined counterattack. Diakos tried again, but a burst of enemy machine gun fire cut him down along with a reservist second lieutenant and four soldiers. Diakos was the first Greek army officer to die in World War Two.

Despite the valiant gestures of sporadic resistance, the bulk of the Julia Division continued to roll south towards Metsovo. Papagos realized he had to stop it, and quickly: if the Greek defence at Kalpaki were to be outflanked, the war might well be lost for Greece. First, however, the Julia had to be accurately located. For this, the creaky old observation aircraft of the RHAF were called into service. One of them, an ancient French-built Breguet XIX biplane piloted by Sergeant Yannis Katsoulas of 2 Observation Mira happened upon the Julia's lead columns bypassing Mount Smolikas on their way to Metsovo. Now a more determined counter-movement could be planned.

Visconti Prasca, too, had to admit losing contact with the Julia, which he blamed on storms blowing down the radio antennas. In a conversation with Pricolo he brushed the problem aside. 'Tell the Duce to relax,' he said. 'The Greeks haven't attacked so far and won't.' The men of the Julia, he added, had orders to 'attack, always attack, without regard to the flanks, every column, every man, even, on the attack'. Pricolo wasn't fooled by the bombast. In an unusually frank discussion with Mussolini the following day, he opined that Visconti Prasca was close to 'taking leave of his senses'.[23]

The boastful general, in fact, was about to fall, and hard. On the very day he was talking to Pricolo the Greek 1 Cavalry encountered some forward units of the Julia. Girotti, thinking that the Greeks had more forces in the area than they actually did, ordered a tactical withdrawal to Samarina. Meanwhile, the Julia's 8 and 9 Alpine Regiments had advanced to Distrato and the north bank of the Aoos River, and thus the whole division was strung out and vulnerable. Colonel Dimaratos, the 1 Cavalry Commander, decided to strike at Samarina to snap the Julia in two. At dawn on 3 November, unsupported by artillery (the ground was so uneven there was nowhere to place the batteries), the 2 Cavalry Reconnaissance Group, including the mechanized section and backed up by a mere twenty infantrymen, fought their way into Samarina, overcoming strong Italian resistance. Retreating, the Italians set fire to the town, leaving behind five dead and eleven prisoners. The Greeks captured wireless transmitters and some weapons, but were disappointed to find no food – the Italians, too, were plagued with serious supply problems – so they had to survive on tiny rations of bread and cheese, supplemented by a few olives.

The Greek seizure of Samarina was the first serious setback to the Julia's advance, confining Girotti's area of operations to a wedge-shaped salient west of the town and abutting the Aoos River. Girotti, headquartered at Distrato, ordered a frontal attack on Vovousa, the next town on the way to Metsovo in the Aoos Valley. The 8 Alpine Regiment flung itself heroically against the slender Greek line at Vovousa, to be repulsed with heavy loss. This was the signal for Vrachnos, the Greek commander in the sector, to hit back at the enemy headquarters at Distrato. Dimaratos of the 1 Cavalry sent the battered but willing 1 Company of the Fifty-first Battalion to block the eastbound roads. Dimaratos himself, with parts of the Fifth and Seventh Battalions, moved at dawn on 5 November on Distrato itself. As the town, nestling between two strategic heights, was in a good defensive position, Dimaratos elected not to waste men on a frontal attack. Instead, he would try to split the front between the 8 and 9 Alpine Regiments of the Julia.

Girotti moved to protect the main road west to Konitsa – his only way of escape if his march on Metsovo were to come to grief, as it showed serious signs of doing. At 5.00 am advance units of the Greek 1 Cavalry overcame an Italian position and took thirty prisoners, but remained pinned down for seven hours by a furious fusillade from the Italian Gemone and 14 Artillery Regiments on an adjacent height. In the afternoon the Greek Seventh Battalion came up, triggering a ferocious bayonet battle that ended in the Greeks driving off the Gemone and 14 Artillery and placing themselves in the rear of the 9 Alpine, cutting its connection with the 8. That evening the Greeks were reinforced by the arrival of the Fifth Infantry Battalion.

Distrato was now in a Greek vice. Girotti's attempts to outflank the Greeks on the right of the Italian position had come to nought. He had received word that the Bari Division was on its way to help him, though by 5 November only one battalion of the Bari had reached the battlefield to make any kind of contribution to the fighting. Only the height of Gomara (2,020m) east of Distrato remained in Italian hands. And the Greeks were concentrating for a decisive blow.

On 6 November Lieutenant General Papadopoulos, the II Corps commander, arrived on the scene and ordered a dual attack: to split the line of the 8 Alpine on the north bank of the Aoos River and drive the Italians from the Gomara height. With the 8 Alpine in disorder, Papadopoulos hoped to pile the pressure on the 9. To do the job he had three infantry battalions (one of which was fatigued), the 1 Cavalry Regiment and 300 skirmishers. At dawn the Greek Seventh Battalion charged the heights west of Distrato four times but was hurled back each time. On the fifth attempt the Seventh succeeded, sending the Alpini fleeing and leaving behind their weapons. The Greek attack on Gomara took rather longer. One company of the 1 Cavalry and two companies of the Fifth Battalion had managed to secure a precarious foothold on the hill by the afternoon. Sixteen cavalrymen found a way behind the Italian flank and captured several loads of supplies into the bargain. The 8 Alpine clung stubbornly to the crest of Gomara until nightfall.

Early on 8 November the Greek cavalry renewed its attack all along the line. The Seventh Battalion moved to cut the Distrato road but encountered a wall of Italian resistance. The 1 Cavalry, too, was meeting formidable fire. Girotti was throwing all his resources into breaking the Greek noose slowly tightening around his division. As the day wore on, the combat became murderous. The Greek cavalrymen charged repeatedly through a storm of shellfire; men and horses alike, weak with hunger and lack of sleep, died together. One Greek military historian has well written: 'These luckless animals, who understood nothing of the senselessness of human beings, endured the privations with exceptional fortitude ... For the cavalrymen, the horses were not just dumb beasts. They were real comrades in arms, their other halves.'[24]

Towards evening a troop under Second Lieutenant Grigorios Karathanasis made the first fatal breach in the Italian line. The exhausted Italians abandoned the Gomara height, but as the road to Distrato was now blocked by the Greeks, they headed south, leaving eleven prisoners and several machine guns and mortars, plus eleven pack mules. The three-day battle at Gomara had cost the Greeks eleven dead, including the valiant Second Lieutenant Karathanasis, and seven wounded. Temperatures in the mountains were plunging. Rain was turning to sleet and snow. Italian and Greek alike cursed the penetrating cold and ubiquitous mud. The Greeks had little to eat but hard bread and olives, which they had to share with their horses. If ever there was a time to rest it was now. Yet the Italians were falling back, and the pursuit could not cease.

In his attempt to meet the Greek pressure on his left, Girotti had weakened his position at Distrato, with the result that two Greek platoons were enough to take the town by assault on 8 November, netting sixty-one prisoners. Girotti had no choice now but to take the only road open to him, the westward mountain road to Konitsa, about 50km away. Under constant artillery bombardment and machine gun fire, the Julia fell back west along the Aoos River, in the direction of the villages of Armata and Pades while the Greek 1 Cavalry occupied Distrato and sent advance units to chase the Italians in the direction of Armata, which the Greek horsemen took on 9 November with barely a shot being fired. While more columns of Italian prisoners were sent trudging to the rear, units of the 1 Cavalry advanced up a narrow goat path to Pades, where the Italians were dug in and another battle was joined.

The 1 Cavalry's 2nd Reconnaissance Group, which had led the attack on Pades, sent two platoons around the village to cut it off. The 8 Alpine managed to keep Pades until the afternoon, but ripped up by furious Greek bayonet assaults, they had to pull out. During the battle Corporal Christos Mariotis led his squad against a house full of Italians, blasting the door away with a hand grenade and bursting in with fixed bayonets to finish the job. Twenty Italians threw up their hands. That done, Mariotis and his squad charged another house. This time a bayonet killed him, but his men exacted enough revenge before fifteen surviving Italians threw down their weapons in front of the body of the brave Greek NCO.

From Pades a very narrow and winding road leads to Konitsa. Girotti's Alpini put up sporadic resistance during their withdrawal. At the village of Elefthero the 8 Alpine held off the Greeks for seven hours, its gunners firing at point blank range until the last shell, before leaving 300 dead and 700 prisoners. To all intents and purposes that was the end of the 8's career as a proud military unit. Girotti was later inclined to blame the Italians' lack of provisions for his retreat, saying that if his men had been adequately supplied, 'the fight could have continued.' This is hard to square with his simultaneous admission that Greek noncombatants joined their troops in harassing the Julia along its retreat, a sign that the Italian discomfiture was not merely a matter of hungry soldiers; the entire Greek locality, military and civilian, was against him. Rather more accurate is the official Greek report which, while acknowledging the effects of fatigue on the otherwise formidable Julia, attributed its defeat to the excessive demands of mountain combat in foul weather which eroded divisional morale wholesale.

The remnant of the Julia straggled into Konitsa in a pitiful state. The black hat feathers of the Venetians drooped limply in the rain. Boots were weighed down with layers of mud and peeling in the moisture, and the once-proud grey-green uniforms soiled and torn. Faces were grubby and unshaven, eyes red from lack of sleep and constant battle. As for Girotti, he could think of nothing better to do than put Konitsa to the torch. Six days later, on 16 November, the Greek 3 Cavalry Regiment entered the town after overcoming a final futile stab at resistance by the 9 Alpine.[26]

If Girotti truly believed that the Julia still had a chance to turn the tables, the lives of his brave soldiers paid for the delusion. As evidenced by his later report, he simply could not bring himself to admit to being tactically beaten so early in the campaign. The assignment for his vaunted division had been to divert the Greeks' attention from the main attack in Ioannina by forcing Papagos to split his forces. Yet from the moment Greek cavalry attacked him in the mountains, soon to be joined by artillery, he knew that his original objective of reaching Metsovo had become impossible to attain. In just two weeks of mountain fighting, the Julia Division had lost one-fifth of its strength. In fact, it was out of the fight. Re-forming at Berat inside Albanian territory, its dispirited men sang bitterly in a three-line stanza reminiscent of Dante:

> *On Berat bridge a flag of black*
> *To mourn the young men not coming back*
> *Of the Julia sent in to the attack.*[27]

Much the same dirge could well have been sung all along the Italian line. The Siena, Ferrara and Centauro divisions, having been stopped dead at Kalpaki, were in full retreat to the Albanian frontier, pursued not only by the triumphantly yelling Greek troops but also by peasants of both sexes. One of them recalled seeing grey-green uniforms fleeing over the slopes 'like ants'. Villagers picked among acres of dead Italians, taking weapons, personal effects and food. Many of these country folk felt quite entitled to the scavenging, as they had made serious personal contributions to the war effort. Women had been willing to trudge up to the front for many hours a day through the freezing rain, rifles and ammunition cases lashed to their backs, returning exhausted to their fireplaces to spend the evenings knitting socks for the soldiers. It was not uncommon for young children to follow their mothers laden with an artillery shell or two.

The Julia's elimination sent shock waves throughout the Rome political and military establishment. In one blow the strategy of the high command in Albania switched from offence to defence. From Visconti Prasca's optimism, the mood swung to the other extreme. In fact, Visconti Prasca's time was up, his bubble well and truly burst.

His own contribution to the sudden soul-searching was to lash out at the Duce's rotund air force chief in Albania, General Ranza, for failing to provide air support. He had a point. The Regia Aeronautica's Albania-based squadrons were not hampered solely by the atrocious weather. So parlous was the air force administration that there was not even a functioning telephone line between Ranza and the Fourth Air Force headquarters at Brindisi. Communications were handled by an overworked liaison officer shuttling by air between Brindisi and Tirana. Air operations themselves were ordered in impossibly general terms, with little specific emphasis on particular targets. While the battle for Kalpaki was at its height and the Julia Division was suffering its first reverses, Visconti Prasca was still dreaming of forging southwards to Preveza 'with or without the three new divisions' he had been promised.

But Badoglio and Roatta knew better. They had never cared for Visconti Prasca's character in the first place, and now they saw their chance to get him out of the way. Badoglio feared for the Albanian positions around Korce inside Albania, as the Greeks appeared to be massing for a counterattack across the frontier. Visconti Prasca replied that he could assemble the Parma and Venezia divisions to protect the sector, as well as the reserve Piemonte, with the Bari and Arezzo on their way. 'I believe the situation is not worrisome,' he cabled the staff chief, while at the same time calling for more light tanks and 'aircraft in mass,' as long as temporary difficulties such as persistent bad weather could ease.

Three divisions – that's all Visconti Prasca claimed to need to hold the line. Badoglio and Roatta, knowing rather more of the truth from the embattled front, must have shaken their heads in disbelief. Was this the same general who, not a month before, had assured all and sundry that the way to Athens would be a walkover? Besides, there simply weren't that many more tanks available for him. It must have been obvious by now even to Ciano and Mussolini that the Army's initial grand hopes for a conquest of Greece had gone badly wrong.

The Duce's remedy was to reorganize the whole army in the field into four corps. On 6 November Badoglio received orders (the evidence suggests that he had little choice in the matter) to form the Arezzo, Parma, Venezia and unblooded Piemonte divisions into the Ninth Corps on the left of the front abutting the Yugoslav border and Greek Macedonia. Attached to the corps would be the Julia (or what was left of it), joined by the Bari, with the Tridentina in reserve. The Ninth Corps' task was to maintain a defensive position until, hopefully, Bulgaria could enter the war on the Axis side. The fatigued and bloodied Siena, Ferrara and Centauro, still reeling from their debacle at Kalpaki, were formed into the Eleventh Corps that would rest until reinforced by three more divisions. Three other reserve divisions would be waiting in the heel of Italy to be fed into the campaign as needed. The whole reorganization would have to be complete within one month, and General Ubaldo Soddu, the deputy chief of the general staff and undersecretary for war, was sent to the front to administer it.

Once in Albania, Soddu tried to unfoul the Italian tangle. Nasci, the Twenty-sixth Corps commander, was pessimistic, perhaps excessively so, and no doubt aware of what was happening to Girotti on his right flank. Soddu asked Nasci to be patient for 'five or six' days until the mess could be sorted out. To stem a feared Greek counterattack, the Taro and Tridentina divisions were deployed south of Korce. The feather-hatted 4 Bersaglieri Regiment received orders to ship out from Italy, while the Morbegna Alpine battalion of the Tridentina was airlifted in to boost the Italians' mountain-fighting capabilities already seriously dented in the hapless Julia. A degree of chaos attended all these changes. Typical was the predicament of the Modena Division which, hurriedly withdrawn from the French front in August and re-trained for a possible attack on Yugoslavia, was partly disbanded in September and then hurriedly patched back together with elements of other divisions, arriving in Albania on 10 November and being deployed around Gjirokaster, while its 41 Infantry Regiment was detached to the rugged defiles of Kelcyre (Klissura). Generally, supplies and logistics failed to keep up with the confusing movements, with the result that the Italian troops were perennially lacking something, from canned food to boots to support artillery. The 5 Alpine Regiment's horses were inadvertently left behind on the docks at Brindisi.

For two days Soddu also had to put up with an incessant bombardment of telegraphed orders, advice, pleadings and cajolings from Mussolini that culminated in the removal of Visconti Prasca from supreme command on the Greek front and official replacement by Soddu. To his unpleasant surprise, Visconti Prasca was demoted to Eleventh Corps commander. (Some in Rome had wanted him to be kicked even lower down the chain of command.) Yet he quickly recovered his morale, especially after receiving reports of successful cavalry penetration by the Aosta and Milano divisions on the coast after the Kalamas River bridgehead had been secured. On 10 November he wrote to Soddu that the Raggruppamento del Litorale could wheel left to entrap the Greek forces at Kalpaki if it could be moved fast enough.

Soddu's reply has been described by the leading Italian military historian of the campaign as a 'cold shower': 'Let's be realistic,' read Soddu's telegram, couched in the best old-style military courtesy. 'All the directions You indicate, Excellency, are of the best, yet they are not the directions that would best resolve the operations ... Improvised actions employing piecemeal forces will not have, and cannot have, a good result.' The patently false quaintly capitalized pronoun and term 'Excellency' were merely a polite mask for what was in essence a stern lecture on tactics. Soddu rubbished Visconti Prasca's suggestions that all the new Italian arrivals be focused onto the central sector for a decisive thrust at Ioannina, and corrected his odd lingering impression that the Greeks were still militarily weak. Visconti Prasca wasn't even given time to reply to the telegram. The following day, as the Julia Division was being whipped to bits in the mountains near Konitsa, Italian state radio announced that Visconti Prasca had been removed from command of the Eleventh Corps, to be replaced by an old rival of his, General Carlo Geloso.[28]

Was Visconti Prasca a scapegoat for a broader incompetence in the Italian political and military establishment? He himself was heartily convinced of it. But Mussolini was also in a difficult position; it would be damaging to his image to have to admit that his judgement of persons was flawed. So Visconti Prasca had to be nicely got out of the way with as little fuss as possible. At the end of November he was dismissed from active service – sent 'on absolute leave' as the terminology went. Playing a part in his precipitous fall was the army brass's low opinion of him, combined with Badoglio's lethal jealousy of his closeness to the Duce. They were undoubtedly glad to see his boasts deflated, his overweening confidence brought low in the mountains of Epiros.[29]

Meanwhile, Churchill had moved quickly to meet Metaxas' call for help. The first British servicemen had begun arriving as early as 2 November. One of them was the head of the British Military Mission, Major General Michael Gambier-Parry, MC, who had just flown in on a Short Sunderland flying boat with nineteen anti-tank guns as baggage. Prince Peter took an immediate liking to the man, who appeared to genuinely want Greek-British military cooperation to run smoothly. Unfortunately, he did not get his wish. This was largely because Lieutenant General Papagos, the Chief of the Greek Staff, took his dignity seriously and under no circumstances did he wish to be seen as susceptible to taking British orders.

An early point of friction was what to do with the Greek 5th Division based in Crete. In the eyes of the British command in North Africa, the 5th Division needed to be kept close at hand in Crete in case it should be needed on that front. Papagos, on the contrary, wanted to ship it up to the front in Epiros post-haste. There were some discussions of how to arm the Cretans in case the division should move out – the mass production of crude petrol bombs was one possibility being considered. Changing the British mind was a cable from Admiral Cunningham, the British Mediterranean Fleet commander, that his ships were quite capable of protecting Crete, and thus the 5th Division could safely be sent north.

It was a victory for Papagos who also brushed aside Gambier-Parry's suggestion that 'twelve artillery pieces' should remain in Crete. The news from the front, moreover, was good. The Julia Division – Papagos' biggest concern – had been neutralized in the mountains and the main body of invaders had been hurled back at Kalpaki. Prince Peter, who served as the interpreter at Gambier-Parry's often-fractious meetings with the Greek commander-in-chief, dined on 8 November with Richard Dimbleby of the BBC who was eager to be sent to the battlefront. That same evening, Gambier-Parry was jubilant. 'Today we saved Greece,' he enthused to Prince Peter, only to add, 'unless, of course, we lose Crete in the meantime.'[30]

Dimbleby was only one of a corps of eager journalists clamouring to see some action to report. From the first, the international media had taken a keen interest in what was already being framed as a classic David-Goliath fight. Foreign (especially American) news correspondents, being by nature a distrustful and cynical bunch, at first dismissed the Greek cause as hopelessly quixotic. Like their counterparts in London during the Battle of Britain, they were overawed by Axis military might, naive adherents of the doctrine that God is invariably on the side of the biggest battalions. One American journalist, hastening to Athens by train from Bucharest soon after war was declared, observed columns of Greek soldiers winding their way to the front, 'bright-eyed' and eager, but with rumpled and ill-fitting uniforms. The journalist's first reaction was one of pity. What chance would these insouciant boys have against the Duce's war machine?[31] Later, the foreign press corps would come to have a good deal more respect for the Greek fighting man.

The RAF put in a much-needed appearance to beef up the slender resources of the RHAF. On 3 November whatever Air Chief Marshal Sir Arthur Longmore, the RAF commander in the Middle East, could spare from his forces began landing at Eleusis and Tatoi fields near Athens. These were, initially, eight Bristol Blenheim I light bombers of 70 Squadron plus a few battle-worn and already obsolete Gloster Gladiators of 30 Squadron. They were later joined by four more Blenheims and Vickers Wellington bombers from 70 Squadron, which were at once sent into action to hit Italian supply ships in the Albanian port of Sarande, across the strait from Corfu. The question of accommodation became acute. Seven Greek generals had to give up their offices in the Grande Bretagne to RAF officers. The RAF commander in Greece, Air Commodore John D'Albiac, DSO, promised up to forty more bombers and thirty-five fighters, not to mention much-needed batteries of 37mm Bofors anti-aircraft guns for the RHAF airfields. Metaxas feared that not even that might be enough.

As the RAF began to bomb Italian shipping at Vlore and Sarande, the Greeks were cheered by news of the Fleet Air Arm victory off Taranto on 12 November, where the redoubtable British 'stringbags' – Fairey Swordfish torpedo-bombing biplanes – decimated the bulk of the Regia Marina's heavy ships. But the RAF's initial daylight raids on Vlore were proving costly. On one of the first such attacks on the air base at Vlore, three Blenheim Is of 30 Squadron were met by the Fiats of 364 Squadriglia. Captain Nicola Magaldi, the flight commander, drew a bead on the Blenheim skippered by Sergeant G. W. Ratlidge and raked it with fire, killing the upper gunner, Sergeant John Merifield.[32] All three bombers, despite their extensive damage, managed to make it back to Eleusis. Merifield was given a hero's state funeral in Athens, attended by the king and filmed by newsreel crews.

The appearance of the RAF meant that the Regia Aeronautica's air superiority was now about to be seriously challenged. But 364 Squadriglia was in action again the following day, against a flight of 70 Squadron's Wellingtons over Vlore. Lieutenant Alberto Spigaglia and Warrant Officer (*Maresciallo*) Guglielmo Bacci claimed credit for destroying two Wellingtons, those of Sergeant G. N. Brooks, which blew up in mid-air, killing all on board, and Flight Lieutenant A. E. Brian, two of whose crew parachuted into captivity. Greek anti-aircraft fire on 9 November downed and killed Second Lieutenant Pietro Janniello of 363 Squadriglia. Blenheims of the RAF's 84 Squadron bombed the *squadriglia's* base at Gjirokaster and were away before the base fighters could be scrambled properly.[33]

The British staff officers' relationship with their Greek counterparts was often a tricky one. The British naval attaché, Rear Admiral Charles Turle, found himself constantly frustrated by the paucity of information the Greeks saw fit to give him. True, naval operations at this stage were taking a distant back seat to land and air activity, but Turle as a result was led to believe that the situation in Epiros was worse than it actually was.

While the Greek army was mustering its strength for a counterattack on the Italians over the Albanian border, Papagos was considering suggestions from D'Albiac that the RAF continue bombing the supply ports of Vlore, Sarande and Durres – and perhaps as far afield as the Italian port of Ancona – while Turle suggested moving Royal Navy units up the Albanian coast to block further Italian landings. On 10 November Papagos scotched Gambier-Parry's idea for a grab-bag of Albanian, Polish and Free French volunteers to beef up the British mission in Greece on the grounds that the Greek war effort came first. He also vetoed Gambier-Parry's request to visit the front. At that moment, writes Prince Peter, D'Albiac entered Papagos' office to announce that a couple of dozen enemy vessels had been located in the port of Vlore and that two Wellingtons were to attack them that evening. Papagos, noted the prince, 'looked very pleased.'

D'Albiac showed an unexpected side of himself a few nights later while watching his Wellingtons take off for a new raid on Vlore and Durres. With him was King George, and the mood was sombre. As the rumble of the bombers' engines faded into the night, and the king was about to get into his limousine, D'Albiac shook his hand and said: 'You will be wondering, Your Majesty, if all this is worth it. In my view, the best thing we could do is abandon our colonies and the British Empire and stop fighting for them!'

Prince Peter, standing next to the two men, was nonplussed. Here was a senior British officer apparently rubbishing a good deal of what Britain in 1940 was fighting for! In the car on the way back, King George puzzled over it. (Only later, after the war, would the anti-colonialist sentiments of some of the British military establishment come into the open.[34]) However, there was little time to brood over this apparent eccentricity as the news from the front was improving day by day.

Chapter 4

Mud, Blood and Cold Steel

Soddu assesses the situation – Keitel chides the Italians – the Greeks invade Albania – 'You've never seen a puppet like me!' – the Greek I Corps gains ground – Italian morale plummets – Mussolini's dismay – Korce falls to the Greeks

The crash of the bombs falling on Athens' industrial districts and port of Piraeus, and the banging of anti-aircraft fire, became a daily backdrop to the lives of young Sotiris Kollias and the other villagers of Kalyvia. Sometimes the blasts would be loud enough to rattle windows. The village and its neighbouring communities, in fact, provided a refuge for the homeless of Piraeus and the bombed districts. 'There wasn't a house that didn't provide shelter to some family from Piraeus,' Kollias recalled. Not that Kalyvia itself was out of danger. Sotiris and his pals were playing in a field when an Italian aircraft roared overhead spraying the kids with machine-gun fire. By sheer chance no-one was hit.[1]

Such hazards, however, were not much when compared with the growing jubilation among all Greeks as the Duce's armies were being pushed back much sooner than anyone imagined. Greek state radio resounded to the sultry voice of singer Sophia Vembo, who had since 28 October turned her talents from romantic pop tunes to patriotic ditties. Even Italian songs were transformed into Greek musical weapons. For example, 'Regina Campanella' was re-worded in Greek to pour utter scorn on Mussolini, Ciano and anyone unfortunate enough to be wearing a grey-green uniform. It became an immediate hit on the radio and in packed theatres.

After its triumph at Kalpaki, the 8th Division was assigned to the I Corps to prepare to chase the Italians into Albania. On the other side, the Ferrara and Siena Division commands had to deal with collapsing morale among the troops, some of whom would flee at the mere sight of an enemy patrol. That said, however, it must be stressed that at no time was the Italian fighting man anything less than the equal of the Greek or any other nationality in valour and endurance. If the Italian soldier was poorly led and supplied, it was not his fault. No less an observer than Major General Katsimitros paid generous tribute to his adversary:

The Italian infantry under competent command fought well; the Italian soldier, especially in defence and in capable hands, was a very good warrior.[2]

Soddu, faced with the task of nursing his beaten forces back into fighting shape, had recourse to a bit of inventive diplomacy with Mussolini, who continued to insist (at least in public) that the war in Greece was winnable. Inspecting the remnants of the Julia Division, Soddu reported back to the Duce on 12 November that 'this superb unit is as proud and solid as ever thanks to its granite alpine troops'. He was able to say this as some parts of the Julia had fought extremely well, and still displayed some fighting spirit when a senior general came to visit. Yet the despatch enabled Mussolini, in an address to fascist party officials six days later, to deny the claims of 'Greek propaganda and its British spokesmen' that the Julia had suffered any major reverse at all!

The 47th Bari Division was hurriedly diverted from its original mission to occupy Corfu to replace the Julia in the mountains. The troops were green, but successfully fended off Greek moves to recapture Konitsa. Soddu, meanwhile, counted the cost so far: 372 dead, 1,081 wounded and 650 missing in the first ten days of conflict. Soddu's strategy was to hold on to the gains secured in the west by the Raggruppamento del Litorale while forming a line inside Albania to defend the towns of Berat and Kelcyre between the frontier and Tirana. On the left of the front, Nasci's Twenty-sixth Corps was maintained in position to strike the Greek flank in case of a counterattack. Nasci's main job, however, was to defend the key Albanian town of Korce (Koritza to the Greeks), yet Soddu was concerned over that whole sector's weakness. Meanwhile, Italian reinforcements were pouring in. By 12 November three alpine battalions, the Val Fella, Val Tagliamento and Val Natisone, had been airlifted into Vlore, while two battalions of the 5 Alpine Regiment, the Edolo and the Tirano, were flown and shipped to Albania respectively. More light tanks for the Centauro trundled ashore at Durres. But all the new arrivals continued to be plagued by disorganization. The battalions, in the words of an Italian officer, 'were sent hastily to unknown locations where it was hard to distinguish where the enemy was.'[3]

The Raggruppamento del Litorale, meanwhile, was up against stiffening Greek resistance. By 10 November its gains south of the Kalamas River had all but been wiped out. Lieutenant Fontana of the 3 Grenadiers was having to call on reserves of fortitude.

> We have to be strong [he wrote]. Events have not been what we enthusiastically expected. We have to remain tough. We need to give time for the new troops arriving from Italy to organize a defence at a line in the rear. Winter is nearly here. There are no roads. The ports are inadequate.

The rain has been tormenting us for a month. Yet we are contesting the enemy's territory millimetre by millimetre. He will pay dearly for his audacity.[4]

As a measure of military spirit when the going is tough, Fontana's diary entry is admirable. Yet one must wonder what Greek 'audacity' he was referring to, since he knew as well as anyone that his side had started the war. It must have been the shock of finding that an adversary who, he had been told, would dissolve in the first days of war was actually hitting back, and hard. This ran counter to all the propaganda that Fontana and other well-meaning Italian soldiers had been fed for months. That despite that shock he continued to fervently fight for his country – he would be wounded in early December – says much for his soldierly qualities.

Badoglio, meanwhile, had the unhappy task of explaining his military's failure to Field Marshal Wilhelm Keitel, the head of Germany's high command, the *Oberkommando der Wehrmacht*, in a mid-November meeting. Keitel fretted that now Germany would have to expend men and resources to step in where Italy had stumbled, as Greece by now had become 'an important Allied air and naval base'. Badoglio made weak excuses, blaming his political leadership for the blunders. In Rome the Duce was ebullient, insisting to General Armellini that the Italians still could, if they punched hard enough, be in Arta and Preveza in December. They were never given the chance to find out.

At dawn on 14 November Papagos gave the order for the Greeks to advance all along the line. By that date his forward units had penetrated into Albanian territory, in front of the 49th Parma, 19th Venezia and 29th Piemonte Divisions. On the right, the III Corps under Lieutenant General George Tsolakoglou made threatening moves on the Devoli River valley in southern Albania. The Devoli Valley winds between the masses of 5,000ft Mount Ivan to the east and the similarly-sized Mount Morova to the west. The valley was Papagos' objective, but to get there he had to face off with Geloso's Eleventh Corps and Vercellino's Ninth Corps massed in the area of Erseke. There had been a last-minute hitch when the commander of the West Macedonia Army Department, Lieutenant General Ioannis Pitsikas, hesitated to move on the key Devoli Valley sector, fearing he would have no reserves in case of an Italian counter-attack. It took a direct order from Papagos to get him to move.

The Greek surge began with the 15th Division of the III Corps moving between the Greater and Lesser Prespa Lakes up against the border with Yugoslavia. Softened up by a shelling, the Italians in the sector at first gave way but stiffened in higher ground in the foothills of Mount Ivan. After a three-hour battle the 15th Division broke the Italian line but was stalled at the mountain. At the same time the 9th and 10th Divisions moved against the lower slopes of Mount Morova, advancing steadily under fire and capturing a few villages and strategic heights. On the evening of 15 November the Greeks were in possession of most of the mass of Morova overlooking the Devoli Valley from the west. In response, the Italian 53rd Arezzo Division rushed to beef up the Morova-Ivan line. To meet this threat Papagos inserted his 13th Division between the 9th and 10th, and continued the push.

Morale among the Greek troops was about as high as it could get. Few of those eager young men who had hung in bunches from the backs of trams to get to the recruiting offices had dared to entertain even the wildest hope that Greece might not only resist the invader but even defeat him. It was a matter of overriding national honour more than anything else. It was a universal feeling that Greece had no choice but to fight, whatever the chances. And now incredibly, after a mere two weeks, victory over an Axis power appeared to be in sight. And that was not all. The Greeks had not only driven the invader from their land; they believed they were actually in the process of re-occupying what was a part of Greece of old – Northern Epiros, where a substantial ethnic Greek population still lived despite the region's being part of Albania. Generations of teachers and politicians had dinned into malleable Greek minds the powerful irredentist message that it was only a matter of time before Northern Epiros fell again into the bosom of the homeland. And now it seemed to be happening.

An astounding instance of morale was witnessed by a practitioner of the traditional Greek shadow play, featuring flat puppets manipulated behind a back-lit screen. In those years the shadow play was at the peak of its popularity with children and adults alike. When the wounded began to stream into the hospitals of Athens, shadow players volunteered to set up their screens in the hospital wards to entertain the men. Such was the enthusiasm among the maimed and blinded soldiers – some of them already breathing their last – that the player in question often began his performance in tears. One day when he was gathering up his gear he was stopped by a laughing shout from one of the beds. 'Hey! In all your years of playing I bet you've never seen a puppet like me!' The player turned to see who was talking. It was a young soldier whose arms and legs had been blown off.[5]

Up in the cold and fog of the Albanian front, Private Miltiades Nikolaou of the 42 Evzone Regiment whiled away his homesickness by observing the rugged countryside around him as he slogged northwards day after day. Thirty-two years old, and having left behind a wife and two daughters, Nikolaou scribbled his impressions in a diary. On the morning of 17 November, after a 40km forced march, Nikolaou observed a column of Italian prisoners. The sight shocked him. 'I was moved more than I have ever been in my life,' he wrote. 'They were barefoot, naked or with disgusting torn clothes, unshaven and in a lamentable state.' The prisoners cried that they were hungry, but neither the pitying Nikolaou nor anyone else could do much for them. Another 40km forced march later, Nikolaou saw the first graves of dead Greek soldiers. At the same time news reached his platoon that a squadron of Greek cavalry had been wiped out. Balancing this were reports that the Greek front was moving ahead and that hundreds of Italians had been captured along with their vehicles and motorcycles. 'Our air force and the British are chasing them,' he wrote.[6]

The RHAF was doing its bit well. Its objectives on 14 November were to hit the Italian air base at Korce with thirteen aircraft of 32 and 33 Bombing Mirai. The first wave smashed five Italian aircraft on the ground, with a second wave destroying ten more. One bomber of 32 Mira was hit by flak and blew up. While that was happening, agile Fairey Battle light bombers of 33 Mira sneaked in from Corfu at low level, pounding the base at Gjirokaster and destroying about a dozen enemy aircraft on the ground. Squadrons of fighters were hurried up to the frontier to provide cover for the III Corps advance. The following day a large Italian bomber force attacked Florina RHAF base, but without inflicting any real damage, a fact that led the commanding officer of 31 Mira, Squadron Leader Grigorios Theodoropoulos, to wonder whether the Italian pilots had been trained well enough.[7]

The bombers of 33 Mira were sent against the Italian positions between Morova and Ivan, but were jumped by Fiat CR42s of the Regia Aeronautica's 363 Squadriglia. The result was two Greek Battles destroyed, another disabled, and four RHAF airmen dead. A similar reception awaited 31 Bombing Mira when it was sent to hit Italian artillery along the Devoli River. The enemy gunfire went wide, but one returning plane was hit by friendly fire inside Greek territory, killing the plane's observer/navigator.

The Greek airmen's sacrifices over the Devoli Valley were not in vain. Soddu brought up the 2nd Tridentina Alpine Division, bringing the Italian strength in the Devoli sector to five divisions, but Pitsikas' West Macedonia Army Department advanced to occupy all of Mount Morova on 21 November. The Tridentina fought the 15th Division to a brief standstill, but by that time Greek artillery fire was ranging as far as the Korce-Erseke road and the Korce air base. The Greek 13th Division got into a spot of trouble when some units got lost in the rain and darkness and ended up withdrawing, momentarily exposing the flanks of 9th and 10th Divisions. The 13th's 23 Infantry Regiment suffered considerable casualties and its commander, Colonel Evstathios Rokkos, was dismissed and indicted for a court-martial. The mishap also cost Major General George Razis, the Divisional Commander, his post. To maintain morale the new Divisional Commander, Major General Sotirios Moutousis, rode right up to the front line to personally observe from his horse where his heavy artillery shells were falling.[8] Mount Ivan, the height on the other side of the Devoli River, fell a day later. The way to the key town of Korce was opening up.

The Greek mobilization had been completed on 11 November, and thus Papagos could better calculate which forces, and in what strength, he could deploy in various sectors. On the left of the West Macedonia Army Department's line where it joined with the I Corps' right in the form of the Cavalry Division, the Greeks penetrated the Albanian frontier and took Erseke on 21 November – fighting hard all the way. On the left, north of Kalpaki, the bulk of the II Corps had yet to come up. To mask this potential weakness from the enemy, Papagos ordered an aggressive advance by the I Corps' 8th Division and 3 Infantry Brigade, joined on 17 November by the 2nd Division, which was thrown into the fight without having time to rest from a 200km march. The I Corps' assignment was to push as far as possible into Albania, aiming for the town of Tepelene that stood on the Vojussa River (the lower reaches of the Greek Aoos). This way a line could be formed between Tepelene and Korce and the river valley road cut. For this, the 8th Division was reinforced by the 39 and 40 Evzone Regiments, one battalion from the 2nd Division battalion, and two from the 3rd Division which would serve as the link with the II Corps to the east.

The I Corps attack was to be three-pronged: the right prong would be provided by elements of the 8th and the Cavalry divisions to strike at the Italian position at Mertzani where the Aoos River enters Albania and becomes the Vojussa; the middle prong would be the bulk of the 8th Division moving on the border post at Kakavia; the left prong would be made up of other 8th Division units to mop up remaining Italian outposts as far as the coast.

On the right the Greek cavalry came up against stubborn Italian artillery fire that kept it pinned down on 14 and 15 November with considerable casualties. On 16 November, when the remnants of the Julia were abandoning Konitsa to the flames, a regiment of Greek cavalry rode along the Aoos Valley heading for the frontier at Mertzani. At the village of Mazi they were held up briefly by an Italian detachment, but managed to arrive at the frontier on 19 November. The way into Albania was blocked by a strong Italian force that offered stubborn resistance that took two days of close-order combat to overcome. With the border at Mertzani breached, the 8th Division in the Kalpaki sector could move forward again. In a series of one-two punches, the 8th and 2nd Divisions moved to clear the road to Kakavia. They encountered serious resistance at Delvinaki by the Italian 2 Bersaglieri Regiment backed up by armour, but that, too, was overcome. The toughest obstacle for the Greeks was Repetista Hill, an Italian artillery position defended fiercely for seven hours in the face of incessant Evzone charges that eventually drove the Italians from the height. Nearly 130 prisoners were taken. In the west the so-far successful Raggruppmento del Litorale had to share the fate of its fellow units, abandoning Igoumenitsa on 17 November. The Greeks forded the Kalamas River in a surprise attack three days later, eliminating the Italian salient in the west. The I Corps three-pronged attack had succeeded.

An unexpected logistical problem for the Greeks was what to do with the flood of Italian prisoners. Shiploads of them were sent from the ports of Epiros round to Athens, where they disembarked and were forced to march to their prisoner-of-war quarters. Few onlookers were inclined to jeer. The Italians, they found, were pretty much like themselves, of similar appearance and character, easy to get on with and sharing the same love of good wine and song. Reports from the Greeks at the front had spoken of well-behaved prisoners, many of them frankly relieved to be out of a war they had never believed in from the outset, and willing to cooperate with their captors as long as it could get them back home.

Prince Peter, whose linguistic attainments included a command of Italian, accompanied Gambier-Parry and Colonel Jasper Blunt, the British military attaché, to a POW camp near Athens.

> The men [the prince wrote later] seemed to be happy and relieved to have survived and be out of the war, but also a bit put out, as they assured us they didn't know why the war was being fought. '*È una guerra politica*' ('It's a political war'), they would repeat, as if by those words they could deny responsibility.[9]

For the Greeks at home the sight of the Italian prisoners was the first concrete sign that they were winning, as the press and radio, not to mention soldiers' letters home, were strictly censored. Communiqués from the General Staff said very little. For example, the Greek public learned nothing of the victory at Kalpaki until many days after it happened.

The renewed Greek push of 14 November coincided with the onset of the Balkan winter. Morova and Ivan and other heights were already capped with snow. Five days into the offensive, Greek artillerymen found that persistent fog and low-lying cloud hampered their targeting. Yet the drive on Korce had a high priority. To prepare for it, Papagos re-formed the 9th and 10th Divisions into Division Group K under Lieutenant General George Kosmas who spent two days preparing his units.

Confusion was rife on both sides as the Greeks pushed towards Korce. The first interim objective of Division Group K was Erseke, held by Colonel Giuseppe Azzaro's 1 Bersaglieri Regiment. There were clashes on the Erseke-Korce road, but apparently on orders from Nasci (the record is disputed here); Azzaro retreated, leaving Erseke exposed along with the left flank of the Bari Division and the whole of Geloso's Eleventh Corps. (Nasci and Azzaro later faced a board of inquiry.) To plug the gap that had opened up Geloso threw together a detachment consisting of a Finance Police battalion and two Blackshirt battalions, but the Bari remained dangerously exposed. The division had been transferred to the newly-formed Eighth Corps under General Emilio Bancale who on 19 November ordered a tactical withdrawal from a bridgehead at the Sarandaporos River. Geloso tried to countermand the order, but in the resulting confusion all semblance of order was lost as Greek shells rained down on the Italian positions. Wounded and dying men were left untended because of a lack of field hospitals and medical equipment. Extreme courage and resigned despair reigned in the same units. The 84 Infantry Regiment, for example, carried out a fanatical bayonet charge against the Greeks on 18 November, but it was thrown back and its commander, Colonel Luigi Zacco, killed. Green reinforcements sent to attack the Greeks on Morova were cut down before they could even fire a shot. Hill 1900, a key position on the Morova slopes, changed hands time after time. Second lieutenants found themselves in command of battalions. Alpini airlifted to Korce air base came under deadly shellfire as soon as they got off the Luftwaffe Junkers Ju52 transports. About 100 of them, seriously wounded within minutes of their arrival, were put back on the planes for home.[10]

Geloso's next idea was to form a new defence line around Gjirokaster, but morale throughout the army was now very shaky. Vercellino, the Ninth Corps commander based at Elbasan, was on the verge of despair. 'We have no communications and virtually no transports,' he messaged to anyone who cared to listen. 'I can no longer furnish the front line with the very few mules still available.' Geloso admitted to having 'no reserves worthy of the name'. The Centauro and Bari needed an urgent rest and refit in the rear, he said, while the once-proud Siena and Ferrara had been reduced to 'a fistful of men' each.

The Siena in particular was in poor moral shape. During the retreat over the Albanian border Captain Fernando Campione, a divisional information officer, tramping with the others over the rough mountain tracks, passed the bodies of soldiers mangled by Greek artillery.

> Another infantryman lies on the road [Campione wrote in a memoir after the war]. His hands are clenched tight. A shell fragment has ripped his belly open up to his right side, where the coagulated blood forms a vast and dirty stain on his tunic. They bury him that evening, probably by the river, at the foot of a lonely mountain.[11]

Discipline in the Siena was in serious danger of breaking down. Some soldiers took to obliterating consciousness by drinking heavily, others to stealing what they could of the Albanian villagers' livestock and food. Captain Campione saw one soldier driving a herd of sheep in front of him. The ignominious withdrawal of the Siena continued until by 2 December, 'more than two thousand soldiers of the line [were] killed and wounded, or missing and sick.'

In the west, after the battle at Repetista the I Corps Commander, Lieutenant General Panayotis Demestichas, pondered his next moves. His objective was to send the 8th Division driving through southern Albania to capture the town of Gjirokaster (where many ethnic Greeks lived) and push on to Tepelene. At the same time the 2nd Division would take a parallel eastern route through the valleys, following the Vojussa River to take Permet and Kelcyre. Separating the two columns would be the long mass of Mount Debelit, some 7,000ft high at its summit. Katsimitros suggested that the 2nd Division take a more westerly route along the Drina River, without having Mount Debelit between that division and his own. Demestichas said he would think about it.

Meanwhile, the enemy remaining west of the Kalpaki sector had yet to be cleared. Katsimitros' division dislodged the Italians from Mount Kasidiaris west of Ioannina by a series of costly bayonet charges. On the Kakavia road the Greeks ran into a detachment of Bersaglieri who with their bicycles had just been flown into Vlore and hurried to the front. The feather-hatted Bersaglieri, made up largely of military college volunteers indoctrinated with the ideology of a new Roman Empire, eventually cracked, but their morale had not suffered. Those captured were unrepentant prisoners, boasting to their captors that more of the Duce's cannon, tanks and aeroplanes were on their way and that they would win in the end.[12]

On the right the 39 Evzones spearheaded the 2nd Division's drive towards the border at Bourazani, along with four batteries of mountain artillery. It was the same story as at the Kakavia road – a fanatic Italian resistance eventually overcome by Greek artillery and bayonets. Early in the afternoon of 20 November a treasure trove of Italian cannon, anti-aircraft guns, bicycles and motorcycles numbering in the hundreds, signalling equipment, ammunition, food, boots and even barbed wire coils, fell into Greek hands.

An Italian pocket remained on the slopes at Limni, where on 19 November the troops rounded up a group of schoolgirls and led them weeping to a schoolhouse. The intention of the Italians in marshalling the girls is not clear. Greek sources indicate the girls might have been prospective rape victims. At that moment Evzones appeared on the ridge above, galvanizing the villagers of Limni into action. Men and women alike took up axes and cudgels and chased the Italians through the village. Young boys picked up abandoned rifles and used them, killing about a dozen of the enemy.

The single Italian detachment now remaining in Greek territory was a part of the Ferrara Division hanging on to the height of Prophitis Ilias overlooking the Kakavia border crossing, along with some Bersaglieri and a few tanks. Greek artillery fire failed to budge it, so Katsimitros decided on another concerted three-pronged attack.

On the morning of 21 November some progress was made with attacks on Prophitis Hill, strongly held by the Bersaglieri who had orders to hold on at all costs and did so. After a day of stalemate, the following morning the Greeks charged with their well-used bayonets through a fiery hell and took the hill, with the slowly retreating Italians contesting every inch. At nightfall the Italians were still in possession of Visani, the last Greek village before the border.

Katsimitros, concerned that the enemy might be consolidating his positions farther north, ordered fresh assaults for dawn the next day. A frenzied Evzone attack, in the teeth of stern enemy resistance, managed to cut the Kakavia road in the Italians' rear. That evening the remnants of the Ferrara were finally compelled to pull back in a hurry. The Ferrara commander, General Giannini, narrowly escaped capture. The advancing Evzones were amazed to discover, in addition to satisfactory quantities of ammunition and radio equipment, a hastily-abandoned officers' club with guitars hanging on the walls and trays of freshly-baked bread.

As the exhausted yet elated Evzones were shepherding their prisoners to the rear, a Greek colonel came upon one Evzone supporting a wounded Italian with difficulty.

'Why are you carrying him by yourself?' the officer asked. 'Why don't you get a couple more Italians to help you?'

'We shouldn't let him die, colonel,' the Evzone replied. 'Blood's running from his leg. Whether he's Italian or not, it's the same thing.'[13]

The Raggruppamento del Litorale, meanwhile, had also been driven back from its gains of the first few days of the war, in the face of the Greek I Corps. The Raggruppamento tried to mask its retreat by setting fire to Igoumenitsa and executing three city councillors on 16 November. Greek forces forded the ever-swollen Kalamas River four days later, employing boats that came under incessant Italian mortar fire.

The Regia Aeronautica bombed the bridge at Menina, while some of the Greek cavalry horses attempting to cross the river were drowned in the onrush. Slowly and agonizingly, the Siena, Ferrara and Centauro rolled back the way they had come less than a month before. Many of the Centauro's Fiat tanks got stuck in the mud and had to be abandoned.

Mussolini was, of course, increasingly dismayed at the reports from the front. Yet owing to the nature of the regime he had built up, he could hardly admit it to the Italian public, in large segments of which he had inculcated the belief that he could do no wrong – or, if he did, it was somehow not his fault. It was in this frame of mind that he addressed a grand meeting of regional fascist party bosses on 18 November. To mask his concern, he chose a line between total denial and being economical with the truth. First he launched a rambling and vitriolic attack on Britain and its Greek ally. He praised (as he should) the ability and tenacity of the Italian soldiers, but his mood became ugly when he turned to the sore point – the 'subtle enemy' that Greece had proved to be.

To underpin this accusation he came up with a unique piece of historical fiction. The day before the unnamed Evzone in Albania tried to save the wounded Italian prisoner's life, Mussolini snarled that the Greeks 'hate the Italians like no other people' and always have done. In petulant tones he claimed that Greece had offered military bases to the British and French (though Metaxas had been bending over backwards to avoid such overt displays). In case any of Mussolini's listeners might be thinking about the Italian reverses at the front – by now the fate of the Julia Division must have been common knowledge – he urged them not to believe 'Greek propaganda and its British spokesmen' and to continue to have faith that General Soddu would save the situation – 'the 372 fallen, the 1,081 wounded and 650 missing in the first ten days of combat on the Epiros front will be avenged'.[14]

Soddu, at the front, was thinking in far soberer terms. His front-line defence against the advance of the Greek Division Group K was the 48th Taro Division under General Gino Pedrazzoli, but that was hurriedly pulled back as it became clear that the Greeks now had a clear preponderance of forces. By 19 November, the day after Mussolini's bombastic speech to the fascist party chiefs, Vercellino had come to the conclusion that his Ninth Corps couldn't hold the Morova-Ivan sector. Soddu agreed, and ordered a general pullback to a position about 50km north of Korce, around Pogradec. Soddu's excuse to Badoglio (or perhaps it was close to the truth) was that he was merely exhausting his men trying to hold on to Korce and that the aim now was to 'attach to second positions with the units about to arrive'. Badoglio commended Soddu for his good sense, but not so Mussolini. Only the previous day, the Duce had boasted to his fascist party chiefs that he still had the means 'to break the back of the Greeks'. Now Soddu as well, after Visconti Prasca, had proved incapable of carrying out the grand plan. His days, too, were numbered.

And how could Mussolini face Hitler now? The issue pressed on him, for the Fuehrer had just written an I-told-you-so letter to him in a highly critical vein, blaming him for delaying the attack on Greece, losing the initial battles, and as a consequence tarnishing the reputation of the Axis, politically and militarily. The humiliated Duce put on a brave face, telling his regional chiefs that 'the worst is over ... Italy is preparing thirty divisions with which to annihilate Greece'.

Soddu's problem was to mask the withdrawal to Pogradec by making it look like a retrenching manoeuvre. This was Badoglio's recommendation when Soddu asked him for advice. As for Mussolini, he was in a self-confessed 'black week'. Loth to leave such a large piece of the Albanian pie in enemy hands even for tactical reasons, and embittered by Hitler's scornful letter, he could only weakly suggest to Soddu that he not make any hasty decisions. Left essentially without any guidance, Soddu had no choice but to evacuate Korce on the night of 21 November. The Tridentina, Piemonte, Parma and Arezzo Divisions left first. The last unit to leave, the 4 Bersaglieri Regiment, had the unhappy task of leaving behind considerable quantities of arms and supplies.

During the march out of Korce, Italian morale drooped. The battalions of Albanian volunteers, until recently deemed so important to the Italian effort, were nowhere to be seen. 'Two divisions of our troops that had been stationed in defence of the Greek-Albanian border at Korce have had to retire to a line west of the city, after eleven days of fighting,' read War Bulletin 168, issued the following day. 'Our losses have been notable. On the other hand, the enemy's losses are perhaps heavier. Our reinforcements are concentrating on the new line.' Meanwhile, wounded soldiers were contracting gangrene and dying for lack of medical attention. Soddu hoped that the promised reinforcements would arrive soon, but nearly a week later he was still waiting.[15]

The Italians tried their best to mask their withdrawal from Korce, but Papagos had cottoned on to what was happening the previous day, when he received a Yugoslav intelligence report that 'a large column,' up to 20km long, was observed moving north from Korce to Pogradec. Greek air reconnaissance quickly confirmed the fact that could only mean one thing: Nasci, threatened by a Greek pincer movement from the Morava and the Prespa Lakes, was clearing out of Korce. Tsolakoglou of the III Corps ordered the 15th and 9th Divisions to probe the approaches to the town while Kosmas' Division Group K sped up its advance from the south. At dawn on 22 November all three units proceeded cautiously, not encountering any of the enemy. One regiment took Mount Ivan with no opposition, while the northwest foothills of Morova were secured. In the late afternoon a 9th Division battalion and company under Colonel Begletis entered Korce to wild displays of joy by the ethnic Greek population. 'I report that at 5.45 pm today a detachment under my command entered Korce and liberated it,' Begletis messaged the General Staff.

The jubilation in Korce was nothing compared to the delirium in Athens. The news of the fall of Korce arrived by a deafening ringing of church bells throughout the capital. Athenians surged through the flag-choked streets embracing one another and anyone wearing a British, Australian or New Zealand uniform. A crowd gathered in front of the Grande Bretagne hotel clamouring to see Metaxas who hesitated to come to his window as the news had not yet been confirmed and a premature celebration might have serious consequences for his regime's credibility. Soon, however, there came a confirmatory message from General Pitsikas. The prime minister duly appeared at a window, beaming. He barely was able to enunciate seven words: 'My dear people, Korce has been taken ...' when he was drowned out by thunderous cheering. Back inside his office he kissed his ministers on the cheeks 'like children'.

King George chose the seizure of Korce to make his own contribution to soaring Greek morale. In a brief address to 'the armed forces and the nation' he stressed that Greece had the war forced upon it, and the resulting sense of rightness had given wings to the soldiers' feet.

> The importance of the material factor has been much-bruited these days [the king said]. Without in the least underestimating it, we believe in the overwhelming power of the moral factor ... Whatever and however many the phases of this great struggle which the Greek Nation has engaged in, and however many trials it has yet to face, there is one fact that cannot be doubted: the final and permanent triumph of justice and honour.[16]

The king's speech was the second such emanating from an Allied leader in 1940, following Churchill's famous 'blood, sweat and tears' address of earlier in the year. It would be tempting, and reasonable, to attribute the inspiration directly to Churchill's example. Yet it is hard to avoid the conclusion that for perhaps the first time in Greek history since the Persian Wars of the fifth century BC, the nation was emotionally and politically united by an act of naked aggression. Hence such stirring and fighting words could be expected to emerge naturally from anyone ruling Greece at the time. One cannot overestimate the effect on military and civil morale of the king's closing phrases (and contrast them with Mussolini's bluster to his own people four days earlier):

> To those heroic boys I send My heartfelt greeting and hope that the same courage and high ideals warm their breasts. And victory is ours, since right is totally ours.

Chapter 5

The Teeth of the Blizzard

Britain's 'journalistic' war – General Heywood arrives – Gambier-Parry 'takes' Gjirokaster – Pogradec captured – Greece's strategic dilemma – Battle of Buna Wood – Cavallero replaces Badoglio – ordeal of the Siena – the Duce pours in reinforcements – perils of winter combat – the lines freeze – a colonel's suicide

International military experts predicting the swift fall of Greece (and incidentally, an equally swift fall of Britain in the summer of 1940) were dumbfounded by the news of the fall of Korce. As Athens erupted in joy, Captain Prince Peter allowed himself hardly a blip in his busy schedule. To top it all, he had just received word from his wife in Istanbul that she was pregnant – a situation hardly calculated to enable an overworked officer to collect his mind in wartime! In the ornate headquarters offices in the Grande Bretagne Hotel he was juggling the treacherous diplomatic undercurrents that always afflict a nation at war. The king and the high command, for example, never could quite figure out the attitude of the British. King George had been puzzling for some time over D'Albiac's unexpected *cri de coeur* at Tatoi; it was probably the first time he had been exposed to that wave of anti-colonial sentiment that would sweep Britain after the war and help deliver the death blow to the Empire. At times it seemed as if the British in Greece looked on the war against the Axis as an Eton playing-fields game rather than a life-or-death struggle. The country seethed with amateur spooks who sometimes got underfoot. There was a brief flurry of concern when the British Military Mission suspected the French Vichy-controlled embassy in Athens of radio-ing war intelligence to the Japanese consulate in Alexandria – a story almost certainly spurious. Those signals, it was hinted darkly, had resulted in the downing of two RAF Wellingtons over Vlore, but the supposed connection was never proven. On the other side was the German military attaché's office, which fed scraps of information to the Greeks designed to fuel concern over a German reaction.

Fortunately for the Greek army, Prince Peter's immediate superior as chief of general staff intelligence was Colonel Apostolos Perivoliotis, a brusque and no-nonsense man who had little time for trivia. It seemed to him that the British brass in Greece were concerned more with what the papers at home would write about them than with cooperating with the Greeks quietly and efficiently. In one tense meeting Perivoliotis told Colonel Blunt to his face that the British had a superficial 'journalistic conception' of war; the Greeks, on the other hand, 'do not fight symbolically, but hard and true.' (Prince Peter managed to avoid translating that part of the exchange.)

Papagos, in dire need of British aircraft to bolster the advance into Albania, and worried over rumours that Germany might send paratroopers to stiffen the Italians, could not afford to alienate the British too much. But he fretted that his allies were prone to complaining too much over issues such as Greek airfields, which were deemed too small and bumpy to handle British aircraft in any sizeable quantity. There was also the pressing issue of what to do with the masses of Italian prisoners and captured ordnance. The explosive Perivoliotis had little time for such British concerns, which he thought detracted from the pressing business at hand – beating the Axis. The British, in the view of Perivoliotis and not a few others, needed to be reminded that in Greece at least, they were not the boss.

There were also murkier issues to deal with, such as leaks to foreign correspondents. Scoop-hungry journalists are not normally respecters of national security, especially in a country that isn't their own. In Greece in 1940 a good many British officers inhabiting the bars of Athens were flattered by the correspondents' attentions – there's nothing like getting one's name in the papers to impress the folks back home – and induced by liberal alcohol into loosening their tongues. Towards the end of November Metaxas himself had to intervene in a most egregious breach of security. Reuters had apparently gleaned – through the bribe of a fur coat to a government official – news of a highly secret Greek amphibious commando landing behind the Italian lines on the Albanian coast. The report had blown the operation and the commandos had been captured. Metaxas ordered all contact cut between the Reuters correspondent-in-uniform and his Greek sources.[1]

Such developments may have undermined Gambier-Parry's position. The Greeks suspected that despite his hearty exterior and genuine desire to cooperate, he wasn't experienced enough in the murky world of high strategy, where cunning and intuition were more important than mere spit-and-polish soldiering. Gambier-Parry's previous posting as head of anti-aircraft defences in Singapore had not equipped him for the difficult job he was given in Greece. A request therefore went out to London for someone more suitable to head the British Military Mission and the result quickly arrived in the person of Major General Thomas George Gordon Heywood.

General Heywood, 'tall and stocky with ginger hair and a moustache of the same colour' was almost a caricature of the rapidly-disappearing imperial

76 *The Defence and Fall of Greece 1940–41*

officer class. His most conspicuous feature was a gold-rimmed monocle hanging by a black ribbon. The monocle was not the only thing that raised the eyebrows of the king, Metaxas and Papagos; Heywood had a perfect command of French 'which he appeared to speak better than his mother tongue'.

Gambier-Parry wanted to do one last thing before leaving – visit the front. As the correspondents continued to pester the Greek military authorities to be allowed up there, Prince Peter received the green light to escort Gambier-Parry and his aide, Captain Charles Mott-Radcliffe, for a visit. They set out by jeep early on 29 November, spending the first evening in Kozani being wined and dined by General Pitsikas at West Macedonia Army Department headquarters. At a briefing the following morning Gambier-Parry was given a digest of the news so far, including the failure of the Italian attempt to move on Ioannina in a pincer movement. Pitsikas claimed that his army had been unable to chase the Italians as far as he had liked because of a shortage of weapons, and asked Gambier-Parry if Britain could send him some. The British officer politely declined, saying it wasn't part of his remit, and that the request would have to be routed through the Greek high command.

The following day, 1 December, the party drove to Kastoria; on the way they learned of the capture of Pogradec over the radio. The day after that they were held up by slow-moving Greek military lorries churning up the mud on the way to Korce via Florina. At some points they had to get out and push the jeep through the sodden ruts. They arrived at Florina in time for a welcome official luncheon. There the party learned that snow had blocked the only road into Albania, and they would have to give priority to columns of lorries waiting for the snow to clear. There was no choice but to return to Kastoria and try their luck with the direct route into Albania from that town. The jeep was now showing serious signs of wear and tear from the execrable roads; tyres burst one after the other. Prince Peter and his party had to hitch a tow from an army vehicle into Kastoria, where they waited for the jeep to be repaired and the temperature continued to plummet. By the evening of 3 December, after wearily tailgating behind a long and slow column of anti-aircraft guns being moved to the front, they crossed the border and made Korce after dark.

Greeting them at Korce was the III Corps Commander, Lieutenant General Tsolakoglou, a tall and scholarly-looking figure who cordially gave them dinner and led them to their reserved rooms at the Palace Hotel. Gambier-Parry, to his consternation, found that the rooms lacked heating and warm water. When Prince Peter went to enquire why, the Greek hotel proprietor sullenly told him nothing could be done. This was an obvious lie, so the prince dealt with the situation by ordering an Evzone guard to requisition heating fuel by force. The hotel proprietor's attitude was a mystery. Less than two weeks before, had not the whole ethnic Greek population of Korce turned out to deliriously welcome the Greek army as liberators? Now, these very same people didn't even want to know. The following day a local gendarme enlightened the prince: the good people of Korce had, at some point, suddenly become afraid that the Greeks' good fortune might not last and that the Italians would soon be back – with reprisals. 'They thought,' Prince Peter wrote, 'that we were there thanks to some quirk of good luck and that this luck wouldn't hold much longer.'[2] Nothing better illustrates the pervasive mentality of paranoid suspicion and inconstancy that bedevils the Balkans to this day.

After a morning touring the Korce battlefields Gambier-Parry heard from Major General Agamemnon Metaxas, the commander of the 15th Division, II Corps, about how he had turned the Italian position of Korce by ferrying men around the shore of Great Prespa Lake on requisitioned fishing boats, earning the nickname 'Admiral' in the process. After lunch the party moved on to Pogradec, to observe the 17th Division attacking Italian artillery positions on Hill 924. A constant stream of wounded men flowed back from the battle, blue with cold but impressing Prince Peter by their sheer spirit. Some of them, even in their pain, joked that the 'Centaurs' (a reference to the Centauro Division) were running faster than usual 'because they had four legs!' It was dark when they arrived at 13th Division headquarters at Podgorie, the night sky lit up in the north by artillery flashes.

Their next stop was Erseke, the headquarters of Division Group K whose commander, Kosmas, showed them around. On the way back to the Greek border they stopped to watch an encounter between a squadron of Italian bombers and RAF fighters. One Italian plane went down trailing thick smoke. Others droned over the road in formations of three, dropping their bombs on villages and vehicle columns. The village of Leskovik was almost levelled. When the party arrived there, they came upon a grim scene:

> We went to the emergency field hospital in a local school filled with wounded [Prince Peter wrote]. There was blood everywhere, even running down the steps. The major [in charge] begged us to drive the wounded to Korce in our vehicle. But there were so many wounded it wouldn't have been possible. I realized the man had suffered a nervous breakdown. Colonel [Alexander] Asimakis [a West Macedonia Army Department staff officer attached to the party] sternly told him off. I thought that attitude rather heartless, but soon saw that the reprimand had its result, and the major recovered his self-control somewhat.[3]

Dead soldiers mingled with disembowelled horses and mules. Gambier-Parry, noticing one horribly mangled mule thrashing about in agony, asked a gendarme to shoot it, which he did.

That evening they were back in Greek territory at Konitsa. There the II Corps Commander, Papadopoulos, appealed for British weapons to Gambier-

Parry, who had to fob him off with the same reply he had given Pitsikas. Their next stop was the I Corps headquarters at Zitsa. Near Ioannina they passed a field hospital where the wounded men erupted in cheers when they saw British uniforms. On 7 December Gambier-Parry got to meet Katsimitros, the redoubtable 8th Division commander, and then said he wanted to speed up to Gjirokaster to get close to some actual fighting. The jeep entered the Drina Valley, splashing through shallow streams, the sound of rifle fire echoing from the heights on either side.

They arrived on the outskirts of Gjirokaster to find the attack on the city by the 4th Division under way. Major General Leonidas Steriopoulos, the Division Commander, advised them to stay back but Gambier-Parry wasn't to be cheated of his experience. The party joined the 4th Division advance units which slowly penetrated the outskirts, meeting no resistance, and suddenly found themselves in the central square of Gjirokaster which had just been evacuated by the Italians. Masses of people stood about dumbly, including bemused Albanian gendarmes in Italian uniforms. There was a café nearby and Gambier-Parry very Britishly strolled into one and sat down, ordering a coffee and cognac.

As a waiter jumped to serve them, Prince Peter looked anxiously around; for all he knew, a sniper somewhere was drawing a bead on them, conspicuously seated as they were. Shooting from the nearby hills echoed through the streets. Peter expressed his worries to Mott-Radcliffe. Gambier-Parry laughed. Even if they did get shot, he joked, tossing down his brandy, 'at least we've got somewhere. We're in Gjirokaster and we got there with the first troops.' The townsfolk dumbly gathered in the square to watch them as they drank, paid the waiter, got back into the jeep and headed south for Ioannina. The party was back in Athens the next day.[4]

Demestichas' I Corps was able to enter Gjirokaster thanks to diversionary advances along the mountain roads flanking the Drina Valley. The slow resistance of the 5th Pusteria Alpine Division and the 37th Modena was what Prince Peter and Gambier-Parry had been hearing on the way up. Another major Albanian town had fallen to the Greeks. The advance had been possible because the 3rd Division had turned the heavily-defended Kakavia crossing from the south, enabling the 4th Division to slip through.

On the far left of the Greek front, the last Italians were driven over the border on 26 November, but not without cost. To speed up the advance a raiding party of the 10 Corfu Regiment was landed on the coast to attack the Italians from the flanks and rear. The raiding party, however, was all but wiped out, though the Italians were spooked enough by it to order increased air patrols over Corfu. Greek progress up the coast was slow and arduous, hampered by unceasing rain and swollen rivers, but by 6 December the port of Sarande was in Greek hands. This made the Greek war effort immeasurably easier, as now the Greeks had an Albanian port through which they could channel men, arms and supplies to the front rather than having to send them on the long and punishing overland route. Soddu had meanwhile formed a new defensive line along the ridges south of Pogradec, with the Taro Division in front. Papagos gingerly deployed the 9th and 13th Divisions forward along the line of the Devoli River with the 10th Division on a parallel course to the west. Two more divisions, the 11th and 15th, made up the second line.

The 9th and 13th encountered the Taro but couldn't make progress because of air attacks. Stymied in front of Pogradec because of a shortage of anti-armour weaponry, the Greeks tried a flanking movement in the hills to the west of the town. On 30 November the 13th Division overcame the Italians while the 17th Division was brought up to relieve it. On 4 December Pogradec fell to the Greeks, the second key Albanian town to do so. Four days after that, the 10th Division cut the road leading from that sector to Korce and controlled the Mount Ostravitsa massif. The II Corps advanced slowly along the Vojussa River, aiming to capture Permet by 5 December.

At the onset of December the Greeks could be justifiably proud that in less than a month they had cleared their lands of the Axis invader. It was something that even the wildest optimists could not have foreseen, even in the heady days following 28 October. But this very fact created a new issue: what was the Greek war aim to be henceforth? The homeland had been defended successfully, and its occupied parts taken back. But after 25 November, when the last men of the Siena had crossed back over the Albanian border north of Filiates, the Greek war had turned from a defensive one into something that required rather more of a justification – a technical aggression into Albania.

Of course, plenty of justification could be sought, on political as well as military grounds. Merely repelling an invader is often not enough; conditions must be created along the border so that an invader cannot come again, and this most often takes the form of a counter-occupation of part or whole of the neighbouring country. It could be argued in Athens that Albania had ceased to be an independent country since Easter 1939, when the Italians had marched in and taken over. Thus as Albania was technically a part of Mussolini's Italy and as strong Italian armed forces remained in the country committed to regaining their lost ground, the war could by no means, at that stage, be considered 'won'. It had to go on.

Just how far the Greek high command was aware of this subtle overnight changeover from defensive to offensive war is a matter of conjecture. Papagos, in his ponderous memoir, gives little indication of his own thought processes except to indicate that the high command (i.e. himself and probably Metaxas, too) agreed that the recent triumphs of Greek arms should be followed up 'as far as their means allowed'.[5] In concrete terms, this referred to an objective corresponding to a line roughly from Sarande and Gjirokaster in southwest

Albania to Korce and Pogradec in the east near the Yugoslav border. This line would pivot on Pogradec, slowly sweeping like a scythe up to the vital port of Vlore. The resulting area would contain the southern third of Albania which conveniently corresponded almost exactly to 'Northern Epiros', an ethnically-Greek region that the Greek schools, church and media had been hankering after for decades. Was an irredentist aim being pursued under a strategic mask?

The Greek army might be winning, but the average Greek soldier, cold and wet and incessantly on the march, was not having an easy time of it. There was a limit to anyone's endurance in those inhospitable crags and execrable weather. The main concern of Private Nikolaou of the 42 Evzones, shivering in his tent at Leskovik, was that he wasn't getting any letters from home. The fall of Korce and Gjirokaster rated no more than passing mentions in his diary, with no comment whatsoever. Italian aerial bombing killed eighty-eight men in his sector on 5 December. A few days afterwards he was shaken at the sight of a disembowelled horse. Then a rumour spread around the regiment that Saint Nicholas had appeared to the artillery and told the gunners the war would be over in nine days. Of more mundane concern, the men had to boil their lice-infested uniforms in whatever containers they could find, such as fuel cans. Freezing sleet whipped over the tents around the clock. At night Nikolaou wept with discomfort and homesickness.[6]

Metaxas was keenly aware of what his soldiers were going through. 'I feel for my boys in the army,' he wrote in his diary on 1 December. 'Would that I could be there with them!' The next day he received 'moving telegrams' from the fathers of fallen soldiers. 'Here is the example for our thoughts.' Yet he knew that the advance must go as far and fast as possible before real winter set in, and he carried his C-in-C Papagos with him. As a sign of his concern for his men Metaxas had relayed a personal encouragement to the leftish young writer and academic Kanellopoulos, who had joined the flood of volunteers after the capture of Korce and on 30 November mustered as a private in the 13th Division. Before he could fire a shot in anger, the War Cross (Fourth Class) was pinned on his tunic as a mark of appreciation from Metaxas. He was also given the job of editing an army newspaper, *Achris* (Until), which brought him into contact with senior officers on a more or less equal footing. Whatever the discomforts of the Albanian front, Kanellopoulos deemed they were better than the jails and internal exile to which the Metaxas regime had consigned him before his change of heart. Motivating him was a burning desire to serve his country, a desire which overrode political allegiances and beliefs. He would find himself in the spotlight much earlier than he imagined.

The West Macedonia Army Department planned to advance farther and chase the Italians out of Pogradec, but the men were worn out. Papagos was unmoved. 'Troops' fatigue understandable but enemy condition worse,' read the directive from headquarters in Athens. 'Cannot risk allowing enemy to regroup.' Tsolakoglou, the III Corps Commander, also wanted to forge ahead. The pivot of the Greek line, it seemed, had to be farther north than Korce. Without waiting for approval from the top, on 25 November he sent four battalions plus heavy and mountain artillery to occupy Podgorie dominating the road to Pogradec, where the Italian Ninth Corps was entrenched in exceptionally well-concealed positions, designed to prevent an outflanking from the east.

The 18 Regiment of the 13th Division was picked for the initial assault on Pogradec on 29 November. The obstacles were formidable. First, the regiment had to cross the Cerrave River at the bottom of a deep gully. Second, the prevailing mist masked the Italian artillery muzzle flashes, making their positions hard to locate. The Greeks scrambled as best as they could down the south bank of the gully and up the other side, grabbing at shrubs and one another for support, but little progress was made. From his observation post, General Moutousis, the Division Commander, wondered what was holding his men up. Mounting his horse in the bitterly cold afternoon he rode up to the line to find out. The left of the 18 Regiment had been advancing in spite of the obstacles, he said. Why wasn't the right moving? Whatever reply he received wasn't satisfactory and so he barked at the regimental adjutant: 'The flag! Bring it here! Sound the bugle for a charge.'

The regimental flag was duly brought up and unfolded with reverence and hoisted to flutter in the wintry Albanian afternoon. At the sound of the bugle the 18 Regiment's battalions fixed bayonets, rose, and charged the virtually invisible enemy position. Within minutes a sea of khaki had swarmed down the gully and up the other side – right into a murderous curtain of fire from the Venezia Division. Men fell like ninepins. Moutousis vainly peered into the smoke of battle to see whether any of his units had pierced the enemy line. He couldn't even direct his own artillery fire. At one point he thought he saw an enemy muzzle flash. 'Get me a cannon!' he roared.

A 105mm mountain gun was rolled up. Moutousis, an experienced artilleryman, ranged the distance with his eyes alone and snapped out the firing coordinates. The cannon thundered, and after a few minutes a giant flash pierced the thick smoke – one of the shells had fallen on an Italian battery and blown up its ammunition. As night was falling, the Italian fire slackened. The following morning Moutousis seized the heights around Pogradec, forcing the Italians to evacuate that town that same evening. The bells rang in Greece again.[7]

The Italian pullback from Pogradec was partly attributable to the fact that there was no point on the whole front on which a unit could be anchored, to form a pivot for other movements, as the Greeks had done around Korce. Individual units were thus vulnerable to being exposed and forced to withdraw. Around Pogradec the Greek 9th Division occupied one height after the other, fighting often in blinding snowstorms. The fresh 17th Division under

Major General Panayotis Basakidis had been brought up to replace the battered and bruised 13th, which was retired into the reserves. The 17th Division's 31 Regiment hurled itself against Hill 1532 held by the Arezzo, whose men had orders not to give an inch. A company of 31 Regiment managed to scale the height using ropes and get in the defenders' rear. A savage bayonet slashing match ensued, with the Arezzo clinging on tooth and nail. Such was the polar cold that Greeks and Italians, bayoneting one another, remained upright in their deaths, pinned together in grotesque frozen sculptures. Hill 1532 eventually fell to the Greeks, who took some 400 prisoners.[8]

With Pogradec gone, the Italian objective was now to protect Elbasan, a headquarters town about 50km south of the Albanian capital, Tirana. The Taro Division was rushed up to the front to join the Piemonte and Arezzo, which were digging in across the Shkumbin River valley. In the central sector the Greek II Corps had been slowly, in the gradually worsening weather, slogging its way up the Vojussa Valley towards Permet and the village of Frasher, a key point to link with the III Corps left. It was hard going against the Italian armour which had the run of the valley. In the end, the Greeks' well-practiced artillery scored several gains. But while the Cavalry Brigade moved on Permet and Frasher from the south, the 1st Division, which was supposed to support the operation on the right, was pinned down by Italian shellfire. The terrain was rough in the extreme, with no patch of level ground that could accommodate more than about half a dozen men abreast. Proceeding with great care in order to keep the units connected and hide from enemy artillery spotters, the 1st Division crawled through the defiles towards Frasher. As the cavalry attacked on the left, the division's forward units charged and took Hill 1300, along with a load of supplies, arms and prisoners. An Italian company, seemingly isolated at the bottom of a ravine, raised the white flag. A Greek company moving in to round them up came under withering fire and had to scatter to battle positions. The Cavalry Brigade encountered serious opposition at the Legatice River, a tributary of the Vojussa but the position was turned from the right and the road to Permet was open.

In the western sector the Italians planned to form a new line of defence between the towns of Tepelene and Kelcyre, a front 18km long. Until the line could be consolidated, however, the Greek advance had to be delayed by any means. It was a wise move. The Greeks, in addition to risking serious exhaustion from a month of incessant fighting, were short of anti-armour weaponry. They were also subject to incessant attack from the air. The heights overlooking the Drina Valley, through which the Greek I Corps had to march, were formidable, offering infinite scope for snipers and gunners. Before the corps could move, though, the II Corps on the right had to take Polican to the east of the valley. The move succeeded; after a partial encirclement from the height of Mount Nemerckes, the Italians evacuated Polican and the Greek northward drive could resume.

The toughest Italian resistance was encountered at the Kakavia border post. While in the east the West Macedonia Army Department and III Corps had been forging ahead after Korce, the 8th Division had been unable to make much progress in the western sector. The Ferrara Division had been reinforced by the 42nd Modena Division which, by a numerical coincidence, found itself facing the 42 Evzones, Private Nikolaou's regiment. The Ferrara, plus units of Albanians, was entrenched with artillery in the Buna wood, throwing back Greek attacks. The Greek infantry, temporarily without effective artillery support owing to the terrain, had to cope with the fire of eight Italian batteries ranging in on them. There was stalemate until two Greek light artillery batteries managed to get within 400 metres of Buna wood. This enabled Greek infantry units to outflank the wood painfully slowly until 26 November when the I Corps artillery was again able to get into suitable position and rain down shells on the Italians and Albanians who had positioned themselves in the village of Voblo, holding the ethnic Greek families hostage while fortifying the houses. Regardless, Greek artillery levelled the village, house by house, with remarkable accuracy. By the time the Albanians surrendered, however, a mere four civilians had died in the rubble, while about a dozen were injured. When a Greek officer apologized for the need to shell the place, the villagers took it in their stride. 'It's war,' they shrugged. 'Soldiers get killed. We get killed. As long as you got rid of those Albanian buggers, the village is happy.'[9]

Still Buna wood held out. Every tree, it seemed, hid an Italian gun. Seeing progress on the other fronts, I Corps Commander Demestichas fretted. Katsimitros replied that his 8th Division had arguably been the most heavily-engaged division since the war began, in action almost daily, and his men were justifiably worn out. Besides, there were 800 Italian prisoners to accommodate and feed. Behind the Ferrara were stationed battalions of Blackshirts with orders to machine-gun any soldier fleeing to the rear. In the Modena seven men were shot and five officers court-martialled for cowardice. The division commander threatened personally to shoot any shirker. Nonetheless, in one final spasm of energy the Italians were cleared out of Buna wood, leaving behind trails of ammunition, canned food and bodies to be picked over by the wheeling vultures.

On 28 November the 3rd Division under Major General Telemachos Papadopoulos was able to join the 8th Division, going straight into battle. After some initial success Papadopoulos was forced to retire under the pressure of an Italian counterattack out of Libohove. At the same time Italian bombers attacked the Greek position at Polican, spreading fire and destruction. Men died; pack mules laden with ammunition were blown to pieces. While that was happening the Italians on the 8th Division front were re-forming on Hill 669, four battalions and two in reserve.

Bravely as his men might be fighting, the Duce had little sympathy for them. His reaction was one of mounting rage at what was beginning to look like a series of unstoppable reverses for Italian arms. Most unlike his opposite number Metaxas, he appeared to have not the slightest feelings for his men; on the contrary, he was so callous as to suggest along Darwinian lines that the hellish conditions served the function of toughening the Italian army by weeding out the weaklings. He fumed and threatened to send senior officers before a firing squad. He didn't actually do so, but chose as his sacrificial victim the one man who had never had his heart in the Greek campaign from the outset, who had been indifferent to its every preparation and who was, consequently, a perfect scapegoat – Marshal Badoglio. The chief of staff, of course, had been proven absolutely right all along. But for a senior soldier, showing up the political leadership for fools is not the way to drape the end of a military career in glory. Attacks on Badoglio began appearing in the tame fascist party press. An elliptical editorial in the journal *Regime Fascista* read:

> We are certain that [the defeat of Greece] will be realized, even though a lack of providence and some unreasonableness in the General Staff has allowed Churchill [to succeed] ... Yet all the evils will not go for nought. The reaction will be greater, and the discomfiture of the enemy will be greater.[10]

Such opaque language was typical of the official attempt to re-brand the defeats in Greece and Albania as mere wrinkles in high command tactics rather than a result of a basically and fatally flawed strategy in the first place. Yet it pointed the finger, clearly and most unfairly, at Badoglio who, indignant, demanded an explanation from Mussolini. The Duce could only lamely reply that the article had been the newspaper's initiative, not his. The marshal tried to get his own rebuttal printed in a Rome newspaper, but the copies were confiscated. Nonetheless, hand-printed copies of Badoglio's defence secretly circulated among the main military commands.

Whatever Badoglio's attempts to set the record straight, he knew he was beaten. Requesting four days' leave, he spent it relaxing and hunting, and composing his letter of resignation from the army, in his country home at Monferrato. Badoglio probably expected his letter to galvanize King Vittorio Emanuele into intervening on his behalf. But the king by now had long abandoned any pretence at occupying an independent throne, and besides, he was not as supportive of Badoglio as the marshal thought he was. In the highest circles, Badoglio's supposed incompetence as the cause of the Greek debacle had become solidified as established fact.

Yet Mussolini was curiously unwilling to let him go. When the marshal returned to Rome on 27 November Mussolini chose to ignore the resignation letter and claim that as the news from the Albanian front was supposedly 'better', Badoglio could stay on as chief of staff if he liked. The only explanation for this see-sawing is that the Duce feared the effect on public opinion if the head of the nation's military establishment were to be sacrificed. Armellini, close to Badoglio in the upper hierarchy, knew first hand that Badoglio had 'lost the confidence of the Duce'.

Badoglio himself by now was visibly ravaged by depression. On 3 December the king met him and was shocked at his haggard appearance. 'Badoglio made a disastrous impression on me,' the king reported. 'Physically destroyed, intellectually dulled.' The marshal had meanwhile regretted penning his resignation letter and begged to have it disregarded. On 4 December Mussolini informed him tersely that he was going to be replaced by General Ugo Cavallero, but first Cavallero was going to be sent to Albania to assess the situation there. When Badoglio bridled, the Duce snapped: 'Very well, as of this moment you are free to go.'[11] Though the humiliated and broken Badoglio had no way of knowing it then, his big moment in Italian history was yet to come.

The choice of Cavallero as chief of staff reflected the need to reconcile the military with the fascist party. Relations between those institutions had come under strain because of the Badoglio affair. Short and stout in appearance, Cavallero was a faithful fascist with one of the sharpest and most original minds in the army. An accomplished mathematician and linguist, fluent in English and German, first in his class at the military academy and a general at thirty-eight, Cavallero nonetheless was known as a busybody of sorts, with an interest in politics and finance, among other things. Being the father-in-law of Jacomoni, the governor of Albania, probably had something to do with his latest promotion. And he loathed Badoglio, a feeling that was mutual.

At the front, Soddu was in difficulties. Apart from the fall of Korce and Pogradec to the Greeks, Geloso's Eleventh Corps was coming under irresistible pressure from the Greek scything motion in the western sector. Geloso advised a quick withdrawal to a line north of Sarande and Gjirokaster; Soddu agreed, but didn't want the pullback to be too hasty. Nonetheless, Hill 669 was abandoned without a fight. The Greeks in the centre were able to infiltrate various points in the Italian positions. On 1 December the Julia Division was attacked in flank, opening up a gap in the sector of the 41 Modena Infantry Regiment into which the Greeks surged to take Permet and secure the entrance to the Kelcyre Valley.

As for the Siena Division, its ordeal was far from over. The first part of December, in the memory of its survivors, was one long and terrible march. Scores of pack mules gave up the ghost out of exhaustion, their bodies blocking the muddy paths, cargoes still tied to their backs. A typical battalion, after a spell on mountain patrol, would present this spectacle, recorded by Captain Fernando Campione:

> The major in command drags his frostbitten feet. On his pallid and grim face you can read the tragedy of the days and nights spent in the cold and snow. He coughs continuously, and while you pity his physical state and obvious exhaustion, at the same time you must admire his serenity.[12]

Such conditions tend to place a considerable strain on morale, and it often takes only a single incident to push it past the breaking point. This came on 17 December when a false rumour of an impending Greek attack sowed panic in the Siena's 32 Regiment and triggered a flurry of confused defensive activity at Himare to meet a Greek advance that never materialized. Instead, at least forty men contracted frostbite while waiting in the snow. 'It's not the fighting that kills, but the exhaustion that frightens and makes us cowards,' Campione noted.

Throughout December Italian reinforcements continued to pour in. Their journey – by rail down the Italian peninsula and then on the freezing deck of a troopship across the Adriatic – was not a happy one. The ejection from Greece was by now common knowledge, whatever their senior officers might tell them, and they generally did not sail happily to the front. Few ordinary soldiers want to be fed into a losing battle. By the time the 1 and 2 Alpine regiments arrived at the port of Durres, their men hadn't had a hot meal in days. Italo Pietra, a lieutenant in the 1 Alpine, witnessed a surreal scene at Durres. The first thing he had noticed after getting off the ship were 'ugly voices in the offices and shops' speaking of nothing but the bad news from the front. While his regiment's Mondovi Battalion was standing on the waterfront in the icy, driving wind, awaiting orders about where to stay the night, a captain appeared with the news that the chief of staff was about to arrive 'for a few minutes' talk with the officers'.

A little while later a roly-poly little general officer emerged from a corner of the square, passing briskly in front of the officers, shaking each man's hand with a question and a smile. It was Pietra's first view of Ugo Cavallero, and the impression the new commander made was a curious one:

> [His] short stature, fat and short-legged, his voice, the glasses on top of his nose and his green scarf didn't help one realize who he was ... What was notable in the dark hour was his serenity.[13]

After Cavallero delivered a brief pep talk in which he defined the task of the 1 Alpine Regiment as 'blocking the torrent of Greeks up there in the mountains,' the men piled onto lorries for the arduous drive up to those threatening mountains, past Gramshi and into the Tomorica Valley. Part of the way they had to get off the trucks and slog for hours 'in mud nearly knee-deep,' to reinforce the 5 Alpine Regiment of the Tridentina Division. Some of the men of the 5 Regiment were in a pitiful condition indeed, swathed in bloody bandages, their unshaven faces crawling with lice. Pietra attempted a few words of encouragement to a young soldier whose feet were so frostbitten, 'they looked like potatoes,' but was rebuffed. 'We don't need courage from anybody,' the soldier replied sullenly, limping painfully on his way. Another man of the regiment tried to keep warm by filling his helmet with the steaming brains of a newly-dead pack mule and putting it on his head. The men's helmets themselves were seen as too shiny – perfect targets for enemy snipers – so it was customary for the men to urinate on them to dull their shine and then smear them with dirt.[14]

At the top, morale was scarcely any better. Soddu was affected, and as a result was given to changes of mood unsuitable for a general in the field. The decline was visible to his chief of staff, Colonel Salvatore Bartiromo, who contemptuously told the general to his face that he was about to 'tie his name to the worst debacle in our history'. Becoming more unnerved by the day, Soddu messaged Roatta on 4 December, pouring out his pessimism: 'Operations are critical. In numbers and morale our troops are in a precarious state, services are deficient.' Reinforcements were coming in far too slowly, he fretted. 'We cannot entertain the possibility, not only of a recovery, but even of an equilibrium.' That same day Soddu telephoned a staff officer in Rome with the suggestion that operations be halted and 'a political solution to the conflict' be explored.

In view of the military situation, Soddu's suggestion was an eminently sensible one. If nothing else, it indicated a sensitivity to wasting his men's lives in what had become an unmanageable conflict. But of course, in Rome the reaction was one of outrage. In Ciano's eyes Soddu was throwing down his sword in the face of the enemy. Mussolini himself waved the transcript of Soddu's telephone call in the face of Pricolo, the Regia Aeronautica Chief. 'Have you seen this?' he fumed. 'It's a proposal for a proper armistice. Rather than ask the Greeks for an armistice I'd rather us all go to Albania and die at our posts.' With the Duce's resolve behind him, in the afternoon of 4 December Cavallero flew to Elbasan to take charge of the campaign.

Mussolini's own violent mood swings, a permanent character trait, were not helping. The Duce cursed himself for believing the enthusiastic fantasies of Visconti Prasca. One day he might fume and rage, while the next he would be sunk in despondency and toy with the idea of Hitler's brokering an armistice with Greece. On one of the latter occasions Ciano threatened that he would 'rather put a bullet in [his] head than telephone to [Joachim von]

Ribbentrop,' the German foreign minister. Ciano despised Ribbentrop. Just two weeks before, he had been on the receiving end of a humiliating dressing-down by the sneering German. Besides, he still could not bring himself to accept that Italian arms could suffer a defeat by a supposedly inferior enemy. He was loth to give up without more of a fight. Yet the inescapable conclusion seemed to be that if Italy wanted to beat the Greeks, it would need German help. So Ciano had to swallow his wounded pride and instruct his ambassador in Berlin, Dino Alfieri, to go cap in hand to Ribbentrop, which he did on 7 December. Ribbentrop was haughty and dismissive, so Alfieri the following day went over his head to the Fuehrer himself.

Alfieri's description of the mess in Albania must have been convincing, for Hitler fell silent with shock and anger. Hitler's disappointment at the performance of the Italian army vied with an alarming realization that he would have to use his own arms and men to pluck Mussolini out of the mud, disrupting his wider strategic plans. In the end Hitler promised to send Luftwaffe transports to Albania. Shortly afterwards forty-nine Junkers Ju52 transports landed at Vlore and Durres with fresh Italian troops and supplies.

On 10 December the German military attaché in Rome, General Enno von Rintelen, flew to Albania on his own fact-finding tour. In the light of Alfieri's grim report, he was surprised to find Cavallero and Pricolo quite upbeat. A decisive thrust was being prepared for the spring, they told the German officer, and thanks very much, but the Fuehrer's help wouldn't be necessary after all. Italy had enough men, weapons and aircraft to do the job. Hitler must have shaken his head in disbelief when he read von Rintelen's report. Whom to believe, the whingeing ambassador or the jaunty Italian generals? Understandably, he shelved plans to send German troops to Albania. But the issue of German help would be raised again soon enough.

Soddu, meanwhile, was rapidly proving to be the wrong man for the job. Having climbed through the ranks mainly as a desk man, he lacked the steel spine necessary in a senior soldier. Setbacks and bad news affected him overmuch. Thinking that by his rank alone he could put matters right against the Greeks, instead he had come up against the brutal realities of war, and they had stunned him. The attitude was little different in Rome, where Roatta had the task of kicking into action a complacent military establishment that had fondly imagined, as Soddu had assured Albanian functionaries, that Korce would be recaptured by Christmas. Additional divisions were hastily remustered to be fed into the deadly ice-grinder of Albania. Mussolini ordered his air force to prepare to raze to the ground 'any Greek town of more than 10,000 inhabitants'. More than that, to Roatta's despair, the Duce insisted on attending to every detail of the re-mobilization. Not a day or night passed without fresh orders from Mussolini to hurry up. As soon as any troopship, transport plane or any kind of floating craft became available, troops were packed on to it. Roatta wrote later:

> As soon as any mode of personal transport became available, be it warship, steamship, or aeroplane, the men boarded, sometimes in small lots, and set out. Heavy weapons, radio stations, kitchens, coverings, baggage, medical materials, ammunition, animals and vehicles followed, via appropriate means of transport, whenever possible.[15]

The result, of course, was an influx of reinforcements armed only with personal weapons and lacking any kind of backup – and in a bitter Balkan winter to boot. More than 30,000 pack mules and their handlers remained in Italian ports, unable to find ships.

The end came for the ragged remains of the Siena when, after the debacle at Himara on 17 December, a battalion of the 17 Motorized Bersaglieri, the feathers in their hats waving in the wind as they drove up, blocked the Siena's retreat with orders to shoot anyone who continued to head rearwards. For some proud men of the Siena it was the final humiliating come-down, and they countered it with a rare heroism. Lieutenant Giulio Venini wrote to his mother:

> If my Country requires the greatest sacrifice of me, that of my life, believe me, I will do it with the most complete dedication, in the knowledge that father [killed in World War One and decorated posthumously] did it also. And I know that through our end you will be able to find a reason for pride and the strength to bear the sacrifice, indeed great, that the Country has asked of you.

Venini's grim forecast for himself would come true within a few days. Cadets in Italy's military academy had been told (not without a measure of truth) that there are few better ways of dying than being struck in the heart by a bullet in the sunshine. But, noted Antonio Cantore, a surgeon lieutenant in the Julia, 'no-one had thought that you could die in the mud, your face sinking into the mire.'

Cavallero studied the situation carefully. His idea was to hold the course of the Shkumbin River, a natural barrier that spans the width of Albania from the northern approaches to Pogradec in the east to the Adriatic Sea in the west. It was vital to keep hold of Elbasan and its military base, just north of the river and a mere fifty or so kilometres from Tirana. But more mundane concerns intruded on his thinking. The army's quartermaster-in-chief, General Antonio Scuero, warned that supplies of victuals, light ammunition and woollen underwear were exhausted. Artillery shells were in very short supply, while the stock of medical equipment was low. Vercellino of the Ninth Corps was scathing. All he had was some light artillery which he knew was heavily outgunned by the Greeks. He had taken some heart after a rearguard action by the Venezia Division re-took a strategic height south of the Shkumbin, but soon realized that was only a flash in the pan. The air force, he fumed, was 'a bluff,' concentrating on faraway targets and not doing enough to support the army. Soddu thought Geloso's Eleventh Corps could make a stand in the Kelcyre Valley, but changed his mind after the Greeks harassed the Siena rearguard unceasingly.

Mere hours after arriving in Albania, Cavallero absorbed all this information and consequently decided on a general withdrawal to the Shkumbin to give his men a week's breather. That same evening Cavallero and Soddu got on the phone to Mussolini. Soddu blustered and grovelled at the same time, assuring the Duce, sickeningly, that he had recently viewed a battalion of Blackshirts who 'sang praises in Your name'. In a false display of toughness he claimed he had dismissed divisional commanders for incompetence and sent Colonel Giovanni Manai, the commander of the 41 Regiment of the Modena Division, before a court-martial for opening up a fatal gap in the division line.

Cavallero, rather more pragmatic, requested a faster rate of reinforcement. Geloso told him that his corps had enough men and materials for at most eight more days of rearguard combat. Italian losses had been grievous. The 8 Alpine Regiment of the Julia, which had been hounded out of Epiros in the first days of the war, had suffered a casualty rate of 80 per cent. The Bari Division had been hacked to a shadow of its former self, its 139 Regiment in total collapse because of a lack of bullets and hand grenades. On 1 December Girotti had begged for the devastated Julia to be retired for a complete refurbishing.

Frustratingly for the Italians, Cavallero's order to withdraw and reform at the Shkumbin came after a series of valiant rear-guard actions that gave the Greeks considerable trouble. Though the Greek II Corps had taken Permet on 3 December, the Italian line of defence across the Kelcyre Valley was hardening. As the 10th and 11th Divisions braced to try and break the line, farther to the west the I Corps was making laborious progress from Kakavia up the Dhrin Valley, along a hugely extended front of 65km. It was easier going along the coast, but the Greek advance was brought almost to a halt by bitter fighting on the road to Gjirokaster. Along that road stood Hill 669, held by elements of Geloso's Eleventh Corps. Geloso had just issued an order threatening the old Roman punishment of decimation for any officer or enlisted man caught fleeing the combat area out of cowardice – every tenth soldier in that man's unit was to be shot. In snow 3ft deep the Eleventh Corps men held fanatically onto Height 669, repulsing the most desperate of assaults by the Greek 8th Division. Soldiers of both sides were later found frozen to death in the height of combat, their rigid fingers tight on the triggers.[16]

To try and turn Height 669 from the east, Lieutenant Colonel Pausanias Katsotas led a patrol through the dark, snowy and inhospitable landscape. Pack mules sank up to their bellies in the mud, slowing down the men. Arriving at a village at night, Katsotas rallied whatever Greek troops he could find there and any civilian volunteers who could carry a machine gun or ammunition box and led them up a steep slope to a height from which in the morning the main road to Gjirokaster would be in view. As Katsotas held his position a sharp order came down from I Corps headquarters for Height 669 to be cleared without delay. But the snow was now some 5ft deep and the 8th Division was stalled a mere 100m from the Italian position. Enemy shells rained down, dyeing the snow red with blood. Katsotas signalled headquarters that he couldn't make any progress and intended to try again at dawn. For him, as for every man in his division, to take Height 669 became a matter of honour. Major Ioannis Paparodou, the heavy artillery battery commander, sneaked in front of his own lines to set up his firing observation post, leaving a dozen kilometres of wires trailing behind him to divisional artillery headquarters.

The new assault on Height 669 began at 2.00 pm on 3 December, the men swarming like black ants over the great white slopes and toppling over among the shell bursts. Geloso's men again held, but it wasn't until the following day that a break in the weather enabled Height 669 to be turned, with the help of Katsotas' detachment. The Greeks who took the hill found the summit to be strewn with scores of enemy dead clogging the trenches with their dead mules, slaughtered by Major Paparodou's close-range heavy artillery fire. More Italian dead and wounded littered the paths behind the summit. At least they had obeyed Geloso's ruthless orders. Before the day was out, Gjirokaster was in Greek hands and the bells around Greece rang joyously yet again.

On 5 December the Greek 3rd Division marched into Delvina and took Sarande, Albania's southernmost port, a stone-built town on a bushy slope overlooking the north coast of Corfu. Next to fall was Dervican, where hundreds of ethnic Greek youths flooded the streets with huge Greek flags to welcome the incoming 4th Division. Next on the Greek list was Tepelene, to keep the scythe blade moving up from its pivot at Pogradec. Tepelene nestles in the Dhrin riverbed between beetling heights that are natural defences. For two months the Italians had been fortifying the approaches to Tepelene with gun emplacements and machine gun nests hewn into the mountainsides, ringed with miles of barbed wire and manned by tough Alpini. The first Greek probes began on 15 December but were forced to halt because of incessant blizzards, but not before units of the 4th Division routed the Italian 42 Infantry regiment, whose commander was killed.

By now the weather was inflicting far more casualties on both sides than the enemy. Major General Leonidas Stergiopoulos, the 4th Division commander, had to confess on 17 December that 'in all my military career, including a campaign in Russia [1918] ... I believe that never has our Army been so sorely tried.' Incessant hunger and lack of sleep had turned the soldiers' eyes into hollow holes. Boots rotted and fell away from the men's feet. Scores of men suffered frostbite as a result, especially in the advanced posts. Two captains in Stergiopoulos' division collapsed senseless from hypothermia and had to be carried to the rear. Cavalry horses and pack mules suffered just as much as the men, dozens drowning in mountain torrents or stumbling and plunging over cliffs.

All too often, frostbite could mean a slow death for the sufferer. The first symptoms were deceptively mild and could be mistaken for a sprained ankle or a foot swollen from marching. The afflicted foot then would swell more and become heavy and red. This would be accompanied by a sharp tingling sensation, as if hundreds of red-hot pins were pricking at the skin. Then the foot would turn a ghastly greenish black as it swelled yet more, opening up cracks out of which oozed a mixture of blood and pus. At that point the foot would turn completely necrotic, dragged along the ground, an unfeeling and lifeless stump. Depending on how quickly the condition was treated by the field medics, lethal gangrene might be avoided. Or not. Amputated toes, fingers and feet piled up outside the hospital tents. 'A man would lose the sense of the world around him, think he had been transported to Hell and that he would be tormented there with no hope of return, condemned for eternity.'[17]

It was not uncommon for a battalion of, say, 800 men to lose two-thirds to frostbite. In some cases companies were down to twenty or so effectives. There were numberless cases of soldiers getting lost from their units and wandering alone, perhaps wounded, in the snowy wastes until they died somewhere of cold and hunger or, if they were lucky, were discovered by a patrol or a supply train, sitting on a rock and sobbing from fear and pain. And perhaps, if he was the thinking type, wondering what had happened to the patriotic enthusiasm with which he had marched off to war just a few weeks before.

In the 42 Evzones Private Nikolaou and his mates had to scrounge what extra food they could from friendly Albanian villagers, sometimes a pot of beans, sometimes – if they were particularly lucky – a chicken or two or even a goat. Stumbling and slipping over the rock-hard ice, the men would try and give themselves sparks of hope with wild and unfounded rumours. One that enjoyed a few days' popularity was that Mussolini had been toppled by Badoglio and the king, but reality would always return with a vengeance.

Sufferings aside, operations had to go on. On the Adriatic coast, Major General George Bakos' 3rd Division aimed to seize Himare, the next key town on the way to the important port of Vlore. Three battalions of *granatieri* (grenadiers) blocked the way at Borsh where a high ridge comes down to the sea. It was an ideal defensive position, and the grenadiers made full use of its advantages, fortifying it with light and heavy artillery, mortars and machine guns. Bakos pondered the problem. There was no way of turning the position, since the Borsh Ridge continued inland, rising as it did so. His artillery was unable to find a suitable place to support an attack, yet Bakos ordered the 12 Infantry Regiment forward at 7.30 am on 15 December in the teeth of a snowstorm. The attack on the left was beaten back with some loss, while on the right considerable resistance was encountered from the revived Siena Division backed up by Blackshirts.

Bakos resumed the pressure the following day, one of the bloodiest of the campaign. The lines in front of Borsh surged back and forth all day. The 12 Infantry's field officers were decimated. Bakos, watching the action through his field glasses, noticed a major leading a fanatically courageous charge on a machine gun nest and ordered that the officer – if he survived – receive a battlefield promotion for valour. It took two more days of relentless attacks – finally involving the ever-trusty bayonet, for the position on Borsh Ridge to be taken, at the cost of twenty-one of the regimental officers and 350 enlisted men. Himare was taken a few days later.

A few kilometres to the northeast of Himare lies the small town of Kuc, which had to be prised from enemy hands if the coast at Himare were to remain secure. A surprise bayonet attack was ordered for dawn on 19 December. As the bugles sounded and the Evzones pulled the pins on their grenades, the Greeks overcame the first line of Italian machine gunners before they were properly awake. The rest of the Italians, though, quickly got their act together and manfully opposed the Greek attack, retreating only slowly, and inch by inch. By dusk, however, Kuc was in Greek hands along with some 200 prisoners. Yet the position was by no means secure, as the surrounding hills were full of Italian units that could at any moment counterattack and retake the town.

One of those units, however, the 141 Blackshirt Battalion, was surrounded. Lieutenant Colonel Thrasybulos Tsakalotos of the 40 Evzone Regiment sent an Albanian through the lines with a message to the Blackshirts. 'Gentlemen,' Tsakalotos wrote in French, 'your resistance is futile. Your regiment has been decimated, captured and broken. You must present yourselves to a major [on my staff] who has orders to receive you kindly.' The 141's officers considered the alternatives; if they held out, they could receive food supplies from the air. But twelve hours later the Blackshirts agreed to give themselves up – twenty-nine officers and 677 enlisted men. The Italians left more than 300 dead at Kuc. The regimental flag of the 40 Evzones was decorated for valour.

But another chief strategic factor had now entered the lists, and that was the Balkan winter. As the lines in Albania gradually froze – perhaps literally – into immobility, Metaxas felt that he could slow the pace. The impressive string of victories which his boys had earned him did not swell his head. On the contrary, he was giving serious thought to what the next steps might be, and was coming up against a big question mark. 'I don't really see a way out,' he confessed to his diary in December. The winter aside, he was well aware that for any further Greek military success to occur there would have to be a coherent strategy to define what that might be. To keep on marching into the snow and ice of the Albanian mountains, leaving a steady stream of dead and frostbitten wounded, would make no strategic or moral sense. As a military scholar he of course was familiar with history's examples to avoid: Napoleon's 1812 disaster in Russia and, more recently, the ill-advised and ultimately catastrophic Greek incursion into the wilds of Turkey in 1922, where the sheer inebriation of 'advancing' had blotted out common sense. Unlike many of his countrymen (and the British, for that matter), Metaxas did not cultivate a contempt for the Italian fighting man, whom he knew to be as good as any. Yes, the macaroni boys were on the run now, but how far could they be expected to run? At any point they could very well counterattack an overextended Greek line, and he had to be prepared for that eventuality.

Such ruminations were apparently lost on Papagos, whose prestige was now at its apex. By mid-December he was concentrating on securing a 250km line across Albania, from Pogradec in the east to the port of Vlore in the west, with forces that now began to outnumber those of the enemy. On the right, the West Macedonia Army Department ranged the III Corps and Divisional Group K, including the 9th, 10th, 13th and 17th Divisions, to hold the Korce-Pogradec sector up to the Yugoslav frontier. The II Corps held the central sector on either side of the Vojussa River with the 1st, 11th and 15th Divisions plus 5 Infantry Brigade. On the left Gjirokaster sector, and as far as the coast, stood the I Corps with the 2nd, 3rd and 4th Divisions, with the much-handled 8th Division and 3 Infantry Brigade in reserve, along with the 5th and 16th Divisions and the Cavalry Division.

Cavallero concentrated most of his strength in the centre. Vercellino's Ninth Corps and Geloso's Eleventh Corps were anchored on Mount Tomori overlooking the Kelcyre Valley and the Tomorica Valley to the north, the obvious Greek routes for an advance on Tirana. Farther on the Italian right was Rossi and the Twenty-fifth Corps, reformed after its recent discomfitures. Between them stood the battered Eighth Corps whose commander, Bancale, had serious doubts about its fighting efficiency. The Tomorica Valley was held by just 700 men of the Finance Police (*Guardia di Finanza*) and whatever battleworthy bits were left over from the Julia Division. The total Italian force numbered some 160,000 men, of whom 100,000 were in the front line.

Nasci and the Twenty-sixth Corps on the left of the line tried to stem the West Macedonia Army Department's advance by deploying the Piemonte and the 3 Battalion Finance Police, but the snow beat him.

> Twenty men frozen to death [Nasci reported] and dozens of cases of frostbite have drained the last moral energy from men who for more than a month have been penned up in temperatures very much below zero.

The sentry posts of the Cuneo Division were connected by a wire which every so often would be tugged by the men in one post to see if those in the next were still there. Sometime there would be no tug in reply, and men would be sent to investigate, to find the hapless sentry frozen to death at his post, a veritable pillar of ice. Understandably, many soldiers preferred capture by the Greeks to such a fate.

Nasci realized that the Greeks were far more familiar with mountainous territory than his own men and could always employ local guides and provisions, freeing them from concern with supply lines and thus enabling them to take the offensive more flexibly. However, the Greeks were not about to employ the techniques of semi-guerrilla warfare. Besides, what had happened to the vaunted Albanian 'friendship' which the Italian high command had assured the men would be strewing flowers in their path, so to speak? Instead of flowers, there was knee-deep frozen mud.

The businesslike Cavallero's main concern was to regularize the supply chain. The gradual settling down of the front into snow-bound immobility after 9 December helped him cope. One of his first orders, issued on 15 December, was to ensure that units embarking for Albania did so with their full complement of supplies and equipment, including pack mules and provisions, instead of hurrying the men over first and leaving the rest of the supplies to find their own way. If the general had been left alone, he might have accomplished much. But the Duce hammered him with a salvo of peremptory cables. One of them blamed the virtual destruction of the Siena Division on 'the infiltration of a few Greek patrols' resulting in the abandonment of Himare – an accusation supposed to have come from Carabinieri units. 'This cannot but give fresh fuel to the morale of the Greek people and army.'

Mussolini, in short, would rather blame the supposed timidity of his generals and soldiers rather than admit two unpalatable truths: one, that his own judgement had proven terribly wrong, and two, the Greeks had simply proved to be the better fighters. The Italian commanders, given the circumstances, had no choice but to adopt a strong defence-based tactic as the only realistic answer to the Greek offensive. Just what that meant was a matter of lively debate. Senior officers disagreed on what the tactic ought to entail and besides, almost all feared losing the Duce's favour. Soddu was merely the most obsequious of them. When the pressure became too much he would retire into another world to compose film music. 'The jealousies among the generals are worse than those of women,' Ciano wrote disgustedly in his diary. 'Geloso has gone soft.' Only Vercellino maintained any degree of ability and sound judgement, and yet he was sometimes depressed to the point of tears.[18]

As a result the image of the senior officers among the Italian junior officers, NCOs and men plunged dramatically. Absurd threats of summary executions for cowardice failed to revive the fighting spirit. Desertions increased. General Mario Arisio, the Third Corps commander, had to send home three battalions of Blackshirts from Sicily and Calabria as totally demoralized. When the renowned Blackshirts began to crack, then was the time to worry. There were still, of course, plenty of instances of valour and even heroism in the field. The commander of the 47 Infantry regiment, Colonel Felice Trizio, fell during a fighting withdrawal; his second-in-command, Lieutenant Colonel Adalgiso Ferrucci, had been killed four weeks earlier. On 8 December a counterattack on a Greek probe in the Pogradec sector had cost the life of Colonel Rodolfo Psaro of the 7 Alpine Regiment, Pusteria Division. Colonel Gaetano Tavoni, the commander of the 9 Alpine Regiment, Julia Division, died of wounds after leading his regiment through six weeks of hell.

At home the fascist party mobilized the public for a Christmas relief drive. Women took to knitting woollens for the troops. Mussolini firmly believed that the war against the Greeks had become a matter of prestige for himself. That was the sole standard by which to formulate strategy. At the outset it had been the conquest and occupation of Greece. Now the job of the Italian army in Albania was to salvage the image of the Duce and of Italy's membership of the Axis. This change of emphasis was responsible for one of the more satisfying developments in Rome: as the fascist party had been the prime drum-beater for the Greece campaign, was it not fitting that the party chiefs in their flamboyant uniforms be sent to the front? They were, after all, supposed to be paramilitary organization, imbued with the discipline and courage of soldiers. Their presence in the war zone, Mussolini felt, would show up the defeatist professional soldiery and encourage the troops in the line.

Thus paunchy high party officials such as Dino Grandi, a former foreign minister and ambassador to London, found himself in the uniform of an Alpini major, along with Giuseppe Bottai, the Education Minister. Others were made into lieutenant colonels of infantry. They were all sent to the front with neither luggage nor orderlies. Ciano was officially inducted into the Regia Aeronautica as a pilot (in which he already had some experience) on three-engined Savoia-Marchetti SM79 bombers. The Duce's sons, Bruno and Vittorio, were already among the aircrews. The air force appointments were made over the head of Pricolo, who could only stand supinely by when bombing targets were set and changed at the whim of whichever inexperienced officer was allowed to make decisions. There were soon complaints that Ciano was able to pull enough clout to have fighter escorts on his missions and leave other crews without, especially as the SM79 was lightly armed and vulnerable to enemy fighters. As a result, many Italian bombers unloaded their ordnance on Corfu as an 'easy' target not too far from the bases in the heel of Italy. These curious military appointments, needless to say, were not of the slightest benefit to the conduct of operations, which by now had coagulated into positional immobility.

The Greek drive had come to a halt after the capture of Himare on the coast. Like Cavallero, Papagos used the oncoming winter to settle the line of farthest advance. On 20 December the II Corps arrived in the northern Korce sector, beefed up by the 15th Division, but not without some skirmishing with Nasci's troops. Three days later the II Corps overran an Italian machine gun emplacement belonging to the 8 Machine Gun Battalion. Strong forces of the 155 Blackshirt Battalion and Modena and Pusteria Divisions engaged Greek forces for the next three days. But that was all the II Corps could do, as heavy snow had cut many lines of communications and supply. The engineers had a herculean task trying to repair collapsed bridges over raging mountain rivers.

Private Nikolaou of the 42 Evzones was relieved to be ordered to stay behind when his platoon was ordered on patrol. He had recently been appointed as the company cobbler, and boots were constantly in need of repair. An Albanian peasant family prepared him a hearty breakfast of salted meat and pickled vegetables as the weather raged outside. He sat in front of the fire in the company of two young Albanian girls knitting socks. On 18 December, however, his regiment was ordered to get ready to march up to the Kelcyre Valley sector. His hosts were sad to see him and his mates go. In the morning of 23 December:

> I woke up not feeling well and very sad, I don't know why. [The previous day he had come across the graves of two Greek soldiers in a churchyard.] Despite the snow today, the artillery never stopped pounding through the night ... At noon we killed two birds and roasted and ate them. I prayed at Saint Nicholas' church and promised the Virgin Mary I'd hold a mass for her when I got home.[19]

That Christmas was the most miserable Nikolaou had ever experienced. On Christmas Eve he awoke with severe diarrhoea but nonetheless had to march along with the rest. Snow got into his boots, freezing his feet and legs up to the knee. The company was billeted that evening in a little stone house where everyone, officers and men alike, gave themselves up to a good case of Christmas blues. Christmas morning dawned with the sight of mules frozen to death; before expiring, in their hunger they had tried to gnaw wooden boxes and even their own saddles. All that day the men marched without knowing where they were going, and then had to retrace their steps all the way back. That night they slept – or tried to sleep with the incessant flea bites – in a cave. Boxing Day brought more marching, until on 28 December the 42 Evzones arrived at the entrance to the Kelcyre Valley.

On Christmas Eve Private Kanellopoulos of the 13th Division resting at Podgorie received an unusual request for an ordinary soldier. The divisional provost-marshal needed a lawyer to defend Colonel Rokkos, the former commander of the 23 Regiment, who was to go before a court-martial that afternoon on charges of dereliction of duty. Rokkos was accused of breaking off the action at Hoxhiste in Albania on 18 November, leading his regiment to the rear and opening a serious breach in the 13th Division's formation. The formal indictment charged Rokkos with 'losing composure and giving way to panic'. If found guilty, Rokkos would almost surely face a firing squad. Kanellopoulos jumped at the chance. Though a mere private, the 38-year-old scholar had become known and respected among the officers as a capable attorney with a well-trained tongue. Moreover, he was convinced that Rokkos was being made a scapegoat for failings higher up in the division.

Rokkos had not been well-liked among his fellow officers, and consequently, as the tribunal session began in the old mosque of Podgorie, the atmosphere was against him. The trial, presided over by Colonel Evstathios Liosis, lasted seven hours. Kanellopoulos, assisted by a reserve second lieutenant, worked hard to counter hostile testimony by a battery of battalion-level officers, worming out of them a consensus that Rokkos was not a coward, and whatever his mistaken actions on the night of 18 November, they were not of a nature as to cast doubts on his personal qualities. As a technical staff officer before the war, Rokkos simply had inadequate experience of field command and this, rather than cowardice, had moved him to make his decisions. As midnight approached, Kanellopoulos wound up his passionate defence of the 23 Regiment's former commander with a clever reference to the holy day about to dawn:

> The star which the Three Kings saw in the east is now, sirs, at this moment over your own heads. The light it emits is the Grace of Jesus Christ. The Grace addresses itself to your spirits and your hands; to your spirits in order to enlighten them; to your hands in order to offer it to your unfortunate brother-in-arms.

A few minutes into Christmas Day the court-martial issued its verdict: the first count of cowardice was dismissed, but the second count of incompetence was upheld. Rokkos was sentenced to three years in prison. Kanellopoulos, like the good lawyer he was, at once requested a suspension of the sentence, but he was turned down. Colonel Rokkos, a broken man, was escorted out of the mosque by military police and Kanellopoulos to a temporary house of detention. He stumbled along in the snow and darkness, barely able to stay upright. He appeared not to hear the encouraging words of Kanellopoulos, who kept telling him that all was not lost, that his case would certainly be appealed up to the Commander-in-Chief himself and he had a good chance of serving out the war. He should consider himself lucky, Kanellopoulos said, to have escaped the firing squad. Kanellopoulos describes what happened next:

> Rokkos isn't listening. He's in utter confusion. He beats himself and tells us he cannot survive. I try to soothe him but it's impossible. We take our leave.

In the morning, as Kanellopoulos was about to settle into his Christmas breakfast, a lieutenant came in with the news that Colonel Rokkos had taken his own life.[20]

Chapter 6

Fiats and Gladiators

Italian air power – the Greek air force pounds Italian bases – dogfights over the mountains – attrition of Greek crews – 'Pat' Pattle flies in – Papagos demands more British help – Longmore reads the riot act – Fairy Tale Valley – the 'carosello infernale' – the RAF bears the brunt

From the outset, and unlike the Greek Army, the Royal Hellenic Air Force was heavily outgunned and outclassed, and would become more so as the conflict progressed. At the outbreak of war the Regia Aeronautica outnumbered the RHAF's front-line strength by three to one. The Italian air force at the time was one of the best-trained in Europe. Italy's aerospace industry, coddled by the Mussolini administration, was turning out redoubtable aircraft such as the Fiat G50bis *Freccia* (Arrow) monoplane fighter, the Macchi C200 *Saetta* (Lightning) fighter, the CantZ 1007bis bomber and the trimotor Savoia-Marchetti SM79 and SM81 bombers. Many Italian combat pilots had honed their air-fighting skills in the Spanish Civil War. In the 1930s Italy had experienced a surge of interest in air sports and aviation in general, encouraged by Mussolini's own attainments as an aviator. It was part of the Duce's broader drive to re-mould the Italian people into a warlike nation like the Romans of old.

The Regia Aeronautica had been an independent service since 1923. It was lucky to have contained pioneering thinkers such as Major Giulio Douhet, who worked out the strategic bombing doctrines that would find their full fruition later in the war. Marshal Italo Balbo refined Douhet's ideas to come up with the idea of a massed bomber force that could penetrate enemy territory like a mailed fist. Balbo became hugely popular in Italy thanks to his flying-boat team's highly-publicized international flights, including a tour of America. Well might Mussolini boast to his fascist party cadres on 18 November:

> The Italian air force is always at the peak of its task. It has dominated and continues to dominate the skies. Its bombers can reach the most distant of objectives, its fighters are making life difficult for the fighters

of the enemy. Its men are truly men of our time: their characteristic is a calm intrepidity.[1]

Mussolini had some cause to boast. In terms of numbers, aircrew and firepower the Regia Aeronautica looked good and was good. But what he didn't mention was that the senior air force command was ill-equipped to aggressively command such a force. The air force Chief, General Pricolo, was allowed nothing like free rein for his task. Worse, he wasn't even told of the plan to invade Greece until the critical high-level meeting of 15 October, which he hadn't even been invited to attend! One might justifiably wonder what had happened to the innovative strategic ideas of Douhet and Balbo. The only possible answer is that the attack on Greece was simply not conceived in air terms. Visconti Prasca's visions were of an exclusively army triumph; there was also a lingering contempt for Greece and Balkan nations generally as not having air forces worthy of the name, and hence not requiring specific air planning to any major degree. Pricolo fretted at this, but seems not to have had the strength of character to do anything about it – he, too, just wanted to keep his job.

As the Greek air force was thought to be a flimsy adversary, the Regia Aeronautica employed obsolescent biplane fighters in the first phase of the Greece operation. About half of the available fighter force consisted of Fiat CR42 *Falco* (Falcon) biplanes and older Fiat CR32s, the latter already at the end of their career. The CR42 was about a match for the Greeks' PZL24 and Gladiator. Eighty examples of a newer all-metal monoplane fighter, the Fiat G50bis, were available, plus twelve of the even better Macchi MC200. The Italian bomber force included the menacing-looking three-engined Cant Z1007bis *Alcione* (Halcyon), an aircraft that could take a lot of punishment and was highly manoeuvrable. Fifty examples of the Cant Z506B *Airone* (Heron), a seaplane version of the Cant Z1007, were also in service. Also lined up on Albanian airfields were squadrons of Savoia-Marchetti SM81 *Pipistrello* (Bat) bombers. The SM81 was in the process of being superseded by the sleeker and more durable trimotor Savoia-Marchetti SM79 *Sparviero* (Hawk). Eighteen Fiat BR20M *Cicogna* (Stork) twin-engined bombers were also operational. The Regia Aeronautica's planes were organized into *squadriglie* of nine aircraft each, which was slightly smaller than an RAF squadron or Greek *mira*. Three *squadriglie* made up a *gruppo* (somewhere between a squadron and a wing), and two *gruppi* made up a *stormo*, or wing.

The Royal Hellenic Air Force had been an independent arm for eleven years, producing its first crop of nine graduating aircrew officers in 1931. Through the politically turbulent 1930s the fledgling air force had experienced its ups and downs. Both the army and navy looked down on the upstart service as little more than a flying club for well-to-do young men. The RHAF College, known as the Icarus School, had narrowly escaped being closed down in 1932. The air force's survival was assured only in 1934 with the creation of the General Air Staff. Still, even in 1940, Greek air operations were under the full control of the army, in the person of Major General Petros Ekonomakos.[2]

On 28 October the RHAF could field four air observation and army cooperation *mirai*, three of naval cooperation aircraft, four of fighters and three of medium bombers, totalling some 160 planes, though perhaps two-thirds were serviceable. The main fighter was the Polish-built PZL24, a rugged machine but rapidly being outclassed in Europe. Before the war Greece had managed to buy a dozen modern Bristol Blenheim IV bombers and another dozen single-engined Fairey Battles from Britain, and a similar number of Potez 63 bombers from France. The naval cooperation *mirai* had the advantage of modern British Avro Anson patrol bombers. When war broke out Greece had ordered 107 additional modern aircraft such as the redoubtable Supermarine Spitfire, the American Grumman F4F Wildcat and the Martin Maryland bomber. It never got to receive them.

The immediate operational need of the RHAF was to repel the waves of Italian bombers while employing the army observation squadrons to keep track of the invading Italian land forces. The fighters had an unequal fight on their hands from the start. The first real aerial encounter of the war took place on 30 October, when a few Henschel Hs126 observation aircraft took off to locate Italian troop formations and had the worst of an encounter with five Fiat CR42s. One Henschel went down, killing its observer, Pilot Officer Evangelos Giannaris, the first Greek airman to die in the campaign. Another Henschel went down that same morning, killing its two-man crew, while Italian bombers hammered the port of Patras.

The Greek aircrews learned how to fight the hard way. 'We didn't know how to fly then,' said Flying Officer George Doukas of 24 Pursuit Mira later. 'We couldn't even shoot. We knew nothing of firing distances or angles of attack. We went to war ... as if we were on parade. We were blown out of the sky.' Greek pilots had very little, if any, training in evasive manoeuvres. To compound the problem for the Greeks, the Italian bombers would come in at high altitude – at least 20,000ft – which was at the limit of the PZLs' and Gladiators' operational ceiling. It was a rare sortie that didn't see some Greek airborne casualty.

Units of the crack 53 Land Fighter *Stormo* (Wing) had arrived at bases in Albania on 1 November – 150 *Gruppo* (Group), comprising 363, 364 and 365 Squadriglie. Their pilots were a bit disappointed in having been given the Fiat C42s to fly, especially as the *stormo* had specifically trained for the new Macchi MC200 fighters, and were naturally quite proud of the fact. But the Macchis were kept safe at Turin while the older biplanes were fed into the war against Greece. While 365 Squadriglia was transferred to 160 Gruppo

Autonomo at Tirana, 364 was stationed at Vlore and 365 at Gjirokaster, sometimes interchangeably.[3]

As the Siena, Ferrara and Centauro Divisions were advancing on Kalpaki, Metaxas himself telephoned the RHAF's bomber chief, Group Captain Stephanos Philippas, at his headquarters at Larissa. An enemy column was rolling towards Doliana, Metaxas barked, and had to be stopped that very night 'even if no-one comes back'. Philippas detailed a flight of 31 Bombing Mira to do the job. The 31 Mira CO, Flight Lieutenant George Karnavias, gulped. None of his crews had ever flown a night operation before. But orders were orders. As night fell, three of his pilots climbed into their twin-engined Potez 63s and headed off into the mountain blackness. One of them was Flight Lieutenant Lambros Kouziyannis, wounded in the head on the previous day's mission. He jumped out of his hospital bed to join the operation, ignoring the protests of his CO.

The pilots' only guide on the way, apart from their glowing instruments, was the dim candlelight from the clifftop Meteora monasteries to starboard. The crews had to shield their eyes from the bombers' white-hot exhaust shooting from the engine housings. The lights of an Italian column approaching Kalpaki became visible as the Potez 63s roared over Ioannina and its shimmering lake. Kouziyannis, his head bandaged, bombed the column, defying a hail of flak on the dive. On his way back he got lost and found himself over blacked-out Athens rather than his base at Larissa. His bomber ran out of fuel over the city, but managed to glide the few miles to the base at Tatoi. He had just cleared the airfield fence and was breathing a prayer of thanks when he collided with a parked trainer in the darkness. The concussion crippled Kouziyannis for the rest of his life.

As the Italians continued to bomb Thessaloniki and other cities, killing scores of civilians, Greek bombers sometimes gave as good as they got. Early in November 31 Bombing Mira took off from Athens to bomb the Italian base at Korce. A formation of Blenheims under Flying Officer Constantine Margaritis pounded the base, killing nineteen airmen who had gathered in the ops room for a briefing, and wounding twenty-five others. Two Italian fighters were damaged on the ground. The Fairey Battles of 33 Mira were equally audacious, sneaking into Albanian airspace and shooting up Italian columns. Those planes, though, were primitive. The pilot of a Battle could communicate with his gunner/observer in the back only through a speaking tube – engine noise permitting, of course. Maps were scarce; the only available map of southern Albania had to be rotated among several crews.

The Fiats of 365 Squadriglia continued tangling with the inexperienced Greek airmen, to the latters' cost. On 4 November Second Lieutenant Lorenzo Clerici and Sergeant Pasquale Facchini pumped streams of bullets into a couple of Breguet XIXs of 2 Air Observation Mira that were strafing the troops of the Julia Division, sending one of them spinning down in flames.

Greece's three bombing *mirai*, 31, 32 and 33, were only gradually introduced to the principles of tactical air warfare. Their task at the outbreak of war was to act as long-range artillery in support of ground operations, a task made easier as the RAF gradually took over the strategic bombing of enemy targets in Albania. These missions took a steady toll of aircrews. One of the Blenheim IVs of 32 Mira was downed over Gjirokaster on 11 November. The Blenheim IV was one of the few modern bombers in the RHAF's armoury and the loss of even one was significant at a time when the Regia Aeronuatica, in response to the Italian setbacks in the ground war, poured some 250 more fighters into its Albanian bases. Metaxas confessed to having nightmares about the erosion of the air force's firepower.

The main reason why the Greeks had to advance quickly on the eastern part of the front to capture Korce was that it was a base from which Greece's cities were being regularly bombed. The Blenheims of 32 Mira and Battles of 33 Mira were sent to soften up Korce on 14 November, in advance of the Greek III Corps thrust, destroying fifteen enemy aircraft on the ground in two waves, for the loss of one more 32 Mira Blenheim – probably to one of Italy's more renowned airmen, Second Lieutenant Maurizio di Robilant of 363 Squadriglia. Flight Lieutenant Panayotis Orphanidis was returning to Larissa from the Korce raid when he found a Fiat CR42 stuck on his Blenheim's tail, firing intermittently and weaving to get a better shot. The Blenheim was the faster plane, but it couldn't quite shake off the pursuer. More than 160 bullets smashed into the bomber's fuselage and wings, holing the fuel and oil tanks, which luckily were nearly empty, and wounding the gunner. Orphanidis knew that the Italian would have his best chance as the bomber slowed down to make the turn to land at Larissa. So instead of making the turn he continued on and across the eastern Greek coast, setting a course for Sedes base at Thessaloniki. Somewhere over the water the Fiat, apparently low on fuel, gave up the chase.

As Orphanidis and his friends were trying to flatten the Korce base, six of the smaller and more agile Battles of 33 Mira swept at low level from Corfu and snaked between the mountain ranges to stage an audacious raid on the Gjirokaster base. Despite the flaming wall of flak they had to penetrate, not one Battle was hit (though 363 Squadriglia reported a damaged 'probable').[4] Typical of the effect on the RHAF's morale was a letter by Pilot Officer Yannis Kipouros to his mother after the operation: 'I know that one day I might plunge to earth defending my beautiful country,' he wrote. 'What are the Italians defending? ... The joy I feel when completing a mission is indescribable.' Kipouros (who was to disappear without a trace on a mission in a few weeks' time) was venting a more general optimism among the Greeks, as mid-November was seeing the tide turn on the ground, with the Julia Division knocked out and the rest of the Italian army stalled before Kalpaki.

The RHAF's army cooperation and observation *mirai* were active in their obsolescent but hardy Henschel Hs126 monoplanes, strafing and harassing Italian columns inside Albanian territory. A large Italian bomber force struck at the advanced Greek base at Florina, the headquarters of 31 Mira, but without hitting a single aircraft or major installation. The 31 Mira CO, Squadron Leader Grigorios Theodoropoulos, wondered whether the enemy were 'just unlucky, or inexperienced and hasty'.

While the Greek drive on Korce was getting up steam, the Fairey Battles of 31 Mira were ordered to hit the Italian forces on Mount Morova and Mount Ivan, the high points defending the southern approaches to the town. The raid was not unopposed. Performing prodigies of flying in this sector was di Robilant of 363 Squadriglia who scored a devastating hit on Flying Officer George Hinaris' plane, killing his gunner/observer and forcing him to bale out, his flying suit on fire. Hinaris was saved by falling into a stream, though he was badly burned. In the same action Di Robilant accounted for Flight Lieutenant Dimitris Pitsikas' Battle, which managed to limp to a landing at Ioannina, though by that time Warrant Officer Aristophanes Pappas, the gunner/observer, was dead in the back seat. While that was going on, three Potez 63s of 31 Mira attacked enemy artillery positions in the Devoli River valley. Vladousis' plane was hit by his own side's anti-aircraft guns. His gunner/observer already dead, Vladousis jumped from the stricken plane into a maelstrom of fire from the wheeling Fiats and the Greeks on the ground. To identify himself to the latter, he took a letter from his mother from his pocket and as he floated to earth he waved it like a white flag, yelling, 'I'm Greek, you fellows!' at the top of his voice.

Once down, he was saved from toppling over a cliff by a sergeant whom he recognized as an old school friend. As Vladousis was chatting with the local sector colonel, the captain of the offending anti-aircraft battery burst in with profuse and embarrassed apologies. The officer, it seemed, had no idea that the RHAF had twin-engined bombers such as the Potez 63 in the air – all he knew about, apparently, were the antique Breguet XIXs. Anything more modern than that, it was assumed, had to be Italian. Relaxing, Vladousis took off his flying overall and in that way he told the army something more about the indomitable spirit of the air force, for underneath it he was wearing his full dress uniform. To the thunderstruck colonel Vladousis quipped, 'Since we never know if we're going to come back, we might as well dress properly.' Just as many airmen carried (and still carry) personal talismans as psychological defence mechanisms against worrying too much about death, the dress uniform was almost Spartan in its significance. It was like Leonidas' Spartans combing their hair before the fatal encounter at Thermopylai. So Vladousis, if he was going to meet death, was determined to do it with dignity.[5]

Two days before the fall of Korce 32 Mira was sent to bomb the base at Gjirokaster. Pilot Officer Alexander Malakis, perhaps because of a navigation error, bombed nearby Permet by mistake. The attack flattened an Italian military hospital, killing at least fifty patients. Next door to the hospital an ammunition dump exploded and burned for three days. While Malakis and his crew were decorated for the raid, Rome howled about a gross violation of the Geneva Convention. What actually happened is disputed to this day. Malakis claimed to have bombed by mistake, as Permet resembled Gjirokaster. The Greeks, moreover, asserted that the ammunition dump – ostensibly the real target – had been deliberately placed next to the hospital to deter attacks. This 'explanation', however, implies that Permet could have been the legitimate target after all. And certainly there was no lack of Greeks in uniform whose memories of Italian aggression were quite fresh and thus not overly scrupulous about what they hit.

The suddenness of the Greek advance on Korce caught the Regia Aeronautica by surprise. Hours before the base's capture, a SM79 bomber collided with three Fiats while trying to take off. It was abandoned to the Greeks who repainted it with blue and white roundels and added it to their bomber force. The Battles of 33 Mira were sent to harass the retreating Italian column but came under attack by a swarm of Fiats which forced the Greeks to break off the operation. One Battle was seriously damaged and its gunner/observer wounded.

The undoubted heroics displayed by the outgunned RHAF drew the admiration of Metaxas, but he fretted that the loss rate could not be sustained for very long. Even with the help of the RAF from the early days of November, and even when the ground campaign began turning in the Greeks' favour in the middle of the month, the air war was giving Metaxas serious jitters. Grateful as he was for what British aerial help could be spared from the Middle East theatre, he could only gloomily observe his own airmen and planes dwindling mercilessly.

More British aerial help arrived on 18 November in the form of 80 Squadron, equipped with Gloster Gladiator IIs. Led by Squadron Leader William Hickey, the fighters touched down at Eleusis along with a lumbering Bristol Bombay transport carrying ground crews and spares. From that day the boys in RAF blue were given hero status by the grateful Athenians. Understandably, the crews that first night took full advantage of the adulation in the form of endless free drinks and meals, but Hickey himself wasn't free to join in the fun, having to receive his orders from the Greek High Command. These were for 80 Squadron's B Flight under the South African-born Flight Lieutenant

Marmaduke 'Pat' Pattle to fly on to Trikala in central Greece the next morning, refuel, and carry out the RAF's first fighter patrol in Greek skies.

Pattle and his flight, plus his CO Hickey, landed at Trikala to find the crews of the RHAF's 21 Pursuit Mira 'enjoying a meal of bread and cheese and olives ... washed down with a very strong-smelling but sweet-tasting wine,' which they shared with the Britons.[6] Thus fortified, three of 21 Mira's PZL24s led Hickey and nine of 80 Squadron's Gladiators on their first familiarity flight over the northwest Greek mountains. By the time the formation reached the Italian base at Korce the PZLs had to turn back because of a lack of fuel, leaving B Flight to see what it could pick off.

The eagle-eyed Pattle, leading the flight's second section, was the first to see four Fiat CR42s of 150 Gruppo climbing to intercept them and signalled to Hickey. As both pilots went into an attacking dive, the Fiats scattered. Pattle got onto the tail of one of them and coolly blasted it at 100yds – the first of the redoubtable South African's many kills in the Greek and Albanian theatres of the war. Over Korce airfield Pattle expertly evaded an attack by a 154 Gruppo Fiat G50 monoplane fighter, of the kind that was now being fed into the campaign in increasing numbers, and a few minutes later downed another CR42. At that point low air pressure knocked out the Gladiator's guns, so he had to fly wildly around the sky getting out of the way of aggressive Italians until the gun pressure could build up again, but by that time his fuel was low and at tree-top height weaved his way through the mountains to Trikala, where 80 Squadron was feted as having accounted for nine Italian fighters and a couple more probables. As a reward, the pilots were put up at Trikala's best hotel.[7]

After that triumphant RAF debut, the weather stepped in. Constant rain for forty-eight hours, and low-lying dense cloud for another forty-eight, held up all operations. Nonetheless, on 25 November Pattle took up half a dozen Gladiators to patrol the Korce area, but couldn't entice any of the enemy to tangle with him. The next day B Flight of 80 Squadron was ordered to move to Ioannina, where conditions were drier and the battlefront nearer. In a clear but freezing sky Pattle's section spotted three SM79 bombers escorted by twelve CR42s well inside Greek airspace. As the section under Flight Lieutenant Edward 'Tap' Jones dived on the bombers, Pattle led his own six planes against the Fiats, which tried to fight back, but abandoned the encounter after Pattle had sent two of them spinning into the ground on fire.

It was during these first encounters that Captain Nicola Magaldi, the CO of 364 Squadriglia who had fired the shots that killed Sergeant Merifield in his Blenheim, was jumped by nine of Hickey's Gladiators and killed in his turn (perhaps by Pattle himself), to be awarded a posthumous gold medal for valour.[8] The following day ten Fiat CR42s of 364 and 365 Squadriglie found themselves entangled with more Gladiators just south of the Albanian border.

One Fiat and one Gladiator collided in the melee, killing both pilots. (The RAF victim was probably 80 Squadron's Flying Officer Bill Sykes, the first British fighter pilot to die in the Greek campaign.) Captain Giorgio Graffer, the commander of 365 Squadriglia, was killed (posthumous gold medal award) – the second 150 Gruppo squadron commander to be killed in as many days. Two Fiats and one Gladiator were lost, with two more Fiats and three more Gladiators damaged.[9]

Two days before the fall of Korce the Greek General Staff met to discuss air strategy. Present were Metaxas, Papagos, RHAF Operations Chief Group Captain Stergios Tilios and Group Captain Arthur Willetts on behalf of the RAF. The meeting came not a moment too soon, as by now it had become clear that the Greeks and British had worrisomely differing concepts of what the term 'air strategy' meant. To the Greek military, as in all second-string European countries which had not had combat experience in the 1930s, an air force was little more than a set of artillery pieces with wings, to send over a trajectory beyond the visibility of land guns and drop high explosive on the enemy. True, any officer could perceive the distinction between a bomber and a fighter operation, but it was seen in simplistic terms as offence (bomber) and defence (fighter). More sophisticated missions for fighters such as escorting bomber formations had not yet been thought of. Though Metaxas can take credit for perceiving the importance of an air force in the first place, Greece could boast no Douhet or Balbo in the theoretical sphere.

Willetts may or may not have been aware that Air Chief Marshal Sir Arthur Longmore, the RAF commander in the Middle East, had sent D'Albiac detailed instructions on how to maintain the relationship with the Greeks. They read, in part:

> You will have the status of an *independent air force command*, but, although not under the control of the Greek General Staff, the conduct of operations of the RAF should, as far as practicable ... conform as closely as possible to the Greek plan for the defence of the country.

This was a diplomatic way of trying to bridge the differences, but in case the Greeks didn't get the message, Longmore was coldly specific:

> You are not to allow bombers to be used for artillery or to participate in actual land operations unless the military situation becomes so critical as to justify the *temporary* diversion of our bombers from strategic bombing to support of the Greek land forces ... *The possibility of a sudden and complete collapse of Greece must not be lost sight of.*[10]

In plain words, helping the Greeks was all very well and noble, but if it meant frittering away men and aircraft on a cause that may well be doomed, then that help would be of little use. Britain of course, had to consider the wider war theatre. In practical terms, that meant that the Greek request for RAF Hurricane fighters, for example, had to be refused. The old stringy Gladiators had to suffice for the present. Besides, the Wellingtons and Blenheim Is of 70 Squadron were deemed quite good enough to hammer the Italians in Albania.

As a ranking RAF officer in Greece, Willetts must have been aware of these directives. Morale was high at the meeting, as Korce was about to fall any day. But a curtain of tension fell when Papagos duly called for British air support to hit the retreating Italian ground troops. As Prince Peter recalled later, at that point Metaxas turned to Willetts with the observation that he knew there was going to be an Italian air attack that day. Papagos, overhearing the aside, gently reprimanded his own prime minister in Greek that he had just spilled a secret to the British. For a commander-in-chief, and in the face of an iron leader such as Metaxas, this was skating dangerously close to insubordination. It can only be explained by Papagos' panic that the RAF might balk at being a Greek flying artillery arm and insist on operating as it saw fit.

Willetts, though not understanding Greek, guessed what the muttering was about. Such was the passion of the Greek vengeance against the Italian aggressors that Papagos wanted RAF planes not only to bomb the Italians out of their positions, but also to mercilessly strafe them as they retreated. This didn't sound right to Willetts, who, encouraged by Metaxas' observation, said on the record that the RAF would be better employed in fighting off the expected Italian air raids. After a lunch break Papagos reiterated his demand as if nothing had happened. This time D'Albiac was present. After sitting through a turgid speech by Papagos detailing the string of Greek victories on the Albanian front D'Albiac reluctantly agreed to send bombers to hasten the Italian withdrawal somewhat, but he drew the line at machine-gunning the fleeing enemy.

Papagos alternated between impatience to keep up the pressure on the Italian army and worry that his logistics setup lagged behind developments on the front line. Still, Gambier-Parry was quite unprepared for what he heard on his next visit to Papagos. If the British were to send troops to help Greece, the Greek C-in-C said casually, 'they would be welcome'. British airmen now were not enough; grounds troops would be useful, too. Gambier-Parry replied that he would officially forward the request to the proper quarters. There was also the foreign press corps in Athens, demanding loudly that they be allowed at the front, and Metaxas still had not made up his mind about whether he wanted them there. To the Greeks, if not to some of the British, this was still not a 'journalistic war'.

As Greek forces closed on Korce D'Albiac mostly cooperated with the Greek air demands. He was loth to run counter to the prevailing spirit of optimism and didn't want to be the fly in the ointment of victory. On 21 November Papagos presented a 'shopping list' to D'Albiac: the RAF was asked to bomb not only the Albanian port of Durres but also Bari, Brindisi and Ancona on the Italian mainland, and, while we're at it, why not Rome itself? The urgency was that an Italian army corps was reported about to disembark in Albania and had to be stopped. D'Albiac agreed, ordering a bombing raid on Durres for that evening and targeting Bari and Brindisi the following night, 'weather permitting'. Rome was, delicately, not mentioned again.

The weather refused to cooperate for the planned raid on Durres, but on 22 November few cared to quibble about it, for the capital was consumed with the happy news of the fall of Korce. Yet one of those few was Papagos, who complained to D'Albiac. The air commodore promised to bomb Durres that same evening, with some of the twenty-five Blenheim bombers of 211 Squadron scheduled to arrive from the Middle East that afternoon. Later that day Willetts told Papagos that three 211 Squadron bombers would be heading for Durres that night.

'Papagos jumped from his chair,' Prince Peter recorded. 'What?' he cried. 'Just three?' Willetts apologized for not having any more for that night, but pledged a bigger force for the following night. Willetts also politely refused to agree to a request by the Greek C-in-C that the RAF bomb the roads south of Gjirokaster, on the grounds that it would be a 'tactical' rather than a strategic strike and thus outside the British remit. The group captain could stand firm against the weight of Greek brass because that same day Air Chief Marshal Longmore had arrived in Athens to see for himself what was being done with his precious planes and crews.

Longmore hit the Greeks like a cold shower. His first meeting with King George went rather badly. With Prince Peter present, the king fulsomely praised Britain's air help to the Greeks and, perhaps unwisely, mentioned a need for more. The crusty air chief marshal, unimpressed by the crowned head before him, replied gruffly that the king was wrong in automatically counting on the RAF's help as his (Longmore's) overwhelming priority was to keep Britain's air force fighting in the Middle East. In Longmore's narrowly functional view the Greek sideshow was nowhere near the RAF's prime concern and the Greeks had to be constantly reminded of that. Essentially, Britain was doing Greece a favour having little to do with Britain's prime strategic tasks, and losing young men to boot. The king came away from the meeting grumbling about Longmore as 'a very unpleasant man'.

If the Greek king came off the worse from the encounter with Longmore, Papagos could expect no different. But at least Papagos, an able officer, put up some sort of spirited response. After being lectured by Longmore about the secondary nature of the Greek front to Britain's strategic concerns, Papagos replied that he saw strategy on a wider scale; in a unified war effort, he opined, every theatre of war was related to every other. For example, he said, an effective strategic bombing of Albania would help reduce the Italian pressure in

North Africa. This argument of the interconnectibility of war fronts appeared to make some impression on the parade-ground Longmore, who softened even more after encountering the same reasoned arguments from Metaxas himself.

> [Longmore] replied that he agreed, and that despite the dearth of means which he had at his disposal he promised to do what he could. He said he would see to it that more British-built and American-built aircraft became available. Metaxas' eyes lit up behind his glasses as he saw he had scored a success with the air chief marshal, and he assured him that with the help of the RAF and Royal Navy ... Greece would stand up to Hitler if the situation warranted.[11]

Yet the elements are deaf to the concerns of soldiers, and once more bad weather saved Durres from a British bombing. D'Albiac, to placate a touchy Papagos, agreed to bomb Tepelene, Gjirokaster and Pogradec, then still in Italian hands. In support, the RHAF's Gladiators of 21 Mira would be stationed at northern Greek airfields in preparation for deployment at the captured base at Korce. But Papagos continued to fret about Durres, where Italian reinforcements were, perhaps at that moment, coming off the troopships. Gambier-Parry, to lighten the atmosphere, brought in a spurious message to the king from Lord Halifax, the British Foreign Secretary, to the effect that the Italian military leadership was supposedly on the verge of revolting against the fascist party.

As the meeting progressed, news arrived that the RAF had bombed columns of enemy vehicles at Vlore. Orders went out that forward airfields be activated, in particular one located at the bottom of a gorge-like valley at Paramythia, a few miles south of the Albanian border. Paramythia field nestled alongside the bed of the Acheron River, which the ancient Greeks believed to be the entrance to Hades. The landscape is certainly portentous. Great crags soar thousands of feet on either side. The pilot of anything as large as a twin-engined bomber had to be careful to negotiate landings and climb-outs, which of course could not be done in foggy weather or at night. After take-off a Blenheim or a Wellington pilot needed to make a series of tight climbing circles before clearing the peaks. The first British airmen to use Paramythia were the pilots of 815 Naval Air Squadron, Fleet Air Arm, whose ancient-looking but agile Fairey Swordfish torpedo-bomber biplanes could negotiate the approaches with rather more ease. The British quickly dubbed Paramythia 'Fairy Tale Valley', inspired both by the unearthly beauty of the place and the Greek word *paramythia*, which actually means fairy tales.

The great merit of Fairy Tale Valley was that the Italian air force didn't know about it. The strip was devilishly hard to find by visual aerial reconnaissance alone. The naval pilots were under strict orders to use Paramythia as a facility for over-water operations against the Italian fleet only. The Swordfish could slip in and out from the coast undetected, but 815 NAS was strictly prohibited from tangling with the Regia Aeronautica over Albania or Greece. If the Italians saw Swordfish in the air they would realize that the Fleet Air Arm was using a base in Epiros, and Fairy Tale Valley would be blown.

At the daily air strategy meetings Papagos suggested that the RAF's Gladiators move up to the base at Ioannina, as their present base at Trikala in central Greece was often under cloud and a target of Italian bombers. Group Captain Tilios, the Senior Greek Air Commander, said he suspected that security leaks had resulted in the Italians bombing the airfields at Kozani and Florina. D'Albiac and Willetts nodded in agreement. The incident with Reuters and the capture of the Greek amphibious commando team in Albania was having its repercussions in Athens, and the Greek security services were paranoid. Gambier-Parry, the British Military Mission head, was on the point of being replaced as lacking experience in the security sphere. The RAF, on the contrary, was becoming increasingly indispensable to the Greek air war despite Air Chief Marshal Longmore's inhibitions.[12]

It was fortunate that Hickey and Pattle and the rest of 80 Squadron were giving excellent accounts of themselves over the front, not only giving the RHAF priceless tips on air combat but also raising Britain's military profile in Greece. By early December the squadron at Ioannina had been joined by more Gladiators from 112 Squadron. There were regular patrols over Gjirokaster in southern Albania, which was now in Greek hands and hence a key Italian bombing target. Pattle, meanwhile, had developed an innovative technique for dealing with the SM79 in particular. Stalking the three-engined bomber from the rear, he would deliver a carefully-timed burst of fire – lasting half a second, no more – into the plane's fuel tank situated between the fuselage and the port engine. For the next ten seconds he would stay on the bomber's tail while its fuel sprayed out. At the right moment Pattle would fire a second burst into the fuel cloud, and the SM79 would blow up. It wasn't long before all his squadron mates had learned the trick.[13]

For the RHAF, though, the attrition through December was becoming serious. By now it was easy for the Regia Aeronautica's bombers to brush by whatever defences the RHAF could put up. Malakis and his crew, the ones who had pulverized the Italian military hospital at Permet, were lost eleven days later. What remained of 1 Army Cooperation (Observation) Mira was blasted on the ground at Kozani and Florina thanks to a daring raid by 364 Squadriglia led by Captain Edoardo Molinari, an Italian ace, and followed by a formation of SM81s. A similar fate befell 2 and 4 Army Cooperation (Observation) Mirai at Florina, which had to be abandoned. The Italians raided Corfu virtually unopposed, killing at least two hundred civilians.

Reinforcements from the RAF's 112 Squadron gave the Greek fliers a bit of a reprieve, and an opportunity to retire a few of the more battered PZLs.

1. Ioannis Metaxas (*right*) and Lieutenant General Alexander Papagos (*centre*). (*Hellenic War Museum*)

2. Young Sotiris Kollias's sketch of Italian bombers over Kalyvia, 28 October 1940. (*with permission*)

3. Greek conscripts go off joyously to war through the streets of Athens, 28 October 1940. (*Hellenic War Museum*)

4. Greek cavalry fords the Kalamas River, November 1940. (*Hellenic War Museum*)

5. The village of Elefthero, where some 300 Italians of the Julia Division were killed during on their retreat, November 1940. (*Author's photograph*)

6. The remains of a bicycle used by the Italian Bersaglieri, in the Kalpaki Museum. (*Author's photograph*)

7. Greek troops in the snows of Albania, December 1940. *(Hellenic War Museum)*

8. Greek artillery is placed in position in Albania. *(Hellenic War Musem)*

9. Greek soldiers pose beside a captured Fiat tank of the Centauro Armoured Division. (*Hellenic War Musem*)

10. Ground crew refuel a RHAF PZL24 fighter. (*Hellenic War Musem*)

1. The rebuilt Mertzani Bridge over the Aoos River today, with the Albanian border behind the first line of hills. (*Author's photograph*)

2. The rear deck of the RHN destroyer *Queen Olga*. (*Hellenic War Musem*)

13. Commander Athanasios Spanidis on his submarine, the *Katsonis*. (*Hellenic War Musem*)

14. Germans go over the top to attack Fort Rupel 6 April 1941.
(*George Mermingas collection*)

15. Germans pinned down in front of the Metaxas line. (*Hellenic War Musem*)

Zur frommen Erinnerung im Gebete

an den Gefreiten

Franz Rothmeier
von Bodenstein

bei der 1. Kompanie eines Infantrieregimentes

geboren am 20. Juni 1907, gefallen am 6. April 1941 bei den Kämpfen an der griechisch-jugosl. Grenze, bei einem Spähtruppunternehmen, beerdigt in Carevo-Selo.

Im heißen Kampf im Feindesland,
Traf dich die Todeswunde,
Die lieben Dein im Heimatland,
Traf schwer die bittere Kunde.

Karl Rieder, Nittenau.

16 (*above left*). Major George Douratsos, commander of Fort Rupel. (*Hellenic War Musem*)

17 (*above right*). Death notice of Gefreiter (Private) Franz Rothmeier who fell at Fort Rupel, 6 April 1941. (*George Mermingas collection*)

18. Field Marshal Wilhelm List, commander of the German Twelfth Army. (*Hellenic War Musem*)

19. A Greek officer (*centre*) surrenders Fort Rupel to the Germans. (*George Mermingas collection*)

20. A German 92mm howitzer at the Rupel National Memorial. (*Hellenic War Musem*)

Pattle was always on hand to give the inspiring example, ranging far and wide out of Ioannina with his spectacular air fighting skills. On 3 December he added to his roster of kills by downing two slow-moving Meridionali Ro37 observation planes – soft targets, but kills nonetheless. The PZLs continued their robust works against the Fiat CR42s, but these latter were now being rapidly superseded in the Albanian theatre by the G50 and the even more redoubtable Macchi MC200 *Saetta*. Greece's own pot-holed airfields were almost as hazardous as the enemy, writing off about one plane per week. Moreover, with the Italian army retreating farther into Albania and flying weather worsening, the RHAF's remaining warplanes and crews were hard-pressed to maintain their range and operational endurance.

The RAF's bombers continued to meet stiff opposition over Vlore, with the Blenheims of 211 Squadron coming under nightly attack from all three *squadriglie* of 150 Gruppo. One of 211 Squadron's skippers, Flight Lieutenant George Doudney, got off very lightly indeed when a bullet penetrated his flying helmet but not the contents. The Gladiators of 80 Squadron gave as good as they got, but more often than not 150 Gruppo's Fiats clawed their quota of RAF bombers regardless. Two of 84 Squadron's Blenheims were shot down by 365 Squadriglia on 7 December, only one crewmember surviving. A 211 Squadron Blenheim was sent plunging in to the sea off Sarande on 18 December, killing the crew. Four days later Major Oscar Molinari of 160 Gruppo disposed of two Gladiators.[14]

Shortly before Christmas the temperature plummetted so low at Ptolemais airfield that the oil froze in the engines of the PZLs of 22 and 23 Mirai. To forestall the oil lines rupturing, engineers tried to warm them over bonfires, but to no avail. Thanks to an old delouser obtained by a resourceful engineer officer, the engines were steamed into operation, but even then the snow on the runway was too deep for the fighters to take off. As *squadriglie* of Italian CantZ1007s and SM79s droned overhead on their way to bomb Thessaloniki, the RHAF's Fighter Chief, Wing Commander Emmanuel Kelaidis, ordered that the PZLs be dismantled and sent overland to the milder conditions of Sedes, about 150 miles to the east. In a remarkable feat of determination that entered Greek air force annals as the 'Engineers' Epic', ground crews forced their ice-numbed fingers into action to unscrew the wings from twenty-two PZLs. The semi-dismantled planes were then towed 26km in a blinding blizzard through wolf-infested hills to the nearest railway station for loading on flatbeds to Thessaloniki and Sedes. There were three such laborious processions. Within days the planes had been reassembled to fight again.[15]

Despite such manifestations of an indomitable Greek air spirit, it was the RAF that now was bearing the brunt of the war in the air. Longmore's initial fears of Britain's becoming over-involved in the Greek effort had been overtaken by the pressure of events. The Italian aircrews were well aware of the shift in power. The Greek fliers had been brave enough, but the RAF's fighter boys showed their experience. The Gladiators of Hickey and Pattle regularly engaged the Italians in what they ruefully termed a *carosello infernale*, an infernal carousel. On 20 December a formation of six SM79s was broken up before it could bomb an advancing Greek column. Over Gjirokaster on 23 December the dogfights resumed. Hickey and Pattle dived into 364 Squadriglia escorting a formation of SM79 and Breda Br20 bombers and scored a couple of kills in quick succession. The escorting CR42s, however, managed to stay out of range of the Gladiators' guns, forcing Pattle and his wingmen to try some dangerous manoeuvres in a sky filled with flaming tracer. But Hickey that day ran out of luck. Either Captain Luigi Corsini or Sergeant Major Virgilio Pongiluppi fired the fatal burst into Hickey's Gladiator, though the 80 Squadron CO might well have survived had he not been machine-gunned to death as he drifted down. In a few weeks he would have returned to his wife and children in Australia. Two other Gladiator pilots were wounded, and five of 80 Squadron's aircraft seriously damaged.

The Blenheim bombers of 211 Squadron continued their attacks on enemy targets over Christmas, to be met by 150 Gruppo's fighters. On Boxing Day 364 Squadriglia eliminated a Blenheim that was bombing the Vlore-Himare road, while on New Year's Eve di Robilant and Sergeant Enrico Micheli downed a Blenheim flown by Sergeant S. Bennett, killing its crew.[16]

While the bulk of the RHAF was deployed over the Albanian front and over Greece's vulnerable towns, its naval cooperation arm was quietly keeping the Aegean Sea lanes free of enemy submarines. The air force had three maritime *mirai*, 11, 12 and 13, the last-named equipped with modern Avro Anson patrol aircraft. The sinking of the *Elli* in August, in fact, was the last successful instance of enemy submarine action in the Aegean Sea until the German conquest in spring 1941. The Ansons and the ageing Fairey III seaplanes protected many a shipload of Greek troops as they were transported to the front from Crete and the islands. Some managed to drop a few bombs on Italian naval installations in Rhodes and the Dodecanese islands.

Meanwhile, D'Albiac – perhaps with one eye on the publicity it could entail – decided to send a few RAF planes to drop packets of toys and sweets for the children of Corfu on Christmas morning. Hardly had the presents been dropped than the Regia Aeronautica bombed the port of Corfu, killing eighteen people having their Christmas dinner. D'Albiac, incensed, gathered together what crews he could from 211 Squadron and sent them off from Tatoi to plaster Vlore that night. The Blenheims were lucky enough to encounter two Italian warships just entering the port and raked their decks with machine gun fire, veering away before the Italian flak crews realized what was happening. The Italian Christmas Day raid on Corfu left a bitter taste in Greek mouths. 'The bastards!' Metaxas scrawled in his diary that night.

The end of December saw more losses in 31 Mira, whose Blenheim IVs were being decimated. The fighter squadrons weren't in much better shape, as bad weather over Albania often prevented them from shooting up the retreating Italian columns. In a little over two months of war, thirty-one RHAF aircrew officers had been killed and seven wounded, plus four NCOs killed and five wounded. Just twenty-eight fighters remained in battleworthy condition, mostly PZLs and Gladiators, while the number of front-line bombers was down to seven. Regardless of the successes of the Greek army in Albania, the air force was on the ropes. The RAF, by default, was about to assume most of the responsibility for the air defence of Greece. For the Greek leadership this was not as welcome a prospect as one might think. For, in Metaxas' mind at least, it could not help but bring closer the day that Hitler would see Britain becoming more heavily involved on Greece's side and decide to make his own 'big brother' move and intervene on Mussolini's behalf. If that happened, he knew the game was up. As long as his army was pushing back the Italians in Albania, Metaxas could gamble that the war would end in some kind of armistice line and Greece could get its breath back for a widening world conflict whose outcome at that stage could not be known.

Chapter 7

Metaxas: 'Let Us Fall Like Men'

Winter fatigue in the lines – Papagos calls a halt – the Italians guard Vlore – Cavallero builds a defence – German threats – Major Reid plays at spying – the war council of 4 January 1941 – Prince Philip's advice – the Wolves of Tuscany are tamed – the Greek II Corps seizes Kelcyre – 'There's only one way! Attack!' – the British insist on an expeditionary force – Metaxas in a dilemma – his illness and death

At the end of 1940 the Greek army had eleven infantry divisions, two infantry brigades and a cavalry division strung across a front of about 180km, from Himare on the coast to Pogradec by the Yugoslav frontier. The line lurched inwards where the Greek II Corps had lagged behind the general advance around Kelcyre. As the weather hardened, so had the Italian resistance. Cavallero had built up his strength methodically, without fanfare. Confronting the Greeks were nine infantry and two Alpine divisions, many of them fresh (the 53rd Arezzo, the 2nd Alpine Tridentina, the 48th Taro, the 37th Modena, the 5th Alpine Pusteria, the 4th Alpine Cuneense, the 33rd Acqui and 11th Brennero). In addition, new Italian units included the 2 Bersaglieri Regiment, the 8 Alpine Regiment (rebuilt from its discomfiture as part of the Julia), two battalions of the 16th Pistoia, one battalion of the 56th Casale, seven battalions of Blackshirts, two machine gun battalions and the 7 and 19 Cavalry Regiments.

The Greeks now probably outnumbered their foes in the field. Though Papagos later insisted otherwise, Italian official records show that Cavallero had between 100 and 105 infantry and Blackshirt battalions totalling some 10,600 officers, 262,000 enlisted men, 32,800 horses and mules and 7,500 motor vehicles. The Greek army, on the other hand, probably totalled up to 135 infantry and cavalry battalions.[1] Yet Papagos could not let the recent Greek successes go to his head. Italian weaponry was not, as has often been claimed, superior to that of the Greeks, but each Italian division had nine artillery batteries to the Greek division's six. The Greek still totally lacked effective armoured vehicles of any kind, which is why Greek attacks tended to avoid flat land where the Centauro's tanks could operate. As the Italian front shrank, new troops could be sped to where they were needed by lorry, while the

Greeks had to march for days in the snow and ice. And of course, the Regia Aeronautica was superior in the skies.

In the last week of December Papagos sent the rested 13th Division to occupy the Pogradec sector in place of the 17th, which was placed in the West Macedonia Army Department's reserves. On the I Corps front, the 4th Division was replaced by the re-formed and rested 8th, while the 5th and 16th Divisions were held in reserve in the Korce sector. The short-term objective now was to consolidate the supply and communications lines while the II Corps prepared for a planned offensive to straighten out the middle sector of the front by hopefully capturing Kelcyre. The 6th Division on the Bulgarian border was prepared for transfer to the Albanian front.

Temporarily improving weather on 30 December gave an opportunity for the II Corps to try for its immediate objective. The 15th Division in the centre began the attack at 6.45 am – without the usual preparatory artillery barrage – supported by the 1st Division on its left and backed up by eighty pieces of light and heavy artillery. Facing them were three Italian divisions, the Acqui, Julia and Bari, plus regiments of Alpini and Blackshirts. Surprise was complete. After a fight lasting a little more than an hour the defenders abandoned their lines, leaving scores of dead, nearly 300 prisoners, eighteen pieces of mountain artillery and munitions enough to last for weeks. On the left, the 1st Division punched its way to its own objective by 11.00 am, with the Italian casualties estimated at between fifty per cent and seventy per cent. On the left of the Greek line progress northwards from Kuc up the Shushice River valley was slow and bloody.

Tsakalotos' 40 Evzones were in the process of trying to secure the heights east of Himare when, on 6 January, Papagos called a general halt to operations on the Albanian front. The decision came not a day too soon for his long-suffering soldiers who were now slogging through conditions rarely suffered by armies in modern times. Pack mules dropped dead of the cold where they stood, icicles hanging from their tails. Incessant snowstorms ripped tents from their guy lines; the men of the 2nd Division were in constant danger of being buried alive by the snow wherever they could encamp. Bread rations were down to one-eighth of the normal daily amount. The 4th Division lost twice as many men to frostbite – 2,711 – than to enemy action, and 2,800 mules. By some miracle, the men of the 4th Division took the town of Nivica, capturing an entire 580-man battalion, a feat explainable only by the fact that the Italians were fully as fatigued as the Greeks.

Papagos issued his order to halt reluctantly. He knew that his troops needed to continue the èlan of their initial success, winter or no winter, and that once they stopped advancing, lethargy and perhaps even defeatism would set in. Prince Peter suspected something of the kind. He knew the Greek mentality well enough.

> We Greeks, admittedly, are wonderful when we attack, advancing heroically [he wrote], without thinking for a second of the dangers. While we are going forward we have exceptionally high morale. But when we stop and are obliged to remain in a defensive position, then it's another story ... The Greek soldier is too restless to stay in the same place and is soon disheartened unless he is given the constant stimulus of movement and success. He needs to feel that he is sweeping all ahead of him all the time.[2]

The prince was right in assuming that in an army, nothing erodes morale like stagnation and immobility. His diary records an instance of one Evzone company that reacted in disbelief when the officers told the men to start digging trenches: 'What?' the men cried. 'You mean we're staying here?' As long as they were surging forward, the losses and frostbite and hunger could be handled. Most Greek soldiers believed they were superior to the British who, it was often quipped, 'can't fight without their jam and tea'. (A barb aimed later by the British against the Americans who supposedly couldn't fight 'without their ice cream and air conditioning'.)

But by 15 December the issue had become academic; the hideous weather conditions had rendered any further meaningful advances in Albania virtually impossible. Were the Greek gains between then and early January – the capture of Kuc and some relatively minor adjustments along the II Corps front in the centre – justified in light of the casualties and tribulations of the troops? Papagos in his memoir claimed that the late-December attacks were necessary 'in order to create a suitable base for later offensive operations'.[3] In short, the winter would pass and the Italians would still be within attacking distance of Greece, so the farther back they could be pushed, the better.

The weakening of the Greek offensive as 1941 approached heartened the Italian command. Just before Christmas Soddu, still in nominal command, suggested that with the Greeks now in possession of Himare and the head of the Shushice Valley and threatening Kelcyre, the Italian forces should maintain 'an aggressive stance to improve our position and give the enemy the impression that a major offensive is in preparation on our part'. The newly-arrived **Cuneo Division** was sent to block the way to Vlore, now just 35km from the Greek line. But barely had the division got itself together than its commander, General Carlo Menotti, was ordered to split it up to plug gaps elsewhere on the front. Its original task of recapturing Himare was quickly forgotten as the aggressive Greek thrusts of late December revealed the folly of dismembering divisions for *ad hoc* requirements.

It was a snowy Christmas in Rome and Mussolini, looking out of the window of his comfortable, centrally heated Palazzo Venezia, delivered himself of the Darwinian opinion that he liked the snow because it would kill off the weaker of his countrymen and hence 'improve this mediocre Italian race'. By way of explanation, the Duce had long been in the grip of a severe inferiority complex vis-a-vis the presumably 'tougher' northern Europeans. What seems not to have occurred to him is that, on the contrary, it was not the weaklings but the best and bravest of his country's youth who were being consumed in the icy hell of Albania. Italian records show that frostbite had put some 13,000 men out of action by the end of December. Like their Greek counterparts in the same mountains, the Italian troops dreaded what they called *la morte bianca* – the white death. Those afflicted would be carried on their comrades' shoulders through the snow, and then on carts bumping over the muddy rutted tracks, for hours of jolting agony until they could reach a hospital worthy of the name in Tirana or Vlore, or be lucky enough to be shipped or flown home.[4]

Mussolini spent part of Christmas Day compiling another long telegram to Cavallero urging him to stay on the ball. As Italian bombs fell on Corfu, Cavallero perused the telegram.

> It is evident [the Duce wrote] that the enemy has two strategic objectives: one in the centre to divide [our] army corps and try to encircle them, [and] one on our right which in particular favours the British wish to occupy Vlore.

Vlore – that was the port to be held on to at all costs. Once the Greeks and British seized it, the supply route for men and provisions into Albania would be fatally cramped. The only way to ward off that possibility, Mussolini, said, was to re-take the initiative in the field. The Greeks had been allowed to enjoy their string of successes for too long. He also gave vague recommendations for 'a reordering of the old divisions, starting with the Ninth Corps,' which would occupy two months of the deepest winter, and then, the soldiers' morale duly revived, they would see that 'the wind direction has changed and then the Greeks will receive a cudgelling'.

Cavallero, an intelligent man, cannot have believed this torrent of false optimism. Yet he was also intelligent enough at first to keep his doubts to himself. And there were plenty. The news from North Africa was not encouraging; Marshal Rodolfo Graziani's forces were being seriously discomfited. The bad news from there and Albania made it a particularly sad Christmas for the Italians. 'The legend, or the illusion, of our military power was gloomily going up in smoke,' writes Cervi.[5] Cadet morale was sinking. Nearly half the graduates of the national military academy were applying for posts in the less-dangerous Carabinieri. Whenever the Duce's image appeared on cinema newsreels, audiences which had once applauded wildly now remained silent. Radio newsreaders made faces in the studio while intoning the regulation praises of Italian arms. It was not a situation designed to lift the national spirit.

The Duce's Christmas cable to Cavallero, bypassing Supreme Commander Soddu, was a sign that Soddu's number was up. On 29 December Soddu was recalled to Rome 'for consultations', the real meaning of that fatal phrase becoming apparent when on the following day Cavallero was confirmed as commander of the troops in Albania while retaining his formal post as Chief of the General Staff. Cavallero knew perfectly well what Papagos was planning and how to counter it. But he continued to be bombarded with control-freakery from Mussolini. Not all of the Duce's admonitions were unrealistic; for example, he wisely urged that fresh divisions arriving in Albania should not be broken up to fill emergency gaps. Yet such was the confusion behind the Italian front lines that the Cuneo Division, for example, was dismembered before it could even begin its task to retake Himare.

Cavallero shrugged off the Duce's aggressive promptings. Some of his divisions, such as the long-suffering Julia, were down to somewhere near 1,000 men. Since the start of the war the division had lost 153 officers and 3,844 enlisted men. He knew that Papagos' forces had greater manoeuvrability and would resume the offensive when the worst of the winter had passed. Therefore his strategy for the new year was one of defence. His first concern was to throw a shield around the key port of Vlore, followed by another one at the approaches to Tirana. The six divisions of the Eleventh Corps were assigned to the first; thirteen divisions including the Ninth Corps were to protect Tirana and northern Albania.

In order to mask this defensive strategy Cavallero planned a snap attack on the Greek lines on the coast around Himare for 5 January. Spearheading it would be the newly-arrived Legnano Division under Colonel Vittorio Ruggero, while the Pusteria, Siena and 7th Lupi di Toscana (Wolves of Tuscany), were to hit Greek II Corps positions in the centre. The Legnano made some progress, but was quickly immobilized more out of premature exhaustion than anything else. The Wolves of Tuscany were newly arrived in the Albanian theatre, yet before they could act the Greek 15th Division got its blow in first and seized the snowy height of Spadarit overlooking the Kelcyre Valley.

By the beginning of 1941 the Greeks had already penetrated between thirty (in the west) and eighty (in the east) kilometres into Albania, and could well have fortified that line before the worst of the winter set in. By any military standards, it was a remarkable achievement for eight or nine weeks of war. Metaxas' original war aim, the expulsion of the invader from the homeland, had been accomplished in a matter of days. More than 10,200 Italian prisoners were in Greek hands. If there was ever a time to stop and take stock of the strategic situation, it was now. But bigger shadows were by now looming over the Balkans. Italy's reverses had embarrassed the Axis and encouraged its enemies everywhere. Could Hitler be expected to sit back and accept it? He already knew, of course, that the British were heavily involved in Greece. The problem for the Greeks was how not to make it too obvious.

Hitler had delivered a strong hint of what was to come on 20 December, when his ambassador in Athens, Prince Victor zu Erbach Schoenberg, called on Metaxas to ask him bluntly if the pervasive British presence in Greece was in any way aimed at Germany. The ambassador, of course, knew very well what was afoot, but wanted to have something in black and white to send to Berlin. 'If you harm us in the Balkans,' Metaxas replied with a nice lack of dissimulation, 'of course.'[6]

Metaxas may have put on a brave face, but he was rattled. He had to keep British uniforms away from the Axis spies along the Yugoslav and Bulgarian borders at all costs. It was all right for someone such as Gambier-Parry to be escorted on a courtesy visit to the Albanian front, but at least one other British officer was known to have clandestinely visited Thessaloniki, earning the ire of Papagos. King George wondered whether such stunts were deliberate in order to provoke a German reaction. To be fair to some British officers, many didn't relish languishing in the Grande Bretagne Hotel while the Greeks did the real fighting. One Major Buckley of the British Military Mission fretted to Prince Peter that he was frankly bored with pushing a pen all day.

> [Buckley] revealed to me [Prince Peter wrote] that he and others had been sent as advisers for mountain warfare operations. But who, he asked me, knew better about this warfare than the Greeks? ... The Greeks knew much more than the British, especially in the difficult and unknown terrain of Epiros and Albania ... I had the impression that the situation was getting on his nerves.[7]

The Greeks were right to be jittery. There were spooks and spies of every conceivable kind everywhere. An example presented itself during the funeral of Prince Peter's aunt, Princess (and grand duchess of Russia) Maria of Greece, who had died after a harrowing railway journey from Italy through Yugoslavia on the floor of a goods wagon crowded with refugees. The officiating priest was one 'Father Dimitrios', an English monk who had supposedly embraced Greek Orthodoxy and had spent some years in the autonomous monastic community of Mount Athos. As a result 'Dimitrios' had become identical to a Greek priest in speech and bearded appearance and profound knowledge of the ancient Orthodox liturgy. Unbeknownst to most who came into contact with him, his real name was David Balfour. He was a British agent whose second job beneath the black gown and cylindrical hat was to gather intelligence for London. (Balfour was soon to abandon Orthodoxy and don the uniform of a British Army officer in Egypt. As for Gambier-Parry, after leaving Athens he arrived in Egypt, to be promptly captured by an advanced

German patrol in the Western Desert. The man who had with satisfaction watched the Greeks gather up columns of Italian prisoners himself languished as a POW of the Italians until September 1943.)[8]

Metaxas had no doubts about what he would do if the Germans attacked; Greece, he assured the British, would stoutly uphold its share in the alliance. 'But that doesn't mean,' the prime minister added in an aside to Prince Peter, 'that if the British reach the North Pole we'll follow them there'. The prince spent long and fatiguing days acting as a two-way interpreter between Greek officials and senior officers on the one hand, and the British on the other. Part of his multi-faceted job was to take custody of the personal effects of RAF crews killed on missions and hand them over to D'Albiac's staff. The case of a crew that had crashed near Agrinion particularly haunted him:

> It was a sad task to note down these few objects [the prince wrote], as I was constantly thinking of these boys' families. Their names were: Flight Sergeant Harry Taylor and Sergeant N.A. Hallet[t]. The address of the former's mother was: Mrs F. Taylor, 30 St John's Street, [Ely?] Cambridge and the other address: 14 Fifth Avenue, Heaton, Newcastle-on-Tyne.[9]

On Christmas Eve Major General Balfour Hutchison, Deputy Quartermaster-general of the Middle East headquarters, flew into Athens and went into an immediate meeting with Metaxas to determine Greece's war materials requirements. Metaxas suggested that some of the Italian war booty in North Africa be made available to the Greeks, and Hutchison agreed. On Christmas morning, about the time the tragic Colonel Rokkos put a bullet in his head in Albania and D'Albiac's bombers were dropping goodies to the children of Corfu, Hutchison received the Greek shopping list: for the Royal Hellenic Navy 266 anti-aircraft guns and nearly 800,000 shells, 6,000 helmets, 100,000 blankets, 25,000 pairs of boots and 29,000 metres of khaki uniform fabric. For the RHAF 100 anti-aircraft guns, 300 machine guns for ground defence, 5,000 pairs of boots, 16,000 blankets, 4,000 pairs of thick gloves, 1,000 helmets, 5,000 oxygen masks, 20,000 pairs of goggles and 10,000 Verey flares.

It was the Greek army that had the lion's share of requirements: urgent replacements for the French-made rifles and machine guns, 100 lorries a month and 500 anti-armour rifles, snow ploughs and dinghies, 200,000 pairs of boots, 500,000 pairs of socks, 50,000 water flasks, 100,000 blankets and 100,000 tents and as many mules as could be spared. The army's list also included twenty-five tons of tea and four million cans of food. Those present, including senior officers, were mildly surprised to see that Hutchison didn't bat an eyelid and calmly promised to do what he could. There was at least some hope that most of the requirements might be delivered. Five days later, sixteen shiploads of the equipment arrived from Britain. Hutchison also gave the green light for a

Greek officer to go to the Middle East and see what could be culled from the captured Italian war materials.

On 28 December a striking figure strode into Prince Peter's office, a tall, blond officer sporting a short moustache, decidedly non-regulation corduroy trousers and suede shoes. The apparition introduced itself as Major Miles Reid, commanding a select outfit known as H Squadron GHQ Liaison Regiment, known as the Phantom, presumably because its existence was some sort of official secret. H Squadron was a battalion of jeeps equipped with powerful transmitters to inform London of the goings-on in Greece in real-time, as it were. As the sartorially correct prince couldn't help commenting on the visitor's unconventional dress, Reid breezily replied, 'In our army, my dear fellow, a lack of imagination in dressing betrays a marked lack of individuality.'

Reid was one of those self-important types who believed they could teach the Greeks a thing or two, when the contrary was actually true. Prince Peter distrusted the man from the first, and was not about to give free rein for Reid's Phantom jeeps to trundle about where they liked. To ingratiate himself with his hosts, Reid exuded charm. He had great admiration for the Evzones, he gushed, and to press the point he had little Greek flags made to sew on his men's uniforms. None of this made much impression on Major General Christos Karassos, the second Deputy Chief of the general staff, who took it on himself to find out what this Phantom business was really about.

Metaxas learned what the British really wanted on 30 December, when he met General Heywood, D'Albiac, Crown Prince Paul and Major General Paraschos Melissinos, Papagos' staff chief, in Melissinos' office. As the German threat from the direction of the northern Balkans was intensifying week by week, Churchill desperately wanted to send a British land force to Thessaloniki as a deterrent. Metaxas was dead against the idea. Far from being a deterrent, he believed, the laughably inadequate British force would merely provoke Hitler. When Prince Peter briefly entered the room to deliver some documents to Melissinos, he received the impression of 'great turmoil and disagreement'.

On New Year's Eve Metaxas pressed the British for a more convincing explanation of why they wanted a force in northern Greece. He demanded of D'Albiac why the RAF wanted a base in Thessaloniki when the Larissa base was equally good for operations over Albania, and closer to the front to boot. The air commodore lamely replied, according to the ubiquitous Prince Peter, that the RAF crews could find Thessaloniki more easily. Then what about the Luftwaffe? D'Albiac said he didn't believe the Luftwaffe could do much in the winter weather lashing the Balkans. 'What will the British do if Germany attacks?' Metaxas demanded.

'Don't ask me,' D'Albiac shot back. 'Ask the British ambassador.' Then the Englishman softened and came to the real reason for his meeting: an RAF team had scheduled a football match with the Greeks for New Year's Day, he said, and he fondly hoped that the prime minister himself would attend! Metaxas' reply is not recorded, but his German-trained mind must have recoiled at such displays of Eton playing-field insouciance, especially when Prince Peter came under pressure to ask the Greek king to attend as well!

New Year's Day found Private Nikolaou of the 42 Evzones listening to the incessant sound of distant cannon fire. Whatever sleep he had been able to get was filled with dreams of his family. He began his diary entry of that day with a fervent prayer that the whole thing might be soon over: 'I wish that all our Army might pass this year [1941] at peace in our homes.'[10] In Athens Prince Peter was emerging from the Dutch ambassador's home at dawn after a dinner party to be greeted with the news that another British plane had been shot down. In the Tomorica Valley the Tridentina Division played cat and mouse with advanced Greek units. Lieutenant Peppino Antolini, a platoon leader in the 5th Alpine Division, was keeping a wary eye on 'a red house, about a kilometre distant, where there was a Greek advanced position'. His night patrols were filled with dread of possible enemy ambush. Back at base, his longer-serving comrades would regale him with the 'frightening things' that had happened to them before he arrived.[11]

By contrast in Athens, the power and influence game was in full swing. Reid called on Prince Peter again and requested outright that H Squadron be allowed to carry out reconnaissance in Greek Macedonia. True to the public-school adventure tradition which he embodied, he planned to operate in disguise out of Alexandroupolis, the largest Greek town in the northeast and just a few miles from the Turkish frontier. There was no way General Melissinos would allow this, and the request only deepened the suspicion among the Greeks that the British were secretly pushing their own agenda for a force in the north.

Papagos addressed a general Greek-British war council on 4 January. Starting with a summary of operations so far, he said the Greeks had begun the war with 129 battalions of infantry and 128 artillery batteries, and were now down to 109 battalions and ninety-eight batteries. The Italians, having started out with sixty-six battalions and 156 batteries, were now at ninety-five and 108 respectively. Both sides' losses and present strength were about equal, though a fresh Italian division, the Brennero, had just disembarked, and other enemy reinforcements were on the way. The Regia Aeronautica still had the run of Albania's skies despite the RAF's efforts. The immediate Greek land objective was to continue the great scything movement with its pivot at Pogradec and seize the prize of Vlore with the left wing. The enemy would thus have only Durres left in the north through which to receive supplies and troops.

'The centre of gravity of operations is on the left of the front,' Papagos told Metaxas, Heywood, D'Albiac and Turle. The Greek I Corps would make the attempt on Vlore, supported by the II Corps which if necessary would carry out a feint in the direction of Berat to the northeast. That was the plan but, as the commander-in-chief promptly admitted, the troops were nearing the limit of their endurance. Yet was a rest advisable? The Italians, he pointed out, could replenish fatigued men and units faster than the Greeks could. Thus the Greek army was faced with two alternatives: to immediately move on Vlore with the extant forces, or spend about three weeks restoring the army's strength, adding the 5th Division to the I Corps, and then advance 'with all our strength'. In the meantime, independent efforts by the II Corps to improve the position at Tepelene and Kelcyre would continue.

Metaxas wanted a bit more information, so Papagos said the first alternative, an immediate move on Vlore, would prevent the Italians from massing reinforcements, but it could only be done if the Greeks and British had some measure of control of the skies. This was still far from being the case. According to Greek intelligence, the Italians were organizing the citizens of Vlore in the town's defence. A lack of transport lorries in the Greek army also meant that the 5th Division would need time to move up to the front line. 'The main thing,' Papagos said, 'is to cut the line of enemy communications between Italy and Albania, both by sea and air, and to get more lorries.' The army would remain on the offensive.

As Papagos had made plain to everyone that Vlore was now the main Greek strategic objective, he was baffled by the British reluctance to step up air raids against the port and cut it off by sea. Most likely, the British saw the halt to the Greek advance as the first sign of a fatigue that could only worsen. Metaxas sought to disabuse them of that impression. 'The Greek attack is simply slowing up,' Metaxas told those around him. 'It is not suspended. You must understand this.' The Italian air force, he added, was still a formidable adversary and enemy ground forces were continuously increasing. Therefore, he said, turning to the British, more transports were urgently needed to keep the Greek troops on the move.

The next few minutes of the meeting were consumed in an academic discussion of how strong the Italians could potentially be in Albania. Papagos said that the capture of Vlore would cut the enemy's strength by half. At least a dozen Italian ships were in the port at any one time, unloading supplies. 'If I could use the airfield at Araxos,' put in D'Albiac (who about this time was promoted to air vice-marshal), 'Vlore could be better attacked. When can it be ready?'

'At the beginning of February,' Metaxas replied.

'All right, then we'll attack Vlore by night and day.'

Araxos, at the north-western tip of the Peloponnese, would be good for D'Albiac's bombers as they could follow the western Greek coastline by moonlight right up to the target. However, he said he would need perhaps a dozen more Wellingtons, but didn't know whether Longmore in the Middle East would be able to spare them. Papagos was concerned also about the Greeks' lack of anti-aircraft guns which made Greek units sitting ducks for Italian strike attacks, to which Heywood replied that a paltry twenty-two Bofors guns were on their way; they were all that Churchill apparently could spare. Metaxas asked Turle if the Royal Navy could not do more against the Italian navy which had the run of the Dalmatian coast. Turle replied disingenuously that he was afraid the Allied naval forces in the area – all of two British and two Greek submarines – might become confused and attack one another!

And so the meeting went on, Metaxas and the Greeks pressing anxiously for signs that their allies would be more generous with equipment, and the British fending off the pressure diplomatically (and in the case of Rear Admiral Turle, ludicrously), not wanting to commit too much to a nation that could well find itself on the ropes in the spring. It was D'Albiac who brought up the issue that was greatly exercising Churchill's mind – when can the British appear in Thessaloniki? The RAF, he said, badly needed Sedes airfield for its Wellingtons and Blenheims, which were stationed too far south at Larissa. Metaxas, evading the issue, suggested Paramythia, but D'Albiac said it wasn't suitable for bombers (not true) and there wasn't enough room for billeting the men (partly true). The air vice-marshal added that he would go to Egypt to try and scrounge another squadron out of Longmore. 'I can't promise anything, but I'll try,' he said.

Metaxas asked about the whereabouts of 200 lorries ordered urgently from Britain. 'That's secret,' Turle replied archly, 'but I can tell you. They're at Gibraltar.' Metaxas hit the roof. By way of apology, Turle explained that the lorries were to have been sent on to Pantelleria island in the middle of the Mediterranean by destroyer convoy, but the destroyers had been diverted to hunt a German U-boat in the Atlantic.

'Then what about those lorries captured from the Italians?'

Heywood fielded that one clumsily. 'I don't know. I've cabled Cairo to ask.' Metaxas didn't accept that as a responsible reply and claimed to have word from his consul in Alexandria that thirty Italian lorries were on the point of being shipped to Greece but the shipment for some unknown reason had been stopped. The Greeks' sense of desperation was becoming uncomfortable. 'They don't understand that we can't do everything,' Heywood muttered in an aside that Prince Peter caught. Turle meekly cited the danger to convoys in the Mediterranean and the meeting broke up.

D'Albiac was also becoming discouraged. He knew that his bomber crews were becoming frustrated with the lack of results on their Albania operations. His despondency communicated itself to the king, who wondered if the air vice-marshal was losing his nerve. To add to the problems, British servicemen in Greece were establishing a reputation for drunkenness and mayhem (similar to the 'lager louts' of a later time). Senior officers said they were afraid the incidents might give Britain a bad name, which was partly true.[12] Then there was the indefatigable Miles Reid, who hankered to go spooking in disguise in the northeast – he received permission, but on condition that he wore civilian clothes and had a driver. The neutral Americans, too, were becoming emotionally involved in the war. The cowboy instincts of Major William Crowe, the American air attaché nicknamed 'Battlefield Bill', came to the fore when he asked to be allowed to go on an air raid or two as an observer. His wish appears to have been granted.

The day after Papagos called a halt to ground operations in Albania, he authorized Miles Reid to make his spying trip. Reid would be closely watched. It was clear what the British were trying to do – establish an intelligence network in northern Greece that would give advance warning of a German attack through Bulgaria. Metaxas was determined to put a halt to what he saw as Britain's unauthorized meddling in national strategy. 'We're either allies and cooperate,' he snapped at General Melissinos, 'or they treat us like a colony!' But Reid was allowed to go not north but south, to Corinth, to play his spy games.

The Greek trepidations are understandable, given that they and the British had differing concepts of what the war was about. To the Greeks, and Papagos in particular, it was a matter of hammering the invading enemy, be they Italian or German, and keeping their country free. Full stop. The British had a more nuanced and complicated approach. Greece was for them a mere corner of the global struggle against Hitler. The blitz on London was at its height, and for all anyone knew, the Germans had not yet abandoned thoughts of invading Britain. The forces assigned to Greece had to be balanced delicately against those required in more urgent theatres and to defend the British Isles. Yet the Balkans loomed large in Churchill's thinking. They had done ever since his ill-fated decision to launch the Dardanelles campaign in 1915, a debacle which haunted him for twenty-five years. Already he was notorious among his advisers for hatching 'ten ideas every day, one good, nine bad'. In the words of a recent biographer, he was 'forever seeking to land troops on the flanks of the enemy'.[13] To Churchill, the Balkans were an early form of the 'soft underbelly' of Europe, a definition which he later assigned to Italy and the south of France.

The rationalization was that a British foothold in Greece would deter Hitler from thrusting south to seize Crete and thus threaten strategic communications with the Middle East theatre of war. As subsequent events in 1941 would show, it was a gross miscalculation. Hitler simply wasn't the type to be deterred from anything, and had, moreover, the military muscle to back him up. But Churchill, too, was determined, and so the British force would have to come. But what was to be its size? Metaxas, for his part, believed with good reason that whatever the British sent simply wouldn't be big enough to stave off a Wehrmacht punch through Bulgaria. If Metaxas could stay on Hitler's good side (he had urged King George to send a reluctant New Year's good wishes message to the Fuehrer) then he could win the war in Albania and hopefully have enough forces left to meet a German incursion. Papagos encouraged him to think along such lines. When Papagos outlined his ideas to Lieutenant General Sir Archibald Wavell, the C-in-C Middle east who called at Athens on 3 January, Wavell cleaned his spectacles and (one imagines) cleared his throat. It was one thing to talk in terms of classroom military theory, he began, and quite another to tackle reality, and the reality was that all he could spare for the Greeks at that juncture was one artillery regiment and a mechanized unit consisting of about sixty tanks.

This, of course, would be too small to be of any practical use, Metaxas protested. On the contrary, such a token force could do untold harm by provoking a German attack. That also was why Metaxas vetoed D'Albiac's request for RAF airfields in northern Greece – they, too, would be a provocation. The result was that Churchill and those under him could not really make up their minds how to use Greece in the wider war struggle. Nonetheless, Heywood tried every possible way to wangle British soldiers into northern Greece, a tactic that was getting seriously on the nerves of Metaxas and Papagos.

In the middle of January a slim and dapper young man in a Royal Navy officer's uniform appeared in Prince Peter's office. Oh no, the prince thought, not one more pushy Brit. But he looked up to see his cousin Prince Philip, serving on HMS *Valiant* in the Mediterranean. 'Why are you doing liaison and not at the front?' the future Duke of Edinburgh and husband of a future English queen said.

'I think I'm more useful here,' Peter replied. He and Philip helped compile a memo for Papagos, but when his cousin left, Philip's words started Peter thinking. What *was* he doing acting as a glorified interpreter for Greek and British officers who were at loggerheads more often than not? Already unmarked Luftwaffe reconnaissance aircraft were probing the blue skies high over Athens, leaving white contrails in their wake.

The war was coming closer to the capital. One morning the air raid sirens wailed. Waves of Italian bombers darkened the sky over Piraeus; the explosions were clearly audible to Prince Peter who was having lunch with the king. After the raid the prince went to the anti-aircraft battery on Lykavittos Hill to find an Italian bomber crewman sitting in an interrogation room smoking nervously. Of the other five members of his crew, one had been killed by fighter attack, three had jumped into the sea and drowned, and the fifth was wounded and also in captivity. They had been picked up trying to swim to shore. One RAF pilot was killed trying to land his damaged fighter.[14]

On 22 January Prince Peter set out for a tour of the Albanian front with Colonel Blunt, the British military attaché, and Private Ventris Pavlidis, a Greek member of the attaché's embassy staff. They spent the first night at Agrinion, where they received the welcome news of the fall of Tobruk. At Arta the prince visited a hospital run by General Papagos' wife and came across one of his former NCOs with both legs blown off. On the way to Ioannina they passed columns of newly-arrived British-made lorries on their way north.

Papagos was also in Ioannina at the time and not in a good mood. The British insistence on wanting to send officers to sniff around northern Greece angered and mystified him; they had been given detailed ordinance maps of the area – wasn't that enough? Of more immediate concern, reports from the 6th Division indicated that some 4,500 men were out of action because of frostbite. The following day Prince Peter and Blunt, escorted by 'a major who bore a remarkable resemblance to Mussolini', were taken to see the vast stocks of captured enemy equipment. From there they were taken to see some Italian prisoners held in the storerooms of the 8th Division.

At Kalpaki the party saw the hulks of the Centauro's tanks and called on General Kosmas, the I Corps Commander, at Dervicane. The prince put up for the night in a stone cottage over a chicken coop and donkey stable. Inured to such Spartan conditions from his explorer days, he bathed in ice-cold water the next morning and breakfasted on goat's milk and black bread. He couldn't help noticing a very pretty young girl who had remained by his side, wordless, all the previous evening and now had appeared again. This time she looked a bit crestfallen. It took some time for the penny to drop; apparently her family had hoped to get her into the prince's bed and thus secure some reward. You didn't get handsome, full-blooded royals coming through every day!

On the way to Gjirokaster Pavlidis scanned the clear sky for enemy aircraft. Dodging air raids, they lunched in the officers' mess of the 4th Division which had suffered 2,200 cases of frostbite. Blunt and Major Bill Barbrook, who knew the area well, having served in Albanian King Zog's police force in the 1920s, were objects of curiosity among the locals. 'What village are they from?' one old lady asked Prince Peter.

'They're British, madam.'

The woman's brow furrowed. 'The Turks came here,' she mused, 'and Austrians and French and Italians and Serbs and Greeks. But British? I can't remember having seen any of those here. What are they?'

When the prince's party arrived at 2nd Division headquarters, Major General George Lavdas was preoccupied with the Italian drive to retake the Kelcyre sector. Staff officers were on field telephones shouting orders to unit commanders to hold their positions. One of them was Major George Grivas, a Cypriot who was later to gain fame – or notoriety, depending on one's point of view – as the EOKA leader who would fight British rule in Cyprus in the

1950s. Grivas chafed at his rear-echelon job; he wanted to be right on the front line where the lead was flying, but had to content himself with briefing Prince Peter and Colonel Blunt.

It had got through to the senior officers at the front, meanwhile, that the British were aiming for an Allied Balkan front on the model of the First World War, and sometimes the appearance of Blunt brought bitter feelings to the fore. When Blunt spoke airily of opening a front in Sicily, General Kosmas smiled bitterly. 'Tell Colonel Blunt,' he told Prince Peter in Greek, 'that the British are completely incapable of invading Sicily or doing anything else in Italy. If he doesn't know that I'll tell him myself!' Before the mood could get ugly, Prince Peter excused himself to go and shave. At that moment Italian aircraft roared overhead. As bombs exploded all around, the party fled for shelter under a flimsy Ottoman-era bridge, the prince still grasping his razor. Among the chaos he glimpsed an old peasant woman sitting outside her house carding wool and watching the raid impassively, making no attempt to protect herself.

'Weren't you afraid of getting killed?' the prince asked the old woman when the bombers had gone.

'Afraid?' the woman said, laughing. 'I've seen many wars, my dear boy, long before you were born. The Turks were the worst. I was young then and didn't want to die. But now I'm old and what's the difference if I die now or a bit later?'

It was a very muddy and sticky journey back to Ioannina, with the roads churned up by the lorry columns. On the way they helped an Italian prisoner set upright an overturned lorry that was blocking the road. When told of his country's reverses in Albania and North Africa, the POW smiled good-naturedly. '*Molto bene!*' he laughed sardonically. 'Very good! We can have our Duce to thank for that!'

As long as the Italians held Kelcyre and the salient around it, the Greek scythe was seriously dented. The cutting edge had to be straightened as far as possible and the II Corps was given the job. While the rest of the Greek front was more or less inactive, the II Corps 15th Division, observed by a handful of American news correspondents, led the first dawn attack without artillery preparation up the foothills of Trebescines. The attack ran into determined resistance by the Julia, which was dug in behind a strong series of battlements. During the afternoon a spirited Greek bayonet charge broke the line. The Wolves of Tuscany (7th Division) under General Ottavio Bollea came up too late to be of any help. While that fight was in progress, the Greek 1st Division stormed through shelling and air attacks to take four hills overlooking the valley road, an objective accomplished by nightfall. The 7th Division of the II Corps fought its way into Kelcyre on the morning of 9 January, achieving a major objective.

The fall of Kelcyre was a major setback for the Italian Fourth Corps of General Mercalli and in particular the Wolves of Tuscany. Somehow Mercalli and General Bancale's Eighth Corps got in each others' way with the result that the Wolves arrived late at the scene of battle and were stopped dead in their tracks. Whatever reputation the Wolves had until then vanished in the smoke of the shell bursts. One divisional officer later told Pricolo, the Air Force Chief, what it was like:

> After a march of more than 30km the division was sent to occupy its assigned positions, at night, with no officer in charge and the promise that the soldiers would find warm food on the spot. After more long hours of a fatiguing climb the troops reached the spots marked on the map, but they weren't easily recognizable and some were even occupied by the enemy. The hot food, of course, was just a wish. The division, without having even completed its deployment, had to fight off violent Greek attacks early in the morning and all the following day ... without the possibility of air cover.[15]

Unfairly perhaps, but in the hard way of soldiers, other units unofficially renamed the *Lupi di Toscana* the *Lepri di Toscana*, or Hares of Tuscany. (The Greeks had an even better word play on the term. By changing just one syllable, *Toscana* becomes in Greek *to skane* – they're running away.)

Prince Peter witnessed the subsequent morale in the Wolves of Tuscany when he visited a group of Italian prisoners in Ioannina. He remarked to the senior Italian officer, a lieutenant colonel, that he could not have been happy to be fighting a war as good as lost.

'Certainly not,' the lieutenant colonel agreed. 'It's a political war. And this is the result.' Prince Peter smiled in sympathy. 'It's the truth,' the Italian insisted. 'I like to be honest.' (*'Mi piace di essere sincero.'*)

Peter wondered aloud if there were any Wolves of Tuscany there. An Italian NCO jumped up and called out for them: *'Lupi! Lupi!'* ('Wolves!') The scene is worth lingering over for a moment, as illustrating what can befall a proud unit in a mere few days. Prince Peter's narrative gives one the distinct impression that the call had derisory overtones. A few of the *lupi* duly appeared, still wearing the bronze wolf insignia on their tunics. They didn't appear to very happy.

Colonel Vincenzo Carla, the Commander of the 140 Infantry regiment, was put on a charge for abandoning Kelcyre precipitately, but later cleared. General Achille D'Havet, commanding the Bari Division, was shortly afterwards relieved of his command for the same reason. Cavallero's own ire fell on the Julia Division, which he believed had again not performed up to standard. 'It is necessary to close the gap even if you have to go personally,' Cavallero furiously messaged Girotti (who had meanwhile been promoted for having been defeated by the Greeks). 'If this position is breached, we cannot hold on any longer ... It is the Country which demands it! And if you have to die, then I'll come and die with you. Make this one last effort, I implore you in the name of Italy.'[16]

The note of desperation that emerges in this message shows how hollow the supposed army reorganization had been. On 16 January Mercalli – ordinarily a stolid officer not given to excitability – reported that his Fourth Corps was being 'attacked on all fronts ... communications are completely cut ... need urgent air intervention to alleviate enemy pressure.' Kelcyre, it was obvious, was going to stay in Greek hands. Cavallero was unmoved. 'The notion that the Greeks are exhausted is false,' he noted. He intended to give his units a rest until the end of February, and then resume what he could of the offensive. The Duce would give him no reprieve. Italy's military reputation hung on it.

The chronicle of the attacks of the Greek II Corps north of Kelcyre is replete with names of obscure Albanian heights taken one by one after desperate bayonet charges. There is the story of the Greek 90 Infantry Regiment which charged a hill in a sub-zero dawn only to find the few Italian defenders stiff and unable to move from the cold. Men and beasts continued to succumb to the polar environment. Such were the howling winds that tents could not stay pegged down. Somehow by 25 January the II Corps had attained its objective of eliminating the Italian salient at Kelcyre and stabilizing the line on the height of Mali Spadarit. Meanwhile the I Corps under Lieutenant General George Kosmas on the left had secured its own part of the Trebescines range, overlooking the southern Albanian plain that stretches as far as Vlore.

Private Nikolaou and his unit were sent on a four-hour night march through the freezing mud to boost the Kelcyre defences. On the way he found someone selling oranges from a lorry and bought a couple. As hundreds more Italian prisoners filed back through the lines the 42 Evzones slept through the following day oblivious to the drone of the aircraft above and the crump of bombs. That night Nikolaou and his friends broke open a parcel of cakes and cognac that someone's family had sent from Athens.

> Patrols, mud, snow and constant rain [wrote Nikolaou in his diary]. The damned weather has shut us inside our tents and we're all pining for our wives and children. Very bad weather. I've got heart trouble and there's no doctor.[17]

Nikolaou's cardiac preoccupations sent him to a sympathetic medic who diagnosed simple rheumatism, giving him a couple of weeks off duty. Even so on 19 January he had to march with the rest of the regiment to the new advanced II Corps position north of Kelcyre. When they arrived after three hours, enemy shells screamed down, triggering panic. Nikolaou and a couple of his friends holed up in a cave and tried to sleep. The next day he counted lice crawling in his vest. Night and day the booming of Italian artillery echoed over the peaks.

Cavallero, well aware of the open road ahead for the Greeks if they should take Tepelene, kept up the opposing pressure with nine divisions – four of them relatively fresh and untried – and incessant air and artillery strikes. In the race for reinforcements and supplies the Italians had the upper hand. Cavallero calculated that after a month or so more of heavy winter he could concentrate a hammer head against the Greek II Corps line. Earlier in the month he had dismissed Soddu's pessimistic suggestion that the Italians give up Vlore and form a defence on the Shkumbin River some 80km to the north and almost at the gates of Tirana. Cavallero – as of 13 January the official commander-in-chief in Albania – intended to hang on to the port of Vlore at all costs and retake Kelcyre if possible.

Mussolini continued to snow Cavallero with aggressive memos. Every day that a counterattack on the Greeks was delayed, the Duce fretted, the Germans' opinion of Italian arms was deteriorating. 'This action,' the Duce urged, 'must be begun and conducted with extreme energy, and must *eliminate every motive for the world's speculation on Italian military prestige.*'[18] This, again, was the Italian strategic motivation – nothing more than staving off military shame! In the same message Mussolini claimed that Germany 'is ready to send a division' to Albania, but it would be his 'desire and certainty' that Cavallero's efforts would render such proferred help superfluous. In closing, Mussolini strangely appeared to have learned some sort of lesson after all: 'The battles of modern armies are too complex to be directed from afar.'

To be fair to the bedevilled Duce, he may well have felt stirrings of remorse for his cavalier dismissal of the Italian soldier as too soft. Partly in compensation he spent increasing amounts of time in a spartan farmhouse near Bisceglie in the heel of Italy, about equidistant from Rome and Albania, but with less than ideal communications with either. This way he believed he was, to some infinitesimal degree, sharing the privations of his troops. He was not a happy man. Ciano, his son-in-law and foreign minister, was in a blacker mood still, knowing full well that he had been the most gung-ho proponent of the attack on Greece and that the Italian people were not forgetting that uncomfortable fact; if ever a man had egg on his face, it was Ciano.

There was also unmistakable patronizing from the Germans. General Enno von Rintelen, the German military attaché in Rome, had made more than one trip to the Albanian front and had come away with questionable impressions. The German suggestion was to change the direction of the offensive. Instead of butting its brains out in the centre, the Italian army should switch its attention to the northeast in the Korce sector, with the Ninth Corps joining with a German alpine division to move on Florina and Thessaloniki, coordinating with a German drive from the Bulgarian frontier – a plan dubbed

'Operation Cyclamen'. It was a good plan, but Mussolini, and every other Italian who valued his pride, realized it would relegate the Italians to a mere auxiliary force, as was already happening in North Africa. Operation Cyclamen was quietly dropped.

Cavallero, of course, needed no prodding from higher up. But try as he might, he couldn't untangle the chronic disorganization in the Italian commands. On the left of the front stood the Ninth Corps and Third Corps (Piemonte, Taro, Arezzo and Venezia Divisions), in the centre was the Twenty-sixth Corps with three divisions (Tridentina, Parma and Cuneo). From the centre to the right of the front, in that order, stood the Eleventh and Fourth Corps (Pusteria, Pinerolo, Bari, Julia and Wolves of Tuscany), the Eighth Corps (with a single division, the battered Siena, due for reserve status around Berat), the Twenty-fifth Corps (Brennero, Centauro, Ferrara and Modena) and a special corps under General Messe positioned to block a Greek advance on Vlore. Facing the Greek I Corps were fresh Blackshirt battalions and the 3rd and 110th Machine Gun Battalions dug in north of Himare. The Italian navy operated virtually unhindered off the coast, shelling the Greek positions. It was all very impressive on paper. But when in reality the *Cacciatori degli Alpi* (Alpine Hunters, 22nd Division) with their skis tried to take some peaks of the Trebescines they found it tough going. The 300-strong Monte Cervino ski battalion found its maps almost useless in the snowy wilds. One consequence of the frequent confusion in the Italian formations was that the front-line divisions were daily bleeding prisoners. One day Private Nikolaou looked up to see 400 prisoners being led away; the next day's catch was double that. (There was also the occasional other, more sinister, procession – of Greek soldiers convicted of cowardice. On Epiphany Day Nikolaou watched nineteen being marched to the rear, five of them to be shot, the rest to be locked up for the rest of their natural lives.)

On 18 January the Duce called to the Palazzo Venezia Colonel Salvatore Bartiromo, Cavallero's deputy chief of staff. The Greeks had eliminated the Italian salient around Kelcyre and he demanded to know why. 'You have to move,' Mussolini urged. 'Grab the enemy's attention, give up this passivity.'

'Yes,' Bartiromo replied dully and dutifully.

'You've got the divisions.'

'The divisions are not complete.'

In reply to Mussolini's question about the number of men taken prisoner, Bartiromo admitted that the 77 Regiment of the Wolves of Tuscany was missing. (In fact, most of its men had been rounded up by the Greeks at one stroke.)

'Bartiromo!' the Duce snapped, interrupting the hapless staff colonel's excuses. 'There's only one way. Attack! Attack! I've been telling you this for two weeks.'

'I know that His Excellency Cavallero has that desire,' Bartiromo replied in the best administrative waffle, 'but something is always missing, in this case munitions.'

After a brief exchange about the whereabouts of the munitions ships Mussolini returned to the theme: 'Bartiromo, you must counterattack, break this spell that for the past ninety days has made us lose territory. We'll end up in the sea. The Greeks will soon reach the Shkumbin River.'

'No time must be lost,' Bartiromo agreed.

Mussolini had his reasons for being impatient. The following day he was to travel to Salzburg to meet Hitler. 'I'm going to Germany,' he told Bartiromo. 'The first thing they're going to ask me is whether I'm going to stop at the actual line. What am I supposed to answer?' The good staff officer, of course, had no clear answer, and so the Duce dismissed him and set out for Salzburg, 'dark in countenance and nervous,' as Ciano noticed him. The fate of the crack Wolves of Tuscany particularly depressed him. According to Ciano he was wont to murmur to himself at times: 'If anyone on 15 October [the date of the crucial war meeting] had forecast what has actually happened, I'd have had him shot.'[19]

At Salzburg Hitler at least had the courtesy of masking his contempt for his failed Axis partner. Mussolini returned to Rome pondering the possibility of achieving some face-saving victory before the Germans felt obliged to step in. What he found, instead, were more messages of reverses and disorganization from Cavallero. But by the end of February, Cavallero reckoned, twenty-five divisions in good condition would be in place and a move could be made on Korce to improve the Italian position for an expected Italian-German offensive in northern Greece in the spring.

Before that could be achieved, though, the Greek position around Kelcyre needed to be cleared. The Twenty-fifth Corps, spearheaded by the newly-arrived 58th Legnano Division, counterattacked on 25 January, backed up by the Centauro's armour and twenty-six battalions straddling the Dhrin River. But many of these battalions contained green troops who broke against the stout Greek defence. The following day, the Italians launched a pincer movement on Kelcyre from the west and south. The western thrust made progress almost to the main Kelcyre-Berat road, while the southern thrust surprised the Greek lines which, however, only just held. Nikolaou watched the action unfold:

> Today we saw our first battle at close quarters, right across from us on the Klissura [Kelcyre] peak. In the snow the Italians made their attack that continued until 2 o'clock. You could see our artillery just mowing them down. The battle is still going on.[20]

Kelcyre seemed safe for the time being but Papadopoulos, the II Corps Commander, was worried about the new Italian pocket west of the town. The 42 Evzones and other units were coming under constant air and artillery attack. Demestichas of the I Corps was also worried about his own right; he sought, and received, permission to transfer the units defending Kelcyre to his own corps to better coordinate the action.

The Italians threw themselves in vain against the Kelcyre sector for four more days, not making any progress but denying the Greeks any progress of their own. On the morning of 29 January the Greeks were making an effort in the driving snow to secure some peaks of the Trebescines range when news arrived from Athens that stunned the army and changed the whole game.

Through the winter Metaxas had not been in the best of health. His diary for the period is full of pessimistic and fatigued entries. On 4 January he despaired over the equivocal British attitude: 'From the British abandonment, from the Germans aggression.' Three days later: 'How can I describe all the examples of love and devotion? But I'm not exalting myself. I remain humble, and the only great one is God, and in Greece her people.'

The British alliance to him was now developing into a dangerous two-edged sword. Churchill was clinging to his dream of a powerful Balkan front that would include not only Yugoslavia but also Turkey and perhaps even Bulgaria. But Turkey was already heavily involved in an intricate diplomatic game that would keep it neutral throughout the war, while Yugoslavia was by no means as secure as Churchill imagined. On 15 January Heywood had suggested sending one British anti-aircraft regiment and a tank company to Thessaloniki. In a meeting with Metaxas he had turned up the heat.

> You have completely opposite views to our government' [Heywood told Metaxas]. He repeated it three times during a long but smooth discussion in which I [Metaxas] carried the day. I assured him that we will never make a separate peace and we will fight to win, but for our honour only. That [otherwise] we would prefer to be destroyed. Palairet shook my hand. Wavell congratulated me. Both very moved.[21]

Metaxas' combative spirit – all too rare among leaders in any age – certainly moved the soldier in Wavell, but the less savoury political side had the upper hand in London's calculations. Metaxas, for all his resolve, couldn't help wondering with a corner of his strategic mind whether the British might have a point after all. From the same diary entry, later that evening:

> Dead tired. I've done my duty. A thought occurs to me. If we maybe brought even a small force to Thessaloniki would we draw the Balkans with us? Would we? We would not, because everyone knows England's weakness! But ... should we not try it anyway? A terrible dilemma. But

what can I do? The Germans, even if they are quiet now, will start again in the spring. Let's wait. If the British had even five divisions available with ample mechanical equipment ... But they have nothing.

Metaxas was right about the precariousness of Yugoslavia. The following day he received a message from Prince Paul of Yugoslavia to the effect that the prince was prepared to resist the Germans if they crossed the Danube; however, if the British moved up to Thessaloniki he would 'revoke this pledge'. The message from Belgrade, at least, was clear. 'This evening very melancholy,' Metaxas wrote. On the following day, 17 January, the pressure was beginning to tell:

> The British insist on coming to Thessaloniki with small artillery forces. Am working out my diplomatic actions. I assured Paul of Yugoslavia there will be no British front at Thessaloniki unless the Germans cross the Danube and enter Bulgaria. Told the British (first Palairet and then Heywood) not to come to Thessaloniki with small forces unless the Germans cross the Danube. The issue may end here. Worked till late at night. Nana [his ailing wife] is better.

On 18 January Metaxas addressed a formal letter to the British government, delivered through Palairet. His mind was made up. He would stick to his guns.

> We are resolved to meet, in every way at whatever sacrifice, any German attack, but in no way do we intend to provoke it, unless Great Britain could supply us the required aid in Macedonia ... The proffered aid (24 field guns,12 heavy artillery pieces, about 40 anti-aircraft guns and 65 light and medium tanks) is completely inadequate, especially in the total absence of infantry. [This force] would amount to a provocation that would entail an immediate German attack against us.[22]

In view of Paul's hesitations, Metaxas suggested that Britain re-think its whole northern Greece plan in such a way as to 'avoid the attention of the Germans'. He also said Allied air cover over northern Greek disembarkation ports would have to be substantially boosted. He ended the letter by saying that Britain's forces in the Middle East could in no way solve the strategic problem presented by the Balkans. 'We will do our duty to the end. It is up to the British government now to take into account our suggestions which come from devoted and faithful friends.'

This, even more than 28 October 1940, was Metaxas' finest hour. His iron sense of honour and duty shines through like a burnished Spartan shield. He had made up his mind that the British were essentially unable to help Greece effectively and that the British proposals would actually make matters worse for his country. Of course, he could not repudiate the British alliance. But his disappointment with Britain's weakness and occasional duplicity runs like a bitter thread through his diary entries and his letter to London.

'The issue may end here,' Metaxas had written in his diary on 17 January. That sentence came true for him in a way he would never have expected, for it was his last diary entry ever. The next day he arrived at the Grande Bretagne headquarters complaining of a sore throat. His doctor gave him some medicine and suggested he take the day off. He refused and worked until 3.00 pm, perhaps drafting the noble yet sad letter to the British government. The next week he spent at home trying to recuperate from what was diagnosed as a throat infection. The infection turned into an abscess that aggravated an old kidney condition caused by a bad tooth.

With the kidneys knocked out, septicaemia set in and Metaxas sank into a coma. Before slipping away he is said to have murmured: 'My hopes [rest] with the Greeks.' Ioannis Metaxas died at dawn on 29 January.[23]

The news plunged Greece into shock. Here was the saviour of their country, felled by a common microbe at the height of the struggle and at the very pinnacle of his fame. His final illness had been kept from the people, which made the shock all the greater. As the nation grieved, the king quickly appointed a former central banker named Alexander Koryzis to fill the vacuum as prime minister.

Prince Peter and Colonel Blunt got the news as soon as they arrived in Ioannina that evening from their tour of the front. The prince at once saw Papagos, who assured him that the war plans would continue unchanged. The C-in-C never ceased to be suspicious of what the British were up to. He feared that the shadowy Major Barbrook, in particular, was scheming to go across to Thessaloniki clandestinely and intended to do all in his power to stop him and others of his ilk.

Chapter 8

Apocalypse On Hill 731: The Spring Offensive

Greek morale is dealt a blow – battles in the snow – new setback for the Julia at Mecgorane – Anglo-Greek friction – the punching-bag prince – Eden fails with Turkey – 'Mr Watt' – Mussolini's fresh hopes – the Spring Offensive – the Duce flies to the front – carnage on Hill 731 – coup in Yugoslavia – reasons for Greek successes

It would be hard to overestimate the anticlimactic impact of Metaxas' death. The diminutive but sturdy prime minister-cum-dictator had embodied the country's struggle as no-one else had. It was simply taken for granted how important a symbol he was. It was his ringing defiance in the lonely wee hours of 28 October, his iron determination and the overwhelming sense of national rightness, that had given wings to the Greek troops' feet for three giddy months of incessant victory, had kept the men going in the face of obstacles and hardships that would have utterly broken up an army with a lesser degree of morale, as the Italians had found out the hard way. Now, under the grey wintry skies, whom could the Greeks look up to as their protector? A mild-mannered banker? Who would supply the leadership now that the Germans were looming more dangerously by the day? And what would the leader's fall do to the morale of the troops in Albania? In one sudden tragic twist of microbial misfortune, Greece's greatest war asset was no more.

To delve into the various conspiracy theories that inevitably arose around the death of Metaxas would be beyond the purview of this book. The Italians at once blamed the British for doing away with him, as he had been the prime obstacle to Churchill's grand plan for a Balkan front. The line was repeated by the Germans and by communist movements during and after the war. As in most theories of this kind, there can be no definitive proof or disproof. Suffice it to say that there is not a shred of evidence that would implicate Britain in eliminating a national leader who not only had his people with him but also had earned the admiration of the great bulk of public opinion in the Allied world.

Up in the snowbound II Corps on 30 January, Miltiades Nikolaou, now a corporal, heard 'a rumour' that Metaxas had died. 'I don't know how true it is, but it has really had a big effect on the army's morale,' he wrote. Of more concern to him was the plague of tormenting lice which didn't let him sleep. The snow was 10ft deep on Mount Trebescines. Mule trains were immobilized, while valley bridges were swept away by raging rivers. Supplies became scarce and frostbite cases multiplied.

Papagos, meanwhile, had transferred his general staff from the comforts of the Grande Bretagne Hotel in Athens to the relative rigours of Ioannina, to be near the front. With every day that passed, and now Metaxas was gone, the chances mounted that the Germans would attack through Bulgaria. For the past three months Papagos had been gradually denuding the defences on the Bulgarian border to beef up the Albania offensive. Now was the time to put some of them back. By a string of orders on 6 and 7 February Papagos packaged the I and II Corps into a larger unit, the Epiros Army Department, made up of a total of nine divisions: the 1st, 2nd, 3rd, 4th, 5th, 8th, 11th, 15th and 18th. Placed in command of the Epiros Army Department was Lieutenant General Markos Drakos with authority to coordinate operations on the left and centre, leaving Papagos to concentrate on the right of the front up to Bulgaria. One of Drakos' first orders was for Kosmas' I Corps to advance to form a junction with the II Corps left at Mount Trebescines where an enemy offensive was expected and the Greek line most tenuous.

The opposing lines in Albania had by now become snowed up. What little action there was consisted of rectifications to parts of the lines. Papagos set the starting date for an advance to consolidate the Kelcyre sector for 13 February, hoping the worst of the winter would be over by then. As the II Corps would need its 5th Division reserve for the task, the 17th Division would be transferred as a reserve from Korce, to be replaced there by the 6th Division 'borrowed' from the West Macedonia Army Department. The date for the advance arrived, but with no let-up in the weather. Nonetheless, over the hesitations of the staff of the 5th Division, the division's 43 Regiment inched forward to seize a few more of the endless peaks of Trebescines, known to the officers only as numbers (heights in metres) and the number of men lost in securing them. On one of those, known only as Hill 1178, Greeks and Italians alike lost several hundred men without any clear tactical advantage. Some battalions took twelve hours to trudge through ever-driving snow to reach an objective that was just a strange name on a map. The Italian 59th Cagliari Division and the 7, 16, 29, 30 and 85 Blackshirt battalions resisted every step of the way with considerable losses. Within five days the 5th Division's offensive fizzled out and the situation along Trebescines was just as stalemated as before. And the prize of Vlore was no nearer than before.

While this was in progress new Italian units were being fed to various sectors of the front. Mostly they were Blackshirt units: the 24th Legion on the Greek I Corps front, the 112 Battalion and 36th Forli Division in the

Pogradec sector, and the 1 Customs Guard Battalion and 93 Blackshirts plus the 1st Torino Alpine Division on the Mount Tomori front near the centre. By now Lieutenant Antolini, the nervous subaltern of the 5 Alpine, was commanding a platoon of Special Forces *arditi*. In early February he received orders to move northeast to a new position along the Guri i Topit mountain range. The move was made, of course, on foot, 'in mud almost chest-high'. They spent the first night shivering on the tombstones of a cemetery infested with giant rats. The problem when Antolini and his men arrived at Guri i Topit was that the Greeks were already holding the heights. 'The Greeks are on top and we're below,' Antolini wrote in his diary. 'Not a good situation to be in.' Yet the fact that he had been able to reach his position in the first place was encouraging. 'I believe the Greeks haven't got many weapons left, otherwise they would have driven us all off.' Yet, as so often, the enemy was of less concern than the brutal weather:

> We're living in ever more inhuman conditions, badly dressed [Antolini wrote on 10 February]. Last night's blizzard piled up so much snow as to make provisioning impossible. We're on reduced rations.[1]

Greek attempts to take a few more strategic heights were hurled back. Drakos, the Epiros Army Department commander, told the C-in-C frankly that Tepelene could not be taken by the II Corps in its present state of exhaustion, and it would take at least three weeks to replace three of the most fatigued divisions. Papagos would not hear of it, and Drakos found himself replaced as Epiros Army Department commander by Lieutenant General Pitsikas, transferred from command of the West Macedonia Army Department. Tsolakoglou of the III Corps was put in Pitsikas' place, and the corps itself temporarily disbanded, its divisions being placed under the control of the Army Departments directly.

Papagos' motives are not hard to divine. Typically, he makes no mention of them in his stony memoirs. But for some time now he had been aware of the constant enemy build-up, observed from the air and confirmed by intelligence reports. He knew that a new offensive was about to fall on his II Corps front. He could not afford to give an impression of weakness by withdrawing tired divisions and letting up to a month pass to enable the enemy to retrench, as Drakos had suggested. Besides, a few more positions on the road to Vlore would provide a better buttress for the Italian offensive.

One such was the Mecgorane Ridge north of Kelcyre, crawling with the Centauro's light tanks and well-concealed artillery. Major General Anastasios Roussopoulos' 17th Division was given the job of taking it. At nightfall on 2 March a team of sappers began to dig an anti-tank ditch 10ft deep and 20ft wide across the main Kelcyre-Berat road. At 11.00 pm a small detachment crept through the darkness to a hilltop overlooking the ditch. So as not to arouse enemy suspicion, they kept intact the telephone line connecting two Italian outposts on either side of the road. The digging continued into the next day and night, with the Italians of the Julia Division suspecting nothing. At 11.00 pm the first Italian tank, trundling towards the outposts with supplies, tumbled into the ditch. At that moment the enemy telephone line was cut. Three soldiers sent to repair it found themselves staring down Greek gun barrels.

The Italian command at Mecgorane sent teams to find out what was amiss. The patrols were repulsed in a flurry of midnight fire. The following morning, 4 March, another Centauro tank avoided falling into the ditch at the last moment; by now the Italians were aware of the Greek trap but could do little about it. A battalion-strength unit sent to clear the road found itself outnumbered and surrendered after a token skirmish. Three tanks were captured, and the Greeks were now in control of 9km of main road north of Kelcyre. Girotti writhed with shame at this new setback for the Julia. 'This unhappy event,' he wrote cringingly in a subsequent general order, 'shows that the required vigilance at all times was not shown, and it is thus a lesson for the future.'[2]

But Mecgorane Ridge was still in Italian hands, and at 9.00 am on 7 March, after an artillery barrage, the 17th Division surged forward in two columns. By 10.45 am the advance troops had come within a kilometre and a half of the ridge, and by 6.30 pm it was in Greek hands. Greek shelling wrought havoc among the Italian troops, more than a thousand of whom, including twenty officers, were trudged off to the POW camps, for a Greek casualty figure of less than a hundred. For two more days the snow and ice on the slopes of Mecgorane Ridge was churned up by Greek and Italian shells as the Julia clung stubbornly to one height.

The problem of the sheer number of Italian prisoners was becoming acute. Most were in camps, but some were sent out to farms to help with the work and that way earn some of their bread. Among them were about 500 officers who by the terms of the Geneva Convention could not be put to work. The British Military Mission wanted to ship the officers off to India where the possibility of escape would be minimal. The Greek General Staff claimed that this would violate the Geneva Convention and insisted, correctly, that all Italian prisoners captured by Greek forces should remain in Greek hands.[3]

On the same day as the attack on Mecgorane Ridge, the I Corps tried to gain new positions on the left of the front, but was halted on the western slope of Mount Goriko. Both sides hurled grenades at each other, the one furiously charging, the other furiously defending. The Greeks noticed one Italian soldier upright in his rank.

[He was] fighting like a mad dog, throwing hand grenades one after the other. Then a Greek artillery shell burst next to him, blowing him sky-high. Everywhere, right and left, men were hit and falling, the Italian machine guns mowing them down, it was a savage and hard thing to see.[4]

A Greek mortar platoon located the Italian machine gun nest, opened up on it and silenced it, though the risk of hitting Greek troops was great. At 3.00 pm the Greeks became dimly aware of a familiar and welcome sound through the din of combat: *'Aera!'* – the Greeks' mountain battle-cry. A Greek battalion had wormed its way behind the Italian line on Mount Goriko and was attacking it from the rear. Within minutes the fight was over. Few realized it at the time, but Mount Goriko was the last Greek military offensive success in the Second World War. Papagos, for his part, could only hope that he had enough front-line units and reserves in place before the counter-blow fell.

With Metaxas suddenly out of the picture, Heywood renewed the pressure for a British military presence in Greek Macedonia with almost indecent haste – on the day after Metaxas' funeral, in fact. Prince Peter found himself in his usual role as the harassed middleman fending off mutual British and Greek suspicions. For example, the Greek high command asked the British to shut down their transmitting station at Ioannina on the grounds that it was being abused to send news to British newspapers and other media organizations. Every other day an RAF bomber would crash and the relatives of the victims notified. Then a shipment of 100,000 shells would arrive when the order had been for just 37,000, and that had to be sorted out. There was the indefatigable Major Reid, whose 'Phantom' H Squadron was still swanning about in the countryside under the impression that it was making itself useful. A very poor impression was made by D'Albiac's number two, Air Commodore John Grigson, DSO, a former commander of 55 Squadron, who one day burst into Prince Peter's office livid with anger because, by a clerical error, a request for more RAF planes had been wrongly addressed to Wavell instead of to Longmore – an error that already had been corrected, but Grigson, in an appalling lack of respect for his Greek hosts, not to mention royalty, had barked at Peter as if he were the lowliest aircraftman. 'We have absolutely no connection with the army and you should understand that!' he screamed. Precious service independence apparently meant more to this officer than fighting the enemy. (The prince got his own back later when Grigson mistakenly forwarded a message through him to the Greek air ministry on an army matter. Lifting the phone, Peter told the air commodore of the mistake, adding primly: 'You are aware, I believe, that the air force has nothing to do with the army, and that matters pertaining to the latter cannot be handled by the former.' Grigson had the good grace to laugh and admit he deserved it.)

The German threat was now becoming more concrete by the day. The friendly Turkish military attaché passed on a tip that the Germans had now amassed 450,000 men in Romania and had painted their tanks white for camouflage against the snow. Spies, real or imagined, were always a problem. Wing Commander Lord Forbes, the British air attaché, was astounded to be told that his Greek valet was a double agent in the pay of the Axis and was being closely watched. On the other hand there were extremely helpful British officers such as Major Peter Smith Dorrien (the son of Sir Horace Smith Dorrien who had commanded a corps in France in 1914) who did much to smooth the occasional ruffled feelings between allies.[5]

The British preoccupation with northern Greece sometimes surfaced in odd ways. In the middle of February four British 'malaria specialists' turned up claiming to wish to study the mosquito-borne disease in Greece. International medical institutes had been looking into the matter in previous years, with the result that northern Greece had been malaria-free for a long time. What, then, did these fellows want? The darkest suspicions were entertained by Major Athanasios Korozis, a staff officer, who yelled, 'The British and their demands can all go to the devil!' when asked to stamp the permits of the 'malaria team', which he did anyway. Few realized at the time that Korozis was secretly pro-German, a role that emerged into the open when he formed part of the team that negotiated the armistice with the Germans a couple of months later. Yet it illustrates how nerves in Athens were fraying in the opening months of 1941, as Greeks and British tried in their own ways to delay the inevitable.

Endless problems, most of them petty, strained the liaison office. Prince Peter was in the middle of pondering the 'malaria' issue when he had another turbulent visit from the excitable and buffoonish Grigson who again excoriated him for – shock horror – asking for aircraft from the British army (even though the issue had long since been settled), and then from a senior Greek Orthodox bishop who bizarrely demanded a staff car in order to stir up pro-Greek agitation in southern Albania with the hope of annexing the area to Greece; even more bizarrely, he managed to get one, courtesy of D'Albiac. Then Colonel Stanley Casson of the British Military Mission demanded 'an investigation' after overhearing the Danish ambassador singing what 'sounded like German songs' in a restaurant – the 'German songs' turned out to be harmless Danish folk ditties. And on it went. Small wonder that on occasion the prince was heartily sick of his punching-bag job.[6]

Papagos, besides keeping his long-suffering men on the offensive in Albania, was worried about defeatist sentiment supposedly emanating from careless talk among the British in Athens. At least that's what King George thought, uncomfortably aware of the appeasement sentiments still lingering among the British upper classes and personified by ex-King Edward VIII and Lord

Halifax. The British Military Mission, for its part, blamed German diplomats and 'rich Athenians who care for nothing else but to keep their wealth'. Or did the British know something the Greeks didn't? A further blow to national morale broke on 17 February, with the news that Turkey and Bulgaria had signed a nonaggression pact. On the heels of that came an announcement that Sir Anthony Eden, the British Foreign Secretary, Lieutenant General Sir John Dill, the chief of the Imperial General Staff, Wavell and Longmore were about to descend on Athens to push for a common stand on what to do about the German threat.

The 'big guns' conference took place on the evening of 22 February at the royal palace at Tatoi. Eden reacted with irritation to King George's suggestion that he meet privately with Koryzis – he was there, he said, to discuss military, not political, issues. But in the end Eden agreed to a meeting. Koryzis read him a dignified statement according to which Greece was committed to fighting on, and that any British aid would have to be realistic and strong enough to confront a German offensive. Beyond that, the forty-eight-hour Tatoi meeting accomplished little. Each side took away what it thought it heard, or wanted to believe. Eden rightly took a dim view of possible Yugoslav support for Greece but there appears to have been no clear agreement on what British and Greek forces could do together if Germany attacked through Bulgaria.

Towards the end of February Papagos gave reluctant approval for Major Reid and his H Squadron 'Phantoms' to finally venture into northern Greece, though only as far as the Strymon River. He was not to be allowed anywhere near the Metaxas Line. To make sure he complied with the order, a Greek intelligence major was sent with him.

On 26 February H Squadron set out on its latest schoolboy stunt. To Prince Peter, seeing them off, the spectacle was laughable.

> They were all wearing half civilian dress, half uniforms, seemingly acting with great secrecy, which to me appeared absurd but really alarmed the respectable but suspicious major [who was accompanying them] ... Miles Reid knew French and spoke in that language to everyone ... but in such an officious tone as to be infuriating. The 'circus' got under way soon afterwards, while a crowd had gathered to enjoy the spectacle.[7]

It was now all but certain that Churchill would finally have his way and send a British expeditionary force to northern Greece. The tenor of the meetings with Eden and Wavell, not to mention the private intelligence that the king was obtaining from London, all pointed in that direction. Reports from North Africa indicated that a new and vigorous German general, Erwin Rommel, was reorganizing the Axis forces there and preparing to wipe out the British gains against the Italians. The Wehrmacht's Fifth Army, according to Casson, was about to enter Bulgaria from the north. And then, at dawn on 1 March, the news broke that the Wehrmacht had burst into Bulgaria and was rolling south towards the Greek border. War with Germany was now a virtual certainty.

The next day Smith Dorrien asked Prince Peter to try and locate Miles Reid's outfit, as it had been ordered to return to Athens forthwith – and by air, to save time. Reid and his Phantoms were at Kilkis near the Bulgarian border, a fact not likely to assuage Papagos' lingering and not entirely unjustified suspicion that Axis agents in the area would have noticed Reid's unit and blown the whistle to the Germans. The Phantoms were airlifted back the following day. Eden, meanwhile, had stopped over in Athens after a futile visit to Ankara, and on 4 March sat down to 'a gloomy luncheon' at the British Embassy in the company of King George, Koryzis and Papagos. No-one spoke much.

Eden was right to be put out. Turkey was Churchill's wild card, and it was being played against him. Turkey had been a party to a military alliance with Britain and France. But twice when the alliance was supposed to kick in – with the Italian attack on France in June 1940 and invasion of Greece in October – Ankara on various pretexts had remained neutral. Eden's latest attempt to get the Turks 'on side' for a south-eastern European shield against Axis aggression had failed. Much as Turkish diplomats might admire the Greek military achievement in Albania, they felt no obligation to do their bit in the east. Their reaction to Churchill's appeal, in fact, was one of pure timidity. The Turks claimed to have no modern air force to oppose the Luftwaffe with. Besides, German forces were as yet nowhere near Turkish frontiers, so Ankara could afford to play the waiting game.[8]

Though the British reaction to Turkish wiliness was one of incomprehension and fury, Eden should have known better. It would have been a tall order for the Turks, a proud people with long memories, to forget their enmity against Great Britain, which had stripped them of their Ottoman Empire at the close of the First World War, helped unseat the last of the sultans and, as if that were not enough, had given military aid to the Greeks in their drive to seize western Turkey in 1920–22. If they were to join the side, the Turks demanded a high price: control of Thessaloniki (and by extension the Aegean Sea) plus territory in the Dodecanese islands and even Albania. A good many British diplomats were prepared to give them all that on a plate, but fortunately for Greece, wiser counsel prevailed in Whitehall.[9] Turkey continued to play off the Germans against the British and in fact managed to stay out of the war completely.

The appearance of British troops at Piraeus was expected daily. Bulgarian and Yugoslav attachés were reported going down to the port and waiting at the docksides. The British Military Mission wanted to requisition two more main hotels. Prince Peter and Smith Dorrien were put to work on a hush-hush project involving one 'Mr Watt', who was to be driven over parts of Greece. Very few people knew that 'Mr Watt' was in fact Lieutenant General Henry Maitland 'Jumbo' Wilson, the commander of the soon-to-arrive British expeditionary force, who wanted to take a personal look at the terrain as unobtrusively as possible. The secret was well-kept. 'Watt' conferred with Papagos on 6 March while staff officers pondered the logistical problems of sending the British force north by train.

The growing jitters in Athens manifested themselves in curious ways. On 7 March one Mrs Preston, an Englishwoman serving as secretary to a British logistics major, asked if she could speak privately to Prince Peter. Mrs Preston had been living in Athens a long time. Nervously she asked the prince to close the door and then blurted out: 'I've seen the Virgin Mary, and she asked me to talk to you.'

'Oh, and what else did she say?' the prince replied unperturbed.

'She said,' Mrs Preston continued excitedly, 'that now that Metaxas is dead, the king must take over the government, and if he does, we'll surely win.'

The prince thanked her and assured her he would pass on her message to the king. The episode, however, deepened his eerie sense of doom. That evening he dined at the Glyfada Golf Club, alone with his troubled thoughts.

> Would we resist an attack, or capitulate like France? I asked myself this, and as I strolled along the beach alone after the meal I made a vow to myself that if Greece were to surrender, I would do what General de Gaulle did and continue the fight with whomever would follow me, creating a 'Free Greece' movement like de Gaulle's 'Free France'.[10]

A few occurrences did lighten the atmosphere. One of them involved an unexpected and comic result of 'Mr Watt's' disguise. As Smith Dorrien related it to a delighted liaison office, Wilson in his civvies was about to inspect an Australian 6th Division camp when he was stopped by a tall and rangy Aussie sentry. 'What exactly is it you want?' the guard asked roughly, barring the way in. Wilson calmly replied that he wanted to tour the camp, whereupon the Australian burst out laughing. 'What would you know about these things, mate?' he said, playfully slapping 'Jumbo' Wilson's prominent paunch and very likely adding some mild obscenity. Chagrined, yet unable to reveal his identity, 'Mr Watt' had to humbly back off. (In the absence of any confirming version, this story, though very likely true, must be considered technically apocryphal.)

Preparations for a new front proceeded apace. Papagos ordered plans to be in place to blow up vulnerable road and rail bottlenecks such as that winding through the Vale of Tempe in the shadow of Mount Olympus. The demolition task was given to the 2nd New Zealand Division of Major General

Bernard Freyberg. Prince Peter's own gloom deepened when his wife telephoned from Istanbul to tell him she had miscarried. He could only comfort her with the words that they were still both relatively young and could have other children if they survived the war. (In fact, they remained childless.) The prince learned that the king was thinking of fleeing to America if Greece fell. Peter confronted the king to ask him if it was true. The sovereign was in the throes of anguish. Should he give himself up to enemy captivity, like King Leopold of Belgium and King Christian of Denmark, or flee like the monarchs of Norway and the Netherlands? Peter told him there was no sense in giving himself up and that he personally intended to get out. The king suggested adding Prince Peter to his staff in that case. The idea of going to America was dropped.

Mussolini, meanwhile, took heart from the German preparations. Addressing a meeting of Fascist party officials in Rome on 23 February, he left no doubt of what was in his mind.

> Let it be said once and for all that the Italian soldiers in Albania have fought superbly; let it be said in particular that the Alpini have written pages of blood and glory that would do honour to any army. When the the story of the march of the Julia almost to Metsovo can be told, it will seem like a legend.[11]

This was, of course, mere puffery. True, the Italians had fought courageously – in fact, better than their detractors had a right to expect – but the Duce's true concern lay elsewhere. It was obvious to everyone by now that Germany was about to invade Greece to finish the job Italy had begun. Mussolini, as a result, would not be able to avoid a loss of face. To avoid such opprobrium he would have to coordinate a new attack of his own with the German assault, an attack which would have a far better chance of success this time. A victory for Italian arms, however belated, would give Rome the legitimation it required for an occupation of Greece, even if it should happen in the wake of Hitler's tanks.

> Think of the Punic Wars [the Duce reminded his hearers]. Cannae seemed to have shattered Rome. But at Zama Rome destroyed Carthage and rubbed it off the map and out of history for ever. Our capacity for recovery in the moral and material sectors is simply formidable, and constitutes one of the specific characteristics of our race.[12]

Mussolini concluded his rambling speech by praising the power and endurance of the German armed forces as 'infinitely superior' to what they had been at the beginning of the war. He derided Britain for appealing to the United States for aid (which he believed would never materialize), and confidently predicted an Axis victory in which Italy would have 'a role in the front rank'.

The speech displays a subtle shift in Mussolini's thinking. For the first three months of the war on Greece he had in turns been patronized and humiliated by Hitler, whose military analysts had not hidden their scorn for the way in which the Epiros and Albania campaigns had been conducted. Now, towards the end of February 1941, we find him praising the Germans to the high heavens and renewing the breast-beating that had been missing so conspicuously earlier in the winter when the news from Albania had been invariably bad. Had he finally realized that the only way he could politically survive an all-but-lost war was by chaining himself to Hitler? Yet he also desperately needed to show his people, at least, that his military could still win battles. Hence the elaborately-planned and much-bruited Spring Offensive (*Offensiva di Primavera*), scheduled to spring into action on 9 March.

Unlike Badoglio and to a certain extent Soddu, Ugo Cavallero didn't expend too much grey matter in cogitation over whether the war was 'right' or even winnable. He was a scientific soldier tasked with a specific mission – roll back the Greek gains in Albania. And that's what he would do, period. 'The troops fighting on the Greek-Albanian front,' he messaged the Duce, 'commanders, officers and men alike, have heard your words with profound pride, animated by a single ideal, sacrifice, and by a single will, to win!' The words sound curious coming from a general officer considered to be one of the more level-headed and competent in the Italian military. Did Cavallero really believe his own bombast? It may have been a typically flamboyant Mediterranean mode of addressing a political superior, but Cavallero's optimism was not totally unfounded. If there was anything resembling an original thinker in the Italian army, it was he. The Greeks, he reasoned, were already expecting a counterattack, and on the principle that attacks were normally made at the enemy's perceived weakest point, they would expect Cavallero to make a thrust, say, in the Korce sector. Instead, he would hit where the Greeks least expected – at the strongest part of their front where the II Corps had been making stubborn inroads in the Kelcyre sector, and consequently would be fatigued from the effort.

Cavallero's bold plan was viewed with mistrust by General Alfredo Guzzoni, the former commander in Albania who was now the undersecretary for war, and whose opinion counted for something. Guzzoni argued for an attack by the Ninth Corps on the pivot of the Greek scythe at Pogradec, to hopefully knock the pivot from its bearings and punch a new salient that would outflank the Greek right, forcing the rest of the Greek line to pull back. Guzzoni had support from Mussolini, who had moved back to his spare 'campaign' headquarters at Bisceglie and was badgering Cavallero for 'an offensive in the grand style and with profound objectives'. But Cavallero was not to be rushed. The Italian Army was nowhere near organized enough for such a coordinated drive. He argued instead for a limited but concentrated action in the centre, to be led by the Eighth Corps, now under the command of General Gastone Gambara. Such an action would also hopefully relieve the enemy pressure on Vlore, which had to be kept at all costs. Only in the centre did Cavallero have a strong enough formation to give the Spring Offensive any chance of success.

After weeks of painstaking preparation, and in the face of persistent Greek nuisance attacks in the centre and left of his line, he had, from left to right, the Fourth, Eighth and Twenty-fifth Corps, with the Eighth to move first. Of twelve infantry divisions available in the sector, seven were to blunt the point of the Greek salient on the Trebescines heights: the 59th Cagliari, the 38th Puglie and the 24th Pinerolo in the first line, and the 47th Bari, the 51st Siena, the 22nd Alpine Hunters and the 131st Armoured Centauro in support. (Gambara had asked also for the Julia, but had been refused.) The morale in these units varied. The soldiers were uncomfortably aware that since the beginning of the campaign nearly 5,800 men had been killed. But it counted with some that Italy's military name had been besmirched, and that the balance needed to be redressed.

That consideration, of course, was uppermost in the mind of the Duce himself, who on 2 March decided to go to the front himself as a latter-day Roman emperor-general to see for himself what was going on, raise the troops' morale, and above all save his own image. He did it by putting a flying overall over his resplendent dress uniform and getting behind the controls of an SM79 bomber at Bari to personally fly to Tirana, escorted by two more bombers, two CantZ506 seaplanes and a dozen Macchi MC200 fighters. With him in the cockpit was General Pricolo, the Regia Aeronautica chief, who was to be a keen observer of the Duce's reactions in the days ahead. On hand to greet Mussolini at Tirana were the rotund Cavallero and the equally portly General Ranza, the air force commander in Albania.

Dispensing with the formalities, the Duce wore a preoccupied expression as he got straight into a staff car to be driven to the front. His frown deepened as near Berat he passed a detachment of the Bari on the march and noticed that some of the men's boots were coming apart. His visit to the front had not been announced, but sure enough he was soon recognized, and some of the soldiers began to applaud and cheer. The cheers were redoubled when his car caught up with Siena Division farther south. The Duce stopped to talk to a wounded soldier and wish him a speedy recovery. 'Victory is what is important,' the soldier is reported to have replied with spirit.[13]

> This reception [Cervi writes] revived [the Duce's] morale, as he was very receptive to applause and cheers that made him forget the responsibilities, the failures, the men who died in vain, the frostbite and the disorganization.[14]

Mussolini's small motorcade wound laboriously around marching columns, lorries and ambulances, in scenes that must have reminded him of his own experiences as a *bersagliere* on the Austrian front in the First World War. He would also have been heartened to notice that the march south was being carried out in daylight without fear of enemy air attack. His first stop was at a village house where Gambara had his headquarters. Gambara, one of those officers who made sure to remain in the good books of the Fascist party, strutted and declaimed as he explained his plan of attack to the Duce: while Mercalli's Fourth Corps was to engage the enemy on the left, the Eighth would send the Cagliari Division into the valley towards Kelcyre to get in the Greek rear while the Puglie and Pinerolo would come into the valley behind the Cagliari to mop up Greek resistance. Gambara said he would need 'four or five days' to get the required 50,000 men into position against a maximum 28,000 of the enemy at that point; he would also have a superiority in artillery and aircraft. The Duce listened, his thought processes illuminated by the trademark expressions of 'thrusting his thick lips outwards and rolling his eyes', yet keenly observing his interlocutors' faces for signs of their own inner thoughts. Later that day, as the car progressed, the soldiers' enthusiasm increased until they clung to the doors and running boards of his car in their exuberance and had to be pushed off.

After a night's sleep Mussolini felt better. At General Rossi's Twenty-fifth Corps headquarters he reviewed a regiment of the Wolves of Tuscany and another of the Legnano Division. Their uniforms, he noted, were in order, and their bandages clean. Pricolo noted that more than one soldier shouted: 'We want an offensive, Duce! Just give the order!' But the air force chief suspected, probably correctly, that these were a minority and that much of the supposed adulation was mere pretence. He noticed one man in particular who:

> Remaining apart at the side of the road, continued to eat calmly. He did not look like a very young man, having a strong build and unshaven face. As he lifted his spoon to his mouth he observed his excited comrades, and at times would halt his motion, looking stupefied at the scene which to him was incomprehensible.

When the soldier noticed Pricolo observing him keenly, 'for a moment he continued to eat, then moved slowly, and virtually retreating, was lost to view among the thickets.'

Rossi explained his plan of action to the Duce, who then was driven down into the Vojussa Valley where the rumble of artillery and mortar fire could be heard. Mussolini, however, was concerned about other things. As he was being briefed he suggested that the army issue a press release about his visit to the front. One wonders why such an announcement had not been made public in Italy before that. The simple answer is that cooler minds in the Italian army wanted to wait and see how the Spring Offensive would turn out before alerting the media. Cavallero himself played along with the Duce's enthusiasm, even suggesting that Mussolini himself assume supreme command 'at the right time'. The cautious camp prevailed – as it turned out, wisely. Nothing was told to the Italian public until May, when the entire issue had become academic.

Jacomoni, the Duce's governor in Albania, assured his boss that the Albanian auxiliaries were loyal and full of fight. Cavallero, he gushed, would 'enter history as the saviour of the Greek front'. Thus cheered, Mussolini at 4.00 am on 9 March found himself at what was called Tactical Position 34, a clutch of houses near the air base at Devoli, listening in the pre-dawn darkness to the sounds of an army preparing for a fight, the whinnying of horses and mules, the sounds of engines being started, the milling cacophony of soldiers waking up and preparing themselves for action. Two hours later, as a cold but brilliantly cloudless day was breaking, he climbed agilely up to his observation post at Komarit, about 2,500ft above sea level. The complete lack of cloud meant that the air force would have a field day. The small yard surrounding the sandbagged observation post was crammed with brass – Ranza was there, as well as Geloso, the Eleventh Corps Commander, Gambara in his short *bersagliere* coat, and of course Cavallero. Far below, the Vojussa River glistened like a ribbon of silver.

The mood among Cavallero's men was mixed. Most soldiers, no doubt, were bracing themselves psychologically for the push, acutely aware of the odds involved, trying not to think of past debacles and lost comrades and the icy hells they had been through. True, some were upbeat, especially those who were dedicated fascists. For example, Milan party activists (known as *squadristi*) serving at the front came up with a war ditty:

> *Soon it will fall to us,*
> *Squadristi of Milan,*
> *To surge towards the front,*
> *Bombs and grenades in hand.*
> *And now the war has come,*
> *The Duce does insist*
> *The Greeks will get a taste*
> *Of our mailed fist.*[15]

Within the next few days, the men who sang that song would need to muster every ounce of courage they could find.

The Spring Offensive got underway at dawn on 9 March with a devastating artillery barrage aimed at the Greek II Corps positions – the 1st, 5th, 6th, 8th, 11th and 17th Divisions, though the 6th and 11th were down to barely a half dozen battalions each.

The Duce watched four hundred guns belching rapid fire – at least 100,000 rounds in the first couple of hours, slamming into the mountainsides and blasting villages and monasteries into nothingness. Soon the sky resounded with the approach of squadrons of Regia Aeronautica fighters and bombers to add their bit. By 8.30 am Cavallero's gunners were lengthening their trajectories, closing in on the Greek position on Mount Trebescines to create room for the first infantry units of the Fourth, Eighth and Twenty-fifth Corps to advance.

The dawn barrage caught General Vrachnos' 1st Division on the chin. His troops were jolted awake into an inferno. Anyone daring to raise his head saw the northern horizon as one long flame of cannon fire. Men threw themselves flat and hugged the shaking ground as great fountains of earth and trees erupted, ammunition dumps exploded and telephone lines were cut. When the barrage flagged the dazed men of the 1st Division got up shakily to repel the waves of grey-green uniforms converging on two strategic peaks, Hills 717 and 731. These were the men of the Puglie, who manfully charged the heights, only be driven off in brutal hand-to-hand combat. The artillery barrage, far from denting the Greeks' resolve, seems instead to have fired it to fury. Lines of Italians were cut down under the lethal hoarse chugging of the Greeks' Hotchkiss machine guns, while the Italian aircraft overhead bombed where they could, assuming their crews could see through the smoke.

Over the next few hours the Puglie's 52 Regiment had achieved its objective, while the Pinerolo and Sforzesca Divisions were pressing on Mecgorane Ridge. But the most savage fight took place for Hill 731, where the Puglie wouldn't give up. One battalion butted itself heroically against the height for a solid forty-five minutes until forced to retire, whipped to pieces by the Greek machine guns. The Cagliari Division, which spearheaded the initial assault, came up against such a wall of fire as to cause its officers to wonder whether the foregoing artillery barrage had done any damage to the Greeks at all; its commander, General Giuseppe Gianni, was unwell and hardly in a position to exercise strong command.

A second charge by the men of the Puglie momentarily secured Hill 717, the farthest-exposed Greek outpost, held by a few platoons, lost it, then regained it at about 12.00 pm. A fresh attempt was made on Hill 731 which remained – only just – in Greek hands. Throughout the day six more attempts on the hill came to nought except to leave piles of Italian dead in front of the Greek lines. At sunset the Italians remained in possession of Hill 717, but Vrachnos wasn't overly worried as long as Hill 731 remained in 1st Division hands.

All of this was being solemnly observed at Komarit. The initial communiqués had been moderately encouraging, but when it soon became clear that the first burst of the Spring Offensive was already stumbling, Pricolo, watching at Mussolini's side with a jaundiced eye, feared the worst. From the grim expressions of the officers around him, Pricolo knew that the day was not going well. So did the Duce, who at one point turned to his air force chief. 'If the offensive doesn't succeed within the first two or three hours,' he said, 'it won't succeed at all.' By evening the failure had become obvious. The Duce nursed the darkest suspicions of Gianni, one of 'those generals who become ill right on the first day of the offensive'. Gianni thus became the scapegoat for the failure of the 9 March attack.

Simultaneous Italian attacks on the left of the line came to grief against the Greek 11th and 15th Divisions. The Greeks had intercepted a radio message to the Duce's army urging it to new efforts. 'It is not possible that the Italian army cannot push back the inferior Greek army,' the message read. 'It is a matter of honour. We need to avenge our dead and be worthy of our glorious traditions.'[16] Thus exhorted, the Italian Fourth Corps was nonetheless stopped by Greek artillery. On the Italian right there was similar ill-luck. Again, Greek artillery fire broke up the Twenty-fifth Corps advance in front of the 8th Division at Mecgorane.

The next day broke on the shell-shocked, cold and hungry survivors of both armies clinging to the rocky hillsides for the next round of the Spring Offensive. Early in the morning Cavallero's guns opened up on Hill 731 in what must have been one of the heaviest saturation bombardments of the entire war. A couple of hours later, when the lines of Italian infantry proceeded to pick their way up the cratered hill they were amazed to find the Greeks waiting, dazed and ragged and bloody, and with big gaps in their lines, but still on their feet. Again bayonet and grenade dealt death at close quarters, with fanatic courage displayed on both sides, until an hour later the Italians retreated. Around noon Gambara's Eighth Corps, duly reinforced, tried again, coming perilously near to taking Hill 731, but he, too, was whipped back. The seventh attempt on Hill 731 was made at 6.00 pm, but the 1st Division still held firm. The newly-appointed II Corps Commander, Major General George Bakos, was impressed enough to issue this order of the day to his 1st Division:

> Soldiers of the 1st Division: Since yesterday all the desperate attempts by the enemy have shattered against your steady heroism. Three fresh enemy divisions broke against your lines of steel in the past two days. I am proud to command such heroes. The Country bows in tribute to you. This message is to reach to the last private of the division.[17]

Day two of the *Offensiva di Primavera* opened with the Cagliari and Puglie thrown against the Trebescines lines again, helped by units of the Bari that had so far been held in reserve. The only Italian success of the day was achieved on the Fourth Corps front, as the 11 Alpine Regiment of the Pusteria temporarily gained the height of Mali Spadarit overlooking the road south. Yet even that was ephemeral, as the advance had exposed the regiment's flanks that in turn were hammered, and the regiment had to withdraw. The Puglie, meanwhile, resumed its desperate attempt to seize Hill 731, which now had become a bloody symbol of the entire campaign. Cavallero wanted it as much as Papagos was determined to hold onto it. Its iconic importance began to outweigh its actual strategic value, as the success of the opening stage of the Spring Offensive had been predicated on seizing that height. Cavallero's failure to do it – especially as the Duce was there watching over his shoulder – was acutely embarrassing. If the Duce was to see anything at all positive, it would have to be the capture of Hill 731. An attempt by the Cagliari to outflank the hill came to nothing, as the Greek 1st Division had posted units on the hill flank to guard against that very possibility. The Italians found themselves trapped along the valley road that runs through a ravine, and before the slaughter could reach epic proportions, more than 500 men of the Cagliari raised white handkerchiefs and were marched off to captivity around the bodies of their comrades. One factor in this Italian defeat was the absence of the air force, as the weather had closed in again.

On the left of the front Lieutenant Antolini was part of a surprise attack on the Greek position atop Guri i Topit. His experience was typical:

> The Greek was surprised. I was lightly wounded by grenade fragments. My sergeant had a lucky escape when a bullet glanced off his helmet ... A Greek hurled himself on me with his bayonet extended, but he caught a sleeve of my white tunic without slashing me. I fired my pistol [and] my tunic became red with that poor fellow's blood. We took a few dozen prisoners. Unbelievable but true, we were then ordered to abandon the positions we had taken. Thus the Greeks re-took both heights. I'm sure we are going to pay heavily for this madness.[18]

Mussolini, frowning at the drizzly landscape through his field glasses, was no doubt wondering what he would tell Hitler. He knew now that Germany was planning to move into Greece at the beginning of April. Before then he needed an Italian victory, if only to forestall the prestige that would certainly be Hitler's when the Germans smashed the Greeks. Moreover, the Italian forces in North Africa had just sustained a stunning reverse at Allied hands, and that could not be allowed to become the rule. Albania was the big gamble now. If it cost the lives of thousands of Italian soldiers, so be it. In the final analysis Mussolini was a social Darwinist; the survival of the fittest was all that counted in life. War, in his view, served to winnow out the weak and preserve the strong. Italy had to be strong, *ergo* the casualties didn't count.

The fruitless attacks in the mud and rain continued on 11 March. They followed a predictable pattern. First the artillery would churn up the ground, then the pre-dawn darkness would be split by signal flares and the lines of grey-green would scramble up the snowy scrubland again as shells and bullets smacked into boulders and trees and human flesh. Cavallero seemed to have no other idea than to repeatedly feed his men in serried ranks into the Greek artillery and machine gun nests. Even then the men of the Cagliari and Puglie ran forward bravely, stiff with cold, tormented by lice and dysentery and frostbite, to fight for their country. There must have been some grumbling in the higher ranks, as Mussolini gave orders to Geloso:

> You must absolutely insist. You can't change the operational plan after four days ... You have to attack tomorrow because if the troops begin to put down roots in one place they'll think the action is over ... The Greeks must be under our fire day and night. The antidote to the mortar is celerity in movement ... *A military victory is absolutely essential to the prestige of the Italian army before the end of the month.*[19]

Mussolini's concern that the soldiers, once halted, would be hard to get moving again is similar to Papagos' concern on the Greek side. For both sides, Albania had become a tussle for military and national prestige. While Mussolini wanted a victory to impress Hitler (and by extension his own warweary people), Papagos and his prime minister, Koryzis, needed to maintain Greece's newly-won prestige both among the British and among the Greek people. But the popular mood in Greece was changing. There was no Metaxas now to exercise inspired leadership. The Athenians were getting used to the long lines of sick and maimed soldiers arriving to fill the hospitals. Church bells no longer rang joyfully at the news of Albanian (or ethnic Greek) towns falling to the Greeks. The news from the congealed front could no longer inspire. Food in Athens and other cities was running scarce. The economy was slowly collapsing under the weight of a hard war. And Germany was the big darkening cloud on the northern horizon. A defeat in Albania, however minor, might easily tip the popular mood into defeatism. For all these reasons, the Duce's Spring Offensive had to be smashed.

On 12 March, day four of the offensive, the Alpini of the Trento Division re-took Mali Spadarit and hung onto it desperately. The following day Gambara, at Mussolini's side at the Komarit observation post, ordered the artillery to lay down a creeping curtain of fire ahead of a new infantry advance. The Duce, nodding his agreement, got on the phone to Cavallero who was at the Bari Division headquarters. 'The faster we move, the fewer losses we'll have,' he said. The word 'move' meant a fresh attack on Hill 731, this time to be made by General Matteo Negro's fresh Bari Division. Mussolini respected Negro's military abilities and made clear to him that he expected much. The attack was a resolute one, but as before, all that was accomplished was to pile up more Italian bodies before the barking, death-spitting muzzles of the Greeks' Hotchkiss guns. Mussolini tried the cheerleader tactic. 'They tell me you're doing a good job,' he signalled Negro, apparently oblivious to the terrific human cost of the fruitless head-butting. 'I exhort you to continue that way.'

Then to General Guido Lama, the Eighth Corps chief of artillery: 'I praise the artillery for the impulse they are giving to the infantry. Continue until the Greeks give way.' He messaged Cavallero: 'Very good today. I believe the Greeks have caved in because the action has been conducted with extreme energy, as I said.'

The Greeks, on the contrary, were far from caving in. A typical Italian attack, say on Hill 731, would proceed until a few dozen metres from the Greek positions. Then the chilling cry of 'Fix bayonets!' would echo through the trenches and the Greeks, heavy helmets drawn down over their brows, would leap out of their foxholes, the cold steel glinting in the dawn light. The advancing Italians, having heard the menacing rasp of metal as the bayonets were pulled from their scabbards and clicked onto the rifle barrels, would have their grenades ready in hand. It took courage of a high order to face a screaming downhill bayonet charge, yet it was faced more than once, and for the next half hour or so no quarter would be given. But more often than not, the Italian side would break and stream to the rear to run the gauntlet of Greek shellfire.

By the sixth day of the offensive the strain was beginning to tell. Some Italian units had to be driven forward like the reluctant Persians before Thermopylai in 480 BC, 'like sheep to the slaughter'. Machine gun detachments were set up in the rear to discourage stragglers. By 15 March no fewer than seventeen bloody and fruitless attempts had been made on Hill 731 (except for a brief success by the Bari on the night of 13 March), which had been churned up into a shapeless mass of bare mud and rock, devoid of a single tree or shrub and covered in bodies and parts of bodies.

The much-ballyhooed Spring Offensive petered out after precisely one week, with the Italians no nearer to their objectives than before. Mussolini was smart enough to perceive that the epic battle for Hill 731 had been uselessly costly. 'The result is zero,' he snapped to his commander, who confessed that if the Greek line continued to prove unbreakable in the next day or so, 'then we will have to re-think it.' The Duce's ardent hope, seconded by Cavallero, that the Italians would prove to be fully able to launch a German-style *Blitzkrieg* of the kind he so admired, had been fatally punctured by the Greek bayonets on Hill 731. The Spring Offensive had also revealed the limitations of ground attacks by the Regia Aeronautica. Though plenty of warplanes supported the land attacks when the weather permitted, they could not seem to make much impact on well dug-in positions hard to locate on the snowy mountainsides, especially when they were wreathed in the smoke of battle.

Cavallero and his officers spent the next couple of days in dazed 're-thinking'. His flamboyant and unconventional idea of hitting the enemy where he was strongest now lay in bloody heaps on Hill 731. Gambara urged an immediate suspension of the offensive but Mussolini wouldn't give up that easily. His mood swings continued. 'How is the morale of the troops?' he asked jauntily on the morning of 15 March.

'I cannot say it is very high,' Gambara replied, citing the conspicuous lack of results over the past week, 'but it's enough to keep the effort in place.'

'We have to carry out a war of attrition against a strong adversary,' the Duce said. 'Our success has a name, and that is Kelcyre. If we reach that objective Greek morale will crumble.' The tactical objective now, he said, was to hold on to Tepelene at all costs while making every effort to seize Kelcyre. That said, he travelled to Vlore to visit his daughter Edda who was a nurse on the hospital ship *Po* that had been torpedoed the night before, and had survived along with Countess Ciano.

Mussolini's belief that the Greeks would collapse if they lost Kelcyre is a curious one. If there was one lesson that could have been drawn from the failure of the Spring Offensive, it was that Greek resolve was in a much better state than that of his own troops. Cavallero, Gambara and Geloso pondered the Duce's recommendation but quickly dismissed it. Yet what was the alternative? A shifting of the offensive to the Korce sector would take time to organize, in which time the enemy would be amply tipped off. There seemed no choice but to keep up a certain pressure towards Kelcyre in the hope that some miracle might result in success. Cavallero himself was torn between sober realism and flashes of Mussolinian overoptimism. 'We're not sunk yet,' he intoned to General Alessandro Pirzio Biroli.

> The country demands that after we have made our wall, we will show we are superior to the Greeks. In early April the Germans will enter Greece and the Duce doesn't want that to be the cause of ending the conflict ... The offensive requires the formation of a mass of Alpine troops.[20]

One wonders what the long-suffering Italian soldier had yet to do to prove his commander's theory that he was 'superior to the Greeks'. But Cavallero was thinking primarily of his own reputation and career, at stake in the inhospitable Albanian mountains. He had to put up a front, even if only in words. But his words to Pirzio Biroli were not just empty talk; he really believed he might break the Greeks with one more decisive push. Every day saw some probing action against the Greek defences until on 19 March Cavallero ordered the eighteenth attempt to take Hill 731. The Siena Division was picked for this one, with armoured units from the Centauro to back it up. This attack, like the others, ended up in bloody heaps on the lower slopes of the hill. By 8.00 am all the officers of the leading ranks were dead or captured and most of the Fiat tanks in the rear had either been blasted by Greek artillery or had tumbled down cliffs.

Italian casualties in the space of ten days had been fearsome. Gambara's Eighth Corps had sustained casualties of around 5,000, while the Twenty-fifth

Corps had also lost 5,000 men, and the Fourth Corps around 1,800 – that is, 12,000 men fed into the meat-grinder to no visible advantage. Hill 731 was strewn with the bodies of Greeks and Italians who lay as they fell in their death-struggles. Vultures swooped down on the gruesome carpet of malodorous bodies and body parts, picking obscenely at the gaping wounds and spilt innards.

A curious sight met the Greek defenders on Hill 731 on the morning of 22 March. Three Italian army chaplains, a medical officer and a team of stretcher-bearers approached the Greek lines under a white flag. As they were let through the lines the head padre was blindfolded for security reasons, but not before he could see the sheer carnage around him. The chaplain blanched and began to shake. When his blindfold was taken off at battalion headquarters he covered his eyes with his hands, murmuring, *'Terribile! Terribile!'* in a shocked voice. He was brought round with a dose of brandy. He transmitted a request for a temporary cease-fire around Hill 731 for the Italians to collect their dead, as the spectacle would be bad for troop morale. The request was communicated to the II Corps headquarters which counter proposed a General Staff suggestion for a general truce all along the front. A Greek lieutenant carried the counterproposal to the headquarters of the Bari Division, which in turn rejected it. Twice more the Siena charged the hill, once at midnight on 24 March and the next three hours later. After that, Cavallero finally had to admit defeat.

Mussolini had flown back to Rome on 21 March, 'sickened' at what he had seen. But he was nauseated in a way rather different from the hapless padre on Hill 731. What got to him was the supposed incompetence of his generals. 'They have been deceiving me to this day,' he fumed to Pricolo. 'I profoundly despise them all.' There was now no escaping the fact that Hitler's imminent invasion of Greece would find his ally still bogged down in Albania after five months of conflict, and having lost ground to boot. Returning to Rome with the Duce were most of the Fascist party bigwigs who had been sent to the front in their black uniforms for appearances' sake (but had rarely seen any actual combat), no doubt to their intense relief. But thousands of lesser-privileged men, in ordinary grey-green, would never come back, all that remained of them, in some cases, being a bloodstained rag of a tunic or scrap of a letter from home blown along in the merciless snow.

Unsuccessful probing actions by the Italians finally came to a halt on 25 March. Papagos employed the lull by rearranging his forces from right to left: the West Macedonia Army Department, comprising the 9th, 10th, 13th and 16th Infantry Divisions (plus the Cavalry Division) holding down the Pogradec-Korce sector at the Yugoslav border; and the Epiros Army Department, comprising the II Corps (4th, 5th, 6th and 17th Divisions and part of the 11th Division) and the I Corps (2nd, 3rd and 8th Divisions) up to the coast at

Himare. The battered 1st Division, which had shattered the Spring Offensive against its immovable wall, was sent for a rest in the reserves. To help fill a denuded Bulgarian front, the 20th Division was relocated east to Florina.[21]

By now the first intimations of spring had arrived to cheer the bone-weary troops of both sides. For the first time in months, rays of sunshine broke through the leaden clouds, melting the snow on the lower levels of the Albanian peaks and swelling the rivers and streams. Songbirds appeared in the silver firs and arbutus bushes, heralding an eventual end to the long weeks of frostbite and polar cold. Yet the mood in the Greek army was one of foreboding. From Papagos down to the last private, everyone knew that a German incursion would not long be delayed; some 680,000 German troops were reported to be in Bulgaria, and they certainly weren't there for Balkan rest and recreation. This in turn raised the question of what the whole heroic effort in Epiros and Albania had been for. In October 1940, of course, the jubilation of upholding national honour had erased every other thought. But many Greeks now wondered what use honour would be against Hitler's Panzers and dive-bombers.

Germany's diplomats, of course, fostered this sense of doubt with all the means at their disposal. German officialdom had never ceased to sing the praises of classical Greece as the supposed source of 'Aryan' values ever since inventing the *faux*-ancient mummeries such as the Olympic Flame that opened the Berlin Olympic Games of 1936 (and have opened each Games since). German military officers frankly admired the way the Greeks had dealt with the Italians – though that was no real compliment, as the Germans despised the Italians even more than the Greeks did. On 12 March the German consul in Thessaloniki reported that certain Greek officers had suggested to him that hostilities with the Italians cease, and that one German division replace the Italian army in Albania as a symbolic gesture.[22] The episode suggests that pro-German sentiment among some Greek officers was still alive, though even German diplomats conceded that the Greek military would certainly resist a German invasion, even if such resistance was deemed hopeless.

Mussolini, smarting under the abject failure of the Spring Offensive, was now amenable to suggestions from Badoglio, who seems to have recovered from his depressive torpor. The staff chief suggested that the attack on the Greeks be renewed in eastern Albania, in the Ninth Corps sector. Briefing King Vittorio Emanuele on his Albania trip, the Duce insisted that morale in the army remained high and outlined his latest plan: to launch 'a single division, supported by heavy artillery fire, to make a breach [in the Greek line], and to send a wedge through the breach that can scatter the enemy formation'. Anyone could have told him that Cavallero had been trying precisely this for many bloody weeks, and had got nowhere. Besides, it never happened, because at the end of March the fatal dice were rolled in neighbouring Yugoslavia.

On 27 March a pro-Allied coup toppled the two-day-old pro-Axis Yugoslav government of Prince Paul, replacing it with his brother Peter II who proclaimed a general mobilization two days later. The Greek high command was relieved; Yugoslavia could now be a buffer against a German attack. Moreover, Papagos could rest in the knowledge that the strategically weakest point on the northern frontier, the point where the borders of Greece, Yugoslavia and Bulgaria come together on Mount Kerkini some 100km due north of Thessaloniki, would in the end be safe from the threat of outflanking.

But the pro-Allied Yugoslav regime quickly failed to live up to the hopes which Greece pinned on it. Instead of deploying their forces along a practically defensible front, the Yugoslavs very unwisely strung out their 800,000-strong military along their entire frontier, facing the now-hostile territories of Albania, Austria, Hungary and Bulgaria. Besides, Peter's counter-coup had enraged Hitler, who fumed that he would erase Yugoslavia from the map, carrying out his threat by sending the Luftwaffe to devastate Belgrade. Far from being relatively safe, Greece was ironically now in greater danger than ever before.

Hitler also used the occasion to take over decision-making in Albania, secretly imploring Mussolini to halt all operations against the Greeks and concentrate on the Yugoslav frontier. The Duce gave his orders to Cavallero:

> It is clear that in entering the war against the Axis and in joining its military forces to Greece, Yugoslavia is trying to attack us in the rear and on the flank. It is thus urgently necessary that we prepare our defence and resist until such time as Germany attacks from the east to join with us. This period is estimated at ten to fifteen days.[23]

Two Italian divisions were to be transferred from the front, boosting the number on the Yugoslav frontier to six, plus various independent commands. Cavallero, the good soldier, acknowledged the orders. He initially agreed with a staff suggestion that the bulk of his force withdraw to better defences on the west bank of the Dhrin River, leaving a sliver of Albanian territory in Yugoslav hands, but quickly found such a move impracticable as denuding some vital part of the front. Besides, he baulked at handing over territory uncontested to the enemy. In the end he changed his mind and stayed where he was, except for sending his two divisions to the east. One of them was the Cuneo, where the mood in the Mondovi Battalion, whose orders to attack the Greek positions the following day had just been cancelled, was one of frank relief. Italian intelligence had scored a triumph, cracking the Yugoslav codes and confusing the Yugoslav units near the Albanian border with false orders until the Germans could steamroller down.

Papagos, for his part, kept up the pressure on the Italians where he could. The Greeks attacked almost daily in the Tepelene sector, in attempts to gain as much territory as possible. Papagos himself passes over this period in his memoirs without comment. Cervi, the leading Italian historian of the war, blames Papagos for having 'a mentality of vain conquest' which would explain, at this late stage and with the looming German threat uppermost in everyone's mind, his 'bloody and senseless' attacks on the Italian positions.

Meanwhile, Greek, British and Yugoslav officers met and agreed that Greece and Yugoslavia join forces for a final push against the Italians in Albania to drive them into the sea and remove the threat from that quarter once and for all. Papagos was in the middle of drafting the necessary orders – the Epiros Army Department to advance on Vlore and Berat, while the West Macedonia Army Department cut around in a scything movement to Elbasan and Durres – when Hitler set his own much bigger plans in motion. The Fuehrer, now eyeing the prize of Russia, needed to secure his southern flank before attacking. This meant knocking out Greece as a centre of Allied resistance. All attention now centred on Greece's north-eastern frontier.

It is reasonable at this point to examine the reasons for the Greek successes in Albania. Perhaps the main factor was the sheer fury at being the victim of unprovoked aggression. Such a motive gives wings to soldiers and fills even the faintest heart with a degree of resolve. The Greeks who fought on that front had been to school inundated with what today we might call nationalist propaganda, but in the interwar years was considered a healthy patriotic curriculum in which the history of the Greek Revolt of 1821–29 and Enlightenment ideas of national liberty took pride of place. Metaxas was widely accepted as a dictator precisely because he embodied and tapped into this source of national and ethnic pride. Greece in 1940, somewhat like Britain, was a distinctly martial nation hiding behind a mask of prosperous middle-class values, and hence underestimated by the Axis.

The territory over which the Epiros and Albania campaign was fought was far more familiar to the Greeks than to the Italians, only a small proportion of whom had any familiarity at all with mountains and how to fight in them. Many of the Greeks, especially those from Epiros, were fighting for their homes in a quite literal sense. Local people guided them over every inch of the crags. Some of the Greeks' weaponry was also superior to the Italian; the Czechoslovak-made Hotchkiss machine gun, for example, outperformed its Italian equivalents from the Breda and Fiat plants, was less liable to overheating and jammed less often. Also from Czechoslovakia came the Skoda 75mm and 105mm mountain cannon which were employed to such admirable effect by the Greeks. This equipment was superior partly because it employed toughened steel developed by the Austro-Hungarian Empire in World War One. This also applied to the Austrian-made Mannlicher rifle used by the infantry – light, reliable and tough – and its fearsome steel bayonet.[24]

Chapter 9

Falling Stars

The RHAF is worn down – 80 Squadron's snowy ordeal – air raid on Ioannina – Hurricanes arrive for the RAF – the Regia Aeronautica gets the chop over Berat – Pattle takes over 33 Squadron

At the beginning of 1941 Metaxas had no illusions about what the coming year would probably bring. He could not have known, of course, that he himself had barely a month to live. Yet the fate of Greece worried him far more than any possibility of personal demise. 'For us Orthodox,' he is reported to have told an American journalist, 'death is simply a transition.' The Germans were in Romania and the Italians in Albania had stopped running. The RHAF brass were worried over the appearance in Albanian skies of the new Macchi MC200 fighter that posed a new and serious threat to the RAF Wellingtons engaged in bombing Albanian ports. One of those ports was Vlore, of which the Greek army had yet to come within striking distance. Severe winter weather over the mainland was forcing D'Albiac's bombers to take longer routes off the coast, at the cost of more fuel and more danger.

The RHAF's fighter *mirai*, 21, 22 and 23, were moved up closer to the front along with the army cooperation observation squadrons. One Henschel was shot down early in the New Year while scouting the territory south of Vlore, killing both crewmembers. Such was the reputation of the Greek airmen that sometimes the sight of the Gladiators and PZLs with the blue and white roundel was enough to scatter enemy bomber formations without a shot being fired. But those occasions were exceptions as Greek fliers found their work more than cut out for them. It was devilishly hard, for example, to weave down between the fog-shrouded Albanian heights to under 300ft and get in a strike at an Italian column, which was more often than not defended by flak.[1]

The light bombers of 31 and 33 Mirai were sent in on 21 January to weaken the strong Italian defence at the Kelcyre Valley. Pilot Officer Yannis Kipouros gunned his single-engined Fairey Battle into no fewer than seven bombing runs over the enemy positions, dropping a 100-pound bomb each time, landing behind the Greek lines on an empty tank. Four days later 23 Mira was scrambled to meet two enemy raids heading for Thessaloniki at 20,000ft, the very limit of the PZL's operational ceiling. As his engine raced to maintain height, Squadron Leader Grigorios Theodoropoulos, the 23 Mira Commanding Officer, found that his oxygen mask was blocking his vision. Tearing it off, and trying not to get hit by his own side's anti-aircraft guns, he claimed one bomber before having to land with a hammering headache caused by the lack of oxygen. At the same time, 21 Mira destroyed two Italian bombers over Albania.

Meanwhile, the RAF's 80 Squadron was having a tough time of it, and not necessarily courtesy of the efforts of the Regia Aeronautica. Midwinter in northern Greece is a formidable elemental foe, and the squadron was glad to be relocated to Larissa in the central Greek plain for Christmas. 'Pat' Pattle, for one, grabbed a bit of holiday leave in sunny Cairo. But the respite was all too brief. In the middle of January the squadron received orders to move back to Ioannina, which meant that the equipment and ground crews had to be loaded onto lorries for the long and fatiguing drive over the forbidding mountains from Larissa. One night the convoy got stuck in the snowbound Katara Pass. Had it not been for the hospitality of the local peasants with their blankets and bowls of hot soup, some of the men might well have frozen to death in night-time temperatures plunging past thirty below zero. Three ailing airmen had to be put in a tin bath and dragged on foot ten miles through the snow to the nearest road for evacuation to a hospital.

> Probably never in the history of the Royal Air Force [writes 'Pat' Pattle's biographer, E.C.R. Baker] have airmen undergone such experience and, although great discomfort was suffered by everyone, not a single word of disobedience or even discontent was uttered by the groundcrews – one more tribute to the devotion, determination, courage and comradeship of this fighter squadron.[2]

The death of Metaxas on 29 January coincided with a two-week spate of bad weather that all but grounded the Greek and British airmen, giving them a precious breather. 23 Mira was posted to Paramythia. Squadron Leader Jones, the 80 Squadron CO, got his pilots together early on 9 February, when some cracks finally appeared in the heavy cloud. The Greek army, he said, was aiming to capture Tepelene, a key town on the way to the port of Vlore. 'It's our job', Jones said, 'to keep the sky over Tepelene absolutely free of enemy aircraft.' Minutes later, he was leading his fourteen Gladiators in impeccable formation. Soon they spotted three SM79s, but had orders to avoid tangling with enemy aircraft on the way up, so the bombers were allowed to escape. Over Tepelene Pattle saw five Fiat CR42s cruising along; three of them broke away early, but Pattle hung grimly onto the tail of one of the remaining two, impervious to the torrents of flak tearing up at him, until the enemy plane slammed into a hillside on fire.

The efforts of 80 Squadron at Ioannina did not go unrewarded. D'Albiac that same evening authorized a Distinguished Flying Cross to be awarded to Pattle as 'absolutely fearless and undeterred by superior numbers of the enemy'. There was also a dubious recognition of sorts by the enemy, which only now appeared to realize the importance of Ioannina as an Allied air base. On 10 February the air raid sirens sounded in the town. 80 Squadron kept its Gladiators on emergency stand-by, so that Pattle and two other pilots were able to surprise five CantZ1007s, which bombed the airfield a little too hastily, doing negligible damage. That afternoon, though, a flight of Breda Br20s of 37 Stormo was more accurate, damaging three of 80 Squadron's Gladiators and destroying one belonging to 21 Mira. Far worse destruction, however, was visited on Ioannina itself. The British pilots drove into town after the raid:

> Everywhere they saw the mutilated remains of men, women and children lying scattered among the smoking debris. Others, blood-stained and wounded, were being carried on improvised stretchers, and some, their minds unbalanced by the terrible happenings, were crying, shouting and running around in circles.[3]

The pilots' own hotel in the town centre was somewhat battered, but their rooms were still intact, enabling them to grab a bit of sleep.

The Italians attacked the airfield again the following day. Waves of CR42s swarmed out of the mountain defiles around the lake to strafe the parked aircraft. Greek anti-aircraft batteries accounted for one of the raiders. A Gladiator of 21 Mira was blown up as its pilot was trying to take off for a valiant attempt to hit back. Local people willingly helped the ground crews fill in the craters that afternoon. The bone-weary pilots, having been at taut pitch all day, staggered to their quarters to be greeted by an unusually exuberant Jones. At long last, he said, eight Hawker Hurricanes would shortly be arriving to give the squadron its first real state-of-the-art fighters. Such was the explosion of excitement that 'within a few seconds the room looked as if the Italians had dropped a bomb right in the middle of it'.

The RHAF, of course, had been hard at work as well. As 80 Squadron was fighting to keep the skies free over Tepelene, 22 Mira under Flight Lieutenant Andreas Antoniou (the nearest thing to an ace the Greeks produced during the war) took on no fewer than fifty bombers escorted by thirty-six Fiat CR42s and G50s. Mitralexis, the hero of the ramming episode early in the war, took out two enemy fighters and damaged a couple of bombers.

The air battle over Tepelene and Kelcyre began to heat up when both the Regia Aeronautica and RHAF added a dash of sophistication to their tactics. Eight Greek Gladiators, four each from 21 and 22 Mirai, joined the PZLs of Squadron Leader Yannis Kellas's 23 Mira on a sweep. Flying at 14,000ft, the Gladiator pilots noticed three Italian bombers cruising below, and dived to the attack. At that moment fifteen Italian fighters pounced, apparently out of nowhere. Kellas's squadron, however, had been flying 1,500ft higher than the Gladiators and was able to engage the Italians in a double entrapment. That day both sides reported nine kills each with no loss to their own side! Two damaged PZLs were broken up after landing to provide the parts for a whole new one, an engineering feat that, according to one proud Greek account, left the RAF fitters 'speechless with admiration'.[4]

The Greek bomber command was not faring so well. The Potez 63s of 31 Mira were coming to the end of their career. One of them, after bombing enemy artillery positions north of Kelcyre, was jumped by a formation of Macchis. The two-man crew baled out just before the plane disintegrated under the blistering fire; the navigator-observer survived. Throughout February the bomber *mirai* suffered constant and ill-affordable attrition. The fighter *mirai* were only just getting by, patching up their battered planes as best as they could. A typical *mira* was by now down to about half of its pre-war strength, but pilot morale was undimmed. Mitralexis, for example, maintained his glowing reputation by downing three Fiat G50s.

The first indication that better aircraft might be on the way came on 16 February, when the RAF sent a demonstration flight of Hawker Hurricanes to Greece. The stubby, tough-looking fighters were a cheering sight, giving the Greeks the feeling that the Regia Aeronautica and eventually the Luftwaffe could now be tackled on more equal technological terms. The arrival of the Hurricane was another sign that the age of the biplane was over, the dogfights over the Albanian peaks between Fiat CR42 and Gladiator its swan song. On the bomber side D'Albiac was optimistic: his Wellingtons and Blenheims hit Brindisi, destroying half a dozen or so Luftwaffe Junkers Ju52 troop transports on the ground there. His crews, he said, had noticed a distinct lack of opposition from the Italians in the air. Papagos was a bit more sceptical of the Hurricanes. In his view the slower and older Gladiators were actually better suited to mountain dogfights since they could wind through the ravines with more agility.

The airfield at Paramythia was still undetected by the enemy, and already being put to good use by the Fairey Swordfish torpedo bombers of 815 Naval Air Squadron, Fleet Air Arm, for operations at sea. Group Captain Stergios Tilios, the senior Greek air officer, asked Longmore for some rugged Westland Lysander reconnaissance and special operations aircraft that could operate from short and bumpy airstrips but the RAF had none to spare. A batch of Greek pilots from the Flight Training Centre (EKI) which had moved from Tatoi to Argos to be safe from bombing had been sent to RAF Habbaniya in Iraq for advanced training.

The problem of the division of labour between the Greek and British military establishments continued to be troublesome, and nowhere was this more apparent than in air operations. Papagos and the senior Greek command had by now grudgingly come round to D'Albiac's views on the value of independent air operations against the Italian supply points. No doubt one reason was the noticeable attrition suffered by the RHAF, which could leave no doubt in anyone's mind that the air defence of Greece was essentially now in British hands. 'Apart from the British air force, no other British force, neither land army nor anti-aircraft artillery nor special forces, reinforced the Greek fight against the Italians in Albania,' admitted Papagos in his memoir.[5] The Regia Aeronautica, moreover, still ruled the Albanian skies, and Cavallero was in the middle of receiving large reinforcements by sea. Papagos asked for more bombs on the port of Durres. D'Albiac had no objection in principle, but said his Wellingtons would need more escorts to counter persistent losses over the ports.

By January 1941 the RAF had contributed thirty-nine fighters and eighteen bombers to the Greeks – apart from the RAF's own squadrons. Between then and March the RHAF was reinforced with twelve more British fighters and five bombers. Inevitably, there were disagreements over the value of this aid. The Greek high command was understandably fretting over the fact that, though the army had justly won great acclaim against the Italians in Albania, it was correspondingly worn out, and consequently its chances against the Germans would be close to nil. The British, of course, realized this, and often had to make it painfully obvious that their help had to have a limit – men and resources could not be poured down the maw of a lost campaign, no matter how morally deserving of such aid the Greeks were. The Greeks still thought in terms of glory and reward; the British, on the contrary, surveyed the wider picture through the sobering lens of *Realpolitik* – in the wider European and Middle Eastern context, Greece was still a sideshow.

Some Greeks suspected that the British might be leaving the hard air combat tasks to the RHAF in order to preserve the RAF's strength against the German attack to come; some of this suspicion leaked out to the British press. Papagos, anxious to scotch any suggestion to the enemy that the Greeks and British were quarrelling, made a point of publicly thanking D'Albiac for his bomber boys' help 'to the Greek ground forces'. There was some disappointment, also, over the quality of the planes which the RAF was delivering to the Greeks. The crews of 32 Mira, for example, viewed with dismay their replacement Blenheim bombers – Mark Is, which were actually older and more cramped than their own Blenheim Mark IVs and less easy to exit in an emergency. These were ordered on bombing raids on the Trebescines Ridge.

While 80 Squadron was waiting impatiently for its Hurricanes, it had to use its worn-out Gladiators to escort the Blenheims of 84 and 211 Squadrons operating out of Paramythia. Fairy Tale Valley was a Shangri-la of sorts. A dozen or so tents made up the camp, whose atmosphere was idyllically happy.

One could bathe in the bracing water of the adjacent lake while marvelling at the snowy peaks and flower-covered slopes rising steeply above. Meals were taken sitting on packing boxes in the sunshine, with afternoon tea invariably brewing on a tiny Primus stove. The mayor of the town of Paramythia regularly kept the squadrons supplied with plentiful quantities of tangy and powerful local wine. Airmen slept on the ground in their sleeping bags. Yet the away-from-it-all feeling was deceptive. Everyone knew that in those beetling mountains, behind the fir forests and riot of spring flowers, wolves and bears were tearing at the decomposing bodies of Italian soldiers unlucky enough to get on the business end of a peasant's pitchfork.

Jones accordingly saw fit to move a 'Detached Flight', led by Pattle, from Ioannina to Paramythia so it could better coordinate escort duties with the Blenheims. A few days later, out of the blue, six Hurricanes roared into Paramythia for perfect landings. As Pattle and others ran up to the sleek new fighters, five Wellington bombers droned in one by one, carrying supplies. That first day, Pattle tried out the Hurricane, revelling in its metallic solidity and power, a most welcome change from the stringy fabric-covered Gladiator biplane. Moreover, the Hurricane had twice the firepower of the Gladiator, and at double the rate. As commander of the Detached Flight, Pattle prepared his new Hurricanes for their action debut on 20 February. The Hurricanes were prepared to make a splash. D'Albiac was assembling five RAF and one RHAF squadron to form an Advance Wing under Wing Commander Paddy Coote of the RAF and Squadron Leader Sevastopoulos for the Greeks. On the evening of 19 February nine Blenheims of 84 Squadron touched down at Fairy Tale Valley, followed by two Wellingtons of 38 Squadron and twelve PZL24s of the RHAF's 21 Mira. The big show was on.

The day's mission for 20 February was for the two Wellingtons and a Greek Junkers Ju52 transport, cocooned by seventeen Gladiators as escorts, to fly to the Kelcyre sector to drop food and supplies to the forward Greek lines. While this was underway, 211 Squadron's Blenheims led by Squadron Leader Gordon-Finlayson, followed by others of 84 Squadron, would blast a bridge at Berat, with the six Hurricanes as escorts led by Pattle. The PZLs of 21 Mira, whose range was limited, would stand by to escort the returning aircraft over Greek territory. The weather was good, with only slight cloud over Kelcyre. Half an hour later British bombs were whistling down on Berat, smashing enemy supply dumps as well as the strategic bridge that was the main target. As the Blenheims were turning to leave, Pattle's eagle eye made out four dark green Fiat G50s. Getting onto the tail of one of the chunky but agile Italian fighters, he held on with some difficulty until he could get into a position to press his gun button. When he did so, the Fiat disintegrated into flaming bits. It was the first time he'd actually fired the Hurricane's eight 7.7mm machine guns and the effect amazed him.

Escorting the Blenheims on the return, Pattle looked at the faces of his two wingmen – both were grinning in delight at the flying qualities of their new fighters. But the danger wasn't over, as the RAF Gladiators bringing up the rear had to wheel to repel a formation of Italian fighters on their tails. In the ensuing dogfight three Fiat G50s and one CR42 were shot down; when the RHAF's PZLs joined the scrap, four more Italian aircraft were downed. The Hawker Hurricane Mk I's debut in Greek skies was an unqualified success, and the success continued over the following days. The Blenheim bomber crews took heart from the reassuring presence of the Hurricanes around them, and not surprisingly, the Regia Aeronautica's presence in the skies of Albania abruptly diminished. Frustrated at not finding enough Italian fighters to get at, Pattle would gun his Hurricane's throttle and fly up to strafe an Italian troop or vehicle column or supply ship in the port of Vlore.

But in the meantime the Italians had finally discovered Paramythia, now visible through the melting snow. On 22 March thirty Macchi MC200s hurtled down on the parked RAF Wellingtons, destroying them all plus a Gladiator. The ordinarily idyllic Fairy Tale Valley was wreathed in smoke. Anti-aircraft fire downed three of the attackers. But the Italians also had a cost, as that day one of their aces, Captain Edoardo Molinari, was killed while doing aerobatics in a Fiat CR42.

Pattle had just returned from strafing the Italian advanced headquarters at Fieri when he found two imposing figures in the mess at Paramythia: Air Chief Marshal Longmore and D'Albiac, who stayed for lunch and addressed a few words of well-deserved praise to the pilots. The following day, Pattle's Hurricanes, accompanying a Blenheim raid, accounted for seven Fiat CR42s, two more of which went down after colliding in mid-air. The only damage to the Hurricanes was a bullet hole in Pattle's fuel tank.

Pattle's string of air victories got longer on 28 February, when his section downed at least three Breda Br20 bombers, but then he found himself in the middle of a whirling sky battle, and out of ammunition at that, so he flew back to Fairy Tale Valley and jumped into another Hurricane, returning to the vast dogfight in a matter of minutes. As admiring Greek troops watched from their dugouts and cheered every time an Italian plane fell flaming out of the sky, Pattle raised his kills score by four. Wing Commander Coote didn't want to miss the fun so he 'borrowed' an 80 Squadron Gladiator and got in a burst at a CR42, destroying it. That evening the mess at Paramythia was the scene of jubilation, no doubt fuelled by the mayor's wine. When the initial tally was in, it was found that the RAF's 80 and 112 Squadrons had destroyed no fewer than twenty-seven Italian aircraft, with almost as many damaged. It was believed to be the greatest single air loss by Italy in a single day in the whole war.

While there is little doubt that the Regia Aeronautica suffered a severe blow, care must be taken in evaluating such claims. As in all battles on land and sea, and in the air, confusion abounded. There were several cases of Hurricane pilots mistaking Gladiators for CR42s and Gladiator pilots mistaking Hurricanes for G50s. Some aircraft suffered serious friendly-fire damage in this way, though luckily no-one was killed. Some jittery Italian pilots swore that they had tangled with Spitfires. The Italians made a highly exaggerated claim of seven British kills and three probables. The only British loss, in fact, seems to have been one Gladiator, shot down by Lieutenant Mario Bellegambi of 24 Gruppo. The Gladiator's pilot, Flight Lieutenant Dicky Abrahams, baled out to safety over the Greek lines.

> No sooner had I fallen sprawling on the ground [Abrahams wrote later] than I was picked up by Greek soldiers who cheered and patted me on the back. I thought I was a hell of a hero until one soldier asked me, 'Milano? Roma?' and I realized they thought I was an Iti. They'd didn't realize it was possible for an Englishman to be shot down. So I said *'Inglese'* and then the party began. I was hoisted on their shoulders, and the 'here the conquering hero comes' procession started. We wined and had fun. Jolly good chaps.[6]

(That same night, while the British were celebrating the day's air victories, a devastating earthquake hit the town of Larissa. Hundreds of people perished. As British and Greek servicemen laboured in the rubble, Italian CantZs bombed what was left of the town. Two Greek PZLs joined two RAF Hurricanes to pursue the raiders, downing two of them near Corfu.)

Official recognition was not long in arriving. 'Magnificent,' Longmore cabled. 'Congratulate all.' Coming from him, those three words were laudatory indeed. D'Albiac was a bit more expressive, conveying his 'hearty congratulations' for 'a first-class show'. That evening Greek radio news readers paid fulsome tributes to the RAF, making especial mention of 'the flight lieutenant who led the flight of Hurricanes'. 80 Squadron, in fact, had just topped a total kill score of 100. On 2 March the news came through that Squadron Leader Jones and Flight Lieutenant Nigel 'Ape' Cullen had been awarded the Distinguished Flying Cross.

Thanks to the RAF operating out of Fairy Tale Valley, the Regia Aeronautica's air superiority over Albania was seriously dented. However, Pricolo could still keep a lot of Italian planes in the air. In February alone the Regia Aeronautica carried out more than 250 bombing raids on Greek targets, killing hundreds of noncombatants as far south as Crete. While the number of battleworthy Greek planes was down to the low double digits, Pricolo could call on nearly 400 modern bombers and fighters – more, in fact, than there were pilots to fly them. General Ranza, the rotund air chief in Albania, told Cavallero that just seventy of his 130 fighter pilots were available for flying duties.

The battered RHAF had reached its breaking point on 26 February when Wing Commander Emmanuel Kelaidis, the Greek fighter commander, ordered his squadrons grounded for a hopefully short rest and refit. The previous day, at least three precious PZLs of 21 and 23 Mirai had been lost over Albania. The remnant of the Greek air force by now could only look on from the ground as the RAF was fighting its battle.

The RAF's monopoly on British military activity in Greece came to an end on 2 March – a week before the start of the abortive Italian Spring Offensive – when the British-New Zealand-Australian expeditionary force began to disembark at Piraeus for deployment in northern Greece. What the late Metaxas had feared was coming to pass. But had he been alive, might he have changed his mind? Conditions in the Balkans were much more dangerous in early March than they had been in January. Hitler had demonstrated his resolve to overcome the Balkan states come what may, whether the British entered Greece or not. In fact, the issue of whether the British should be in Greece at all was now academic, as King George and Koryzis had little choice open to them.

Greek air attacks on the *Offensiva di Primavera* were sporadic. 32 and 33 bomber Mirai bombed the Italian lines on 11 March, though without much result, except for the loss of two Blenheims and one of the crews. Wing Commander Menelaos Kinatos, the commander of 33 Mira, volunteered to fly in the place of a newcomer whose wife was visiting the base. 'If I don't come back,' Kinatos told the young pilot, taking out his wallet and taking off his watch, 'give these to my sister.' He and his Fairey Battle didn't come back.

In Ioannina, 80 Squadron waited impatiently for more Hurricanes to replace its remaining tired Gladiators. Pattle was told that his flight would be given a rest at Eleusis near Athens. He was about to protest when his commanding officer, Squadron Leader Jones, casually dropped the bombshell: 'When you get to Athens, Pat, you had better see the tailor about getting an extra half ring sewn on.' That's when Pattle learned he had been promoted to squadron leader and given command of 80 Squadron's keenest rival, 33 Squadron, as well as a bar to his DFC.

The hard-bitten characters who made up 33 Squadron were proud of their insubordinate toughness, and when they learned that an 80 Squadron man was to be their new boss, they didn't take it well. The kill tally of 33 Squadron stood at ninety-one, about a dozen less than 80 Squadron, and the shortfall rankled. Of course, they had all heard of Pattle, and when he addressed his new pilots for the first time at Larissa they were prepared to give him a modicum of respect. The respect, though, turned to indignation when their clean-cut new commander at once berated them as a 'scruffy-looking lot'.

> Your flying, by my standards, is ragged [Pattle said]. Flying discipline starts when you start to taxi and doesn't end until you switch off your

engine. In future you will taxi in formation at all times unless your aircraft has been damaged, or in an emergency.[7]

33 Squadron were not going to take that sitting down, especially from someone whose forenames were Marmaduke St John! One of the pilots, 'Ping' Newton, a cocky Rhodesian, promptly challenged Pattle to a mock Hurricane dogfight. Newton had been flying Hurricanes for at least six months, while Pattle was still relatively new to the type. As the whole squadron watched, Pattle and Newton jousted dangerously at 10,000ft over Larissa. Within minutes, Pattle had outmanoeuvred Newton, sticking on his tail despite the Rhodesian's most desperate efforts to evade. Pattle was gracious in victory. 'You're too smooth at the controls,' he told a chastened Newton. 'You've got to be rough with them in a dogfight.' That was how Pattle established mastery over one of the roughest squadrons in the RAF.

Pattle and 33 Squadron went into action for the first time on 23 March. Thirteen Hurricanes touched down at Paramythia to join 84 Squadron's Blenheims and 112 Squadron's Gladiators on a raid to Berat. There was considerable opposition over the target, as well as low cloud; two of Pattle's Hurricanes were damaged by flak but remained flyable. The squadrons encountered more Fiat G50s near the Greek border; one Hurricane's engine stopped and its pilot baled out. There was just enough time for lunch back at base before 33 Squadron took off again for a raid on the Italian air base at Fieri in retaliation for the Italian attack on Paramythia on 22 February. Fieri was known to be smothered in flak and swarming with G50s, and for one of the few times in his career, Pattle's mouth was dry.

At 25,000ft over Fieri, as the Hurricanes were beginning their strafing glide, a pack of G50s and Macchi MC200s jumped them. The dogfight was fierce, but somehow the Hurricanes managed to return to Paramythia, Pattle the last to get back. On jumping down from his cockpit he made for the ops room in a cold fury. In no uncertain terms, he reminded his pilots that their mission was to strafe the field at Fieri and not get involved in diversionary actions, as the Italians no doubt had planned. He and another pilot had been the only ones to carry out the stated mission.

By early April it was blindingly obvious that the main threat to Greece was no longer the Italian army in Albania, or even the Regia Aeronautica, but the Germans massing on the Bulgarian border and about to invade. The RAF and RHAF squadrons were recalled to bases nearer Athens and in east Greece to be ready for the new fight to come.

Chapter 10

'This One's For The *Elli*!': The Naval War

The Regia Marina and the RHN – the Psara and Spetsai shell the coast – Greek submarines slide into action – the naval conference – the Papanikolis and Torpedo 13 – Iatridis draws blood – Kavvadias shells Vlore – attack on the goats – the submarine war – Cunningham's cryptic smile – Operation Gaudo – Battle of Cape Matapan

In the frantic months of war since October 1940, what had the Royal Hellenic Navy been doing? True to its tradition since classical times of guarding Greece's seas and some 12,000km of tortuous coastline (mainland and islands), the navy did not neglect to build up security as relations between Greece and Italy worsened. A secret order issued on 27 May 1940 detailed the navy's rules of engagement and concluded with blunt instructions to officers and men on the indomitable Spartan spirit expected of them:

> Bear in mind that the reason for existence of the Army, Navy and Air Force is that they should sacrifice themselves to the last man for the country's independence. There is no middle way. Let this powerful foundation be the guide to our thoughts and actions. Enshrined within is the *honour of our country*. To preserve this requires a spirit of self-denial and self-sacrifice. It is required to resist to the end, and to the last man, any attempt to violate National Sovereignty. Fortifications, ships, technical works and in general any war materials are to be blown up by the defenders rather than fall into the hands of the enemy. No-one can win if he is afraid of death.[1]

At the outbreak of hostilities with Greece the Regia Marina had two large *Littorio*-class battleships of 35,000 tons, four *Cavour*-class battle cruisers of 23,000 tons, seven 10,000-ton heavy cruisers, fourteen light cruisers and 102 destroyers and torpedo boats. The whole fleet had paraded off Naples on 7 March 1940, gladdening the hearts of Hitler and Mussolini who were observing from the bridge of the *Cavour*, the pride of the fleet. Flanking them were eighty submarines and scores of minesweepers and torpedo boats. Crowds on the Naples waterfront cheered as the endless procession sailed past. Then, in a carefully staged show of what the Italian navy could do, a squadron of destroyers turned their guns on the old and decommissioned battleship *San Marco* that had been brought out to face its last moments, and quickly pounded it to a smoking hulk.

Against this the RHN could field a mere thirty-seven aging vessels, none of them bigger than a destroyer. The *doyenne* of the Greek fleet was the ancient 9,500-ton *Averof*, the country's first battle cruiser, already thirty years old and now moored at the Salamis Naval Station for crew training. Its record in clearing the eastern Aegean Sea of Turkish warships in the Balkan War of 1912–13 had ensured its survival as an honoured relic. The active Greek fleet consisted of eleven destroyers, thirteen torpedo boats (none larger than 300 tons), six submarines, four minesweepers, two minelayers and a supply ship.

At 2.00 am on 30 October Commander Panayotis Konstas, the commander of the destroyer *Psara*, received orders to take his ship and the *Spetsai* up to the Albanian frontier to bring their guns to bear on the Italian forces. An army lieutenant colonel was to go with them to advise on targeting. Later that morning Konstas received his orders from Commander-in-Chief Papagos, very much preoccupied over the initial Italian advances. Papagos, on the instructions of Metaxas, wanted the Greek destroyers to open fire on the Italian troops to relieve the pressure on the army. At 2.15 pm the *Psara* and *Spetsai* steamed out of the Salamis channel, heading for the Corinth Canal at twenty knots. Only then did Konstas reveal the mission to the crews.

> The Greek Navy [he messaged] has reserved for us the supreme honour of carrying out the first naval operation [of the war]. I am certain that we will not disappoint. Commander Konstas.[2]

It took more than two hours for tugs to tow the two ships through the slit-like Corinth Canal, whose limestone banks rise sheer for hundreds of feet on either side, fighting a contrary current. The ensuing night was tense as the two ships threaded their way carefully through the minefields in the Gulf of Corinth, arriving the following morning off the mist-shrouded northwest Greek coast at the mouth of the Kalamas River. The officers on watch could hear the distant booming of cannon fire. Through their binoculars they could make out the thread of the Preveza-Igoumenitsa road hugging the coast along the base of the hills. At 6.40 am on 31 October Konstas ordered the battle flags raised on both ships, slowed them to seven knots, called out the first targets for the guns to home in on, and gave the order to fire.

The gunners needed no encouraging. 'This one's for the *Elli*!' they shouted as they loosed salvo after salvo. 'This one's for the ultimatum!' Before long the village of Ano Sagiada, where the Italians were believed to have ammunition dumps, was a mass of flame. For half an hour the bombardment continued, the gunners firing methodically and grimly in cold revenge, their faces blackened with cordite, as the two destroyers steamed steadily northwards. On reaching Corfu, they about-faced and sailed back south, turning their guns to port to pound the coast once more.

Half an hour and some 250 expended shells later, the *Psara* and *Spetsai* high-tailed it back south, zigzagging at twenty-seven knots, but the only sign of the enemy was a formation of aircraft shadowing them at a safe height. Unknown to the crews, however, another unseen danger was lurking. The RHN submarine *Papanikolis* was patrolling the area, but Commander Miltos Iatridis, the sub commander, had not been told that friendly warships were about. Near Levkas the *Papanikolis* hydrophones picked up the destroyers' engine noise and Iatridis was on the point of sending a few torpedoes in their direction when something made him hesitate – it was only the second day of the war and giving the order would be a fraught decision, and besides, he had no specific orders to engage. He let the *Psara* and *Spetsai* sail on, unknowing of what almost befell them.

At 9.20 am the ships slowed and stopped to wait for evening before attempting the run home through the Gulf of Corinth where in daylight they would be vulnerable to air attack. After nightfall they bucked and plunged through a stormy sea, arriving at Salamis nine hours later. Barely had the crews time to rest than Italian bombers appeared over the naval station. In two attacks they did little damage. The *Psara* and the venerable *Averof* were moved to a safer anchorage at Eleusis, better protected by anti-aircraft batteries.[3]

Whether the Ionian Sea raid did any appreciable damage to the advance of the Raggruppamento del Litorale along the coast is debatable. But the Greek public was led to believe so and understandably there arose a clamour for more such naval stunts, not least from the navy itself. It was a week in which the Greek army (and to a lesser degree the air force) was getting all the glory on the Epiros front, and the navy yearned for a bigger piece of the action. The action was there, but it wasn't of the kind that made headlines. In fact, the RHN's main task was to ferry troops from the islands to Thessaloniki for despatch to the front. Thirteen troopships and requisitioned island-hoppers began the ferry service on 2 November, accompanied by the navy's entire destroyer force. Some narrowly escaped being bombed in the port of Volos. Many ships had to make the nerve-racking crossing from the eastern Aegean islands at night, in dangerously heavy seas, with the ever-present risk of enemy submarines. The entire 5th Division was transported from Crete in this way. In fact, this unsung operation was to be the most successful RHN action of the whole war. Thanks also to the overhead patrols of the RHAF's naval cooperation squadrons not a single one of the 80,000 men, 120,000 mules and thousands of tons of supplies ferried over the treacherous waters was lost to enemy action in the crucial first months of the war.[4]

But in the first week of November all that was in the future. The navy wanted something more glamorous to do. Metaxas responded by calling a naval strategy conference under King George that met at the General Staff headquarters of the Grande Bretagne Hotel on 11 November. In Metaxas' view, the RHN's task was twofold: to keep protecting the troopships in the Aegean and to try and obstruct Italian reinforcements by sea in the Adriatic. The distance between these two theatres was considerable, and Rear Admiral Alexander Sakellariou, the naval staff chief, wanted to avoid tangling with a superior enemy in the Adriatic, but Metaxas overruled him.

'If the enemy is allowed to transfer reinforcements to Albania without opposition,' he said, 'there will come a time when we can't carry on. Therefore I ask – can the fleet intervene in some way towards a positive result?'

'It is possible,' Sakellariou replied, 'but I don't know how effective it will be.' The Fleet Commander, Rear Admiral Epaminondas Kavvadias, was rather more forthcoming. He envisaged a night raid in the Strait of Otranto, where the Albanian coast juts out towards Italy opposite Brindisi, by all six of the navy's destroyers, which would patrol on either side of a line between Brindisi and Vlore, to see what they could attack, before retiring south of Corfu at dawn.

'Will you fight?' Metaxas demanded of his bumptious fleet commander.

'Of course, if I encounter warships,' Kavvadias replied.

There was the question of whether Admiral Sir Andrew Cunningham's British Mediterranean Fleet, which had so far broadly cooperated with the Greeks, might be of any help in that mission. Sakellariou, distrusting the British – or perhaps knowing that Cunningham had enough on his hands already – said he didn't think so. Metaxas said he'd have a word with Rear-Admiral Turle, the British naval attaché (and later head of the British Military Mission), but he agreed that the operation should go ahead, whether the British co-operated or not. Turle, when consulted, was pessimistic about Cunningham's ability to help; the Royal Navy, he said, was already hard-pressed. Nonetheless, Metaxas couldn't wait; the Italian troopships had to be hit. If he could hold up the Italian advance in Epiros for two weeks, until the full Greek defence could be mobilized, he believed his country just might win.[5]

In the morning of 13 November Kavvadias boarded his flagship destroyer, the *Queen Olga*, to lead his small task force – the *King George*, *Psara*, *Hydra* and *Koundouriotis* – towards the Corinth Canal. They left one by one, at irregular intervals, with orders to spend the night holed up in some of the many convenient inlets of the Gulf of Corinth, and assemble at the Rion Strait. The *Koundouriotis*, however, lurched in the strong canal current and hit a bank, damaging the propellers, and had to return to base. The following morning the four destroyers emerged singly from their hidden anchorages, assembling at the anti-submarine nets at Rion at 3.30 pm. Here they waited until nightfall to cruise outside Patras, where Kavvadias knew Axis spies would be keeping an eye on Greek ship movements. After dark they formed up in a square, 500m between each ship, moving at twenty-five knots.

The full moon limned the calm sea with patterns of silver. There was only one moment of anxiety. At 7.30 pm the radiomen picked up a coded message from the naval observation station on Kephalonia that 'four destroyers of unknown nationality' were steaming north. Kavvadias fumed at the idiot who had sent the message by unsecured simple code. For all anyone knew, their position might have been inadvertently compromised. Some officers urged that the ships go back. But Kavvadias wouldn't be deterred at that stage. If the mission was compromised, then it was just too bad. He, for one, was there to fight.

Off Levkas Kavvadias ordered the ships to zigzag forward, leaving silver dragon's tails of foam in their wake. The long dark mass of the Corfu mountains passed slowly to starboard, and pulses began to quicken – they were entering the area of potential enemy action. Lookouts strained their eyes to scan the moonlit sea, but the horizon was clear as a knife-edge. At 11.17 pm Kavvadias ordered the crews to battle stations. On the ships steamed, approaching the waters off Vlore, but no enemy ship of any kind came in sight. It was well past midnight when Kavvadias, cursing in frustration, ordered his little fleet to turn back. 'For a moment,' the admiral confessed later, 'I wanted to send the Italian admiral a message saying, "I'm waiting for you!"' Decorum prevented him from issuing such a Leonidean challenge. But the RHN had gambled and won; in its small way it had sought out the Regia Marina to do battle and been vindicated.

The RHN took pride in its squadron of submarines: the *Papanikolis*, *Katsonis*, *Proteus*, *Nereus*, *Triton* and *Glavkos*. The only drawback to these French-built diesel-electrics was that they were old, the *Papanikolis* pushing sixteen years. They were fragile craft, and serving in them had its hazards. A few lacked hydrophones which could detect sound waves in water, and even sonar. None of them had anything resembling an up-to-date oxygenation system, and there was a constant shortage of spare parts.

On the first day of hostilities the squadron was ordered to patrol the Gulf of Patras; only the *Glavkos* stayed behind, awaiting a battery replacement. The *Papanikolis* and *Nereus* arrived off Patras to find an air raid in progress, and had to dive several times to avoid detection by enemy bombers. The subs had no orders to attack enemy shipping – merely to patrol and 'gather information', and this has since been criticized. It seems certain that the submarine squadron commander, Captain Athanasios Xiros, had little idea of how to employ his units. The fact that Iatridis in the *Papanikolis* was ready to exceed his instructions if necessary (as shown by the narrow escape of the

Psara and *Spetsai*) proves that the submarine crews wanted a more aggressive stance.

Yet the submarines encountered trouble of a non-combat kind. Shortly after arriving at its patrol area the *Nereus* ran aground in shallow water and had to return to Salamis for repairs. The *Proteus* went out to replace it on 2 November, but found itself hurled about by rough seas which surged into the craft through the conning tower, knocking out the diving controls. Commander Michael Hadjikonstantis only just managed to make it into a sheltered port on Paxi Island, where he waited for calmer weather before turning back to base. The *Papanikolis*, after fruitlessly searching the northwest Greek coast, was recalled to Salamis for a rest on 5 November, to be replaced by the *Katsonis* and *Triton*, one of the newest of the submarines. Cunningham now seemed willing to allow the Greek subs a greater radius of action in the Ionian Sea and the skipper of the *Katsonis*, Commander Athanasios Spanidis, was given the area off Sarande on the Albanian coast in which to hunt Italian shipping. For five days Spanidis didn't spot a thing, until he realized that the Italians would not be so foolish as to risk their supply ships by day. The distance between the heel of Italy and Sarande was small enough to enable small vessels to get through by night, which was apparently what was happening. The Admiralty saw the sense of Spanidis' observations and called off the Sarande patrols.

The *Triton*, meanwhile, had a rather tougher role: to check British intelligence reports of anti-submarine nets and mines stretched around Vlore, and to find out how extensive they were. When the submarine emerged from the Gulf of Patras on its way to its mission, Commander Ilias Verriopoulos, the skipper, expected to be piloted through the minefields at the gulf mouth. No-one was there to do it. After hours of fruitless messaging, Verriopoulos decided to return to Patras to tear a ferocious strip off the naval station personnel there who were responsible for providing minefield pilots. Having to dive every so often to evade Italian bombers, Verriopoulos disembarked at Patras and grabbed a pilot. But night was falling and the pilot couldn't see the buoys marking the safe passages. There was no choice but spend the night submerged and motionless at that spot, the mission already a day behind schedule.

The *Triton* was finally able to enter the open sea at 6.00 am on 5 November. When the sun came up Verriopoulos ordered a dive, both to remain invisible and to escape the choppy surface seas. All day the sub made its way north, surfacing at nightfall. But after midnight the sea got rougher, so Verriopoulos ordered another dive, only to find that the vessel's compressed air ballast system had failed. The skipper ordered a turn-about to shelter in a cove on Kephalonia, where the sub arrived at 3.30 am. As Verripopoulos was considering what to do, a crewmember threw himself up the conning tower steps and through the hatch, jumping onto the rocks ashore. 'What kind of war is this?'

the seaman shouted in a frenzy. 'What the hell are we doing at the bottom of the sea? I want to fight! A gun, a cannon, a sword, anything! Not like this, at the bottom of the sea!' As two sailors grabbed the man and tried to calm him, others tried to repair the compressed air system, but it took some time.

On 7 November the crew received another shock: Italian forces, it was reported, had landed at Katakolo point in the northern Peloponnese, a mere few kilometres away! The report proved to be false – attributed to fifth columnists in the Gendarmerie – but in the fevered atmosphere of early November it was widely believed. The *Triton*'s problem had by now been fixed and Verriopoulos radioed for new orders in the face of this apparent new development. The reply from the Admiralty was for him to proceed with all speed to the area of his original patrol, which he reached on the evening of 8 November. The following morning, off Vlore, Verriopoulos saw through his periscope two groups of small vessels, probably torpedo boats, heading straight for his submerged position. He gave the order to dive, and for the next half hour the *Triton*, its engines off, shook violently in the blasts of the depth charges raining down. When the explosions ceased, and the crew could breathe again, Verriopoulos got out of the area smartly, not surfacing until 7.00 pm.

But the sub's tribulations were not over. When it surfaced the sea was rough and water poured through the hatch. For two more hours the helmsman wrestled to stay on the prescribed course. The air inside the vessel began to get heavy; the air recycling system was breaking down. Then the lighting battery went, plunging the interior into darkness; a short circuit sparked a fire, sending smoke through the cabins. The lights were soon back on, but by now the air was well-nigh unbreathable. With a dive out of the question, the only thing to do was guide the sub like a bucking bronco on the surface through the filthy weather, keeping the hatch open merely for everyone to be able to breathe. At dawn the *Triton* struggled into Sami on Kephalonia, and after perfunctory repairs headed back to Salamis. The *Triton*'s sufferings did not go unmerited. At least it was able to ascertain that there was no anti-submarine net guarding Vlore, proving that Cunningham's concerns might have been exaggerated.[6]

Through November and early December, as the Greek army was notching up its string of victories in Albania, the RHN again began to chafe at the bit. So far the navy had well performed its main task of ferrying troops from the islands to the front. But the public wanted something more spectacular. Metaxas, ordinarily the consummate strategic planner, was himself caught up in the populist clamour for more naval triumphs and chaired a meeting on 12 December on how to bring the navy more into the action. Admiral Sakellariou, the navy chief, was sceptical. There had been talk of organizing a landing on the Italian-held Dodecanese islands in case Turkey moved to grab them when the Italians were defeated. But Metaxas wanted to keep attention concentrated in the west. Fixing his cold stare on his interlocutors, the tall and ordinarily taciturn admiral, a veteran of the Balkan Wars, pulled no punches. The state of Greece's little navy, Sakellariou argued, including 'the six submarines which in any other country would have been mothballed' precluded anything particularly eye-catching. In the aviation sector, all the RHN really controlled were a handful of obsolete Fairey III floatplanes with inadequate wireless batteries and a *mira* of Avro Ansons (13 Mira RHAF, in fact) based at Tanagra where they were stuck in the mud whenever it rained.

The RHN's real problem, Sakellariou said, was that it was split between two fronts, the Aegean and the Adriatic. Housed at Italian naval stations in the Dodecanese were a light cruiser, six new destroyers, fifteen submarines and fifty-one torpedo boats, backed up by fifty bombers and twenty fighters, all well-protected by flak batteries. Ferrying troops and supplies under the noses of that force without a single casualty, Sakellariou argued, was an incredible achievement, especially as the Regia Marina's subs had the run of the Aegean. In the Adriatic, however, the enemy's strength was far greater. The British had decimated the main Italian battle fleet at Taranto on 11 November, but the Italians had enough large capital ships left. Even now, the admiral claimed, the Royal Navy hesitated to probe north of Corfu, as Regia Marina formations were in the area. The most he could do in the west, he admitted, was to use the navy to carry supplies to the Greek troops.

> I would be unworthy of the office of Chief of the Naval Staff [Sakellariou concluded] if I were to counsel offensive operations by our destroyers in the Adriatic, which would inevitably cost us losses and give the Italians a chance at an easy victory ... I would consent to a sacrifice, however great, if I could expect advantages from such an operation. But I'm not going to recommend an action from which very little can be expected.[7]

Kavvadias, the Fleet Commander, then spoke up. This was his chance to shine. In contrast to his cautious boss, he declared with some flamboyance that he, personally, would be 'prepared to undertake any operation which you [Metaxas] might order and bring it to completion'. That was what Papagos, for one, wanted to hear. He asked whether the navy might want to transfer its base of operations to Corfu, but Sakellariou scotched that idea on the grounds that Corfu lacked adequate repair facilities, especially for submarines, and more critically, anti-aircraft cover. A battle for influence was now shaping up between Sakellariou and his ambitious number two. Kavvadias suggested moving the advanced naval base up to the Ambracian Gulf off Arta and asked Papagos for anti-aircraft guns. Papagos flatly refused; he had enough on his plate with the land campaign without having to worry about the sailors' needs. Tempers began to fray. Metaxas calmed the atmosphere by coming down on the side of the navy, urging that it continue its Adriatic patrols. 'The moral effect on the enemy is significant,' he said, 'because our small fleet dares to approach his main bases.' With that, the meeting broke up.

The next Adriatic patrol was scheduled for 14 December. The destroyers *Psara*, *Spetsai* and *Koundouriotis* were available, the others being on duty in the northern Aegean. Commanding the formation again was Kavvadias, whose orders were to disperse the three in inlets of the Gulf of Corinth for the night of 14 December and join up at the Rion narrows at 4.00 pm on the following day. In the teeth of high seas the destroyers crawled up the west coast of Greece, not being able to do more than twenty or so knots. Hail pounded on the hulls as they passed Corfu to the west at night. Then the *Spetsai* radioed that its boiler ventilators had broken down. Kavvadias ordered it to return to an anchorage at Araxos.

There were just two ships now, steaming into the dark and hostile Adriatic Sea. Huge waves crashed down on the lurching decks. The air temperature outside was well below zero. None of the crews, officers or ratings, had anything resembling an oilskin coat to keep out the cold. Occasionally the moon would peep through the ragged clouds to reveal the dark mass of the Albanian coastline to starboard. For about an hour, from 11.30 pm to 12.30 am on 16 December, the *Psara* and *Koundouriotis* sailed back and forth outside Vlore, hoping for some enemy ship to appear through the murk, but Kavvadias again was disappointed and set course for home. At least the daring stunt got some plaudits from the Royal Navy, if nothing else.

The previous evening, the outline of the two ships had appeared in the periscope of Commander Dionysios Zeppos of the submarine *Triton*, also lying in wait in the area. As the Italian-built destroyers were similar in outline to the Regia Marina's, Zeppos couldn't be sure what they were, so he ordered the sub to go under. Despite a list caused by faulty ballast tank valve, the *Triton* continued its voyage, reaching the Yugoslav coast on 16 December. At 11.40 pm Zeppos saw two large merchant ships, their lights on, and prepared to attack. But at the last moment he realized the vessels were in Yugoslav territorial waters and hence immune by international law. At once he suspected that Italian troopships and supply vessels were using Yugoslav waters in their voyages to and from Albania precisely to avoid Allied attacks by sea. In going through those waters, the Italians were compelled by international maritime law to assemble the transported troops on deck for inspection by the Yugoslavs. The Greeks could complain with some justice that the Yugoslavs never bothered to inform their presumed Greek allies of what they saw!

Zeppos' chance came on 20 December when at 12.40 am his periscope revealed a large merchant convoy steaming on the route from Brindisi to Durres, accompanied by four small warships. But the convoy was some six miles away, too far for his stipulated coordinates of action, and out of torpedo range.

At midnight on 22 December the *Triton* was on the surface recharging its accumulator batteries when the lookout shouted that he had spotted an enemy submarine. As the dark shape loomed closer, the deck gunners rushed to their positions. The enemy sub, its crew believing the *Triton* to be one of their own, flashed recognition signals. Zeppos gave the order to dive immediately. As the crew tumbled down the hatch, he hoped to manoeuvre his sub into a position from where he could torpedo the enemy vessel. But the enemy sub commander now had realized his mistake and cut his engines. For some minutes the two submarines stayed absolutely motionless in their positions, each afraid of betraying itself by the slightest sound or motion. Eventually Zeppos decided that he couldn't win the waiting game – his patrol period was now up, anyway – and slipped away with all speed through a sea that was now millpond-calm.

Lieutenant Commander Miltos Iatridis, RHN, was no ordinary crusty naval officer. Short and chunky and hard-living, a sea-dog of the ancient Athenian sort, he courted danger and was unhappy when he couldn't get it. He fretted at peacetime activities, and his promotion as a result had been slow. Service on torpedo boats and destroyers left him unsatisfied. The outbreak of war, however, had found him in command of Greece's oldest submarine, the *Papanikolis*, and rather more in his element. In the months leading up to the war Iatridis had trained his crew to a high pitch of efficiency, consistently winning awards in naval exercises.

Mariners the world over tend to be a superstitious lot. On the sub's first active patrol Iatridis had to put up with an extraordinary example in the person of Leading Seaman Dimitris Katsikoyannis of the torpedo section who baulked at having to handle a torpedo with the number thirteen stencilled on it. In fact, no sub commander except Iatridis had wanted that particular torpedo on board his own vessel! According to a story that may be apocryphal (though Melas describes the incident in some detail), that night, as the *Papanikolis* was nosing through the Rion narrows, Katsikoyannis sought ways to avert the jinx of Torpedo 13. In the sub's tiny iconostasis was an icon of Saint Nicholas, the Orthodox patron saint of mariners, lit up by a dimly flickering candle. The fearful leading seaman fished a few coins out of his pocket.

'Look,' he told the few seamen around him, their faces pale in the candle's fitful light. 'I'm going to put these coins on the icon. If they stick and don't fall, we'll be all right and come back.' He placed the coins on the glass – and they stuck.

Jubilant sailors sought out the skipper on the bridge. 'Sir! Come down and see a miracle!'

'What are you talking about, you fools?' Iatridis shot back. He had better things to do than listen to superstitious crewmen.

'The coins stuck to Saint Nicholas!'

It was a few minutes before Iatridis realized what must have happened; the glass of the icon was grubby and moist from weeks of veneration by the religious among the crew, which involved kissing the glass and breathing on it in prayer. Months of this had left its residue, hence the coins had stuck.

'Go and wash your coins,' Iatridis told a chastened Katsikoyannis, 'and dry them carefully, and then see if they stick.'

The torpedoman did as he was told, and lo and behold, the coins stuck to the saint's visage again. The seamen's eyes stuck out of their sockets, and Iatridis could find nothing else to say but to order them back to their stations and admit that he, too, was hoping for divine aid.

At 4.50 am on 20 December the *Papanikolis* entered the Adriatic danger zone. As it was pushing gently at sixteen knots west of the northern tip of Corfu, the hydrophones picked up the sound of a light cruiser or large destroyer steaming from Vlore in the direction of Taranto accompanied by three aircraft, but they were too far away to attack. That night the moon was brilliant, adding to Iatridis' problems. Manoeuvring so as to keep the moonlight from showing up the sub's profile, and alternately diving and surfacing so as to recharge the batteries and help the seamen gulp down some fresh air, Iatridis hugged the Albanian coast. It wasn't until 1.30 pm the next day that a tempting target finally loomed in his periscope's sights – a large passenger ship with two smokestacks. 'Battle stations!' Iatridis barked. The ship was the *Salerno*, requisitioned to carry mail and supplies to the Italian troops. But the ship, heading away from Vlore in the direction of Italy, was faster than the ancient Greek sub. For two hours the *Papanikolis* strained its engines to keep up, but at 6.30 pm Iatridis had to give up the chase and turn back south.

The moon beamed down brilliantly on the calm sea, as flat as an oil slick, as the *Papanikolis* lingered on the surface for another battery recharge. It was 1.15 am on the morning of 22 December when the lookout in the bow called out that a small ship was dead ahead. Through the mist the lookout made out the shape of something resembling a big trawler, the throbbing of its engine clearly audible, about half a mile away. Iatridis, bent over his charts below, heard the commotion on deck and climbed up. The skipper's immediate instinct was to move on the vessel, whatever it was, and capture whoever was on it. The other alternative would be to dive and get away. But Iatridis was a fighter by nature. For all he knew, he might be sailing into a trap, yet the thought, if it occurred to him, probably wouldn't have bothered him. Here was prey, and he wasn't going to be cheated of it this time.

As the craft got closer, he ordered an Italian speaker among the crew to call through the bullhorn in Italian: 'We are control! Come with your boat and papers so we can inspect you!' By now the boat was almost alongside. Someone who looked like its master got into a lifeboat with one other man and prepared to cross to the sub.

'No!' the crewman called, again in Italian. 'The whole crew has to come over, nobody remaining!' Soon five anxious-looking figures had climbed on the *Papanikolis*' deck. Only then did they realize they had fallen into Greek hands and were prisoners. The vessel was indeed Italian, and two of its crew were defiant. Pistols had to be drawn before they were subdued and locked up until they could be interrogated. The vessel, the 250-ton *Motorella Antonietta*, was searched and found to contain several tons of food and provisions for the Italians at the front, plus millions of lire in soldiers' pay. All of it went up in flames when the Greek seamen drenched the boat in petrol and set it alight – after an unsuccessful attempt to sink it by ramming.

The papers of the *Motorella Antonietta* turned up a bonanza, for among them were secret instructions by the Regia Marina on the precise positions of the minefields off Vlore and how the supply ships could avoid them.[8] Iatridis stepped up the patrols outside the port, to be rewarded on 24 December by the sight of twelve large ships approaching, escorted by six destroyers and fifteen aircraft. One of them he recognized as the *Salerno* that had got away three days before. It wasn't going to escape this time. When he had the *Salerno* firmly in his sights, he ordered torpedoman Katsikoyannis to fire. This was his chance to rid himself of Torpedo 13 which was the first to go. Three others followed at seven-second intervals. When the last was gone, Iatridis ordered a sharp 270-degree turn to port and halted the engines. Soon three muffled explosions were heard through the hull.

No sooner had the crew time to smile in satisfaction than the Italian destroyers were overhead, dropping depth charges. For nine hours the *Papanikolis* zigzagged under the surface, bouncing about in the incessant concussions, somehow escaping the lethal rain. On Christmas Eve night the crew – not to mention the five terrified Italian prisoners – could finally relax. On Christmas Day the sub was briefly attacked by enemy aircraft but suffered no damage. Iatridis delivered his captives to the naval station at the Corinth Canal and steamed home to a hero's welcome. The *Papanikolis*, it turned out, had sunk two troopships, the 15,000-ton *Liguria* and the 20,000-ton *Lombardia*, with considerable loss of life. And Leading Seaman Katsikoyannis could rest secure in the conviction that Saint Nicholas had indeed looked after his frail sub.

The sinking of the two troopships was a mere dent in the constant stream of Italian reinforcements sailing and flying across the lower reaches of the Adriatic. But its impact on the Greek public was far out of proportion to its practical result. The RHN finally had a sinking to its credit. Here, at long last, was payback for the sinking of the *Elli*. When the sub neared the jetty at Salamis it was greeted by a brass band. Iatridis and his crew were hoisted on shoulders in a frenzy of adulation. The other submarine commanders now had a role model to follow.

'This One's For The Elli!': The Naval War   185

One of them, Lieutenant Commander Spanidis of the *Katsonis*, noticed two enemy supply ships moving out of Vlore on Boxing Day. He fired two torpedoes at them but missed. The sub spent the next twenty-four hours hugging the Yugoslav coast in appalling weather. At 1.00 pm on 27 December a ship was sighted off the port of Durres. Manoeuvring to get close, Spanidis got in fact too close to the enemy, endangering his own vessel in case his torpedoes found their mark. After backing water and getting into position, Spanidis, by his own admission, was paralysed by a sudden attack of nerves.

> The small prospects of success [Spanidis wrote in his report] and my previous failed attack had their psychological effect on me and I did not order the torpedoes to be fired.[9]

The lapse indicates the constant nervous strain that submariners were under in those conditions. Spanidis was frank enough to recognize it in himself, and strove to make amends at 8.20 am on 31 December, when he caught the outline of an enemy tanker in his periscope. The ship was just half a mile away when Spanidis ordered his remaining two torpedoes to be fired. The sub's engines were stopped for the crew to listen for the explosions, but none came. Missed again! Cursing, he ordered the sub to surface so it could have a go at the tanker with its guns – a risky move, as the tanker might well be armed. His patrol would be over in less than two days, and he was damned if he was going to return to Salamis empty-handed, especially after Iatridis had been showered with glory.[10]

Now was Spanidis' chance to even the score with his rival. A hail of shells from the *Katsonis'* deck gun raked the tanker's hull as the crew dived into the sea in panic, afraid of a massive explosion. Heads calling for help bobbed alongside the submarine but despite the pleas of his crews, he couldn't rescue them. Already the stricken tanker would have signalled their position. The tanker's demise was viewed through the periscope. A grateful King George promoted Spanidis to commander and awarded him the Gold Medal of Valour. Four other officers received the Military Cross Second Class, and all the petty officers and ratings the Third Class. (The Yugoslav government, however, added a sour note by primly protesting to Athens that both the submarine and its victim were in Yugoslav territorial waters at the time, and shouldn't have been doing naughty actions.) The Greek submarine squadron was right to crow about its record. But disaster would soon follow.

The public acclaim surrounding the *Papanikolis* and *Katsonis* rankled with the commander of the submarine *Proteus*, Lieutenant Commander Hadjikonstantis. Taking his vessel to the Adriatic on 26 December, he vowed to come back with results. That was the last that anyone heard from him and his crew. It wasn't until 10 January that the mystery was solved and Rome Radio described the last moments of the *Proteus*.

It appears that at 10.00 am on 29 December an Italian torpedo boat, the *Antares*, escorting a convoy across the Adriatic, noticed torpedo trails, followed by the sudden surfacing of a submarine about two miles away. As the sub hurriedly dived, the torpedo boat skipper, Commander Niccolo Nicolini, headed straight for where he had last seen it. He was about to drop four depth charges timed to explode at the maximum depth when the sub suddenly nosed out of the water. Nicolini rammed the submarine with his boat, the sub dived again, and he let his depth charges go. The next stage in this dramatic tussle at sea was that the submarine resurfaced with a list, and vanished again. Nicolini dropped seven more depth charges, and soon the surface was littered with bubbles, oil slicks and wreckage. There were no survivors. The sub must have been the *Proteus*. And what Rome Radio conveniently omitted to mention was that it had just sunk two Italian troopships, probably the *Firenze* and the *Sardegna*.

Hadjikonstantis never got to enjoy his laurels. He and his entire crew, forty-eight men in all, were promoted and decorated posthumously. Yet the question remains why he surfaced so soon after firing his torpedoes. The most likely explanation is that the *Proteus*, suddenly lightened of its ordnance, floated up like a cork before the crew could react. This argues for a possible failure of the diving controls at a critical moment, as evidenced by the repeated surfacings. The truth will probably never be known.

While the fate of the *Proteus* was still a mystery, Sakellariou and his number two Kavvadias had put aside their differences and agreed to a British plan to shell Vlore. The RAF from its bases in Greece was already doing some damage to the port, but not enough to seriously hamper the Italian reinforcements. Kavvadias duly hoisted his flag on the flagship destroyer, the *Queen Olga*, on 4 January 1941, and sailed at the head of his squadron consisting of the *Psara*, *Spetsai*, *Koundouriotis* and *King George*. The bombardment of Vlore, it was pointed out, should take place only in case no enemy ships were located in the Otranto strait. The route was the usual one: to proceed singly and at intervals through the Corinth Canal, hole up the following morning, and assemble off Rion at noon. The weather was foul, and sea and sky were one. As the snow-covered heights of Mount Parnassos loomed to starboard, Kavvadias kept his crews busy with drills.

The low cloud was good, as they didn't have to worry about enemy air attack. Through driving rain the ships continued north until nightfall. Looking towards the Albanian coast, the crews could see the artillery flashes from the battles far inland. As no enemy ship had been encountered so far, Kavvadias ordered his squadron to turn its guns on Vlore. The crews were glad to contribute a bit of artillery of their own. But Commander Konstas on the *Psara* was concerned that aiming the guns would present a problem, as bad weather had prevented any aerial target reconnaissance. Moreover, the Italians had fortified an islet in the mouth of the Vlore gulf with scores of guns large and small against the possibility of a British attack from the sea. Also protecting the port was a long, thin, peninsula to the south, also lined with guns. Kavvadias, however, ordered the flotilla to sail in line astern seven miles off the port, heading south, and just when they were in the right position about seven miles out, to open fire.

The guns belched in unison and without stopping, with no answering fire from the shore batteries which apparently didn't want to reveal their position in case bigger ships lurked behind the attackers. When the salvoes were over and Kavvadias ordered a fast withdrawal south at twenty-eight knots, the crews were intrigued by hundreds of little lights flickering far away on the dark Albanian mountain ridges – the Greek army's forward posts to the south of Vlore were signalling their thanks to the navy for the bombardment! Kavvadias himself was in two minds; he had carried out his mission admirably, but had yet to sink a single enemy ship! (He didn't know yet what the submarine commanders did – that the Italian supply ships were hugging the Yugoslav coast instead of going straight across the Otranto strait.)

When Mussolini heard that the Greek navy had dared to shell Vlore, he ordered a retaliation in the Aegean. The specific target was a tiny and barren islet east of Amorgos, inhabited only by a dirt-poor family with a handful of goats. On the night of 6 January two Italian destroyers and five torpedo boats attacked the islet, driving the family in terror to a cave for shelter. Two hundred soldiers leaped ashore, machine guns firing – at no-one. At first light the Italians cautiously approached the family's hut, found it empty, and took away two dead goats as booty.[11]

As the Greek and Italian armies were fighting themselves to a standstill on the frozen peaks of Albania, the waters off Albania were the scene of an equally uncompromising silent war, as Greece's submarines stalked the icy depths and were stalked in return. In the early hours of 9 January the *Triton* came upon the Italian submarine *Neghelli* on the moonlit horizon and fired two torpedoes at it. The *Neghelli* disappeared in a blossom of flame and smoke, as the *Triton's* crew danced and hugged in joy. But Lieutenant Commander Zeppos, of course, had no time to waste in jubilation and ordered a fast escape back to a safe shelter on the island of Ithaki. For his kill he was promoted to commander.

The old and creaky *Papanikolis*, the sub that had inaugurated the string of victories for the RHN, started its fifth patrol on 23 January. Battling foul weather all the way, the sub found itself under attack from the air and dived. Muffled bomb blasts shook the hull, but no damage was done. On the morning of 28 January Iatridis spotted two merchantmen, one of them armed, sailing towards Vlore on a dead calm sea. As he called for battle stations, the two ships abruptly veered away at speed; the sub had been spotted. Zigzagging away from pursuing enemy craft, the *Papanikolis* continued its course towards the narrowest part of the Otranto strait between Brindisi and Durres. All the crew were suffering from stomach trouble, but nonetheless, shortly after midnight a large, dark shape loomed in the periscope's sights, less than a mile away. The shape turned out to be two ships – a supply ship heading for Brindisi, preceded by a destroyer. Iatridis sent one torpedo slamming into each.

By the following morning the weather in the Adriatic had dramatically worsened. Mountainous waves tossed the sub about whenever it tried to surface for a recharge. But when the *Papanikolis* entered its home station on 1 February, it received an enthusiastic public welcome, if somewhat subdued after the recent death of Metaxas. Plaudits even came from the stiff-lipped Royal Navy mission in Greece. Strike four for the RHN's submarines.

The bad weather in the western Greek seas throughout February held up underwater operations, but on 23 February the submarine *Nereus*, commanded by Lieutenant Commander Brasidas Rotas, had just managed to sink an enemy merchantman, when he had to dive to escape a rain of depth charges from two escorting destroyers that pursued the sub for two hours. Knocked about but undamaged, the *Nereus* exited the battle zone for a day or so in order to reload its torpedo tubes and give the crew a rest. At about 10.00 am on 25 February, when the sub was off the port of Vlore, a large ship was seen exiting the port, picking its way carefully among the minefields. Rotas was about to give the order to fire a torpedo when he luckily noticed big red crosses on it and had to let it go.

For the next couple of days the *Nereus* dodged repeated attacks by air and depth charge. The sub had probably suffered a cracked fuel tank and could have been leaking fuel, the resulting oil slick betraying their position. It was a real battle of wits, as Rotas and his crew would occasionally stop and listen on the hydrophones for the sound of pursuing destroyers; the enemy ships, for their part, would alternately stop and halt their engines to try and confuse the sub's hydrophone operator, and thus the deadly cat and mouse game would go on, perhaps for hours. Luckily for the Greeks, the sea began to get rough, forcing the Italians to call off their pursuit. But the towering waves themselves, beating against the rocky shore nearby, would boom in the earphones like the propellers of a large ship, fooling the hydrophone operator. It was a tired crew indeed that returned to Salamis.

Replacing the *Nereus* on patrol was the *Papanikolis*, starting its sixth such mission on 1 March. The moon was high at 4.30 am on 4 March in the battle zone outside Vlore when Iatridis gave the order to dive. The diving alarm failed to sound, so the order had to be repeated the length of the sub. The vessel duly slid below the surface – and almost never came back. Seawater had got into the front and rear battery accumulators, triggering a chemical change that released lethal chlorine gas into the air. Moreover, the inrush of water was upsetting the sub's equilibrium and sending it nose-down to the bottom. Iatridis wasted no time; as the *Papanikolis* began sinking at a faster rate he ordered the immediate emptying of the ballast tanks to enable the sub to surface and the crew to breathe. The old tub failed to respond; the depth gauge showed 15m and sinking, while the forward dip had increased to fifteen degrees off horizontal. Lieutenant Commander Vasilios Arslanoglou, the second-in-command, ordered the forward ballast valves shut, so that the sub could get back on an even keel. The order worked. Slowly the sub righted itself and inched back up to the surface, where the priceless fresh air could blow away the chlorine.

It was some time before Iatridis and his crew could recover from the shock of a probable watery grave. An onboard investigation showed that the seawater entered the batteries because a seaman had forgotten to close the outgoing air vents while diving... By the time the cause was established, two or three tons of water had got in. Many crewmembers were already displaying symptoms of chlorine poisoning: shortness of breath, fainting and disorientation. Iatridis gave them quantities of milk to counteract the effects. Of course, there was no question of submerging now. If it came to battle on the surface, the deck gun would have to suffice. When a hospital ship appeared on the horizon, Iatridis knew that if it spotted the *Papanikolis* it would signal its position to enemy warships. The only thing to do was dive, but how? The sub's air had not yet cleared of the chlorine. One way suggested itself: have everyone wear his gas mask. Iatridis duly gave the order, and the venerable *Papanikolis* survived to sail again.[12]

The *Triton* began the RHN's twentieth submarine patrol on 16 March under Lieutenant Commander George Zeppos, the brother of the previous skipper Dionysios Zeppos. Once in the Adriatic one of the officers who was on a submarine familiarization course began spitting blood. It turned out that he had a bullet lodged in his chest from a firearms training accident and the submarine's foul air had worsened his condition. Zeppos turned back and off-loaded the ailing officer at Ithaki. Back in the Adriatic theatre, Zeppos received a signal that a British submarine would also be operating in the area. The *Triton* duly kept its distance from the Albanian coast. When the sub's hydrophones picked up the sound of propellers, Zeppos assumed it was the British sub in the vicinity. But one look through the periscope told him it was a supply ship flanked by an enemy torpedo boat, with seaplanes flying overhead.

The Italians had stepped up their own patrols in the area, as on 14 March the hospital ship *Po* had been sunk in Vlore harbour by British aircraft. Edda Mussolini, the Duce's daughter, and her sister-in-law Countess Ciano had served on the *Po* as nurses; both were lucky to be picked from the water, but many wounded men had died.[13] But the ships were too far away for a quick strike, and by the time the sub got into position it would surely have been detected. For two days the *Triton* idled fruitlessly off the Albanian coast, and then at 9.40 am on 23 March Zeppos got his chance.

A large convoy, in two lines of ships, was seen steaming away from Brindisi in the direction of Durres and led by a destroyer. Zeppos decided to get in between the rows, approaching from the direction of the sun. He picked out one supply ship, the *Carnia*, towards the rear, lined up his sights and gave the order to fire four torpedoes in close order. The sub lurched in the sudden loss of weight, but the helmsman expertly kept it level at periscope depth. Three of the torpedoes smacked into the *Carnia*; the sound of the blasts through the crew's earphones was deafening. The moment of jubilation on a submarine can only be of the briefest, for immediately afterwards there comes the inevitable ordeal by depth charge. These are by far the worst moments. For two solid hours, with the sub absolutely immobile, the crew lived through seventeen depth charge explosions, any one of which could have blown them to smithereens or drowned them like mice. It was night before Zeppos dared surface to recharge and set course for home. The entire crew of the *Triton* received decorations and Zeppos was promoted to commander.

The RHN's destroyers, meanwhile, were not idle. In early March, when the British expeditionary force was being shipped from the Middle East to Greece, the Greek navy was called on to escort the convoys and protect them from raids by the Italians based in the Dodecanese islands. Here at last Sakellariou's concerns about the Dodecanese could be addressed, though not in the way he had first imagined. An area of particular danger was the Kasos Strait, between the small Italian-held island of that name and Crete. Kasos and its larger neighbour, Karpathos, bristled with Italian guns.

The transfer of British and Empire forces to Greece peaked between 18 and 25 March. The destroyers *King George* and *Koundouriotis* were escorting five empty troopships returning to Alexandria on 22 March when enemy aircraft roared out of the sunset from the direction of Crete. On the *King George*, and in command of the Greek ships, was the head of the RHN's destroyer force, Rear Admiral George Mezeviris, with a retired captain as head of the convoy. As three of the planes dived on the *King George*, the ship's anti-aircraft guns opened up. The lead plane bombed one of the empty supply ships and hit the engine room, but at once fell flaming into the sea. By now the HMS *Salvia*, a Royal Navy corvette at the head of the convoy, had brought its guns to bear, and the second aircraft was damaged before it could attack. The third plane also bombed the stricken supply ship and made off. Thirty seamen were rescued. The *Koundouriotis* was ordered to stay close to a Norwegian tanker whose engine had been knocked out by a near miss, while the *King George* made it safely to Alexandria with the remaining vessels.

In Alexandria the Royal Navy informed Mezeviris that the attacking aircraft were most likely of the Luftwaffe based in Sicily. This was the Greek navy's first intimation of the new direction from which the enemy was about to come, and the war was about to take. The information was confirmed by German war reports. But that didn't improve the foreboding of the convoy chief, retired Captain Constantine Papanayotou, as he reported to Cunningham about losing two ships.

'You realize, captain,' the British admiral replied with a philosophic smile, 'that in war you'll have losses. The fault is mine, as I didn't provide a cruiser for anti-aircraft support. Unfortunately I couldn't, as all my cruisers were on serious business.' Cunningham dismissed the relieved Greek officer with a promise that on the return journey to Piraeus he would be provided with just such protection, 'and you'll see what it can do.' The promised cruiser was the HMS *Calcutta*, which joined up with the *King George* and the troop-laden northbound convoy west of Crete. At the same time the RHN destroyers *Leon*, *Panthir* and *Ierax* were ordered to remain in the Ionian Sea.

The 'serious business' that Cunningham had cryptically mentioned to the Greek officer were in fact a bold plan to entrap a good portion of the Italian battle fleet. The Italians could not be expected to remain idle in the face of the transport of some 60,000 British troops to Greece by sea. In fact, Admiral Angelo Iachino of the Regia Marina had been preparing to strike a blow at the convoys for some time. Operation *Gaudo* was planned with the overall purpose of re-establishing Italian naval power in the Mediterranean after the devastating setback suffered at Taranto the previous November, and hitting the convoys would be a good start. Iachino, however, had little idea of the strength of the Royal Navy in the region. German intelligence, on which Rome relied, indicated that the British had only one battleship in the eastern Mediterranean, and no aircraft carriers.

Had Iachino known the truth, Operation *Gaudo* might well have been binned. Cunningham had at his disposal three battleships (his flagship HMS *Warspite* plus HMS *Barham* and HMS *Valiant*), one aircraft carrier (HMS *Formidable*), four cruisers and several destroyers. Against this line-up Iachino was sailing with the brand-new battleship *Vittorio Veneto*, which on 27 March met up with Vice Admiral Carlo Cattaneo's First Division (the heavy cruisers *Pola*, *Zara* and *Fiume*, each of 10,000 tons), and Vice Admiral Luigi Sansonetti's Third Division (the heavy cruisers *Trieste*, *Trento* and *Bolzano*). Iachino also could call on the light cruisers *Garibaldi* and *Abruzzi*, plus seventeen destroyers, to sweep the waters around Crete where the British convoys to and from Greece had to pass.

Yet the Italians lacked the one weapon which had enabled Britain to survive the Battle of Britain the previous year and come out on top, and that was radar. Cunningham also read intercepts by Ultra, the new code-cracking system. The British commander was thus able to track Iachino's fleet as it steamed to the south of Crete and then, on new instructions from Rome, north to Cape Matapan, dangerously close to the convoy route. In the evening of 27 March Cunningham was apparently relaxing in an Alexandria social club. No-one saw him quietly leave and get straight on board *Warspite* to set sail for the showdown in Greek waters. His first order was to Vice Admiral Henry Pridham-Wippell, who commanded four light cruisers and four destroyers, to sail south from Greece with all speed. The flotilla would act as a lure, to draw the Italians towards Cunningham's main force. Shortly after dawn on 28 March an Italian reconnaissance plane spotted Pridham-Wippell's ships. Iachino ordered Sansonetti to engage that force, which he did at 8.00 am, opening fire on HMS *Gloucester*. The shots missed, and Pridham-Wippell escaped by laying a smoke screen and racing towards Cunningham's force. The battle of Cape Matapan had begun.

Sansonetti's division began to pursue, but Iachino ordered him to stop and turn northwest, as Sansonetti was entering the area of British air cover. What Iachino did not expect was that Pridham-Wippell, in his turn, would turn about and start to chase Sansonetti. Pridham-Wippell was being unnecessarily foolhardy, as his job was to lure the Italians into Cunningham's trap. Instead, he was sailing into a trap himself. And Iachino would have sprung it, had not Pridham-Wippell managed to get out at high speed when the *Vittorio Veneto*'s big guns opened up on him.

Now it was the turn of HMS *Formidable*. Six Fairey Albacore torpedo bombers roared off the deck in the direction of Iachino's flagship. The Albacore looked and was clumsy. Touted as 'new' by the Fleet Air Arm, which was only just equipping with the type, it was in fact an ugly biplane that barely could exceed the top speed of the even more antiquated Fairey Swordfish it was replacing. In fact, it was exactly half as fast as a Hawker Hurricane. The Albacores failed to do any damage to the *Vittorio Veneto*, but the operation did occupy Iachino for long enough to enable Pridham-Wippell's ships to get away. Iachino himself turned to join his main force, while under attack from the RAF based in Crete. Then at 3.10 pm a second flight of Albacores from HMS *Formidable* sent a torpedo into the *Vittorio Veneto*'s vitals, seriously damaging it. The battleship was crippled, but still afloat.

Iachino was still apparently unaware of the presence of Cunningham's main force. He sent away his light cruisers and ordered Sansonetti and Cattaneo to form a shield around the limping flagship with their heavy cruiser divisions. At 7.25 pm a third strike by the *Formidable*'s lumbering Albacores scored a crippling hit on Cattaneo's *Pola*, slowing up Iachino yet more. Darkness had now fallen, and the Italian ships were now sitting ducks on the Royal Navy's radar screens. Cattaneo had detailed the *Pola*'s sister cruisers, the *Zara* and *Fiume*, to shield the shattered ship while the rest of Iachino's fleet continued to crawl northwest. This was the time for Cunningham to strike hard, to deliver a follow-up to the destruction which he had visited on the Italian battle fleet at Taranto four months before. Dodging enemy torpedoes, the HMS *Warspite* and *Valiant* split the darkness with their lightning and thunder, raining shells at 4,000 yards on the *Zara* and *Fiume* and two accompanying destroyers. The *Fiume* was the first to be reduced to a blazing hell, sinking in half an hour. HMS *Barham* opened up on the silhouette of an enemy ship outlined in the searchlight of the destroyer HMS *Greyhound*, but was unable to see the result. The *Zara* now drew the full force of fire from HMS *Valiant* and other heavy ships and went to the bottom at 2.30 am. The *Pola* was boarded and its surviving crew taken prisoner. Cunningham had the idea of towing it to Alexandria, but decided it was too seriously damaged, and turned his guns on it. The rest of Iachino's force got away in the dark, eluding Greek destroyers sent to intercept it.

The relative ease with which Cunningham had overcome the enemy encouraged him to try to pursue what remained of Iachino's fleet. Some officers argued against it on the grounds that the battle had already been won and anything else would be a waste of effort. What made Cunningham change his mind and return to Alexandria was the untimely appearance of Luftwaffe Ju87 Stukas screaming down and hindering efforts to rescue Italians in the sea. His high spirits, however, are understandable. The engagement had cost the Royal Navy just three men killed (the crew of an Albacore that was shot down), while the Regia Marina suffered a loss of more than 2,400 men. Vice Admiral Cattaneo went down with the *Zara*. Some 900 Italian naval officers and men were taken prisoner. For all his enthusiasm to pursue the enemy, Cunningham proved to be a gentleman of war. Before steaming back to his home port he took the trouble to send a message to Rome, and *en clair* at that, with the location of about 350 Italian survivors bobbing about on dinghies and awaiting rescue. With equal courtesy, the Italian naval staff radioed back with the news that a hospital ship, the *Gradisca*, had already sailed from Taranto and thanking Cunningham for his solicitude. Rarely in World War Two was there such respect between foes, a respect that probably saved hundreds of Italian lives. Many Italians were unhappy fighting the Allies, and on occasions such as this displayed their true colours. In fact, within two years Admiral Cunningham would have the honour of taking the surrender of what remained of the Regia Marina.

The battle of Cape Matapan saw the first use of radar in naval combat. The Italians never knew such a thing existed, and were nonplussed. An Italian gunnery officer rescued by the destroyer *Hydra* of the RHN was reported as confessing to the destroyer's skipper:

> In all my years as a gunnery officer I longed for the moment when I could press the button and loose my guns on the enemy. But neither did I see any enemy or even have time to give an order. With one salvo I was in the sea.[14]

Not surprisingly, news of the battle was suppressed in the controlled Italian press, which reported erroneously that one British cruiser had been sunk and that Italian casualties had been light.

Chapter 11

The Allies Arrive

British and Empire forces disembark at Piraeus – green light for Operation Marita – Cavallero lines up his divisions – Papagos' illusions – Greek fatigue begins to tell – planning the Olympus defence

At the beginning of March 1941, despite universal fears of an imminent German attack on Greece, Athens was still careful not to rupture diplomatic relations with Berlin. This was bad for security, as German diplomats were therefore on hand to witness the first units of the British and Empire expeditionary force disembark at Piraeus on 2 March. Some of the supplies were literally unloaded onto the steps of the port city's German consulate, whose staff was understandably very interested in the proceedings.

The incoming troops, destined to hold a line in northern Greece were 1 Armoured Brigade under Brigadier Harold Charrington, the 2nd New Zealand Division under Major General Bernard Freyberg and the 6th Australian Division under Major General Sir Iven McKay (soon to be replaced by Lieutenant General Thomas Blamey). By 21 March Charrington and Freyberg had got their men up to the Aliakmon River which Papagos visualized as a main line of defence when the Germans, as he expected, moved quickly to overrun Thessaloniki. But the Australians were slower in catching up with the rest, and General Wilson, the overall mission commander, was fretting about having to keep on his 'Mr Watt' mask, as the Greeks still shrank from advertising to the Germans that a British general officer was now holding an active command in Greece. Prince Peter has left a vivid description of 'Jumbo' Wilson:

> He was fat, with his wide grey suit with thin white pinstripes hanging from his bulky body. His face was long, like a pear, without very much hair on his head, and he would look at you in a distinctive and penetrating manner over his gold spectacles which he wore on his long, straight nose. An untidy moustache completed the picture.[1]

Papagos may have been in overall command, outranking Wilson, but it was clear that the Greek army was now definitely playing second fiddle in the defence of its country. Papagos had called up whatever reserves he could, though they were not of the calibre of the men who had fought in Albania. Wilson decided to place the Greek 19th Motorized Division, a motley assemblage of captured Italian Fiat tanks, ten British-built Vickers Mark IIIB light tanks, several dozen Universal Bren Carriers and whatever odd motorbikes and private cars could be requisitioned, in the mountainous areas where the Greeks knew how to fight. The 19th Motorized had been formed in January as a belated answer to the Italian Centauro Division, but too late to be of much use in the snow. In March it had been hurriedly pulled out of the Albanian front at Tepelene and rushed 600km to Katerini on the east coast in the shadow of Mount Olympus; on the gruelling route, several vehicles broke down and a few plunged off cliffs. From Katerini, led by Major General Nikolaos Lioumbas, and rather the worse for its journey, the 19th had trundled northwards to Kilkis, where it was destined to face the first and only fight of its career. It was placed in the East Macedonia Army Department, commanded by Lieutenant General Constantine Bakopoulos, tasked with holding the eastern shore of Doirani Lake and the border crossing with Yugoslavia in the valley of the Axios (Vardar) River while keeping an eye out for German paratrooper drops.[2]

Metaxas, as we have seen, had dismissed Wavell's offer of between two and three divisions as hopelessly inadequate and a needless provocation to the Germans. Yet Churchill, as we also have seen, was hard-headedly set on worrying away at the southern Axis flank simply to be seen doing something. Papagos, for his part, maintained a grandiose faith in the Greek army to perform miracles without British help.[3] Wilson was caught between two fires, trying his best to put together a defence which he knew could well be hopeless; but as a soldier, having to follow orders.

Hitler, for his part, sought control of the Balkans right down to Crete for two reasons. First was the need to secure his southern flank for the planned attack on Russia, and second, to secure Greece as a convenient base for attacks on Allied shipping in the Mediterranean, not to mention a vital staging post for reinforcing and supplying Rommel's forces in North Africa. If Egypt and the Suez Canal could be seized, then a most vital link in Britain's imperial connection with India would be severed. Greece would be a base from which a determined attack on this link could be made.

In fact, the Fuehrer had made his plans far in advance. On 13 December 1940, in Directive No. 20, he had ordered the Wehrmacht to prepare twenty-four divisions to roll over the entire Balkan peninsula in the spring – a move that was dubbed Operation Marita. Two months later Bulgaria, sensing that it might finally get its coveted outlet to the Aegean in the wake of the German army, had handed the Germans free passage through the country. In late March Hitler wrote to Mussolini asking him to concentrate all his attention on the Yugoslav border.

I would cordially request, you, Duce [Hitler wrote], not to undertake any operations in Albania in the course of the next few days ... I also consider it necessary, Duce, that you should reinforce your forces on the Italian-Yugoslav front with all available means and with the utmost speed.[4]

Hitler was obviously impatient to get the Italian discomfiture in Albania over with so that he could show his bumbling Axis partner how wars really should be fought.

Operation Marita would provide the example. The German Twelfth Army of Field Marshal Wilhelm List, massed just inside the border in Bulgaria, comprised five armoured Panzer, two motorized and three light mountain divisions and three SS regiments of the all-Nazi Adolf Hitler Division, not to mention an overpowering Luftwaffe. In terms of sheer firepower, List could bring more than 1,900 heavy tanks into action against Wilson's 176, nearly 1,100 artillery pieces against 427 and 1,549 anti-aircraft guns against 228. The Germans also had double the number of mortars than the Anglo-Greek force, backed up by some 1,000 Luftwaffe aircraft, including swarms of the feared Junkers Ju87 Stuka dive bomber, against D'Albiac's forty-five (though some sources put that number rather higher, taking into account the remnant of the RHAF). Against this juggernaut Wilson could field two and a half full divisions, plus the Greek contingent, numbering just under 60,000 men, of whom perhaps 35,000 were front-line troops.

Though the numbers speak for themselves, the quality of armaments, moreover, overwhelmingly favoured the Germans. The Vickers light tanks (not to mention the second-hand Fiats captured in Albania) were tin cans compared to the Panzers even in the mud of an early spring. Wilson knew, of course, what he was up against, and had no illusions. The same cannot be said, however, for Papagos, who pinned great hopes on the Yugoslav army, nominally 800,000 strong, which he expected would help dam a German offensive midway across Serbia. The truth, however was that the Yugoslav army, though large, was ill-equipped and of low morale, riven by ethnic splits (the same ones that would break up the country fifty years later) and understandably reluctant to give up half its territory on the say-so of a Greek general.

To clarify the Yugoslavs' intent and coordinate strategy, Papagos and General Jankovic, the deputy Yugoslav chief of staff, met at the railway station of Kenali on the Greek-Yugoslav border on the night of 3 April. Wilson was there to represent the British and keep an ear to what Papagos was thinking.[5] For four hours the Greek and Yugoslav generals argued their respective points: Jankovic for the need to defend Thessaloniki as vital for Yugoslav sea trade, Papagos for the Yugoslavs to form a line across Serbia, and Wilson sheepishly admitting that all Britain had available just then was an armoured brigade and infantry division. The admission came as a shock to Jankovic, who protested that the British Imperial General Staff had promised the Yugoslavs an armoured division, not a mere brigade.

During the debate Papagos and Jankovic, apparently to mollify the atmosphere, agreed that the Greeks and Yugoslavs could join forces to drive the Italians out of Albania, now that warmer weather had arrived. Jankovic pledged four divisions to invade Albania from the east and converge on Tirana while the Greek Epiros and West Macedonia Army Departments would push from the south. Wilson did not intervene to halt this obvious diversion away from the main task at hand. He probably realized that to start arguing at this point would be counterproductive and moreover, that the planned joint offensive in Albania would be thwarted anyway by events in the east – as indeed happened.

One consequence, however, was that Cavallero, getting wind of the plan, deployed the newly-arrived Firenze Division on the left flank of the Ninth Corps abutting the Yugoslav border, beefed up by the Cuneo, Alpine battalions and cavalry. The Puglie, reinforced by Carabinieri and Finance Guard units, was sent to block the Dhrin Valley, with the Centauro farther to the north. Cavallero's strategy now was a purely defensive one in the first phase. Later, assuming that the Germans would successfully penetrate Greece from the direction of Bulgaria and turn west, Cavallero would serve as an anvil against which List's advancing hammer would smash the Greeks and Yugoslavs. In reply to a German staff officer's question about how long the Italians could hold out in Albania, Cavallero replied, 'about a month'.

The Greek strength on the Albanian front at the beginning of April stood at fourteen divisions and one brigade. From east to west, the 13th, 9th, 10th and 16th Infantry Divisions made up the West Macedonia Army Department (formerly III Corps) holding the Pogradec-Mount Tomori sector. Next to them were, in order of formation, a part of the 11th Division, the 6th, 17th, 5th and 4th Infantry Divisions (II Corps); plus the 2nd, 8th and 3rd Infantry Divisions (I Corps). The I and II Corps formed the Epiros Army Department. The 1st and 15th Divisions and part of the 11th were held in reserve along with the Cavalry Division at Korce, the 20th Infantry Division at Florina and the 21st Infantry Brigade.

Against this line-up were twenty-one Italian divisions (minus those switched to the Yugoslav border). The Ninth Corps held the left of the Italian line, followed by the Third, the Twenty-sixth, the Eleventh, the Fourth, the Eighth and Twenty-fifth on the far right; this last corps included the battered Julia and Ferrara divisions, and the Wolves of Tuscany. This wall of troops, Mussolini noted with pious hope, 'will hold fast in any circumstances.' This time, though without knowing in what sense, he was right.

In the spring of 1941 what the Greeks probably did not realize was how parlous Britain's own position was. The Blitz was in full spate, not only over London but over other major British cities as well, killing civilians and disrupting vital war industries. Hitler's U-boats were tearing into Atlantic convoys, sending food and other supplies to the bottom; in March alone half a million tonnes of merchant shipping were sunk. Churchill himself, though keeping up an indomitable public face, was fighting off fits of depression, his notorious 'black dog', as the dangers that Britain faced 'gnawed at [his] bowels'.[5] Yet he kept his promise to the Greeks, even though the weakening of Britain's Middle East forces may well have helped contribute to the desert successes of General Erwin Rommel's Afrika Korps later in the year.

Though there were plenty of British officers in the expeditionary force prepared to believe they were facing a second Dunkirk, the possibility does not appear to have occurred to Papagos. Still basking in the glory of the Albania campaign, the Greek C-in-C believed that his forces still confronting the Italians on that front could – after disposing of Cavallero with Yugoslav help – veer westwards to threaten the Germans in the flank.[6] The plan, bordering on fantasy, indicates that Papagos may have known dismayingly little about the actual strength of the Germans. It also displayed an indifference to the fatigue of his own Greek soldiers, who he mistakenly believed would be ever ready to advance at his command.

But the Greek army was tired. Dispiritedness was quick to set in. Corporal Nikolaou of the 42 Evzones wrote in his diary on 16 March: 'May God and the Virgin Mary end our ordeal quickly.' Many of his entries contain the same devout wish. The following day, while on patrol he stumbled with horror on the frozen body of an Italian soldier and, typically, felt sorry for the family that must be waiting for him. Nikolaou hadn't been able to change his underwear in six weeks or wash his hair in four months. Legions of lice were his constant companions. He was on constant night supply missions with his team of mules and by day couldn't sleep for the incessant cannon fire. A few days before, his wife had given birth to a third daughter, and he wanted to get home. Instead, he was stuck 'sitting on an Albanian mountainside feeding mules'.[7]

The Italians were quick to try and take propaganda advantage of the stagnation in the Greek lines. Italian aircraft buzzed the lines on 22 March with a couple of tons of leaflets. They were a clever appeal to the Greeks' patriotic instincts with the message that they were suffering in Albania not for themselves, but for the British. Nikolaou picked one up:

> One of them shows a mother grieving over her 17-year-old boy fallen in battle, while [they] have 22-year-old soldiers. It says that we're fighting for England. The other poster shows an English mother putting her children into a posh car, and says the English have sent their children

to America for safety while we're exposing our children to a thousand dangers.[8]

Nikolaou's company was ordered to retire to Konitsa for a rest, though the relief the men felt was tempered by news of the pro-Axis coup in Yugoslavia. 'If that's true, then Greece will surely lose the war,' he wrote, displaying a flash of insight denied even to his commander-in-chief.

Papagos, for his part, seemed unaware of what the ranks were thinking. He was loth to deprive army and people of the aura of triumph they both enjoyed, and to his credit, never considered capitulating in the face of the Germans. He was resolved to fight, Leonidas-like, to the bitter finish. In fact his father's name, which serves as a middle name in Greece, was Leonidas, also his son's name.

> The Greek high command [Papagos wrote in his memoir] decided that even in the event of a German intervention, the main Greek effort would continue to be made in the Albanian theatre of operations, so that the Greek army, whatever the developments on the Bulgarian front, would maintain the position of victors over the Italians.[9]

In the third week of March General Heywood was taken on a tour of the Albanian front. Papagos suspected, rightly, that the head of the British Military Mission secretly wanted to check for any defeatist sentiment among the Greek commanders in Albania. To thwart that, Papagos had ordered every unit commander to assure Heywood that Greece would stay faithful to the Allied cause in case of a German attack. Pistikas, the Epiros Army Department commander, was the first to dutifully give Heywood such assurance. One of the clerks at Pitsikas' headquarters was Private Kanellopoulos, the sociologist lawyer who had vainly tried to get the tragic Colonel Rokkos acquitted of dereliction of duty at the Christmas Eve court-martial. Kanellopoulos, according to one observer, greeted Heywood in the corridor with 'a strange, Mona Lisa-like smile'.[10] Nonetheless, some officers were blatantly insincere. One was General Bakos, the II Corps commander holding down the advanced Kelcyre sector, who boasted to Heywood that 'in all her history, Greece never let down her allies and had no intention of doing it now'. (Weeks later, Bakos would be one of the first generals to surrender to the Germans, so far forgetting his vow as to become a minister in the puppet occupation government.)

Papagos realized that morale, from himself down to the lowliest private, would collapse if the army in Albania was pulled back, even in case of a German invasion from Bulgaria. Yet as winter gave way to spring, Albania was forced on the back burner as indications multiplied that the centre of combat gravity was about to shift. As early as January, intelligence was reporting twelve German divisions in Romania and feverish work underway on throwing bridges over the Danube and into Bulgaria. German intelligence officers in civvies were crawling over Bulgaria; what were they doing there if not scouting for invasion and occupation facilities?

Northern Greece was poorly equipped to meet a threat from the frontier. New airfields were needed at Thessaloniki and other towns, while the ports of Thessaloniki, Kavala and Amphipolis needed upgrading to able to handle the disembarkation of one division a day. Supplies for the Allies had to be stockpiled in such a way as to resemble ordinary Greek military procurements. Greece's trains were requisitioned for military needs. Wavell had estimated that in the best of cases it would take about two months for the required expeditionary force to be assembled and shipped to Greece.

What of the vaunted Metaxas Line along the Bulgarian frontier? In Papagos' estimation it would take at least twelve divisions to adequately man the fortifications, more than twice as many as the Greeks and British together could provide. Even so, there were weak spots in the line, the weakest being on the left, on Mount Kerkini (Beles). Surging through this point, where the borders of Greece, Yugoslavia and Bulgaria meet, the Germans could be in Thessaloniki within hours, cutting off the forces in the east as well as those in Albania. The only feasible solution in Papagos' view was to plan for a withdrawal to a 150km defensive line from Mount Kaimakchalan on the Yugoslav border to Mount Olympus.

That, however, was assuming Yugoslavia would remain upright. If the Yugoslavs collapsed, the whole rear of the planned Kaimakchalan-Olympus line, not to mention the forces in Albania, would be in grave danger. In such a case the line would have to be moved from a northwest-southeast orientation to a roughly east-west one, from Mount Olympus to the Aliakmon River, and from there westwards across the mountains all the way to Mertzani on the Albanian border, where the Greek divisions in Albania would hopefully be able to link up. Either way, the military decision would be politically unpopular, as it would entail abandoning Thessaloniki and a large chunk of its surrounding territory to the enemy without a fight. The morale of the soldiers would inevitably suffer as a result.

When on 1 March German forces began pouring into Bulgaria, Eden and Lieutenant General John Dill, the chief of the Imperial General Staff, had asked Papagos to set in motion his plan of withdrawal to the new lines of defence, a manoeuvre that would take some three weeks to complete. The Greek C-in-C hesitated; it was still far from clear what Yugoslavia would do and, as a consequence, he was by no means convinced the withdrawal plan was necessary. Moreover, he was bitterly against any forced withdrawal from Albania. Instead, he proposed an alternative plan: while the Greek defenders at the Metaxas Line stood firm, from Mount Kerkini to the mouth of the

Nestos River on the Aegean Sea, the 12th and 20th Infantry Divisions plus the 19th Motorized Division would retire to the Kaimakchalan-Olympus line to join the British. If Yugoslavia held out against the Germans, then the units along that line would be rushed up to the Bulgarian front.[11]

Of course, huge uncertainties hovered over all the plans, and by the time of the Kenali railway station meeting, all bets seemed to be off. The pro-Axis coup and pro-Allied counter-coup had come and gone in Belgrade. The chances of Yugoslav survival were very slim. The Turks, for their part, feared a German attack as well and were not going to risk anything that might trigger one. However, the Turkish military attaché in Athens was sympathetic to the Allied cause and hence a useful source of intelligence. Though pessimistic about Greece's chances, he claimed also to be confident that the Turkish army was strong enough to halt the Germans if it came to a crunch.

Chapter 12

6 April 1941: The Saga of Fort Rupel

Erbach delivers Hitler's ultimatum – List's Twelfth Army invades – the Clan Fraser explosion – the attack on Fort Rupel – Bakopoulos calls for a cease-fire – the Greek 19th Motorized Division implodes – the fall of Rupel – German admiration – the RHN and RHAF carry on the war – Pattle goes down – Nikolaou's Easter

> It is the Germans' honour and pride to have such adversaries.
>
> German officer taking the surrender of Fort Rupel

But neither Papagos nor Wilson would be given any more time to think. At 5.15 am on 6 April the telephone rang in the home of Koryzis, the Prime Minister. In a sinister replay of the events of the early hours of 28 October, Koryzis heard that the German ambassador, Prince Victor Erbach zu Schonberg, would call on him in half an hour. The prime minister barely had to time to notify the king and his ministers when the ambassador stalked in, sat down, and began to read Koryzis a long list of German 'grievances' against Greece. The main one was that little Greece had had the temerity to join with Britain, a sin for which the Third Reich had displayed 'excessive patience and tolerance'. Britain, Erbach claimed, was planning to use Greece as a major base of operations against the Axis, and that could not be tolerated.

> For this reason, [the German declaration said], the government of the Reich has already given orders to its forces to drive out British forces from Greek soil. Any resistance which the German army encounters will be mercilessly crushed.

Of course, the declaration continued in the hypocritical manner of all such texts, 'the German forces do not come as enemies ... by expelling the British invaders from Greece, they will provide a service to both the Greek people and the European community'.

German propaganda had cleverly turned the ethical aspect of the Greek situation on its head. The British expeditionary force could, with not too great a mental contortion, be viewed as an aggressor – especially as Metaxas hadn't wanted it in the first place. The Greek army could be viewed in a similar light, as having far outpaced its original mission to clear Greek soil of the Italians and becoming an aggressor in Albania. In this light, the Greeks had really no cause to cry wolf. But to any sane mind, this was casuistry. Metaxas' prescience had turned out to be devastatingly correct. The presence of the British was precisely the excuse Hitler had been waiting for.

That same morning, while the Luftwaffe was bombing Belgrade and killing 18,000 of its people, King George walked into Prince Peter's office in Athens' Grande Bretagne Hotel, looking very pale. 'Can I use your toilet, Peter?' the king said. The prince gestured towards the bathroom door. 'Germany has declared war on us and Yugoslavia', the king added with a bitter, weary smile before closing the door behind him.

'So that's it', Prince Peter thought. 'What now?' Would Athens be next on the terror raid list? There was some hope that the city, as containing monuments from Greece's ancient past which the Germans claimed to so much admire, might be spared. One thing was sure: the Germans would be a far different proposition from the Italian 'amateurs'.[1] An intelligence major was flown up north to see what was going on, but his plane was shot down and forced to crash-land in a field. The major survived but was injured; he returned to tell a tale of utter demoralization in the Yugoslav army. While he was away, waves of Luftwaffe bombers droned over Athens and the large Greek cities. The Athenians looked up anxiously, but no bombs fell. Special mine laying squadrons laid their deadly eggs in the ports of Thessaloniki, Kavala, Volos and Preveza, rendering them useless in a matter of hours. This was professional warfare of the kind the Italians had never managed to get together.

Squadron Leader Pattle and his 33 Squadron were at Larissa when news of the German invasion broke. The Hurricanes were fuelled and placed at readiness for immediate take-off. In the early afternoon the squadron received orders to hunt down Luftwaffe formations over Bulgaria. Pattle sighted his first Messerschmitt Bf109s over the Strymon River valley and dived into them. The encounter was brief; very soon five Bf109s were falling out of the sky, with no casualties in 33 Squadron. That same day three Hurricanes attacked five Italian CantZ bombers over Volos harbour; three of the raiders went down.

33 Squadron's victory triggered a retaliatory raid by the Luftwaffe that same afternoon. Towards sunset a formation of Heinkel He111s, operating from bases in Sicily, came within sight of the port of Piraeus, dotted with allied supply ships riding at anchor. Preceding them were twenty Junkers Ju88s. Earlier in the day, Hurricanes of the RAF's 33 Squadron had shot down five Messerschmitt Bf109s north of Athens, and the Germans were in a vengeful mood. Turbulence over Greece forced some of the Heinkels to

jettison their mines, but the rest of them came out of the sunset to roar down on the massed supply ships, among which were some laden with munitions and explosives, defying furious Greek and Allied anti-aircraft fire. One of the ships was the *Clan Fraser*, packed with 250 tons of TNT destined for a Greek munitions factory and lying alongside a warehouse on the jetty. One of the mines from the Heinkels, instead of falling into the sea, hit the warehouse, blowing to bits an Australian gun crew on the roof and setting the building on fire. The blaze quickly spread to the *Clan Fraser*. The flames shot up to a great height, clearly visible to General Heywood, who was watching from the slopes of Lykavittos Hill. He wondered aloud what was burning so fiercely, and buttonholed Prince Peter to drive him down to the port.

It was dark when they got there, the only light being the intense glare from the burning ship. From the sound of incessant explosions, Heywood was worried that the *Clan Fraser* might contain munitions, though a port official had assured him that the cargo was nothing but uniforms and boots. Not being able to do much, Prince Peter left his car with Heywood and hitched a ride back to Athens with Group Captain Willetts, who had also driven down. It was about 3.20 am on 7 April when, as they were halfway to Athens and about four miles from the ship, a colossal blast shattered the night. The *Clan Fraser* had gone up with its explosive cargo, devastating the entire Piraeus waterfront and killing dozens of servicemen and civilians, including the British assistant naval attaché, Commander John Buckler, who had been in the process of trying to get the stricken ship towed outside the port. An RAF train full of bombs had also blown up. Thirteen smaller ships went to the bottom. Heywood was lucky; he had been in a shelter, but had suffered slight injuries when he was thrown to the floor. Had the explosion occurred twenty minutes earlier, they all would have perished. Pieces of the *Clan Fraser's* steel hull were found five miles away.[2] The entire Piraeus waterfront was soon a mass of flame. Windows were shattered all over the greater Athens area, and people were jolted awake as far north as the suburb of Kifissia, 20km away.

Charged with defending the Bulgarian front was the East Macedonia Army Department (the former IV Corps) under Lieutenant General Constantine Bakopoulos. The Department included the 18th Infantry Division and 19th Motorized Division deployed west of the Strymon River and the 7th and 14th Infantry Divisions to the east, plus the complex of Metaxas Line fortifications. Great hopes had been pinned on this line of forts. It would have been adequate against a Bulgarian army of the 1930s, but against the Wehrmacht and Luftwaffe it didn't have a chance. Yet the Germans had a tough time overcoming the Metaxas Line thanks to the bitter resistance they encountered at the mountain Fort of Rupel on the east bank of the Strymon River. Situated towards the west end of the Metaxas Line, Rupel was in the direct line of advance for von List's main thrust into Greece along the Strymon Valley.

As the threat from the north loomed, the Metaxas Line had been extended westwards to the Axios River in order to shield Thessaloniki. At the close of 1940 it was assumed that the Yugoslavs would remain a large buffer state to the north. But with the rapid Yugoslav collapse at the end of March the western end of the Metaxas Line was left hanging, easily outflankable. Yet any German incursion would still have to get by Fort Rupel dominating the 200m wide Strymon Valley, consisting of 2,500 metres of reinforced concrete surface fortifications and about twice that length of underground bunkers defended by six companies. In the sector of the Greek 14th Division, the fort was defended by 950 men under Major George Douratsos, plus seven 75mm guns, five 35mm anti-tank guns, one 37.1mm anti-aircraft gun, twelve 81mm mortars and seventy-six grenade-launchers.

Before Prime Minister Koryzis was yet awakened in Athens, List's motorized artillery began its bombardment of Rupel and the adjacent forts. The initial barrage lasted for exactly half an hour, giving way at 6.00 am to ten-minute dive-bombing attacks by squadrons of Ju87s, followed by another artillery pounding. Artillery and Stukas alternated their attacks for the next two hours with great accuracy, guided by plentiful reconnaissance photos taken in previous days. The Luftwaffe was completely unopposed in the air, threatened only by the fort's single anti-aircraft gun and the occasional brave Greek soldier who fired his rifle at the swooping planes.

Between the artillery and mortar attacks, and the Stukas' bombing, the Greek defenders were given no chance to rest. Bits of the concrete superstructure began to give way under the relentless hammering. Thick smoke hindered optical communication with the neighbouring forts. In between the bomb and shell blasts, the defenders heard the dull growl of German motorized and infantry units surging over the frontier in their direction. As visibility gradually improved in the morning mist, eighteen assault boats full of German troops and guns floated down the Strymon River towards the fort. These were the advance units of the 125 Infantry Regiment of the Lieutenant General Franz Boehme's Eighteenth Mountain Corps (*Gebirgsarmeekorps*), one of the three army corps making up List's Twelfth Army. Submerged nets caught the first few boats whose occupants were either cut down or drowned. In fact, Rupel's defences were proving surprisingly resilient after the initial hammering. Two German battalions managed with great difficulty to get within 600ft of the fort but were virtually annihilated.

The 125 Regiment continued to come in waves, seemingly impervious to the slaughter that met it. The Greeks would let them advance, sometimes stumbling over the unfamiliar ground, and spray them with machine gun fire when they got closer. At this initial success some Greek troops got carried away and exposed themselves above the parapets to get a better view of the carnage; a few were killed by German shellfire. Around 11.00 am the bulk of the German attackers were pinned down. They rallied for another crack at the fort, preceded by Panzers of the Fortieth Panzer Corps under Lieutenant General Georg Stumme, to be met by more withering fire. Unfortunately, some of the Greek shells had passed their shelf life and many failed to explode. This defect enabled a German detachment to penetrate between Rupel and the outpost of Karatas to the east and under cover of a smoke screen to reach the village of Kleidi in the rear, but not without considerable casualties. At the same time, an attempt to seize a nearby hill was repulsed, with some Germans taken prisoner.

The Ju87s screamed down again in the early afternoon; Greek sources claim the solitary anti-aircraft gun accounted for three of them.[3] A Luftwaffe officer was later quoted as saying that the Greeks, unlike the French, kept their nerve under the Stuka attacks. There followed more fanatical German infantry surges – no fewer than ten until nightfall – all of which were beaten off with heavy loss. The first day's attack on Fort Rupel had cost the defenders twenty-two dead and thirty-six wounded out of a total 950. Three anti-tank guns and three machine guns were destroyed. The massive concrete fortifications did not suffer significant damage. The underground telephone cables were repaired and back in operation overnight. German losses at the end of the first day stood at roughly 100, and twenty-four German prisoners were marched to the rear.

But the German penetration to Kleidi had opened a dangerous crack in the Greek line, enabling units to pour into the Rodopolis Valley from the heights of Beles where the Greek, Bulgarian and Yugoslav frontiers meet. At the same time in the east, List had managed to outflank the easternmost forts of the Metaxas Line and move on to Xanthi and Komotini near the Turkish border. Rupel, however, was the adamantine obstacle to a general German advance, and Bakopoulos ordered that it be held 'until the last'.

The Greek 19th Motorized Division, scouting positions on the southern slopes of the Rodopi mountain range that formed the border with Bulgaria, was in the direct path of the German advance in the east. The 192 and 193 Motorized Regiments making up the division were stretched very thin, having to cover a 30km front with firepower equivalent to just four infantry battalions and fourteen field guns. Communication among units was poor because of a shortage of telephone wire, and the 19th's vehicles, constrained to use the roads by day, were sitting ducks for the Luftwaffe Ju87s, which surprised the 192 Motorized Regiment as it entered the village of Theodorovo that afternoon to reinforce the 81 Infantry Regiment, killing thirty men and wounding ninety-five. Two Universal Bren Carriers, ten Austin armoured cars and ten motorcycles were destroyed.

A few kilometres to the southwest, the 193 Motorized Regiment dug in to shield the town of Kilkis; one of its forward patrols captured a German non-commissioned officer after beating off a German thrust at Kato Sourmena. Field intelligence revealed that the Germans were massing north of the railway that runs along the southern edge of the Rodopi range. The 192 and 193 Regiments were reinforced by two companies sent by train from Thessaloniki. They brought with them orders to abandon their captured Fiat light tanks, the rusting veterans of the Albanian campaign that had by now become a lumbering liability; their personnel would join the Universal Bren Carrier crews making up 2 Open Armoured Company.[4]

Meanwhile Fort Rupel, reinforced overnight by two companies, faced the second day of its ordeal. The morning followed the pattern of the previous morning with German methodicalness: artillery barrages alternating with Stuka bombardments. Thick mist wreathed the surrounding heights, giving an initial advantage to the German armoured personnel carriers of the 125 Regiment. Once they appeared over the last ridge, however, the Greek mortars and guns opened up on them, stopping them in their tracks. The Germans withdrew to the nearby height of Goliama, where supplies were parachuted to them. A Greek attempt to seize Goliama was partly successful. List concluded that frontal assaults were too costly, and instead ordered that select infantry units infiltrate the defiles between Fort Rupel and its adjacent outposts and turn their positions. These detachments came under a withering crossfire from the defenders. German corpses piled up in front of the Greek pillboxes, yet still they kept coming with dogged determination, managing in the end to hoist the swastika on the neighbouring height of Karakitok. Hardly had they time to rest than the Greeks counterattacked with the kind of furious bayonet charge they had perfected against the Italians and drove the shocked Germans from Karakitok with some loss, and captured the swastika for good measure.

The German Thirtieth Corps commander, Lieutenant General Otto Hartmann, went up in a balloon to see for himself what was holding up progress. Floating at 2,000ft, and out of range of the Greek guns, Hartmann saw how formidable the Rupel fortifications were and realized that Stukas could do little against such structures except waste their ordnance. Instead, the dive-bombers would be more useful attacking the outlying artillery batteries. The Ju87s – again unopposed as neither the RAF nor the RHAF could spare any aircraft for that sector – promptly switched to pounding those batteries. The Greek artillery inevitably betrayed its positions while firing in defence of the fort, and one by one the adjacent batteries were silenced.

That night, as German patrols picked up the hundreds of their dead and wounded, the Greek defenders pored over German maps taken from prisoners marking the positions of the Greek guns with great accuracy. The fort's own defences were by and large intact, and supplies of ammunition were adequate.

But in the meantime, resolute teams of Germans had infiltrated into positions around the fort, threatening the whole position of the 14th Division and fighting off Greek attempts to dislodge them. The second day's attacks had cost the Greeks fourteen dead and eleven wounded.

By now Rupel was close to being completely cut off from the rest of the Greek defence. On 7 April whatever resistance the Yugoslavs could put together collapsed, and the entire western flank of the Metaxas Line was turned. Bakopoulos asked for the British Armoured Brigade to halt the German advance down the Axios Valley, and for the RAF to strike the advancing columns, but Wilson was unable to comply either way. Thus the 19th Division was ordered to extend its front westwards for 20km more or so to the Axios River. The last reserves in Thessaloniki were rushed north to beef up the 19th, some of them having to move more than 80km in a single night. The 192 Regiment fell back southwest to form the centre of the new line at Akritas, south of Doirani Lake. One of the reinforcing units was the 1 Infantry Security Battalion, assigned to hold the heights at Metamorphosis, while three companies held the left. The bulk of the 19th Division stayed on the right of the line, stretched out almost to Kerkini Lake.

The thin Greek line was just waiting to be rolled up, and at 3.00 am on 8 April Stumme's Panzers, spearheaded by the 2nd Armoured Division, began rolling towards the shores of Doirani Lake. The Greek 19th Motorized was ordered to block the advance as well as it could at Akritas. The 192 Regiment moved up first, beefed up by two companies of infantry from the 193, but it was too late, because by dawn the first Panzer columns were in sight of Akritas, backed up by aggressive air cover. During the morning the Germans drove the 193 off the strategic height of Obeliskos and soon made short work of the scattered units of the 192 attempting to defend Akritas. Two Panzers were lost to anti-tank fire. At noon the Germans entered Akritas. One column turned northeast to protect the approach to Doirani Lake while the bulk of the German armoured force rolled on towards the town of Kilkis. The remnants of the 192 and 193 Motorized Regiments were swept aside, powerless to resist as they had lost their artillery and anti-tank weapons.

The assault on Rupel resumed on 8 April, with more fruitless and suicidal German attacks in the morning. By sheer pressure of numbers the 125 Regiment and 5th Mountain Division by noon had penetrated well to the rear of the fort. Nonetheless, the defenders at Rupel were determined to obey Bakopoulos' no-surrender order, and throughout the afternoon repulsed incessant German thrusts. The Greek 41 Regiment moved on the Germans occupying Goliama, but failed to dislodge them after hours of trying. Bakopoulos himself, however, appeared to be having second thoughts. With the inevitable staring him in the face, he sent a message through the lines to the commander of the German 2nd Armoured Division, proposing a cease-fire along the line with the Greeks retaining the right to keep their weapons; at the same time he secretly ordered his units to remain in position until the actual signing of the truce. In this Bakopoulos was not quite acting on his own initiative; his somewhat contradictory instructions from Papagos were to 'resist to the end, but accept a truce only when all means of resistance are exhausted'. The commander of the East Macedonia Army Department evidently felt that the second part of the instruction had more weight in the circumstances.[5]

The 2nd Armoured headquarters transmitted the proposal to List, who assented, though with the proviso that the issue of the Greeks' weapons would be settled by negotiations. Thus unopposed, the Germans were in Kilkis before midnight on 8 April and by the following morning their tanks were rolling into the key port of Thessaloniki, Greece's second largest city. With Bakopoulos' withdrawal from the fight, the East Macedonia Army Department ceased to issue orders. This sowed confusion in those units that still didn't know the details. Major General Nikolaos Lioumbas, the 19th Motorized Division commander, saw fit to order a general withdrawal along the only free road south, where what was left of the 192 Regiment joined the main division early in the morning of 10 April. The 193, after putting up a brief fight east of Doirani Lake, surrendered to the enemy that same day. That action was the last by the East Macedonia Army Department. On 10 April the 19th Motorized Division surrendered at Kilkis. Lioumbas didn't stay around to become a prisoner-of-war but fled with a couple of dozen other officers to the hills of the Halkidiki peninsula. Some units such as the 191 Motorized Regiment, which had seen little action so far, dissolved themselves, their men scattering to the hills.[6]

Fort Rupel was now all but isolated. Douratsos knew nothing of Bakopoulos' approaches to the enemy, and in the morning of 9 April his men mowed down more waves of Germans while having a brave go at the Stukas. Boehme, of course, was quite well aware of the cease-fire, yet to take the stubborn fort had become a matter of honour for him. At 3.00 pm the incessant attacks ceased, and the Greeks couldn't quite believe it when they saw the Panzers retreating. Two hours later a German vehicle flying a white flag drove up to the fort's main entrance. The German emissaries informed Major Douratsos of the cease-fire and the occupation of Thessaloniki, and added the obvious conclusion that as further resistance would be fruitless, the surrender of Fort Rupel was required.

'Forts are not surrendered,' Douratsos retorted. 'They are taken.'

The Germans replied calmly that they weren't lying about the cease-fire, and left Douratos until the following morning to think it over. Douratos promptly got in touch with 14th Division headquarters, which confirmed the news. There were further developments: the Wehrmacht, echoing Hitler's admiration of the Greek military performance in Albania, would allow all captured Greek officers to keep their sidearms and pledged that no Greek enlisted man would be sent to a concentration camp.

It would have been natural at that moment for Douratsos and many of his men to think back to Spartan King Leonidas I at Thermopylai, to the resolve of the 300 Spartans to die at their posts rather than surrender, and a good many would have been prepared to imitate the grand example. To have to capitulate after seeing the bodies of one's enemies piled up in front of you is not an easy thing to accept. Some comforted themselves with hopes of escaping to the mountains to continue armed resistance, as many eventually did. Douratsos, thinking in twentieth century rather than ancient Spartan terms, agreed to spare more bloodshed and give up the fort.

The surrender of Fort Rupel brought out an unexpected noble side of the supposedly ruthless Teutonic warrior mentality. The Germans are a people who admire strength and firmness of purpose, even in their enemies. When the battle for Rupel was over they were uncharacteristically fulsome in their praise of the Greeks' fighting qualities. At 10.00 am on 10 April a German officer walked up to where Major Douratsos was waiting to hand over the fort, clicked his heels and saluted. The message from his commander, the officer said, was that 'it was the Germans' honour and pride to have such adversaries'. Douratsos then was taken on a ceremonial inspection of a German honour guard before leaving with his men. The Greek flag was kept flying on the fort. As a reflection on the Teutonic way of thinking, the commanding officer of the decimated 125 Regiment asked who had been the officer whose guns had wrought such destruction on his unit. A young Greek second lieutenant of artillery was brought before him. The colonel stood to attention and pointed to a corpse-strewn slope. 'That is your doing,' the colonel said, with no trace of menace or even regret in his voice. 'In half an hour you knocked 400 men out of action. Congratulations.' The colonel squeezed the nonplussed second lieutenant's hand. As the Greek contingent was marching away from the fort, a German platoon passed them going the other way, and stepped into parade march as a sign of respect. Then the sound of a bugle pierced the air. The Greek flag on Fort Rupel came down and the swastika went up.[7]

Franz Boehme, the commander of the Eighteenth Mountain Corps, was gracious enough to compliment Bakopoulos when the two met shortly afterwards in Thessaloniki, far from the smoke and blood of battle. 'I had heard of the valour and heroism of the Greek army,' Boehme said, 'but I never could imagine the bravery your soldiers displayed. They fought marvellously. Again, I heartily congratulate you.' List himself paid tribute to his foes in his next order of the day, urging his men to 'deal with the Greek prisoners as befits brave soldiers'.[8] The battle for Fort Rupel had cost the Germans more than 300 killed, against fifty-six Greeks.

When the Germans burst over the frontier, officers of the Royal Hellenic Navy's coastal batteries east of Thessaloniki received sealed orders to blow up the installations. The British consulate in the city had supplied the navy with the requisite explosives. With the Germans mere hours away, the sealed orders were delivered to the personnel involved at 4.20 pm on 8 April. Not all of the weaponry was destroyed. After the flag of the coastal battery was ceremoniously hauled down, all portable weapons and aiming equipment, as well as at least one anti-aircraft gun – even down to gun barrel lubricants and pictures of King George – were put on fishing boats already loaded to the gunwales with innumerable pieces of equipment and codes and documents. Just before midnight the shore installations went up in one grand explosion, lighting up the sad faces of the sailors as their boats turned to hug the coast southwards.[9]

Two days later the senior RHN brass met to debate what to do 'if national territory is seized by the enemy'. The king had already decided that in such a case he and his government would have to flee and set up shop in exile. If the army was to buckle under the German onslaught, as was already happening, and the air force was practically eliminated, the navy would be the only service able to follow the government wherever it went. Sakellariou, the navy chief of staff, had already given the issue some thought, and produced a memorandum. The RHN, he said, 'can make available battleworthy units and the necessary personnel to continue the struggle'. Still to be worked out, though, were details such as where the fleet's secure home base would be, how many warships would be available to carry on the war and how munitions and supplies would be furnished.

On 6 April the Greek navy could count on the destroyers *King George*, *Queen Olga*, *Hydra*, *Spetsai*, *Psara*, *Koundouriotis*, *Leon*, *Aetos* and *Ierax*. (A tenth destroyer, the *Panthir*, was being serviced and wouldn't be ready for two more weeks.) Of the submarines, the *Triton* and *Papanikolis* were ready, while the *Nereus* and *Katsonis* would take few days to get into shape – the *Glavkos* would finally also be ready after many months in the repair yard. Added to these were nine naval supply ships and nine requisitioned passenger island-hoppers. The ancient *Averof* was put on standby as well as several ageing torpedo boats. Also, all Greek-flagged merchantmen and passenger ships of 800 tonnes and over in the Mediterranean and Black Seas were ordered to proceed with all speed to Alexandria to place themselves at the disposal of the continuing war effort; smaller commercial vessels were confined to home waters to ensure that the islanders wouldn't starve – a piece of planning foresight that undoubtedly saved many lives in the months to come. Naval personnel remaining on the Greek mainland were to be sent on indefinite leave – meaning that they would have to decide for themselves what to do under an enemy boot – and all confidential navy headquarters documents would have to be destroyed forthwith. Prime Minister Koryzis (who also had the portfolio of navy minister) issued the orders on 11 April.[10]

That morning, however, the naval stations at Piraeus and Eleusis came under attack by Ju87s while Kavvadias, the fleet commander, personally led his destroyers through the narrow channel at the west end of Salamis into open waters. But that wouldn't have offered much more protection, so Mezeviris, the destroyer force commander, ordered the ships to scatter at night through the Aegean in pairs. The *King George* and *Queen Olga*, however, were anchored rather closer to the mainland, and at 11.00 pm on 13 April German bombers droned over the ships on their way to attack Piraeus. An hour later, as the bombers were returning, one of them appeared to change course to fly over the destroyers. Mezeviris, on board the *King George*, ordered the skipper to begin zigzagging while readying the guns. Before the gunners could line up their sights, a Ju87 screamed down on the ship from 3,000ft. The bomb fell wide to port, but close enough to the destroyer to blast a great hole in the hull right on the waterline, lifting the *King George* almost out of the water. Mezeviris' own quarters were turned into a mash of metal and wood. The ship was plunged in darkness and at once began to rapidly list to port. Mezeviris signalled the *Queen Olga* to prepare to tow the *King George* to a safe anchorage while protecting it from further air attack. Enough engine power was restored for the ship to spend the rest of the night limping back to Eleusis, listing drunkenly all the way.

A brave sailor volunteered to enter what was left of the admiral's quarters, flooded with oil and seawater, to see if he could salvage anything of value and managed to rescue Mezeviris' ceremonial sword, dress uniform buttons and watch. The admiral sadly walked off the drunkenly-lurching flagship that had been his home, hoping he might see it again after a major repair job, but he wouldn't be that lucky. A day before it was to move to Alexandria on 24 April, the Luftwaffe damaged it in another attack. The new damage prevented it from being towed to deeper waters to avoid falling into German hands, and so the Germans found it half-sunk in its dry dock.

The defence of Greece in the air was now almost exclusively the task of the RAF, as the RHAF had been whittled down to nearly nothing. Yet the Greek airmen fought on. On the day of the German invasion Antoniou, the CO of 21 Mira, accounted for a Luftwaffe observation Henschel Hs126, while a Bloch of 24 Mira knocked down a Dornier Do17 reconnaissance bomber. Pattle and 33 Squadron were also in the air throughout the following week, taking a steady toll of Italian and German fighters and bombers while escorting the Blenheims of 11 Squadron to targets in Yugoslavia and the Strymon Valley. Sunday 13 April was an especially hectic day. As the Greeks marked Palm Sunday in the gloomy realization that it would be their last as a free nation for some time (if ever), 33 Squadron was scrambled three times. The worst moment was when six Blenheims of 211 Squadron were all shot down over northern Greece, only two airmen surviving (though one of them was killed when the plane flying him to hospital was also shot down). The bombers had been without an escort partly because Pattle's squadron was busy defending the Allied line north of Mount Olympus.

What remained of the Greek bomber force – a handful of Fairey Battles of 33 Mira – attacked Italian positions in Albania. Scattered fighters of 21 and 23 Mirai droned above the Greek troops, showing the blue and white roundel to keep up their morale. But by 15 April the ragged RHAF was down to twelve aging fighters. In the dogfights of that day, a PZL of 22 Mira shot down a Stuka, and a Gladiator of 21 Mira another. But the Greeks couldn't hope to challenge the waves of Bf109s that soon appeared. The 21 Mira Commander, Squadron Leader Yannis Kellas, was seriously wounded when his severely damaged Gladiator crash-landed in a wheat field. But he lived to continue the war in RAF service.[11]

The base at Larissa was now coming under determined attack by the Luftwaffe's III/Jagdgeschwader 77 and II/Jagdgeschwader 26, fighter units employing the deadly Bf109. A few Hurricanes were damaged, but the Greek planes parked at the field, including the few remaining Potez 63 bombers of 31 Mira, some battered Gladiators and the captured Italian SM79, were blasted to bits. D'Albiac flew up to Larissa to deliver more bad news: General Wilson had decided to abandon the Allied position north of Olympus and move right back to the fabled pass of Themopylai. This would mean the abandonment of all the airfields north of that point, including Larissa, leaving just three in the wider Athens area. On the evening of 16 April 33 Squadron packed its equipment and ground crews into lorries for the gruelling night-long drive to join 80 Squadron at Eleusis. It was hard enough going over the hazardous mountain roads without the constant attacks from low-flying Bf109s. Pattle himself made the journey bundled up in the back of a staff car, ill and feverish. He had lost a lot of weight recently, and had his batman move the buttons on his tunic so the others wouldn't see how thin he had become.[12]

At Tanagra airfield near Thebes, eight out of nine Gladiators of 23 Mira based there were destroyed by a lightning Messerschmitt raid. Kellas by then had more or less recovered from his injuries and was ordered to take his last remaining Gladiator down to Eleusis. There were still some Blenheims left in 32 Bombing Mira, and they were sent on what would be their last mission, to drop bread, tea and sugar to the Greek troops on the Albanian front. After that, some of the squadron officers suggested that, as Greece was to all intents and purposes defeated, they should fly on to Crete or North Africa to continue the war under Greek colours. Group Captain Nikolaos Averof, the bomber force commander, vetoed the idea on the grounds that it would look like a dereliction of duty, and besides, the fight wasn't over yet. Not long afterwards, he changed his mind, but by then his Blenheims – not to mention the three remaining Battles of 33 Mira – were smouldering hulks after the Luftwaffe had finished with them.[13]

Flights of Junkers Ju88s attacked Eleusis almost daily, taking a steady toll of Hurricanes and installations. The strain was beginning to tell. Both 33 and 80 Squadrons had been in constant action for more than a month. Pattle was becoming increasingly emaciated and unwell, subject to attacks of fever. Fear churned his insides more often than before. But he was now a squadron commander, and couldn't let down his mates by succumbing to his feelings, especially as he was losing an average of one pilot every few days. He awoke from an uneasy nap on 19 April to see his Welsh orderly standing over him with a cup of tea. The grateful Pattle didn't get the chance to even take a sip when the tannoy sounded with a scramble order. 'Enemy aircraft approaching from the northwest!'

'Better drink that yourself, Taffy,' Pattle said, leaping out of bed and grabbing his flying helmet. Minutes later, he had downed a Ju88. Back in Athens, he availed himself of a good hot bath in the apartment of Tommy Wisdom, the RAF's press liaison officer.

Eleusis was bombed again the following morning, but by early afternoon 'Tap' Jones noticed the sky might be clear enough for an offensive sweep by 80 and 33 Squadrons. Pattle, though he'd had a good rest at Wisdom's flat the night before, was still not feeling well. At 5.00 pm the tannoy at Eleusis rasped that about 100 enemy aircraft were approaching the base. Seconds after the pilots scrambled, Pattle threw off the blankets that had been covering him as he lay shivering with a high temperature on a couch. His adjutant tried to stop him, but he shot out of the door. He couldn't just lie around when his boys were about to put their lives on the line again. As he raced for his Hurricane a Messerschmitt Me110 momentarily stopped him with a rain of cannon shells. Unhurt, he resumed his sprint thanks to the encouragement of a very brave fitter who literally pushed him forward and didn't seek shelter until he had started up Pattle's fighter, unplugged the starter battery and stayed exposed in the middle of the airfield until Pattle was airborne.

Jones was in the control room directing the action. Both 80 and 33 Squadrons had all of fifteen Hurricanes left between them, and all were in the air. Twenty thousand feet over the port of Piraeus a dozen or so Ju88s were dive-bombing a hospital ship.

Newton managed to bag a Ju88, but one Hurricane was shot up so badly it had to return to base; the pilot died of his burns a couple of days later. The others found themselves in the fight of their lives. When Pattle caught up with them he saw one of the Hurricanes climbing to engage a defensive circle of Me110s. That, he thought, wasn't a very smart thing for a fighter pilot to do, as he was drawing a whole swarm of the enemy onto him. Nonetheless, as one of the German planes dived out of formation onto the attacker, Pattle reflexively hit the throttle and rammed the stick forward to go to the Hurricane's aid. He was too late to save the Briton, but peppered the underside of the Messerschmitt, which burst into flame.

The Me110 was a powerful aircraft, beyond the league of the Italian CR42s and even G50s, and even the Hurricane. Heavier and faster than the British fighter, the twin-engined German machine could also outdive it in a fight. Pattle found himself in a maelstrom of them over Piraeus; he managed to flame a second one, and then he was hit. The last man to see Pattle was Flying Officer Jimmie Kettlewell of 112 Squadron, who noticed Pattle slumped forward, apparently unconscious, his Hurricane on fire and diving while two Me110s were still pouring fire into it. Kettlewell got one of Germans, who plunged into the Bay of Eleusis alongside Pattle, accompanying the South African ace in death. They are still there.[14]

Thousands of Greek troops still languished in Albania, absorbed now in the snippets of news emanating from the new north-eastern front. Their grim mood comes through in the diary of Corporal Nikolaou, who was kept trudging alongside his supply mules in the early spring snow. 'All the army thinks of now is withdrawal,' he wrote on 10 April. Younger soldiers reacted in dismay to the news that they would be transferred to the new combat theatre. Morale was further dampened by false rumours that the king had abdicated and the prime minister had resigned. Unseasonal blizzards kept the men in their tents for days at a time, as artillery duels boomed through the nights. The 42 Evzone Regiment began its pullback, along with the mass of the Greek army, on 15 April. Many of the men were ill and wounded, more were hungry. Stooping under the weight of bitterness as well as fatigue – what an undeserved end to so glorious a campaign! – they trudged painfully back to the Greek border, depending on peasant handouts for survival, accompanied by the constant crash of Greek artillery protecting the withdrawal.

On the morning of 20 April, Easter Day in the Greek Orthodox calendar, Nikolaou's company reached Greek territory. Marching all night, they had chanted the Orthodox Easter hymn, the *Christos Aneste* (Christ is Risen) to stay awake and keep up their spirits in the dark wilderness. When they crossed the frontier into Greece one hour after midnight they fired their rifles into the air in celebration. That day they rested and each soldier enjoyed a rare treat of meat, half an orange, one egg, a small crumbly bun and a packet of cigarettes. In the afternoon Italian aircraft came over and bombed and strafed the Greek camp, 'but Christ put forth His hand and none of us was hurt'. The evening brought orders to move on to Kalpaki, where they arrived the following morning after another all-night march – the ninth in a row.[15]

Chapter 13

Final Countdown

Desperation in Athens – confusion in the army – Wilson decides on a quick bolt – Koryzis commits suicide – sinking of the Psara – king and government prepare to leave – Tsolakoglou calls a truce – final shots in Albania – Thermopylai bypassed – Operation Demon – surrender at Kalamata – escape from the Peloponnese – death wrapped in the flag

> In the interests of historical justice I am obliged to point out that of all the adversaries we had to confront, the Greek soldier fought with reckless courage and the highest disregard for death. He capitulated only when all further resistance proved impossible and hence fruitless.
>
> Adolf Hitler, 4 May 1941

With the fall of Fort Rupel and the outflanking of the rest of the Metaxas Line, Papagos had now no choice but to fall back considerably if he had any hopes of halting the German steamroller. The Greek 14th and 18th Divisions, and 19th Motorized Division, had essentially ceased to exist. Many of the men in those units were already melting away into the hills. An uneasy calm settled over what remained of the Greek lines. Indeed, the week between 13 and 20 April saw the vice of defeatist paralysis settle over Greece's political and military establishments. Everyone knew what was about to happen but few wished to believe it. Prince Peter was called into Papagos' office on 14 April and told to close the door. 'Greece is going to be occupied by the Axis,' the commander-in-chief said gloomily. 'That means that we here are going to be taken prisoner along with all the other Greek soldiers.'

Peter reacted in shock. He was expecting, if worse came to worst, to escape with his cousin the king and carry on the war from wherever he was. Papagos, instead, was insisting that as an officer in uniform Prince Peter would have to share the fate of his comrades. When he prince began to protest, Papagos cut him off angrily: 'Those are your orders, captain, to be captured. And as commander-in-chief of the Greek and Allied forces I order you to do it!'

Peter realized that his chief was under tremendous strain, but in all conscience he could not obey the order. 'I'm sorry, sir,' he replied, 'but I will do anything to avoid capture, even if it means going into the mountains as a partisan with a Tommy gun. Wars are different now, and not even you, Papagos, can demand compliance with such an order as long as there is a chance of winning the war.' Papagos looked at him with narrowed eyes for a moment, then dismissed him without a word.

It was King George who found a way out of his cousin's dilemma by appointing him as his adjutant, with orders to follow the king wherever he went. Back in his office, the prince transferred the gold fourragère from his left shoulder, where it had been staff officer style, to his right, indicating his new status. Shortly afterwards, generals Pitsikas and Bakos entered, visibly shaken, to meet with Papagos and ask that he approve a cease-fire in Albania.[1] Pitsikas, the commander of the Epiros Army Department, warned of 'a danger of a complete collapse' of the army's morale.

Papagos at first was inclined to dismiss the fears. It was taking him a long time to tear himself away from the attack mode that had proven so successful a few months before. But there were 200,000 men in uniform languishing in Albania, not knowing what their fate would be. The commanders were as confused as the men. Papagos' past failure to set out a coherent strategic objective in Albania now matured to bear bitter fruit. As early as December 1940, as the Greeks were enjoying the flush of victory after victory, a staff officer reported to Metaxas that the corps commanders already were wondering what the ultimate objective of the Albanian campaign would be – in contrast, apparently, to Papagos, whose sole aim seemed to be to advance *per se*, with little idea of where it would lead. As long as such concerns were limited to senior officers, little damage was done. But in April 1941 the where-are-we-going sense had percolated down to the last private. Papagos, a classic member of the military elite, seems to have made a mistake common to many senior commanders: he lived in a world different from that of the citizen-soldiers he commanded, who once the danger is over wish to return to their families and civilian jobs. Once a soldier stops fighting and has a chance to rest and sleep properly, he starts thinking. Around the campfires and in the tents, like Corporal Nikolaou, he starts asking questions: 'How long are we going to stay in this hell of a place?' 'When is this damn war going to be over?'[2]

In Athens, King George, Koryzis, Papagos and other political and military figures could only hold meeting after futile meeting, coming to no clear conclusion while each day brought fresh news of a German advance southwards and increased the paralysis. There was also the psychological pressure of not wishing to let down the British. Wilson was counting on the Greek army in Albania to rush southeast and hold a defence west of Mount Olympus, but morale and organization in that force were now crumbling irreparably. German patrols in Epiros would meet with groups of Greek soldiers trudging back from the front and, apart from disarming them, would let them go. It suited the Germans down to the ground to see the Greek army dissolving before their eyes. More seriously, outbreaks of mutiny occurred in the 5th (Cretan) and 6th Divisions. A few dozen deserters were caught at the Mertzani Bridge on the border and promptly executed, but that didn't stop the rot. Amid these signs of an army's disintegration, on 14 April Major General Katsimitros of the much-bloodied 8th Division appealed to Pitsikas to consider an armistice with the Germans merely to keep some of the army intact. Pitsikas consulted his I and II Corps commanders, who agreed wholeheartedly, and the following evening a staff officer was sent to Athens to notify Papagos.

When King George got wind of what was afoot, his first reaction was to rule out a truce as the British were still fighting in the north. It would seem cowardly to make a separate peace. Papagos and Wilson met at Lamia, north of Thermopylai, on 16 April. Wilson was pessimistic. He had been expecting the Greek army to come and bolster his left wing west of Olympus, and it hadn't turned up. This, he said, compelled him to fall back from Olympus to a planned defence line along the Aliakmon River, and assume the fabled line of defence at Thermopylai.

Papagos said he would be able to provide Greek troops to cover the British withdrawal, which would include an eventual evacuation from ports on the east coast if necessary. Then he received a nasty surprise when he learned that Wilson had been planning an outright withdrawal for at least three days, without informing Papagos – who was his formal superior – or the Greek general staff, which had the power of veto. Wilson, it seems, had discarded what he considered a piece of official fiction and was taking his orders direct from Wavell. The Greek Army General Staff report issued after the war is damning:

> [Wilson] never communicated to the Greek General Staff his orders to his divisions and did not keep it informed of the tactical situation at the front. General headquarters did not know what the British forces were doing. General Heywood ... when asked, would reply either that they didn't know or assumed the forces were at such-and-such a line.[3]

'The British,' in the hard words of one Greek authority, 'abandoned the standard of conduct of gentlemen by hiding their actions from their Greek allies.'[4]

To be fair to Wilson, he never lost sight of the basic harsh fact of his campaign: that the British force was in Greece to ultimately serve British strategy. As long as it coincided with the Greek cause, all was well and good. But when British interests diverged, as when it was obvious to everyone that the Germans would soon roll over all Greece, Wilson had to think of his men and country first. Then why, it may be asked, did he keep it secret from the Greeks? The answer is probably that, in a typically diffident British way, he didn't want to hurt the Greeks' feelings, especially after they had accomplished so much against the Axis. But he managed to hurt them nonetheless.

Papagos, by contrast, remained faithful to his alliance with the British. On hearing that Pitsikas and two corps commanders were recommending a truce, he was stern.

> The government [he told the staff officer who brought him the news] does not by any means intend to abandon the British, and will not accept any truce as dishonouring Greece as long as British forces remain in the country ... It prefers that the army be dissolved, destroyed or taken prisoner rather than be dishonoured ... This way Greece will retain her honour unbesmirched until such time as Great Britain emerges victorious.[5]

Whatever the divergent strategies of the Greeks and British, here was the Greek commander-in-chief displaying a touching faith in British solidarity – and, moreover, a Churchillian faith in ultimate victory – at the very time when Wilson was in effect sneaking off without telling the allies who had fought so well at Britain's side. It was a lesson the Greeks would not soon forget, with sad consequences for both countries' post-war relations.

Papagos may have been gripped by a sense of military honour. Yet his reply essentially abandoned the eleven Greek divisions in Albania to their fate. When he was reminded of this he wavered, spent several hours thinking it over, and eventually agreed to a truce. It may have been brought home to him finally that the British now regarded Greece as a lost cause and had no intention of staying. Neither, in fact, had the king and government, who were making plans to flee to Crete. On 13 April the old battle cruiser *Averof*, ten destroyers and the remaining submarines were made ready to carry the government to Crete. Two days later Koryzis slimmed his government down to seven cabinet members. The plan was for king and government to set sail from Oropos on the east coast 30km north of Athens on the night of 17 April. But an aggressive defeatism had spread to the RHN, and the crews refused to sail on the designated night. The Aegean was swarming with German aircraft, and many seamen couldn't see why they should risk their lives for a bunch of politicians and even a king. Admiral Sakellariou had a word with the mutineers, and persuaded them to sail on the following night.

At an inconclusive meeting at the Grande Bretagne on 18 April, Wilson said he was willing to hold the line at Thermopylai until 5 May as long as Papagos could pull his forces out of Albania in time to prop up the left wing. In light of Wilson's decision to abandon Greece, the issue sounds academic. King George, for his part, balked at having to leave for Crete that evening, and the departure was postponed. At a second high-level conference at 2.00 pm, the sense of unreality persisted. As the air raid sirens sounded throughout the day, Sakellariou noted that irrelevant small talk dominated the discussion and 'everyone nervously hoped for some divine power to come and halt the enemy at the gates'.[6] Koryzis and Papagos admitted that the Greek military was all but beaten. Wilson said he didn't want the Greek government to desert the ship. Wrangling continued until 2.20 pm when the king said he wanted a private word with his prime minister.

Koryzis was deathly tired. He confessed to King George that as the Germans had now invaded and would in all likelihood occupy Athens, he had failed as prime minister; all he wanted to do was to resign. The king admonished him stiffly that this was no time for a prime minister to lose his nerve and leave the country without a government; indeed, he should consider himself a front-line soldier and keep fighting to the end. But Koryzis was adamant. He was neither a politician nor a soldier, but an ex-banker. He wanted out. Others could carry on the struggle in his place. But neither would the king budge. He ordered the hapless prime minister to stay in his post. At that, Koryzis stooped to kiss the king's hand and said he had to go home 'for some business'. Eyewitnesses saw Koryzis emerge ashen-faced, and without a word, pick up his hat and coat and exit the hotel almost at a run. Prince Peter encountered him at the front door.

> I managed to get a glimpse [the prince wrote], through the glass door, of his face, haggard with anguish. I thought of how weary he must be with all the responsibilities loaded on him at these critical moments.[7]

Koryzis got into his car and was driven home. The king emerged and buttonholed his brother and heir, Crown Prince Paul, and told him that something in Koryzis' attitude worried him and he wanted to make sure his prime minister was all right. Paul drove to Koryzis' house, to be met by the prime minister's distraught wife. Her husband had come home 'very sad', she said, and had locked himself in the bathroom. At that moment a pistol shot sounded from inside. Prince Paul burst in to find Koryzis dead, with a bullet in his head, lying in a widening pool of blood. It was the afternoon of Good Friday, the saddest day in the Greek Orthodox calendar.[8]

Koryzis' suicide climaxed the intense depression that seized the entire country. Morale in the RHN was now crumbling, along with that in the army. With the *King George* knocked out, Rear Admiral Mezeviris transferred his flag to the *Queen Olga*, but he hardly had time to settle in when a mutiny on the destroyer *Aetos* occupied his attention. Lieutenant Commander Ioannis Toumbas, who has masterminded the scuttling of the shore batteries at Thessaloniki, was sent to the *Aetos* to restore order after the captain and two senior officers had walked off. Addressing the surly crew from the bow,

Toumbas said he didn't want to have to arrest anyone at this critical stage, so 'any member of the crew who doesn't realize his duty should leave this ship now. Those who stay will continue the fight out of the country'. All but the three of the *Aetos'* petty officers, and half the ratings, promptly left the ship. Some of the mutineers had sabotaged some of the anti-aircraft guns (though not irreparably). Among them was the ship's purser, who was stopped at the gangplank and found to be carrying a case full of the ship's money; the man was court-martialled and shot. The ugliness also spread to the crews of the *Spetsai*, but it was nipped in the bud with harsh measures.[9]

Such negativity, fortunately, was the exception rather than the rule. When the air raid sirens sounded on Easter Day, 20 April, the *Psara* was at anchor off Megara. The crew had gathered on the deck for the Easter service and looked skywards anxiously, but nothing appeared. At 2.45 pm, just after lunchtime, Commander Konstas was ordered to join a convoy that had been put together to escort the *Averof* to safety at Alexandria. At 6.15 pm, about four hours before the destroyer was due to sail, fifteen Ju87s screamed down on it out of the sunset. As the *Psara*'s anti-aircraft guns blasted away at full strength, bombs fell on the *Queen Olga* and *Panthir* alongside.

Two bombs smacked into the foredeck of the *Psara*, almost severing the bow from the main structure, and knocking out the forward gun control. The Stukas strafed the decks, blasting any crewmembers there literally to bits. 'Heads and body parts were all over', wrote Konstas, trying to describe the hell. The *Psara*'s bow began to sink, though Konstas had the satisfaction of seeing his remaining guns blast at least two Stukas out of the sky.

The Luftwaffe attacks ceased half an hour later. Konstas had the shattered ship towed to Megara, but it was too far gone for repair. The bow was under water and the engine room was flooding. Reluctantly he gave the order for the brave little *Psara* – the first RHN vessel to fire a naval shot in anger by shelling Italian positions in Epiros – to be abandoned. Documents and portable weapons were removed, as well as the ship's emblem with the motto, 'Freedom or Death'. The Greek ensign was left flying on the mainmast. Konstas described his own experience during his ship's last moments, as darkness was falling:

> I go down to my quarters, which are dark and full of water. I light a match to see my way. The door to my bedroom is jammed, so it can't open. I pick up the photograph of my children, say an emotional farewell to my cabin and go back up on deck ... It is time to abandon our beloved ship. We draw away in boats. Now nothing is visible of the ship but the flag fluttering on the mast. It's twenty past seven. The sea is about to cover the mast. We doff our hats and cry, 'Long live the *Psara*!' with tears in our eyes. At the same time we hear the boilers explode, the sea

churns and the hulk of the *Psara* vanishes from our sight ... We leave the place in deep sadness, yet proud, because the *Psara* up to the last moment performed her service to the Country.[10]

When the *Psara* died, forty of her crew died with her. Fifty-seven others were wounded, two lost their wits in the horror and two were missing. It was an Easter the survivors would never forget.

Two days after that, the destroyer *Hydra* was ordered to accompany the submarine *Papanikolis* to Alexandria, along with a Danish freighter carrying munitions. The skies seethed with Luftwaffe reconnaissance aircraft. Between Aigina and the mainland a large formation of dive-bombers approached from the north. Half of the formation – about three dozen planes – peeled off and dived on the *Hydra*. Mezeviris, on the bridge, ordered a high-speed zigzag course and readied the anti-aircraft guns. The Stukas' attack was identical to that on the *Psara* – near-vertical dive bombing followed by a devastating strafing of the decks. One bullet caught the ship's commanding officer, Commander Theodoros Pezopoulos, hatless as he was hastening up from his quarters, killing him instantly. Mezeviris saw him 'slip and sit down on the deck, his back supported by the rail, with his eyes closed and a slight smile on his face, showing the calm of having done his duty till the last'.

Bombs burst around the *Hydra*, immobilizing the engines and putting out of action all but a few light machine guns below the bridge. The ship had not actually been hit, but many near misses had cracked the hull and water was pouring in. The decks were strewn with dead and wounded. When the destroyer was visibly fatally crippled, the Ju87s broke off the attack. Rear Admiral Mezeviris, himself bleeding from a flesh wound, stumbled over the foredeck awash with blood, 'stepping over dismembered bodies' and ordering whoever he met to abandon ship. Only one lifeboat was left, and the most seriously wounded were placed in it. The rest of the survivors had to swim a few hundred yards to an islet called Lagosa (one of the advantages of Greek seas is that a ship is never far from some island or speck of rock in an emergency). A few minutes after the last man got off, the *Hydra* dipped its prow suddenly, its stern rearing up, and went down vertically, carrying Commander Pezopoulos and its dead with it.

An exhausted Mezeviris lay down on the rock of Lagosa for an hour or so. Wounded and soaked men were everywhere. One medic, himself lacking part of a leg, crawled up to the admiral. 'How are you feeling, sir?' the medic said, oblivious of his own life-threatening condition. The men 'cried like children' when they learned that Pezopoulos, a well-liked commander, was dead. As the entire scene had been visible from Piraeus, a host of rescue craft sped to Lagosa. The *Papanikolis*, which had waited in vain for its escort to show up, proceeded unprotected to Souda Bay in Crete. That same evening Mezeviris ordered the *Queen Olga*, *Ierax* and *Panthir* to leave for Crete ahead of schedule. They only just made it.[11]

Admiral Sakellariou was appointed acting deputy prime minister, and his impression of those dark days is not complimentary to his country's political establishment. What remained of the Greek government was by now in a state of total selfish panic. Government ministers, he noted, were clueless, frightened and wholly dependent on what the king would do, 'so as not to lose his favour and keep their posts after the war'.[12] In the view of this crusty old sailor, the politicians' sole care was to save their skins and get out. The fate of the army and navy meant nothing to them.

The British now were more determined than ever to pull out as quickly as possible, but had qualms about appearing to abandon Greece in its supreme hour of need. This was the chief concern of General Wavell, who arrived in Athens on 19 April, determined to manoeuvre the Greeks into okaying a British pullout. He said the British were prepared to continue the fight in Greece as long as the Greeks did the same, but by this time any sober thinker would have realized the issue was academic. Wilson had been promoting the same line, but now Wavell added an ultimatum: the Greek government must decide whether it wanted the British to stay or not. This appears to have been a way of thwarting later criticism that Britain had 'abandoned' Greece. Papagos evaded replying. At this point Palairet, the British ambassador, flourished a telegram from Churchill saying that any British pullout from Greece must take place 'with the full consent and approval of the king and Greek government'. Everyone at that table realized, of course, without admitting it, that essentially the game was up. If Churchill was thinking of withdrawal, then that was it. The formal British insistence on 'Greek consent' was merely a fig leaf to mask an unpleasant truth. At that, King George caved in and gave his approval for the British to evacuate Greece. Wilson replied with a few platitudes about the Greeks' sense of duty, and everyone, relieved that the air had been cleared, went to attend Koryzis' funeral. The charade was finally over.[13]

Up at the front Lieutenant General Tsolakoglou, the Commander of the West Macedonia Army Department (formerly III Corps) decided that it was time to halt the Greeks' crucifixion. Three German divisions were roaring through the Thessalian plain in pursuit of the British. The 1 Motorized Infantry Regiment (*Leibstandarte*) SS-Adolf Hitler under Major General Sepp Dietrich had turned west from the body of the Fortieth Corps and was heading to Metsovo to secure the Ioannina area and prevent a Greek breakout. Dietrich had no difficulty overcoming the weakened Greek 11th Division at the Katara Pass. Pitsikas in desperation telegraphed to the General Staff, but his chief worry was not the Germans but the Italians: 'For God's sake save us from the Italians.' Nothing would be worse than for Cavallero's legions to come storming down from Albania to complete the destruction of the Greeks. To see the defeated and despised foe coming in like a jackal was something no Greek soldier could tolerate.[14] Moreover, Mussolini was demanding that all 200,000 Greeks in Albania be taken prisoner.

General Stumme's Fortieth Corps, meanwhile, had taken Florina but a sudden onset of unseasonal snowy weather briefly halted it. When the weather improved on 12 April the corps, comprising the Leibstandarte SS-Adolf Hitler, the 9th Armoured Division and 73rd Infantry Division, resumed its slow but crushing progress southwards, sweeping aside Charrington's British 1 Armoured Brigade at Kleidi and scattering its units. The Allies had to retreat to regroup at Amyntaion, leaving four out of five anti-tank guns in enemy hands. An attempt by the Australians to stem the German tide came to nothing in the face of the relentless Panzers; the Australians fled, leaving their weapons on the field. Charrington's armour made a spirited attempt to stop Stumme at Proastion; the tank battle lasted through the day, but in the end the 1 Armoured Brigade had to resume its withdrawal south behind a smoke screen.

The Greek 20th Division suffered the same fate trying to block the Klissura Pass for twenty hours with obsolete arms, vainly trying to stop the Germans from entering Kastoria and threatening the rear of the Epiros Army Department. The 13th and Cavalry Divisions covered the withdrawal; the 13th had marched without interruption all the way from Pogradec and was hardly in shape to confront the SS at Lake Kastoria, yet the Leibstandarte was halted in its tracks. Greek and German artillery fought a duel as the 13th Division held on grimly to the west shore of the lake. A final overwhelming push by Stumme's men on 15 April forced the 13th back, even as General Moutousis, the division commander, rode among the retreating men on his motorbike trying to rally them, but in vain.

The battle around Lake Kastoria was the last land action involving the Greek army and the Axis. It was clear now that Greece had been militarily vanquished. Some senior officers in the I and II Corps refused to wait for the dithering authorities in Athens and wanted to treat with the Germans themselves. Pitsikas, though, was afraid to defy Papagos' orders. Tsolakoglou, meanwhile, had sent a confidant to Athens who messaged back that despite the confusion in the capital, the feeling was that a cease-fire with the Germans would not necessarily be a bad thing. Papagos may or may not have known about the message; his memoir throws no light on it. But Tsolakoglou had all the confirmation he needed. At 6.00 am on 20 April – when Pattle was waking up to his last day on earth and the crew of the *Psara* were preparing for the Easter Day service, unknowing of the fire and storm that would soon be unleashed upon them – Tsolakoglou despatched a colonel and two majors representing the West Macedonia Army Department, the I and II Corps, to

Sepp Dietrich's headquarters outside Metsovo to ask for a truce. They drove the distance in the staff car which the British had given the bishop of Ioannina, who was also urging a truce on humanitarian grounds.

Tsolakoglou's move has been the subject of considerable controversy ever since. Apologists for him agree that it was a thankless task, but given the total collapse of Greece, someone had to do it. Besides, time was of the essence to prevent the Italians from trying to cash in on the Greek defeat, and that was a risk no-one wanted to take. Papagos heard of the truce from General Heywood and was 'shattered'.[15] His response, when he recovered, was to at once relieve Tsolakoglou of command and order the army to 'continue the struggle to the utmost of its ability'. A Cadets' Battalion was put on a train to Patras with orders to resist a German move on the Peloponnese. Swift as the reaction was, it was too late. The officer on whom the order would have devolved in the absence of Tsolakoglou was himself absent, having been cashiered by Tsolakoglou! In his memoirs Papagos flatly damns Tsolakoglou as a 'mutineer' who directly disobeyed the orders of himself and the king to keep on fighting.[16]

Tsolakoglou and Dietrich signed the cease-fire protocol, between 'the valiant German army and the valiant Greek army', in the village of Votonosi that morning. The protocol stipulated that all hostilities between the Greeks and Germans cease as of 6.00 pm that day, that German forces would move to position themselves between Greek and Italian units in Albania, that Greek forces pull back to the Greek frontier within ten days and that the men of the Epiros and West Macedonia Army Departments be demobilized and sent home, the officers being allowed to keep their sidearms.

But there was a wild card in the deck, and that was Mussolini, who as soon as he heard of the German terms threw a tantrum. He was going to be cheated of his desire to herd the Greeks into prison camps. It is debatable whether the Duce seriously considered parading Greek prisoners through Rome in chains, like the emperors of old, but there were plenty of rumours that he was. Count Ciano was in Vienna at the time, and relayed the Duce's disappointment to Hitler. The Fuehrer may well have smiled under his toothbrush moustache. Nonetheless, he gave orders for a new armistice to take into account the Italian demands. Barely was the ink dry on the agreement than Dietrich presented the Greeks with the new one, revoking the Greeks troops' non-prisoner status and giving the Italian field command authority to decide on a cease-fire on its front. Tsolakoglou protested, but eventually signed the new protocol 'compulsorily as a prisoner of war and not of my free volition'.[17]

All was not yet quiet on the Albanian front. Cavallero, encouraged by Mussolini's rejection of the Greek-German truce, had ordered 'a penetration without delay in all directions as deep as possible into Greek territory'. The Casale Division thereupon moved on the border post at Kakavia and suffered some casualties before being halted by a German detachment. There followed some confusion as Greek, German and Italian units spent a few days staking out their respective positions, with the Germans sandwiched in the middle.

On 19 April the Greek 28 Regiment, the rearguard of the 15th Division, was encamped near Leskovik, as other units gradually pulled back from Korce along the Erseke road. The road was a river of gloomy, unshaven and unwashed soldiers, the officers indistinguishable from the men, with infantry, cavalry and artillery jostling for position on the potholed strip of tarmac. The Regia Aeronautica, now free of all opposition, droned insolently overhead in menacing formations. Around noon on 20 April the rumour of the armistice spread like a brush fire among the retreating men.

By evening, when they stretched out on the cold ground to sleep in their overcoats, the rumour had been confirmed: at 1.00 pm the following day, their war would be over.

It was a report, however, that brought it own unique troubles. No-one wants to be the last man to die before the armistice bugle sounds. As the sun rose on 21 April, the men gathered up their weapons and equipment, their pots and pans, and disconnected the telephone lines connecting the regiments, and loaded up the pack mules to be ready for when the signal was given. The men glanced constantly at their watches, willing the hands to creep up to 1.00 pm, dreading the unexpected bullet or shell that might come at any moment before then, with the unlucky man's name on it. During the morning an officer rode up on a motorcycle and asked to see the regiment commander, Lieutenant Colonel Theophilos Kontis. 'The Italians want to see you,' Kontis was told.

Kontis, like his men, was dressed in a worn greatcoat and private's hat, his badges of rank invisible. But he couldn't meet the enemy like that, so he opened his trunk and took out his dress uniform with full leather straps and polished boots. Thus bedecked he got into the officer's sidecar and went off to meet the Italians. It wasn't long before he was back. As his men waited impatiently to hear what he had to say, Kontis wordlessly went and changed back into his scruffy old apparel. 'Lay out the wires again,' he said, grim-faced, when he emerged. 'Re-connect with the other regiments. All men to resume positions. Machine guns and mortars to set up again and be prepared to fire.'

The Italians had told him they didn't recognize the truce. 'They're demanding that we surrender. Otherwise they'll take us all prisoner. If the Italians don't cease fire at one o'clock, the war will go on. We'll attack them.'

It was a bitter blow for the men. To one of them, Second Lieutenant Lazaros Arseniou, it seemed 'as if we had tumbled down a mountain when we were just a few metres from the top'. Nonetheless, the men duly prepared for battle. At about the time they hoped their tribulations might be over, the Italians attacked with machine gun fire. The 28 and the neighbouring 16 Regiment held their positions, with the latter even managing to take about fifty Italian prisoners. At nightfall the pullback resumed, reaching the Mertzani Bridge at the border by morning. Arseniou was crossing the bridge with his platoon, when some officers loomed up in the dark. By their peaked caps he saw they were staff officers, since combat officers invariably wore helmets. They turned out to be Germans, one of whom shone a torch on Arseniou, who in turn opened his greatcoat to reveal his second lieutenant's shoulder stars. The German then confided that the Wehrmacht had orders to separate the Greek and Italian armies to enforce the cease-fire.[18]

The roads around Ioannina now were great khaki rivers of shuffling soldiers trying to find their way home by any means, trying not to think of tomorrow. Occasionally a rumour that the Italians were hard on their heels would trigger momentary panic. But the Germans made sure the Duce's army remained in Albania – for the time being. German detachments going the other way ignored the ragged Greeks, many of them bandaged and limping. The soldiers inundated Ioannina and other towns, sleeping rough, begging for food from the locals. Weapons were cast by the wayside, to be collected by the Germans as war booty. What had begun as a great patriotic endeavour just six months before, with the entire Greek nation united under the flag, had turned into a mass moral and physical disintegration.

Corporal Nikolaou of the 42 Evzones finally returned to his family at Distomo on 3 May after a twelve-day travelling ordeal. His company had continued its withdrawal southwards, encountering the first German columns near Ioannina on 22 April. As the armistice had been signed two days before, the ragged Greeks were allowed to go on their way. The next day an officer briefed the men on the armistice terms and gave them some back pay. As the Greeks camped by the scenic lake at Ioannina, a German military committee arrived and confiscated their weapons. Nikolaou observed what amounted to blatant looting:

> I realized what kind of plundering Greece was about to suffer from the Germans. They left no fuel, no vehicle, no food, nothing. On the road I saw other German shameful acts. I saw Germans opening officers' kitbags and seizing pistols, binoculars, cigarettes, gloves, handkerchiefs etc ... [The Germans] stand in the street and take money from civilians and soldiers.

To all intents and purposes, Nikolaou now was no longer a soldier. Sleeping each night in a different location, and one occasion hitching a lift in a German truck, plagued by lice all the way, he got home and tried to resume normal life – that is, as normal as it could be under an Axis occupation where hunger and fear were daily companions.[19]

It was the Germans, ironically, who saved the Greeks from more humiliation at Mussolini's hands. When the Duce had protested at List's lenient and generous treatment of the defeated Greeks, General Enno von Rintelen, the German military attaché in Rome, retorted:

> No-one can deny that the Greek army defended its country with valour and dedication. If that were not the case, the Italians would not have had to fight against it for so many months. And for the German army the penetration of the Metaxas Line was difficult.[20]

As Tsolakoglou's new German masters told him to send envoys to the Italian command requesting a separate truce, he ordered all Greek units to move with all speed south of a line connecting Igoumentsa with Metsovo so as to avoid capture.

Such was the Germans' contempt for the Italians that in many cases they actually helped the Greeks escape, even giving them lifts in their vehicles. Meanwhile, in the morning of 23 April Tsolakoglou had in his hands a draft truce signed by General Alberto Ferrero of Cavallero's staff, to take effect the following day, providing for hostilities to cease on the front of the Italian Ninth and Eleventh Corps. The Duce issued an order of the day: 'After six months of the bitterest struggle, the enemy has laid down his arms, and victory consecrates our sanguinary sacrifices.'[21]

But few in Athens were paying much heed to the Duce's crowing, for events were moving swiftly to their climax. The neutralization of the Greek army now left the Fuehrer's forces free to sweep up the British unhindered. The immediate burning issue was how to evacuate the British and Empire troops – an operation dubbed, with wicked appropriateness, Operation Demon. The obvious initial destination was Crete, 150km over the water, as a way station towards Egypt, 500km away. When news of Tsolakoglou's cease-fire broke, the initial evacuation day was brought forward by four days, to 24 April. For by now the British were retreating pell-mell through the Greek mainland as the Germans hurtled towards Athens. The stand at Thermopylai had been overcome exactly as Xerxes had overcome it in 480 BC – by turning the pass via the valley to the west. The New Zealand Division had held the pass successfully at first, destroying at least a dozen German Panzers, but had to withdraw with the rest of the British force. The Wehrmacht's Eighteenth and Fortieth Corps were roaring down the Thessalian plain, led by the 6th Mountain Division and 9th Motorized Division, trundling over the smoking wreckage of British trucks and other vehicles destroyed by the incessant Luftwaffe raids.

The 19 Australian Brigade halted the German advance in a stiff fight at Bralos, but constant attacks by squadrons of Ju87s forced the Australians, too, to detach. On 25 April the Germans were almost at the gates of Athens, and the British and Empire troops lost all semblance of order as they raced, dodging the Stuka attacks, to their designated ports of departure. Piraeus, now sown with German mines, was out of bounds. That left Rafina and Porto Rafti on the east coast of the Attic peninsula, and Megara to the west. Other departure points were being hastily made ready at Nafplion, Monemvasia and Kalamata in the Peloponnese. General Blamey, the Australian commander, was recalled to Egypt. General Freyberg, the New Zealander, was sent to Crete to prepare for his men's arrival. Only General Wilson was left to manage the increasingly chaotic exodus. To cap it all, on 23 April, while List was overcoming the doomed defence at Thermopylai, King George and his government set sail for Crete. The curtain was lowered.

The mad rush to Porto Rafti in the early morning of 25 April was witnessed by ten-year-old Sotiris Kollias who had drawn his picture of the Italian bombers on the first day of the war. He had insisted on going with his father on a donkey to salvage Allied materials said to be left by the ton at the dusty roadsides. The boy saw columns of lorries full of British soldiers racing along the roads, and other trucks passing other vehicles abandoned haphazardly. Some lorry drivers had lost their way and were careering panic-stricken through the dirt tracks in the vineyards. Local villagers, like Sotiris and his father, carried home everything portable they could find. One man was lugging an entire tent; another had his head inside a sack of sugar and was gobbling down the contents.

Sotiris' father didn't have time to take anything. 'Without warning the sky filled with planes flying low and strafing,' Sotiris wrote many years later. That's when the young boy learned what a Ju87 Stuka was and what it could do. Everyone on the roads leaped wildly for cover. The Stukas made one pass, and then when everyone thought they had gone, came back for another. They flew so low that Sotiris could see the pilots' faces.

Running to save himself, Sotiris stumbled on a dead British soldier.

> His clothes were soaked in blood. Several things had fallen from his pockets, including a small wallet. Somebody picked up the wallet and gave it to me. It contained a few coins, and was stained with blood on the outside. It was of leather, with some designs on the front.

Sotiris Kollias kept the bloodstained wallet at home for the rest of his life.[22]

Some 5,000 men managed to scramble onto two ships at Porto Rafti, 6,100 at Nafplion and 5,000 at Megara. Greek fishing boats gathered up 200 who hadn't been able to board the ships and ferried them to the Royal Navy waiting offshore. About one-quarter of the British force was evacuated in one night, in a Mediterranean version of Dunkirk. To block the way into the Peloponnese, Wilson had placed explosives on the sole road and rail bridges over the Corinth Canal. But on 26 April 800 German paratroopers got there first and tried to disconnect the wires; as they were working they came under fire from two Britons hidden in the undergrowth 200m away. One of them, a sharpshooter, drew a bead from that distance on the explosive charge under the bridge, and fired. He missed. Disregarding volleys of machine gun fire from the Germans, the man fired again. This time his aim was accurate and the bridge plus the Germans on it went up, and then a few hundred feet down into the canal. The Germans lost 237 men in the canal operation, but captured 921 British soldiers and 1,450 Greeks. At the same time, swarms of Ju87s smashed British artillery positions around Corinth.

Sepp Dietrich's Leibstandarte SS-Adolf Hitler moved south from Ioannina on 25 April to secure the Peloponnese from the north and west. Two days later, in the footsteps of the invading Dorian Greeks of 1100 BC, the division met up with the German paratroopers at Corinth. Another German column headed for Nafplion, only just missing the last of the British. The larger part of Dietrich's division boarded a train for Pyrgos on the west coast of the Peloponnese, and from there moved south to Kalamata, where chaos prevailed in the port. Two thousand British troops under Brigadier Charrington and perhaps 8,000 unarmed Yugoslavs, Greeks, Cypriots and Palestinians were crowding to board the last few ships. These men had long since lost the capacity for rational thought; as the SS moved on to capture the thronging mass, a New Zealand NCO rushed at the Germans with his bayonet. Within seconds hundreds of other Allied troops joined him. The melee was soon over, with forty-one SS men dead, sixty wounded and 150 captured by the very men they themselves expected to take prisoner. Two German tanks, two cannon and twelve vehicles were in Allied hands.

Just when Charrington and his men thought they had a sporting chance at getting out unscathed, the Royal Navy vessels waiting to take them on board received urgent orders to sail and meet an Italian fleet reported to be in the area. The 8,000 non-British fugitives milled along the Kalamata waterfront, not knowing what to do. Charrington and his 2,000 men elected to stay and be captured – except for those who decided to chance it by stowing away on fishing boats to the islands. Making Charrington's surrender even more poignant was that the report of the Italian fleet approaching had been false.[23]

Sailing, of course, was no guarantee of survival. The Stukas were buzzing overhead incessantly. The Dutch troopship *Slamat* had been one of the last to sail for Crete on 27 April. Sixty miles north of the island it came under attack by the Luftwaffe. As it began to sink, the destroyers HMS *Diamond* and HMS *Wryneck* sped to its aid, rescuing about 700 men, but the two British warships themselves received the attentions of the massed Luftwaffe and were sunk almost immediately. More than 980 men lost their lives. The sole survivors were one officer, forty-one enlisted men and eight of the evacuated troops.[24]

Operation Demon was completed by 28 April. Of the 62,562 men of the original expeditionary force, 50,732 made it back out. About 3,000 were killed in action (1,500 British, 750 Australians and 750 New Zealanders including some 300 Maoris). Five thousand more troops scattered themselves over the Greek mainland and islands, most of them eventually making their way to the British forces in the Middle East. Up to 8,000 British may have been taken prisoner. All 209 RAF and RHAF aircraft were destroyed on the ground, except for a bare handful – mainly a half dozen Avro Ansons of the RHAF's 13 Naval Cooperation *Mira* – that against all odds escaped to Egypt. Eight thousand British military vehicles were destroyed.

List's Twelfth Army lost 1,420 men killed and 3,400 wounded. It captured 444 light cannon, 431 mortars, forty-nine anti-tank guns, 151,000 rifles, 1,344 armoured vehicles and 2,710 other vehicles, most of them belonging to the Greek army. The Greeks themselves, from the start of the Italian invasion, lost 13,408 killed and 42,485 wounded.[25] Italian losses are roughly comparable. The Greeks also lost 23,000 men captured, though the great majority of these surrendered to the Germans, who subsequently let them go home. Most of the Allied troops made straight for Egypt except the New Zealand Division which stayed to fight in Crete and would play a large part in the impending Battle of Crete.

Prince Peter remained behind after the king fled to Crete, waiting in his office in the now-deserted Grande Bretagne Hotel to see what the morrow would bring. It seems he was resigned to carrying out Papagos' order that he be taken prisoner by the Germans who were expected in Athens any day. Athens, bereft of its sovereign and government, wasn't even the capital any more. Constantine Maniadakis, the public order minister, urged what remained of the General Staff to resign. But General Wilson, who was still in the city, shrank from asking Papagos – his superior – to step down.

'But what will you do if [Papagos] asks you to surrender to the Germans?' Maniadakis pressed. 'Will you continue the evacuation or give yourselves up?' Wilson looked thoughtful.

'If you do as I say you won't have that dilemma,' Maniadakis went on.

'All right, all right,' Wilson replied with a chuckle. 'Tell General Papagos what you want. I'll be no obstacle.' Then, turning to an aide: 'This is the first coup d'etat I've ever done in my life!'

Prince Peter and the minister went to Papagos' home, where the general was ill in bed. Pulling up chairs by his bedside, both men urged Papagos to formally resign as Greek commander-in-chief. Papagos did not demur. Prince Peter asked him if he preferred to go to Crete and join the king, maintaining his military position and avoiding capture.

'I don't want to take that course of action,' Papagos replied. 'I've done my duty, which is to defeat the Italians in Epiros and Albania, and to fight the

Germans.' The king, he said, was making his own decisions, a new chapter in the war was beginning, and others could rise to take responsibility. 'I will stay and share the fate of the army and people.' Papagos was tired. But he was not going to run away from his country. He signed his own resignation on the spot.[26]

With the hasty departure of the British and the dissolution of the General Staff, Prince Peter didn't have a job any more. He cabled the king offering to join him in Crete, but received the reply that he should attach himself to General Wilson's staff as Greek liaison officer. By now Athens was filling with mobs of hungry ex-soldiers turning to petty crime to survive. On 24 April the prince came upon a crowd of suppliers and sub-contractors filling the lobby of the Acropole Hotel that had been taken over by the British, demanding payment for goods and services. Before he knew it he found himself saddled with the tedious task of paying off the claimants with bunches of banknotes thrust into his hands by a departing British officer. Some of the British demanded that Prince Peter find them captured Italian weapons with which to defend themselves on the long sea trip south; he was unable to oblige. Greek ex-soldiers created ugly scenes in the streets. One person was killed when gunfire erupted on a crowded tram; the prince saw a small boy 'wearing a British helmet far too big for him, running as fast as his legs could carry him'.

Later that day the Luftwaffe came over and bombed the *Hellas*, an evacuation ship loaded with 300 wounded men and sundry Yugoslav officers in the port of Piraeus. From the Grande Bretagne balcony the prince and Rear Admiral Turle watched the great columns of smoke rise from the stricken ship. Turle was especially shaken, as the naval evacuation was his responsibility. He seems to have been ignorant, even at that late stage, of the power of the dive-bomber. 'Those Germans!' Turle exclaimed as the wounded on board were blown up or drowned. 'Who could imagine they'd do a thing like that!'[27]

Preparing to leave with Wilson, Prince Peter got his things together and said his goodbyes to the remainder of the royal family who had elected to stay in Greece and face whatever would come, including the cloistered Princess Alice, the mother of Prince Philip and future Duke of Edinburgh. Telephone calls never ceased. The mayor of Athens, for example, wanted a reassurance from Wilson that the city would be spared any battle between the Germans and the retreating British. On 25 April the prince got into a staff car with Peter Smith Dorrien and headed for Corinth. Halfway there, along the winding clifftop road at Kakia Skala, the way was blocked by the heaped carcasses of mules blown up by a German Stuka attack. Holding his nose, Peter helped move a number of the dead beasts to be able to continue.

At the Corinth Canal they came upon the indefatigable Miles Reid, who was acting as a traffic policeman, directing British units south across the canal bridge. 'You'll get caught if you're not careful,' the prince told Reid. A few hours later German paratroopers floated out of the sky to preserve the bridges, capturing Reid in the process. The car passed Corinth at nightfall, the darkening sky red with the flames of the blazing railway station that had just been bombed along with a hospital train. They caught up with Wilson at Argos and proceeded along the coast road to Nafplion, where ships were burning in the harbour, lighting the way. The boom of German bombs echoed through the night.

Prince Peter and Smith Dorrien spent the rest of the night at Myli, a tiny fishing village west of Nafplion, sleeping in the car. They were awakened at sunrise by an anxious staff officer who said that Wilson thought the car was parked in too visible a spot. Smith Dorrien duly moved the car under a larger olive tree. Also at Myli with Wilson were General Heywood, Rear Admiral Turle, Maniadakis and Admiral Sakellariou, soon to be joined by Crown Prince Paul whose yacht put in later in the morning as a German reconnaissance plane droned overhead. Wilson's plan was to get away on Paul's yacht but it was at once apparent that the vessel was too small to take everyone. Then squadrons of German aircraft began appearing in the sky, on their way to bomb and strafe the British and Empire troops still fleeing south. The sound of distant explosions filled the warm air. At lunchtime the officers dined hastily on a deal table set up under an olive tree. Prince Peter marvelled that the British officers, laughing and joking as they ate, could remain so calm while the din of war was all around them. General Wilson's Sudanese valet, a fellow named Ahmed, was busy digging a slit trench when the prince asked him what he thought of Greece. 'Very nice country,' Ahmed replied, 'but too many bombs!'

In the afternoon Smith Dorrien said they could all fit in Paul's yacht if some personal baggage was left behind. The party was busy separating essential from non-essential effects when more German aircraft appeared. One of them strafed the car of Brigadier Guido Salisbury-Jones, fortunately without hitting anyone. Then at 5.00 pm a lone bomber appeared from seaward and launched five torpedoes at Paul's yacht, which sank along with the party's hopes. Wilson got onto his rigged-up wireless to demand an RAF Short Sunderland flying boat to get them off the mainland.

As they waited, the Luftwaffe attacked in waves, probably tipped off about who was hiding under the olive groves. British soldiers crowded for protection around the lorries while the prince found a sewer opening over an irrigation ditch. He didn't know which was worse, to risk a Luftwaffe bullet or cover himself with sewer grime. He didn't have to make the choice, as night fell and the German aircraft made off. Wilson was getting desperate when, as if by magic, a white Sunderland roared up from the south, settling on the water. 'Now what are you going to do?' the prince asked Wilson.

'I'll do what a lot of generals in history have done before me,' 'Jumbo' replied. 'I'll sit on my suitcases.'

Prince Peter was the last to get on board the Sunderland, after he and Smith Dorrien broke up and burned their car to keep it out of German hands. Seventy-five men were crammed into the flying boat's cavernous fuselage and the pilot was wondering how he could get airborne. The prince stretched out on the floor under the chain-smoking Maniadakis' feet, and at once fell asleep, oblivious to the soft rain of cigarette ash falling on his face. The pilot waited until nightfall to take off, but Heywood, looking through a window, saw German units coming down the road from Argos. The Sunderland's growling engines turned over slowly so as not to attract the enemy's attention, moving the great flying boat fifteen miles out to sea. There it waited until 5.00 am, when the pilot pushed forward the throttles and the heavily-loaded Sunderland ploughed a large distance through the choppy waves before finally lifting off. Even then, the flying boat flew almost at wave-top height, its fuselage groaning under the strain, touching down at Souda Bay in Crete at 6.45 am. 'There was never a more welcome sight,' Peter wrote.[28]

Almost at the same hour, in the early morning of 27 April, the first German columns of the 6th Mountain Division appeared in the northern outskirts of Athens. The columns rumbled down deserted Kifissias Avenue – the same road up which Grazzi had driven to deliver his ultimatum to Metaxas a mere six months before to the day – and into the city where a capitulation committee headed by a mere army corporal waited at the junction of Kifissias and Alexandras Avenue with orders to let the Germans through after a token halt. Within a few minutes the German lieutenant colonel in charge of the advance guard had received the formal surrender of Athens, and the lead motorcyclists continued down Vassilissis Sophias, towards the centre, the growl of the engines echoing off the faces of the upscale apartment blocks of Ambelokipi and Kolonaki. One eyewitness said the German riders 'looked neither to the left or the right, sitting upright, like conquerors'.[29] Few were about. The Athenians, numb with defeat, shut themselves up in their homes. The lead column turned left at Syntagma Square, in the shadow of the Grande Bretagne Hotel and headed down Amalias Avenue towards the Acropolis. At 8.45 am a guard detachment under a Captain Jacobi walked up through the Propylaia and past the Parthenon to where the Greek flag was fluttering on the eastern parapet of the Acropolis overlooking the city centre. Jacobi had orders to haul the flag down and replace it with the swastika. And here is where the final dramatic act in the fall of Greece is caught up in the mist of romantic legend.

It was reported, by both German and Greek sources, that Jacobi approached the Greek guard on duty at the Acropolis, a soldier named Constantine Koukidis, and ordered him to take down the Greek flag on the eastern parapet so that it could be replaced with the swastika. Koukidis refused. Jacobi then ordered a German soldier to do the deed, which he did, handing the flag over to Koukidis. Within seconds, before anyone could react, Koukidis wrapped himself in the flag, ran to the parapet and jumped to his death 60m below.

So far, there is general agreement. But just who Constantine Koukidis was has been surprisingly controversial. Most accounts say he was an Evzone guard. Yet recent research has turned up no mention of his name in the Evzone rolls. This has suggested to some that Koukidis never really existed. The Cairo correspondent of the *Daily Mail*, reporting the story on 9 June 1941, mentions merely 'a Greek soldier' and is vague on sources. As by the time the Germans entered Athens the Greek army had ceased to exist as a command organization, what would an Evzone on active duty be doing? Others claim that Koukidis was not in fact a soldier but a member of the fascist EON National Youth Organization whose duties included guarding the Acropolis. It was in his EON uniform that he leapt to his death wrapped in the flag, and his true identity was hushed up in the politically-correct anti-fascist post-war years.[30]

The weight of evidence suggests that Koukidis – whatever the uniform he was wearing – was a real person, and that the suicide story is authentic. Several eyewitnesses saw his body tumbling down the rocks to come to rest on Thrasyllou Street, where a monument to his sacrifice now stands. The witnesses say he was put in an ice-cart and trundled to a burial in Athens' First Cemetery not far away. Such was the dramatic yet humble end of the last hero of the defence and fall of Greece.

Chapter 14

Behind the Wire

A rotten job but someone had to do it – Papagos and four generals are arrested and deported – Papagos' later career – the RHAF carries on the war in the desert – was Pattle the top ace? – Greek and Italian casualties – Prince Peter in Crete and later – fate of the Nikolaou family

General Tsolakoglou agreed to become the prime minister of a German-controlled puppet government along the lines of the Vichy administration in France. His cabinet included General Bakos, the former II Corps Commander, as defence minister, and General Demestichas, formerly of the I Corps, as interior minister. General Katsimitros, the hero of Kalpaki, took a post as labour and then agriculture minister. Major General Nikolaos Markou, former commander of the 6th Division, became deputy public order minister, while Major General Sotirios Moutousis, former Commander of the 13th Division, was appointed transport minister. Athens Radio became a German propaganda mouthpiece, while the press was muzzled and to the regular police force were added Security Battalions, many of them made up of rightwing ex-soldiers. These were of two kinds: those who needed a job and weren't too fussy about whom they worked for, and those who, while resenting the occupation, believed the spectre of communism to be a greater danger. The Germans staged a victory parade before the Tomb of the Unknown Soldier on 3 May. Few turned out to watch, especially as the despised Italians were also taking part. (List hadn't wanted them around, but the Fuehrer insisted, again not wishing to sour relations with Mussolini.) General Geloso, the commander of the Eleventh Corps on the Albanian front, was appointed Italian military governor of Athens, and his corps the Italian occupation force – a bitter pill indeed for the Greeks to swallow. Yet one imagines that Visconti Prasca must have been eating his heart out.

Tsolakoglou was utterly convinced that he was doing the right thing. Greece had been defeated on the field of battle, and this was the logical consequence, to be nobly endured for as long as it would last. The same could be said for the ex-officers he appointed to his puppet cabinet. It was a rotten job, but someone had to do it. 'He confronted the task with the same admirable coolness he had displayed in the face of the enemy,' a sympathizer wrote. Tsolakoglou did what he could for the public welfare, for example, mitigating the threat of mass starvation in the bitter winter of 1941–42 by cracking down on black marketeers. The German-controlled government, under a series of puppet prime ministers, lasted until 12 October 1944, when the last German soldier left Athens to wild rejoicing. Tsolakoglou was promptly jailed and in May 1945 sentenced to death for high treason. The sentence was commuted but Tsolakoglou died in prison of leukaemia shortly after his trial. Bakos was seized and executed by communist partisans in December 1944, during an abortive communist attempt to seize power. Demestichas was sentenced to twenty years in jail.

Katsimitros after the war also served a few years behind bars, but thanks to his brilliant war record was restored to the army roster in 1951 and promoted to lieutenant general.[1]

Papagos' fears that he would be taken prisoner were not realized, thanks to the moderation of the Germans, who told him to stay quietly at home, assuring him he wouldn't be harmed if he didn't rock the boat. But he did. Two years of quiescence were too much for his soldierly spirit; he began to worry that communists and anarchists were seeking to control the budding resistance movement, and decided to form a conservative one of his own. In early 1943 he began hosting a series of clandestine meetings at his home with Generals Bakopoulos (East Macedonia Army Department), Pitsikas (Epirus Army Department), Kosmas (I Corps), Papadopoulos (II Corps) and Panayotis Dedes (West Macedonia Division Group). In a declaration signed on 20 May 1943, the five pledged to maintain 'unity of purpose among the remaining Greek officers ... and thwart any attempt to disturb public order or overthrow the social order [while] reinforcing Greece's continuing struggle ... pledging allegiance to the king and legitimate government'.[2]

But security was not of the best, and Bakopoulos described what happened on the morning of 25 July:

> It was very hot. My wife and two children, with their governess Lemonia, were sleeping on the roof of our house. At about 0530 hours the doorbell rang urgently ... I got up, looked out of the window and saw two men in civilian clothes, a third who was loitering, and a German car. It was obvious they had come to arrest me.

The two men belonged to the Gestapo. One of them, who spoke Greek, assured Bakopoulos' wife that her husband would be back home in a few days after being questioned at the German headquarters. As Bakopoulos was dressing, his young son Alexander came downstairs and 'stood in front of the Germans, frowning and silent'. His little daughter Dora, to lighten the atmosphere, tinkled a few notes on the living room piano, but the hard faces of the Gestapo men were not softened. At that moment the telephone rang. It was Bakopoulos' brother, who called to give the happy news of Mussolini's overthrow. As he was marched into the waiting car, Bakopoulos gained a bit of courage from the news.[3]

In the Gestapo office Bakopoulos found Dedes and Kosmas. Papagos was brought in soon afterwards, and Pitsikas in the early evening. Papadopoulos somehow escaped arrest. The five generals were put on a train which started them on the long and exhausting trip to Germany. Several days later they got out at Koenigstein Castle, a prisoner-of-war camp for high-ranking Allied officers. From there, after some months, they were transferred to a special *Prominenten* section of the Sachsenhausen concentration camp near Berlin. There they came into contact with British officers, to whom Papagos came across as haughty and uncooperative.[4] As the Allies penetrated into Germany in 1945, the five Greek generals and other Allied officers were driven to northern Italy to serve as human bargaining chips for the SS. On liberation, they were flown back to Greece. The 'few days' the Gestapo said Bakopoulos would be away from home had turned into more than two harrowing years.

Papagos was promoted to full general in 1947 and given charge of suppressing the communist rebellion that he had feared. When the Greek national army was on the verge of winning in January 1949, he was upped to field marshal, the only Greek officer ever to achieve that ultimate rank. Resigning from the army in 1951, he decided to enter politics on the strength of the military laurels he had earned, forming the conservative National Rally party on the model of France's de Gaulle (whom he seems to have consciously tried to resemble, even to the supercilious expression and short moustache). National Rally won a landslide in the elections of November 1952, propelling Papagos into the prime minister's chair. But his health was already failing, and he served three years until his death in October 1955, aged seventy-two.

The RHAF, though battered into near-extinction, came out of the campaign covered in glory. Throughout the seven-month campaign the Greek air force lost thirty-seven aircraft, approximately half the number of Regia Aeronautica aircraft destroyed by Greek action. Fifty-two Greek aircrew died. When the Germans marched into Athens just one squadron remained operational – 13 Naval Cooperation Mira with ten Avro Ansons based at the capital. They had lined up on the runway ready at Hellenikon to escape to Crete on 23 April when a formation of Bf109s appeared out of nowhere and shot up half of them. The remaining five dodged the bomb craters and took off. For thirteen tense hours they overflew the Mediterranean and Crete, evading the Luftwaffe, until touching down at the RAF base at Mersa Matruh in Egypt. From there 13 Mira continued the war under British command yet proudly kept its Greek roundels, until joined later by other Greek airmen who eventually made up 335 and 336 (Greek) Squadrons RAF which, besides helping the Allied air effort in the Middle East and later Italy to no small degree, kept the Greek air force flying when its homeland was under occupation.[5]

As for the RAF proper, Squadron Leader Marmaduke Pattle may well have been the RAF's highest-scoring air ace in all of World War Two. We say 'may well have been' as the operational records are by no means complete. Going by strictly official records, Pattle scored twenty-three kills from his first two Italian victims on 4 August 1940 at Bir Taleb el Esem in North Africa to the end of March 1941 when he took command of 33 Squadron. The Air Ministry has no record of his score in the last three weeks of his life, as all the documents were destroyed when the British evacuated Greece at the end of April 1941. All we have of that period is a brief summary of 33 Squadron's activity written from memory and deposited in the Air Ministry's Air Historical Branch. Thanks, however, to research by E.C.R. Baker, we can confidently conclude that Pattle downed at least seventeen more enemy aircraft from 6 to 20 April. This brings Pattle's more or less confirmed score throughout his eight-month combat fighter pilot career to forty kills, with six damaged and three probables, which would make him the top Allied as well as British ace.[6]

In mid-May King Vittorio Emanuele III visited the front in Albania with a triumphant Cavallero in tow. The king stopped briefly at shell-cratered Hill 731, where the smashed bodies of his courageous soldiers had at last been buried. Cavallero had written to the Duce requesting approval to make the hill into a war memorial. If there was one place in Albania where the Italians could truly claim to have displayed great military valour, Hill 731 was it. Yet the place apparently made such a faint impression on the monarch that his aide-de-camp didn't even mention it in his diary. Vittorio Emanuele didn't bat an eyelid when a young Albanian extremist fired four pistol shots at him, puncturing one of the royal car's tyres. Mussolini replied fulsomely to Cavallero's appeal for a shrine, but the matter appears to have been taken no further.[7]

The dead of Hill 731 were among the 13,755 Italians killed in action during the fight against the Greeks. Some 50,880 were wounded, while 12,368 men suffered various degrees of frostbite (some fatal) and more than 25,000 went missing – at least 23,000 into Greek prisoner-of-war camps. Albanian units attached to the Italians suffered fifty-nine killed and sixty-eight wounded. On the Greek side some 13,410 Greeks died on the Albanian front and 42,485 were wounded. Eighteen ships ferrying troops and supplies from Italy to Albania were sent to the bottom, while sixty-five aircraft of the Regia Aeronautica were destroyed, with the loss of 229 airmen. It is a tribute to the skill of the Italian airmen and the quality of their aircraft that Greek and British losses in the air were rather higher than their own.[8]

Cavallero rode on his 'success' in Albania for two more years, heading the Italian Army Staff as *Maresciallo d'Italia*. When in July 1943 the Italians lost Libya to the Allies, Marshal Badoglio, who always despised Cavallero, had him arrested. Badoglio was able to act because the Duce's days of power had also come to an abrupt end, thanks to decisive action by Badoglio and the king. Cavallero appealed to the Germans for support, protesting his faithfulness to fascism and the Axis cause. But at the same time he had taken out insurance by writing to Badoglio that he despised fascism and Mussolini. The Germans faced him with this conflict, which he saw no way to resolve; a few months later he shot himself in the head. In 1948 his son Carlo published Cavallero's war diaries as *Comando Supremo*, a major source of our knowledge of the Albanian campaign from the Italian side.

Prince Peter, still a captain in the Greek army, continued his liaison service with the British in Crete. While there he witnessed a shocking breakdown of discipline among the Allied troops, narrowly escaping being shot by a group of drunken and fatigue-crazed Australians in a Chania hotel. During the Battle of Crete he escaped with the king and the prime minister over the rough Cretan mountains, boarding a British destroyer which took them to Egypt. As aide-de-camp to King George, he briefly served in the Sacred Band, an elite unit harking back to ancient Thebes, returning to Greece on its liberation in October 1944. His chest filled with decorations, he was promoted to reserve lieutenant colonel. Some time afterwards, disillusioned with the partisan savagery of the Greek Civil War, he resigned his commission and went to live in France.

He had never lost interest in Oriental anthropological studies – an interest which may account for his calm and philosophical attitude throughout the hazards of war – and returned to scholarship in the field, penning a number of books and articles in learned journals and completing a doctoral course at London University in 1959. Between 1961 and 1964 he was president of the Interallied Federation of NATO Reserve Officers. He made occasional visits to Athens, where he became an honorary professor at Athens University Medical School.

Prince Peter remained childless. His wife Irina Alexandra Ovchinnikov, whom he had married in a civil ceremony in India in 1939, never visited Greece as the Orthodox Church did not recognize civil marriages at the time. After the Greek monarchy was abolished after many political vicissitudes in 1974, the prince saw no further purpose in having anything to do with Greece. He died in London in October 1980, aged seventy-two. His war diaries, which throw a fascinating light on the defence and fall of Greece, especially his relations with the British, were published in Athens in 1997 thanks partly to the efforts of Papagos' son Leonidas, who for many years served as the head of the household of King Constantine II.

Corporal Nikolaou's premonitions about the Germans came tragically true on 10 June 1944, when German troops burst into his home in Distomo and machine-gunned him, his wife and two daughters to death. His youngest daughter Eleni was the sole survivor. The atrocity was but one small part of a massacre of the inhabitants of Distomo in retaliation for a guerrilla attack. A total of 218 people were slaughtered, including a two-month-old infant. In 2007 Eleni Nikolaou decided to immortalize her father's war diary in a little book. In the intervening years, unsurprisingly, she had been plagued with horrific nightmares, but managed to become a mother herself. 'As many years as might pass,' she writes in an epilogue, 'the psychic traumas can never be healed ... I've found myself in Germany by chance a few times. I may no longer hate those who did me such great evil, but I have contempt for them. And I could never imagine [the Germans] as being Europeans.'[9]

Appendix

Major Italian and Greek operational units and their commanders on the eve of the Spring Offensive, March 1941

Italian

Third Corps	Gen. Mario Arisio
	Divisions: Arezzo, Venezia
Fourth Corps	Gen. Camillo Mercalli
	Divisions: Julia, Wolves of Tuscany
Eighth Corps	Gen. Emilio Bancale
	Divisions: Siena
Ninth Corps	Gen. Mario Vercellino
	Divisions: Piemonte, Taro
Eleventh Corps	Gen. Carlo Geloso
	Divisions: Bari, Pinerolo, Pusteria
Twenty-fifth Corps	Gen. Carlo Rossi
	Divisions: Brennero, Centauro, Ferrara, Legnano, Modena
Twenty-sixth Corps	Gen. Gabriele Nasci
	Divisions: Cuneo, Padova, Tridentina
Special (Coastal) Corps	Gen. Giovanni Messe

Greek

I Corps	Lt. Gen. George Kosmas
	Divisions: 2nd, 3rd, 4th, 5th, 8th and 18th
	Epiros Army Detachment: Lt. Gen. Markos Drakos
II Corps	Lt. Gen. Dimitrios Papadopoulos
	Divisions: 1st, 11th, 15th and 16th
III Corps	Lt. Gen. George Tsolakoglou
(Later West Macedonia Army Department)	Divisions: 6th, 9th, 10th, 13th and 17th Divisional Group K

Notes

Chapter 1
1. Melas 12–4
2. *Op. cit.* 14–8
3. *Op. cit.* 48
4. Quoted in Cervi 41
5. *Op. cit.* 42
6. Karras 124
7. See Woodhouse 231
8. Karras 91
9. *Op. cit.* 95
10. *Op. cit.* 115
11. Veremis (ed.) 142
12. Woodhouse 233
13. Veremis (ed.) 146
14. *Ibid.*
15. Karras 96–102
16. *Op. cit.* 119
17. Papagos I 218–19
18. Karras 120
19. See 'The euthanasia of 4 August' in *Adesmeftos Typos*, 27 October 2002
20. Karras 118
21. Veremis (ed.) 153
22. *Op. cit.* 155
23. PP 20–1
24. Veremis (ed.) 205
25. Karras 119–23

Chapter 2
1. Rendina 610–4
2. Mack Smith 21; testimony of Leda Rafanelli, an early radical associate
3. Korpis *op. cit.*
4. Cervi 45
5. Mack Smith 173
6. Cervi 46–8
7. Mack Smith 72–3
8. Cervi 6
9. Mack Smith 153–8
10. *Op. cit.* 252–3
11. Cervi 50

12. *Ibid.*
13. Gen. Quirino Armellini, quoted in Cervi 51
14. *Op. cit.* 57
15. *Op. cit.* 77, citing Grazzi's *Il principio della fine*, Rome 1955
16. *Op. cit.* 63
17. *Op. cit.* 66 citing Roatta's *Otto milioni di baionette*, 1946
18. *Op. cit.* 51
19. Mack Smith 247
20. *Op. cit.* 254
21. Cervi 75
22. Mack Smith 257
23. Cervi 83–4
24. Niglis *op. cit.*
25. Christodoulou *op. cit.*
26. GAS 8
27. Arseniou 30
28. Cervi 98–105
29. Caution must be exercised in estimating Greek and Italian divisional strengths. Mussolini had taken the novel step of halving the size of his divisions to increase their number, partly to impress the distrustful Germans. A typical Italian division would stand at some 10,000 men, while a Greek division might number up to double that.
30. Papagos I 363–8
31. *Op. cit.* 416–8

Chapter 3
1. Karras 127
2. Terzakis 39
3. Karras 131–2
4. In Mackenzie, C. *Greece in my Life*, London: Chatto and Windus 1960, 122–3
5. Woodhouse 237
6. PP 25–35
7. Cervi 115–6
8. Papagos II 304
9. Carr 3
10. Kollias 23
11. Quoted in Cervi 215
12. *Op. cit.* 122
13. Papagos II 304–5
14. Carr 8
15. Terzakis 52–3
16. *Op. cit.* 51
17. *Op. cit.* 58; Hellenic War Museum
18. Christodoulou *op. cit.*
19. Terzakis 58
20. Cervi 125–6
21. Terzakis 58–9

22. *Op. cit.* 60
23. Cervi 128–9
24. Karykas *op. cit.*
25. Cervi 139
26. Karykas *op. cit.*
27. Author's translation of: *Sul ponte di Perati bandiera nera / L'è il lutto della Julia che va alla guerra / La meglio gioventù va sotto terra.* Cervi 140
28. Cervi 135–8
29. In 1943, with the fall of Mussolini, Visconti Prasca joined the Italian partisans and was taken prisoner by the Germans. After the war he continued to insist that he had been grossly unfairly treated in November 1940. He penned a self-serving memoir, *Io ho aggredito la Grecia* (*I aggressed against Greece*), to justify himself, but the evidence of incompetence continues to weigh heavily against him.
30. PP 37–63
31. Terzakis 42
32. Mattioli 14
33. *Op. cit.* 14–5
34. PP 70–5

Chapter 4
1. Kollias 23–4
2. Terzakis 63
3. Col. Aldo Rasero, quoted in Cervi 144
4. Cervi 216
5. In Spatharis, S. *Memoirs*, Athens: Pergamos 1960 137–40
6. Nikolaou 25–6
7. Carr 35
8. Terzakis 100
9. PP 69
10. Cervi 146–7
11. *Op. cit.* 216–7
12. Terzakis 111
13. *Op. cit.* 114
14. Full text of Mussolini's address in Cervi 303–8
15. *Op. cit.* 149
16. Quoted from *Neon Kratos* magazine, Vol. 4, 1940

Chapter 5
1. PP 87–9
2. *Op. cit.* 88–93
3. *Op. cit.* 97
4. *Op. cit.* 97–100
5. Papagos II 329
6. Nikolaou 32–4
7. Terzakis 116–8
8. *Op. cit.* 128

9. *Op. cit.* 125
10. Quoted in Cervi 154
11. *Op. cit.* 156
12. *Op. cit.* 217
13. *Op. cit.* 219
14. *Op. cit.* 219–20
15. *Op. cit.* 161
16. Terzakis 134
17. *Op. cit.* 144
18. Cervi 171–3
19. Nikolaou 37–40
20. In Kanellopoulos, P. *War Years*, Athens 1964 15–6n

Chapter 6
1. Quoted in Cervi 304
2. For a more detailed account of the RHAF in the war, see Carr *op. cit.*
3. Mattioli 13
4. *Op. cit.* 15
5. Vladousis lived well into his nineties; he died in 2011.
6. Baker 88
7. *Op. cit.* 89–91
8. Mattioli 16
9. *Op. cit.* 17
10. Author's italics
11. PP 81
12. *Op. cit.* 73–88
13. Baker 9
14. Mattioli 17–8
15. Carr 42
16. Mattioli 19

Chapter 7
1. Cervi 176
2. PP 111–2
3. Papagos II 337
4. Cervi 173–4
5. *Op. cit.* 175
6. Karras 145
7. PP 110
8. *Op. cit.* 103; Pitellos to author
9. *Op. cit.* 105; the names and addresses have been transliterated from the Greek and may contain errors.
10. Nikolaou 45
11. Cervi 222
12. PP 142
13. In Keegan, J. *Churchill*, London: Weidenfeld & Nicolson 2002 128–9

14. PP 155–63
15. Quoted in Cervi 180
16. Terzakis 157; Cervi 181
17. Nikolaou 52
18. Cervi 178; author's italics
19. Dialogue in Cervi 185–6
20. Nikolaou 56–7; entry of 26 January 1941
21. Metaxas diary entry for 15 January 1941
22. Quoted in PP 201–2
23. Karras 151–4

Chapter 8
1. Cervi 222
2. Terzakis 168
3. PP 237
4. Terzakis 170
5. PP 187–201
6. *Op. cit.* 212–3
7. *Op. cit.* 230–1
8. For details on the diplomatic wrangling with Turkey, see Weber, F. *The Evasive Neutral*, University of Missouri 1979 59–60
9. *Op. cit.* 60
10. PP 252
11. Quoted in Cervi 321
12. *Ibid.*
13. Cervi does not give a source for this exchange, though it was probably Pricolo, and hence can be considered authentic.
14. Cervi 201
15. *Op. cit.* 224; free translation by the author
16. Terzakis 176
17. *Op. cit.* 178
18. Quoted in Cervi 222–3
19. *Op. cit.* 207; author's italics
20. *Op. cit.* 211
21. Papagos II 350–1
22. Terzakis 189–90
23. Cervi 234
24. Arseniou 81–4

Chapter 9
1. For the later stages of the air war, see Carr *op. cit.*
2. Baker 125–7
3. *Op. cit.* 134–7
4. Carr 50
5. Papagos II 353
6. Quoted in Baker 151
7. *Op. cit.* 157–60

Chapter 10
1. Quoted in Melas 23; italics in the original
2. *Op. cit.* 85
3. *Op. cit.* 82–91
4. For more on the contribution of the RHAF's naval cooperation squadrons, see Carr *op. cit.*
5. Minutes of the meeting in Melas 110–3
6. *Op. cit.* 137–42
7. *Op. cit.* 147–8
8. Hellenic Maritime Museum documents
9. Quoted in Melas 192
10. In fact Spanidis was often heard exclaiming, 'I cannot sleep because of Miltiades's honours!' The phrase had been uttered by the Athenian Themistokles in 490 BC when his fellow-general Miltiades had taken all the credit for defeating the Persians at the battle of Marathon, and the ambitious Themistokles couldn't live with it. Miltiades, of course, was also Iatridis' first name.
11. Melas 212–3
12. *Op. cit.* 216–43; HMM records
13. Cervi 210
14. Quoted in Melas 266

Chapter 11
1. PP 272
2. Christodoulou *op. cit.*
3. Papagos II 364
4. In Shirer, W.L. *The Rise and Fall of the Third Reich*, New York: Fawcett Crest 1960 1082
5. Keegan 132–3
6. Papagos II 355
7. Nikolaou 98–105
8. *Op. cit.* 103
9. Papagos II 355
10. PP 276–7
11. Papagos II 374–5

Chapter 12
1. PP 285–6
2. *Op. cit.* 288–9; Carr 60
3. Terzakis 196–9
4. Christodoulou *op. cit.*
5. Papagos II 411
6. Christodoulou *op. cit.*
7. Details of the Rupel operation in Nikoltsios and Hadia 45–71
8. *Op. cit.* 72
9. Melas 287–90
10. *Op. cit.* 281–6
11. Carr 65–6

250   *The Defence and Fall of Greece 1940–41*

12. Baker 173–6
13. Carr 68
14. Baker 183–7
15. Nikolaou 116–24

Chapter 13
1. PP 301–4
2. Arseniou gives a concise analysis of this phenomenon, 275–6
3. GAS 147
4. Arseniou 280
5. GAS 174
6. Sakellariou 201
7. PP 307
8. *Op. cit.* 307–9; Arseniou (286–7) mentions two shots, though that is improbable for a suicide. He also asserts that Koryzis shot himself in his study and that a journalist found him, not Prince Paul. I have preferred Prince Peter's version as based on Paul's direct eyewitness account.
9. Melas 302–3
10. *Op. cit.* 306–7
11. *Op. cit.* 308–12
12. Arseniou 289
13. Not all British officers shared the defeatism. Brigadier Guido Salisbury-Jones confided to Prince Peter that he wanted both of them to go to Thermopylai and, like the Spartan Leonidas, 'fight till we are killed.' The prince talked him out of it; PP 310
14. Arseniou 293
15. PP 316
16. Papagos II 442–3
17. GAS 227
18. Arseniou 298–300
19. Nikolaou 126–34
20. Arseniou 302
21. Cervi 258
22. Kollias 29–32
23. Arseniou 308–9
24. A ceremony was conducted at the spot on 26 June 2012, attended by relatives of the victims, on board the present HMS *Diamond*. Present was the commander of the Greek Navy, Rear Admiral Constantine Mazarakis, who said he was honoured to 'visit [the Royal Navy] that has such respect for its traditions, its fathers and its grandfathers.' (In 'HMS *Diamond* Remembers Wartime Disaster,' *Britain at War* August 2012.)
25. Figures in Arseniou 309–10
26. PP 320–3
27. *Op. cit.* 328–9
28. *Op. cit.* 329–47
29. Arseniou 310
30. George Mermingas to author.

Chapter 14
1. In 'Occupation Prime Ministers,' *Tote* magazine, issue 22, April 2006
2. Bakopoulos 35
3. *Op. cit.* 39–41
4. See, for example, Smith, S. *'Wings' Day*, London: Collins 1968
5. For details of the RHAF's later war history, see Carr *op. cit.*
6. Baker 7–8
7. Cervi 262
8. Italian Defence Ministry figures in Cervi 267–8
9. Nikolaou 154–5

Sources

The alert reader will by now have become aware that in researching this book I have made use overwhelmingly of Greek sources. The reason I have done this is to bring back the actual atmosphere of the defence and fall of Greece as authentically as possible, especially as, to the best of my knowledge, few if any of these sources have been translated into English. The great bulk of information about the Greek campaign does come from Greek sources, on which all others are based. Exceptions include my use of E.C.R. Baker's *Ace of Aces*, an engagingly-written account of the accomplishments of Squadron Leader 'Pat' Pattle, and Mario Cervi's seminal account of the war from the Italian side. The main sources I have used are:

(G) = available in Greek only

Arseniou, L. *Anatomy of the Epic 1940–41*, Athens & Ioannina: Dodoni 1998 (G)
Baker, E.C.R. *Ace of Aces*, New English Library 1973
Bakopoulos, C. *Five Generals Hostage*, Athens (self-published) 1948
Carr, J. *On Spartan Wings*, Barnsley: Pen and Sword 2012
Cervi, M. *Storia della Guerra di Grecia*, Milan: RCS Libri 2000
Christodoulou, D. 'Greek Motorized Forces in the War of 1940–41' in *Stratiotiki Istoria* January 2012
Greek Army Staff *History of War Operations 1940–41*, Athens 1946 (G) (Referred to in the notes as GAS)
Hellenic Naval Museum *The Silent War: The Action of Greece's Submarines 1940–44*, Athens 1995 (G)
Kanteres, D. 'The German Invasion of Greece and the Dissolution of the Army,' in *Polemos kai Istoria* April 2012 (G)
Karras, N. *Ioannis Metaxas: A Historical-Political Appraisal* (including extracts from the Metaxas diaries), Athens: Pelargos 2003 (G)
Karykas, P. 'Greek Cavalry Halts the Italian Blitzkrieg,' in *Polemos kai Istoria* April 2012 (G)
Kollias, S. *Stories with Aeroplanes*, Athens (self-published) 2010 (G)
Korpis, P. 'Radio Bari' in *Kathimerini*, 26 Oct 2003 (G)
Mack Smith, D. *Mussolini: A Biography*, New York: Random House 1983
Mattioli, M. *53 Stormo*, Oxford: Osprey Publishing 2010
Melas, S. *Flaming Seas*, Athens 1947 (reprinted by Biris publishers) (G)
Niglis, E. 'The Metaxas Line' in *Strati kai Taktikes*, March-April 2012 (G)
Nikolaou, M. *Diary from the Front*, Athens: Kastalia 2007 (G)
Nikoltsios, V and Hadia, A. *Fort Rupel*, Thessaloniki (self-published) 1995 (G)

Papagos, A. *The Greek Army and its Preparation for War*, Athens: Goulandris-Horn 1997 (G) (Referred to in the notes as Papagos I)
Papagos, A. *The War for Greece 1940–1941*, Athens: Goulandris-Horn 1997 (G) (Referred to in the notes as Papagos II)
Prince Peter of Greece *War Dairies 1940–1941*, Athens: Goulandris-Horn 1997 (G) (Referred to in the notes as PP)
Rendina, C. *Storia Insolita di Roma*, Rome: Newton and Compton 2001
Sakellariou, A. *An Admiral Remembers*, Athens: Yiota Sigma (undated) (G)
Terzakis, A. *Greek Epic 1940–1941, 5th edition*, Athens: Estia 2008 (reprint) (G)
Veremis, T. (ed.) *Metaxas and his Era*, Athens: Evrasia 2009 (G)
Woodhouse, C.M. *The Story of Modern Greece*, London: Faber 1968

Index

Abrahams, R. Flt Lt, 170
Alexander the Great, 9
Alfieri, D., 88
Alice, Princess of Greece, 233
Aicardi, G. Lt, 4
Andreini, E. Col, 40
Antolini, P. Lt, 124, 141, 155
Antoniou, A. Flt Lt, 165, 213
Arisio, M. Gen, 96
Armellini, Q. Gen, 26, 43, 63, 85
Arseniou, L. 2nd Lt, 227–8
Arslanoglou, V. Lt Cdr, 189
Asimakis, A. Col, 77
Asimakopoulos, E. Lt Col, 50
Avati, R. Lt, 47
Averof, N. Gp Capt, 214
Azzaro, G. Col, 67

Bacci, G. WO, 59
Badoglio, P. Marshal, 19, 22–7, 43, 55–7, 63, 71, 84–5, 92, 149, 160, 241
Baker, E.C.M., 164, 240
Bakopoulos, C. Lt Gen, 196, 205, 207, 209, 210–11, 238–9
Bakos, G. Maj Gen, 93, 154, 200, 218, 237–8
Balbo, I. Marshal, 100, 108
Balfour, D. ('Father Dimitrios'), 121
Bancale, G. Gen, 67, 94, 130
Barbrook. W. Maj, 129, 138
Bartiromo, S. Col, 87, 134–5
Basakidis, P. Maj Gen, 82
Begletis, Col, 72
Bellegambi, M. Lt, 170
Bennett, S. Sgt, 114
Blamey, T. Lt Gen, 195, 230
Blunt, J. Col, 67, 75, 129–30, 138
Boehme, F. Lt Gen, 206, 210–11
Bollea, O. Gen, 130
Boris III, king of Bulgaria, 29
Bottai, G., 96
Brian, A.E. Flt Lt, 59

Briand, A., 17
Brooks, R.N. Sgt, 59
Buckler, J. Cdr, 205
Buckley, Maj, 121

Campione, F. Capt, 68, 86
Cantore, A. Lt, 89
Carla, V. Col, 131
Carloni, Col Mario, 40
Casson, S. Col, 144–5
Cattaneo, C. Vice Adm, 191–3
Cavagnari, D. Adm, 4, 26, 28
Cavallero, U. Gen, 85–9, 94–5, 97, 116, 119–20, 131–5, 149–50, 152, 154–5, 157–61, 170, 198–9, 224, 226, 229, 240
Cervi, M., vii, 5, 22, 119, 150, 162
Chamberlain, N., 14
Charrington, H. Brig, 195, 225, 231
Christian X, king of Denmark, 148
Churchill, W., 5, 37–8, 58, 73, 84, 123, 126–8, 136, 139, 145–6, 196, 199, 224
Ciano, C., 4, 19, 22, 24–5, 29, 39, 44, 61, 87–8, 96, 133, 135, 226
Ciano, E., 158, 189
Clerici, L. 2nd Lt, 103
Constantine I, king of Greece, 6, 11
Constantine II, king of Greece, 241
Coote, P. Wg Cdr, 168–9
Corsini, L. Capt, 114
Crowe, W. Maj, 127
Cullen, N. Flt Lt, 170
Cunningham, A. Adm, 37, 58, 176, 178–9, 191–3

D'Albiac, J. Air Cdre, 59–60, 74, 108–12, 114, 122–5, 128, 143–4, 163, 165, 167–70, 197, 214
Dapino, V. Col, 42

Davakis, C. Col, 42, 50–1
Dedes, P. Gen, 238–9
De Gaulle, C. Col, 21, 147, 239
Demertzis, C., 8
Demestichas, P. Lt Gen, 68, 78, 83, 237–8
D'Havet, A. Gen, 131
Diakos, A. Lt, 51
Dietrich, S. Maj Gen, 224, 226, 231
Dill, J. Lt Gen, 145, 201
Dimaratos, S. Col, 51–2,
Dimbleby, R., 58
Di Robilant, M. 2nd Lt, 104–105, 114
Doudney, G. Flt Lt, 113
Douhet, G. Maj, 100, 108
Doukas, G. Fg Off, 102
Douratsos, G. Maj, 206, 210–11
Drakos, M. Lt Gen, 140–1

Eden, A., 145–6, 201
Edward VIII, king of England, 9, 144
Ekonomakos, P. Maj Gen, 102
Erbach zu Schoenberg, Prince V., 121, 203

Facchini, P. Sgt, 103
Falkonakis, G. Gp Capt, 41
Ferrero, A. Gen, 229
Ferrucci, A. Col, 96
Flamininus, T. Quinctius, 18
Fontana, G. Lt, 43, 62–3
Forbes, Lord Wg Cdr, 160
Freyberg, B. Maj Gen, 148, 195, 230

Gambara, G. Gen, 150, 152, 154, 156–8
Gambier-Parry, M. Maj Gen, 58, 60, 67, 75, 77–8, 109, 111–12, 121
Geloso, C. Gen, 18, 57, 63, 67–8, 85, 90–1, 94, 96, 152, 156, 158, 237

Index

George II, king of Greece, 8, 29, 38, 40, 60, 73–4, 110, 121, 128, 144–6, 148, 170, 176, 185, 204, 212, 218–20, 224, 230, 241
Gianani, R. Col., 40, 47, 49
Giannaris, E. Plt Off, 102
Gianni, G. Gen, 153–4
Giannini, Gen, 70
Girotti, M. Gen, 32–3, 42, 51–4, 56, 90, 131, 142
Goebbels, J. 14
Gordon-Finlayson, Sqn Ldr, 168
Graffer, G. Capt, 108
Grandi, D., 96
Graziani, R. Marshal, 119
Grazzi, E., 15, 17, 22, 25, 27, 29, 34–6, 39, 41, 235
Grigson, J. Air Cdre, 143–4
Grivas, G. Maj, 129–30
Guzzoni, A. Gen, 149

Hadjikonstantis, M. Cdr, 178, 185–6
Hadjikyriakos, A., 12
Halifax, Lord, 111, 145
Hallett, N.A. Sgt, 122
Hartmann, O. Lt Gen, 208
Hatzilakos, C. Cadet, 41
Hatzopoulos, A. Capt, 3
Heywood, G. Maj Gen, 75–6, 123–4, 126, 128, 136–7, 143, 200, 205, 219, 226, 234–5
Hickey, W. Sqn Ldr, 106–107, 112, 114
Hinaris, G. Fg Off, 105
Hitler, A., vii, 14, 17–18, 20–1, 23–4, 27, 29, 40, 71, 87–8, 111, 115, 120–1, 127–8, 135, 148–9, 155–6, 159–62, 171, 173, 196–7, 199, 204, 210, 226
Homer, 1
Hutchison, B. Maj Gen, 122

Iachino, A. Adm, 191–3
Iatridis, M. Cdr, 175, 182–5, 187–9, 249n

Jacobi, Capt, 235
Jacomoni, F. Lt Gen, 22, 24–6, 31, 85, 152
Jankovic, Gen, 197–8
Janniello, P. 2nd Lt, 59
Jones, E. Flt Lt, 107, 164, 168, 170–1, 215

Kanellopoulos, P. Pvt, 13, 39, 80, 98–9, 200
Karassos, C. Maj Gen, 123
Karathanasis, G. 2nd Lt, 53
Karnavias, G. Flt Lt, 103
Katsikoyannis, D. Ldg Smn, 182–4
Katsimitros, H. Maj Gen, 15, 31–3, 44–6, 49, 61, 69–70, 78, 83, 219, 237–8
Katsotas, P. Lt Col, 91
Katsoulas, Y. Sgt, 51
Kavvadias, E. Vice Adm, 176–7, 180–1, 186–7
Keitel, W. FM, 63
Kelaidis, E. Wg Cdr, 113, 171
Kellas, Y. Flt Lt, 165–6, 214
Kellogg, F., 17
Kettlewell, J. Fg Off, 216
Kinatos, M. Wg Cdr, 171
Kipouros, Y. Plt Off, 104, 163
Kleiamakis, D. Plt Off, 41
Kollias, S., 41–2, 61, 230
Konstas, P. Cdr, 174, 186, 222
Kontis, T. Lt Col, 227
Korozis, A. Maj, 144
Koryzis, A., 138, 145–6, 156, 171, 203, 206, 213, 218, 220–1, 224, 250n
Kosmas, G. Lt Gen, 67, 72, 77, 129–30, 132, 140, 238–9
Koukidis, C. (Pvt?), 236
Kouziyannis, L. Flt Lt, 103

Lama, G. Gen, 157
Lambropoulos, C. Sgt, 48
Lavdas, G. Maj Gen, 129
Leeper, R., 9
Leonidas I, king of Sparta 9, 34, 105, 200, 211, 250n
Leopold III, king of Belgium, 148
Liosis, E. Col, 98
Lioumbas, N. Maj Gen, 196, 210
List, W. FM, 197–8, 206, 211, 229–30, 232, 237
Longmore, A. ACM, 59, 108, 110–13, 126, 143, 145, 166, 169–70

Mackenzie, C., 39
Magaldi, N. Capt, 59, 107
Malakis, A. Plt Off, 106, 112
Manai, G. Col, 90
Maniadakis, C., 232, 234–5
Margaritis, C. Fg Off, 103

Maria, Princess of Greece 121
Mariotis, C. Cpl, 54
Mariotti, L. Capt, 48
Markou, N. Maj Gen, 237
McKay, I. Maj Gen, 195
Melas, S., 5
Melissinos, P. Maj Gen, 123–4, 127
Menotti, C. Gen, 118
Mercalli, Gen, 130, 132, 151
Merifield, J. Sgt, 59, 107
Messe, Gen, 134
Metaxas, A. Maj Gen, 77
Metaxas, I., viii, 5, 20, 22, 29–31, 34–41, 47, 58, 71–2, 75–6, 79–80, 84, 94, 103, 106, 108–109, 111, 114–15, 120–8, 136–40, 143, 147, 156, 162–4, 171, 174, 176, 178, 180, 188, 196, 203–204, 218, 235
Mezeviris, G. Rear Adm, 190–1, 213, 221, 223
Micheli, E. Sgt, 114
Misyris, Lt Col, 50
Mitralexis, M. Plt Off, 47–8, 166
Molinari, E. Capt, 112, 169
Molinari, O. Maj, 113
Moltke, H. von, Gen, 6
Mondini, L. Col, 15, 29, 34–6
Mott-Radcliffe, C. Capt, 76, 78
Moutousis, S. Maj Gen, 65, 81, 225, 237
Mussolini, B., vii, 5, 13, 16–18, 20–1, 23–9, 31, 40, 43–4, 46, 51, 56–7, 61–2, 70–1, 73, 79, 84–5, 87–8, 90, 92, 95–6, 100, 115, 118–20, 124–5, 129, 133–4, 148–53, 155–61, 173, 187, 198, 225–6, 229, 237, 239–41

Napoleon I of France, 94
Nasci, G. Gen, 32, 42, 56, 62, 67, 72, 95, 97
Negro, M. Gen, 156
Newton, P. Fg Off, 172, 215
Nicolini, N. Cdr, 186
Nikolaou, E., 242
Nikolaou, M. Pvt, viii, 63, 80, 83, 92, 97, 124, 132, 134–5, 139, 199–200, 216, 218, 228, 242

Orphanidis, P. Flt Lt, 104
Ovchinnikov, I.A., 241

Palairet, M., 37, 136-7, 224
Papadopoulos, D. Lt Gen, 31, 52, 77, 136, 238-9
Papadopoulos, T. Maj Gen, 83
Papagos, A. Lt Gen, vii, 10, 21, 30, 32-4, 40-1, 47, 51, 54, 58, 60, 63-5, 67, 72, 75-6, 79-80, 94, 97, 108-11, 116-18, 120-1, 123-9, 138, 140-1, 144, 146-7, 155-6, 159-62, 166-7, 174, 180, 195, 197-201, 203, 210, 217-21, 224-6, 232, 238-9
Papagos, L., 200, 241
Papanayotou, C. Capt, 191
Papanikolaou, ERA, 3, 5
Paparodou, I. Maj, 91
Pappas, A. WO, 105
Pattle, M. Flt Lt, ix, 107, 112-14, 164-5, 168-9, 171-2, 204, 213-16, 225, 240
Paul, Prince of Greece, 38, 123, 221, 234, 250n
Paul, Prince of Yugoslavia, 23, 137, 161
Pavlidis, V. Pvt, 129
Pedrazzoli, G. Gen, 71
Perikles, 9
Perivoliotis, A. Col, 74-5
Perth, Lord, 14
Peter, Prince of Greece, viii, 14, 39, 58, 60, 67, 74-8, 109-10, 117, 121-4, 126, 128-31, 138, 143-4, 146-8, 195, 204-205, 217, 221, 232-5, 241, 250n
Peter, Prince of Yugoslavia, 161
Pezopoulos, T. Cdr, 223
Philip, Prince of Greece, 128, 223
Philippas, S. Gp Capt, 103
Pietra, I. Lt, 86-7
Pirzio Biroli, A. Gen, 158
Pitsikas, D. Flt Lt, 105
Pitsikas, I. Lt Gen, 63, 65, 72, 76, 78, 141, 200, 218-20, 224-5, 238-9
Pius XII, 16
Platis, C. Maj Gen, 21-2
Pongiluppi, V. Sgt Maj, 114
Preston, Mrs, 147
Pricolo, F. Gen, 23-4, 26-8, 44, 51, 87-8, 96, 101, 131, 150-1, 153, 159, 170, 248n

Pridham-Wippell, H. Vice Adm, 192
Psaro, R. Col, 96

Ranza, F. Gen, 23, 27, 55, 150, 152, 170
Ratlidge, G.W. Sgt, 59
Razis, G. Maj Gen, 65
Reid, M. Maj, 123-4, 127, 143, 145-6, 234
Ribbentrop, J. Von, 22-3, 88
Rintelen, E. von Gen, 88, 133, 229
Rivolta, C. Gen, 32
Roatta, M. Gen, 21, 23-5, 55-6, 87-8
Rokkos, E. Col, 65, 98-9, 122, 200
Rommel, E. Gen, 145, 196, 199
Rossi, C. Gen, 32, 40, 42, 45, 48-9, 94, 151
Rotas, B. Lt Cdr, 188
Roussopoulos, A. Maj Gen, 141
Ruggero, V. Col, 120

Sakellariou, A. Rear Adm, 178-80, 186, 190, 212, 220-1, 224, 234
Salisbury-Jones, G. Brig, 234, 250n
Sansonetti, L. Vice Adm, 191-2
Sapienza, Col, 40
Scuero, A. Gen, 89
Sevastopoulos, Sqn Ldr, 168
Smith Dorrien, H. Lt Gen, 144
Smith Dorrien, P. Maj, 144, 146-7, 233-5
Soddu, U. Gen, 26, 56-7, 62, 65, 71-2, 79, 85, 87-9, 95, 118, 120, 133, 149
Solinas, Col, 40, 43
Spanidis, A. Cdr, 178, 185, 249n
Spigaglia, A. Lt, 59
Spyropoulos, 2nd Lt, 51
Stalin, J., 9
Stergiopoulos, L. Maj Gen, 78, 92
Stumme, G. Lt Gen, 207, 209, 225
Sykes, W. Fg Off, 108

Tavoni, G. Col, 42, 96
Taylor, H. Flt Sgt, 122
Theodoropoulos, G. Sqn Ldr, 65, 105, 164
Tilios, S. Gp Capt, 108, 112, 166
Toumbas, I. Lt Cdr, 221
Trizio, F. Col, 40, 43, 96
Tsakalotos, T. Lt Col, 93, 117
Tsolakoglou, G. Lt Gen, 63, 72, 76, 81, 141, 224-6, 229, 237-8
Turle, C. Rear Adm, 60, 124, 126, 176, 233-4

Vembo, S., 61
Venini, G. Lt, 89
Vercellino, M. Gen, 63, 68, 71, 90, 94, 96
Verriopoulos, I. Cdr, 178-9
Visconti Prasca, S. Gen, 18-19, 21-5, 27-8, 31, 40, 42, 44, 49, 51, 55-7, 71, 87, 101, 237, 246n
Vittorio Emanuele III, King of Italy, 24, 26, 84, 160, 240
Vladousis, A. Plt Off, 47, 105-106, 247n
Vrachnos, V. Maj Gen, 49-50, 52, 153

Waterlow, S., 14
Wavell, A. Lt Gen, 128, 136, 143, 145, 196, 219, 224
Wilhelm II, Kaiser of Germany, 6
Willetts, A. Gp Capt, 108-10, 112, 205
Wilson, H. Lt Gen, 147, 195-8, 203, 209, 214, 218-21, 224, 230, 232-5
Wisdom, T., 215

Xerxes, King of Persia, 229
Xiros, A. Cdr, 177

Zacco, L. Col, 68
Zeppos, D. Lt Cdr, 181-2, 187, 189
Zeppos, G. Lt Cdr, 189-90
Zog I, King of Albania, 129
Zygouris, C. Maj Gen, 33